Cinematography in the Weimar Republic

The Fairleigh Dickinson University Press Series In Communication Studies

General Editor: Gary Radford, Department of Communication Studies, Fairleigh Dickinson University, Madison, New Jersey.

The Fairleigh Dickinson University Press Series in Communication Studies publishes scholarly works in communication theory, practice, history, and culture.

Publications in Communication Studies

Paul Matthew St. Pierre, *Cinematography in the Weimar Republic: Lola Lola, Dirty Singles, and the Men Who Shot Them* (2016)

Anastacia Kurylo and Tatyana Dumov (eds.), *Social Networking: Redefining Communication in the Digital Age* (2016)

Phil Rose, *Radiohead and the Global Movement for Change: "Pragmatism Not Idealism"* (2015)

Brent C. Sleasman, *Creating Albert Camus: Foundations and Explorations in His Philosophy of Communication* (2015)

Michael Warren Tumolo, *Just Remembering, Rhetorics of Genocide Remembrance and Sociopolitical Judgment* (2015)

Phil Rose, *Roger Waters and Pink Floyd* (2015)

Ronald C. Arnett and Pat Arneson (eds.), *Philosophy of Communication Ethics: Alterity and the Other* (2014)

Pat Arneson, *Communicative Engagement and Social Liberation: Justice Will Be Made* (2014)

Erik A. Garrett, *Why Do We Go to the Zoo?: Communication, Animals, and the Cultural-Historical Experience of Zoos* (2013)

Philip Dalton and Eric Kramer, *Coarseness in U.S. Public Communication* (2012)

Catherine Creede, Beth Fisher-Yoshida, and Placida Gallegos (eds.), *The Reflective, Facilitative, and Interpretive Practices of the Coordinated Management of Meaning* (2012)

Jolanta Aritz and Robyn C. Walker, *Discourse Perspectives on Organizational Communication* (2011)

S. Alyssa Groom and J. M. H. Fritz, *Communication Ethics and Crisis: Negotiating Differences in Public and Private Spheres* (2011)

R. C. MacDougall, *Digination: Identity, Organization, and Public Life* (2011)

Deborah Eicher-Catt and Isaac E. Catt (eds.), *Communicology: The New Science of Embodied Discourse* (2010)

Dan Cassino and Yesamin Besen-Cassino, *Consuming Politics: Jon Stewart, Branding, and the Youth Vote in America* (2009)

On the Web at http://www.fdu.edu/fdupres

Cinematography in the Weimar Republic

Lola Lola, Dirty Singles, and the Men Who Shot Them

Paul Matthew St. Pierre

FAIRLEIGH DICKINSON UNIVERSITY PRESS
Madison • Teaneck

Published by Fairleigh Dickinson University Press
Copublished by Rowman & Littlefield
A wholly owned subsidiary of The Rowman & Littlefield Publishing Group, Inc.
4501 Forbes Boulevard, Suite 200, Lanham, Maryland 20706
www.rowman.com

Unit A, Whitacre Mews, 26-34 Stannary Street, London SE11 4AB

British Library Cataloguing in Publication Information Available

Library of Congress Cataloging-in-Publication Data Available

ISBN 978-1-61147-944-7 (cloth : alk. paper)
ISBN 978-1-61147-945-4 (electronic)

∞™ The paper used in this publication meets the minimum requirements of American National Standard for Information Sciences—Permanence of Paper for Printed Library Materials, ANSI/NISO Z39.48-1992.

Printed in the United States of America

Contents

Illustrations

Acknowledgments

Growing up in Vancouver, I had permission from my mother to stay home from school whenever I liked, which I did often, because even then I knew educational institutions cultivate only mediocrity and conformity, and because I much preferred to watch old American movies on morning television, in hazy transmissions from a cross-border station in Bellingham. I distinctly recall admiring movies like *San Francisco* (1936), starring Clark Gable, Jeanette MacDonald, and Spencer Tracy; *Boys Town* (1938), with Tracy and Mickey Rooney; and *God Is My Co-Pilot* (1945), with Dennis Morgan and Raymond Massey, a Canadian. I did not care about directors and cinematographers back then. After the movies ended, I was concerned only with forging a good letter to my teacher, and in my mother's handwriting, for I was encouraged to do this too, accounting for yet another of Paul's absences. Little did I know years later I would write about letter forgery in Carl Theodor Dreyer and Rudolph Maté's *La passion de Jeanne d'Arc* (1928). So I thank my late progressive mother, for cultivating my interests in film, truancy, and forgery.

Without the help of my expert and diligent research assistant, Matthew Tomkinson, writing *Cinematography in the Weimar Republic* would have been a more protracted and onerous process. He did an outstanding job tracking down rare and obscure data about camera operators, their techniques, and their work with directors. His research formed the armature of the book.

Harry Keyishian, director of Fairleigh Dickinson University Press, has been invaluable in his support of this project from the beginning. The interest he expressed all along in German film has been my inspiration. Thanks for the encouragement and for believing in me over many years.

Viktoria Cseh offered me sage advice from her perspective as a film editor and expert, slipped me a *trick deck* when I most needed it, and suggested the current title. *Danke vielmals.*

1

The Weimar Revolution and German Collaborative Filmmaking

That throughout the 120-year history of film directors and camera operators have worked closely together may be apparent in the plethora of stage set and location photographs of them together at the camera, whether conferring about it or simply posing for the picture. One might recall, for example, the famous images of Charles Chaplin looking through the camera lens on the set of *City Lights* (1931) and of Ingmar Bergman, in the company of his cinematographer, Sven Nykvist, reviewing a camera angle on the set of *Fanny and Alexander* (1982). Chaplin worked with cinematographer Roland Totheroh on thirty-two films, from *Work* (1915) to *Monsieur Verdoux* (1947), Bergman with Nykvist on seventeen films, from *Sawdust and Tinsel* (1953) to *Fanny and Alexander*. It would seem, therefore, that each director worked very closely with his preferred cinematographer on multiple films and that they collaborated on the essential visual property of the film, potentially on every shot selection, camera angle, and lighting choice, as may be evident in the photographs. Yet film-production photographs of this kind are more likely marketing properties, designed to promote the brand of the democratic, hands-on, collaborative filmmaker, in contradistinction to the model of the dictatorial director with total control over production, who dictates shot selection, camera angle, and light source to the cinematographer, and then, sometimes in pantomime for promotional shots, inspects the camera and confers with the operator to confirm his or her demands have been met. Totheroh, having shot Chaplin's films almost exclusively, was typical of the silent-film cinematographer, essentially a camera operator indentured, if he was lucky, to a great director. In contrast, Nykvist, although he worked with Bergman more than with any other director and clearly had a productive collaborative partnership with him, also enjoyed a professional mobility and an artistic independence that allowed him to shoot films for other directors internationally, like Norman Jewison, Richard Attenborough, Nora Ephron, Volker Schlöndorff, and Woody Allen.

In reference to director-cinematographer collaborations, film history is a labor spectrum where the model of the contracted camera operator is conspicuous in the silent era and that of the autonomous cinematographer has evolved throughout the sound era. In the Weimar period of German filmmaking, however, these two models existed not on a dichotomous continuum but simultaneously, in a singularity of labor and visual culture in which the emergence of the camera operator as a cinematographer and a director of photography, as a film collaborator and an independent agent, was not protracted over a century of film history but was concentrated in a fourteen-year period of fierce artistic activity and disabling political and economic instability.

Berlin in the 1920s was the principal site of the interdisciplinary avant-garde of the Modernist movement in the visual, literary, architectural, design, typographical, sartorial, and performance arts in Europe. The Weimar Revolution that emerged in the aftermath of the November 1918 Armistice marking the end of World War One and that established the Weimar Republic, 1919–1933, informed all the arts with both the innovation and the uncertainty of the new laissez-faire politics: Expressionism, Dada, the Bauhaus, Minimalism, Objectivism, Verism, *Neue Sachlichkeit* ("New Objectivity"), and other revolutionary paradigms of the postwar Modern style and Weimar culture. Among all the avant-garde forms of these new stylistically and culturally negotiated arts, the cinema was foremost because, still an emergent formational art, filmmaking had been a radical experimental practice in new visual technologies that proved instrumental in changing how human beings perceived movement, structure, perspective, light exposure, temporal duration, continuity, spatial orientation, human postural, facial, vocal, and gestural displays, and their own spectatorship, as well as conventional organizational standards of storytelling like narrative, setting, theme, character, and structure. Whereas most of the arts mobilized into schools, movements, institutions, and other structures, cinema, a collaborative art, tended to organize around its ensembles of practitioners, as well as stylistically in obsolescent structures like the Expressionist movement. Historically, the silent-film era, 1895–1927, is associated with auteurs, the precursors of François Truffaut and other filmmakers in the 1960s: actuality filmmakers and pioneers like R. W. Paul and Fred and Joe Evans in England, Auguste and Louis Lumière and Georges Méliès in France, and Charles Chaplin and Buster Keaton in America, who, by managing all the compositional, executional, and editorial facets of film production—scripting, directing, acting, photographing, set, costume, and lighting design, editing, and marketing—imposed their personal vision or authorship on the film. The dichotomy of the auteur and the production ensemble established a production hierarchy in most filmmaking. In formative German silent film, however, this hierarchy was less rank or class driven, because collaborative partnerships took precedence over authorship. Whereas in silent-film production in most countries the terms *filmmaker* and *director* were synonymous, in German silent film the plural term *filmemacherin* connoted primarily both directors and cinematographers, along with the rest of the filmmaking crew. Thus, German silent filmmakers' chief contribution to the new medium and art of film was less the representational iconographies of the Expressionist, New Objective, and Naturalist styles than the executional practice of coauthorship and coproduction. Nevertheless, the persistence of daring Expressionist techniques and iconographies as design features in many of the signature films throughout the period—such as Robert Wiene's *The Cabinet of Dr. Caligari* (1920), F. W. Murnau's *The Haunted Castle* (1921) and *Nosferatu* (1922), Arthur Robison's *Warning Shadows* (1923), E. A. Dupont's *Varieté* (1925), Fritz Lang's *Dr. Mabuse, the Gambler* (1922) and *Metropolis* (1927), and Paul Leni's *Waxworks* (1924) and *The Cat and the Canary* (1927)—was uncharacteristic of the avant-garde in other visual arts, chiefly painting, which largely rejected the tradition of Expressionist aesthetics in favor of *Neue Sachlichkeit*'s aesthetics of Verism and Realism. Prominent in this movement toward objective representation were the painters August Sander, Christian Schad, Georg Scholz, Otto Dix, and George Grosz. Jean Mitry notes: "European cinema, freed from the shackles of theatrical representation, developed under the heavy influence of painting. Because the theatre is verbal and the cinema silent, inspiration would be drawn from painting and not from the theatre. For the images to be meaningful, all that was needed was to ensure that they express everything the painting might express, any movement providing an added value."[1] Were German filmmakers, in comparison, late to the dance, hesitant to adopt the Post-Expressionist objectivity aesthetics of the new art movement, when "by 1919 the Expressionists' revolutionary fervor was beginning to be replaced by a growing disenchantment,"[2] or does the medium of film have inherent technical qualities, especially in the formative silent era, when experimentation and innovation were salient, that may have lent themselves to or demanded Expressionist modes?

For example, like photography and theater, film is dependent on natural outdoor light (particularly in the experimental actuality films of the late-1890s) and artificial lighting in its production and development, as distinguished from the representation of light, as in painting. In film light and lighting equipment are the primary tools of directors and camera operators or directors of photography, and also lighting directors, the grip crew, and other members of the ensemble. A pioneer of artificial lighting technology in theatrical performance and in silent film, Adolph Appia (1862–1928) recognized that three-dimensional sets, as distinguished from flat painted backdrop sets, by allowing for the interpenetration of planes of light and shade, imitating the phenomenology of life, evoked a sense of spatial verisimilitude that enhanced the natural narrative properties, or visual grammar, of film, which directors Edwin S. Porter and Sergei Eisenstein were the first filmmakers to exploit. In this regard, R. S. Furness notes the "distortion and tortuous, labyrinthine quality" of the sets in *The Cabinet of Dr. Caligari* and "the twisting streets" of Prague in the two versions of *Der Golem* (1912, 1916) as fundamental to their Expressionist effects.[3] Early German Expressionist film harnessed these technical properties inherent in artificial lighting and the concomitant visual grammar of chiaroscuro for the purpose of enhancing spatial definition, narrative continuity, including narratological dichotomies of good and evil, spectator engagement, and visual literacy, the ability to read the screen and its contents. These properties were more than elements of a style or aspects of a school. They had been intrinsic to the medium of film content and spectatorship from the beginning, particularly the exploitation of chiaroscuro along with vertical and horizontal locations, linear perspective, and other aspects of visual organization as a depth cue in the depiction of a three-dimensional field, and they seemed indivisible from the current phase of its development. German Expressionism had taken film to the edge of a visual spectrum, where the phenomenon of light is synonymous with the modality of lighting, and from this vantage point in the Weimar Republic it exploited the supernatural genre that had the capacity to exhibit this intense exchange of light and dark as its own enduring aesthetic. Even at the end of the era, in America, F. W. Murnau ingeniously fabricated the natural light and physical properties of his outdoor setting entirely on the soundstage in *Sunrise: A Song of Two Humans* (1927), for which cinematographers Karl Struss and Charles Rosher received Academy Awards. Murnau observed, "For some scenes, such as the swamp sequence, the camera went in a complete circle. This created enormous lighting problems. We built a railway line in the roof, [and] suspended a little platform from it, which could be raised or lowered by motors."[4] German filmmakers exploited these basic properties of film throughout the era, in scenarios typically with three-dimensional theatrical sets and sharply defined lighting, properties the camera recorded to dramatic effect, and they continued to test their aesthetic potential mainly in Expressionist visual syntax throughout the Weimar period.

That Expressionism continued to be an experimental mode in film while other visual artists such as painters, sculptors, architects, and photographers deemed Expressionist practice outmoded was an executional paradox typical of German culture at the time, which was characterized by great freedom of expression and for experimentation, but also by incontrovertible economic and political uncertainties that inhibited the promise of lasting cultural and social change and destabilized all emerging aesthetics across the disciplines. Thus, the Weimar period was a precarious interval between the First World War and the event horizon of the Third Reich and the Second World War, when artistic communities, precisely because they were innovative and experimental, were especially vulnerable to economic and political forces. Whereas artistic communities faced constant change and the threat of dissolution, however, individual artists faced the imminent and absolute dangers of poverty, homelessness, insanity, exile, and execution, partly as the consequences of their freedom of expression and association.

For example, amid this economic and political turmoil, and of course for complex personal reasons as well, several prominent artists committed suicide, including Imre von Santho, Walter Benjamin, Walter Hasenclever, Ernst Kirchner, and Balder Olden. Others, such as Otto Freundlich, Erich Salomon, Else Neuländer-Simon, and James Klein, were incarcerated and executed in concentration camps. Many others managed to emigrate from Germany, typically to the United States, including major figures Hannah Arendt, Albert Einstein, Paul Klee, Ludwig Mies van der Rohe, Walter Gropius, Kurt Weill, Bertolt Brecht, and Thomas Mann, and principal filmmakers like Karl Freund, Theodor Sparkuhl, Josef von Sternberg, Ernst Lubitsch, E. A. Dupont, Billy Wilder, and Fritz Lang. Some prominent actors found their careers seriously compromised, such as Brigitte Helm, who withdrew from the film business in 1935, and Emil Jannings, who made Nazi propaganda films starting in 1933, and the photographer and filmmaker Leni Riefenstahl, who directed the Nazi propaganda film *The Triumph of the Will* (1935). Other filmmakers, like cinematographer Fritz Arno Wagner, who died after falling off a camera trolley, and director F. W. Murnau, in a car crash, evoke the Weimar period's tragic ethos.

Yet the art movements of the Weimar Republic were remarkable too for their propitious beginnings. Corresponding to the *Neue Sachlichkeit* movement in the visual arts, the Bauhaus movement in design and architecture made an enduring contribution to twentieth-century aesthetics in Europe and the West. Founded by Walter Gropius in Weimar in 1919, and subsequently based in Dessau and Berlin, until it was shut down by the Nazis in 1933, the Bauhaus typified the Weimar period by spanning it, with art. With the group's emphasis on formal education, traditional crafts, and elemental designs, it emblematized much of the contemporaneous *élan* of German cultural distinctiveness and the aesthetic values of precision, innovation, simplicity, and surprise within a brand-new paradigm of Modernism. The principal link between the New Objectivity in the arts and Expressionism in film is apparent in elemental construction design, in the futuristic architecture and furniture of the Bauhaus, and the demonstrative three-dimensional architectural settings and property furnishings of many Expressionist films, which "tried to convey psychological states through décor,"[5] as well as through lighting, dramaturgy, and spectatorship: "While objects can be put onto the stage in theater and maintain their integrity as inert objects, no such assumption can be made in cinema. An object does not maintain its status once it is in the frame: color or a set are not merely background but part of the experience of the spectator, constituted through the temporal experience of a shot."[6] Compare, for example, these descriptions, of Mies van der Rohe's 1921 design for a pyramidal office building in Berlin, "a prism constructed entirely of glass and steel: transparent, futuristic and highly practical in terms of material and attractiveness,"[7] and of Fritz Lang's film *Metropolis* (1927), in which "futuristic architecture and the apparent emphasis on science fiction are balanced against older motifs such as the destructive class struggle and its resolution in a final appeal to collective labor."[8] As the glass skyscraper was Mies's signature, the celluloid skyscraper, the framework setting as visual content, was Lang's, and also other Expressionist filmmakers'. Like Bauhaus function-based design, from buildings, furniture, and lighting to wall hangings, pottery, glasswork, photography, and other visual arts, notably the paintings of Paul Klee, Gustav Klimt, Wassily Kandinsky, Marc Chagall, and Piet Mondrian, German film, precisely because as a relatively new medium it still had to be somewhat self-explanatory or meta-filmic, in the manner of the novel historically as a genre, was fundamentally architectonic, drawing attention to its design, structure, and composition, the constructivist antithesis of reification, as well as to its performative, its visual display or narrative, in which respect, it might be said, its aesthetic elided form, function, design, and style. In other respects, however, the Bauhaus was quite unsympathetic to the medium of film, in that filmmaking is a form of mechanical production, even though, it can be contended, it involved much handwork in this early phase of its history, as is apparent in the activation of hand-cranked cameras and projectors and in hand-operated executive processes like developing exposed film and editing it.

> Some of the rudimentary optical and mechanical elements of early film production, of which audiences would be aware, were important sources of engagement. Film cameras were hand-cranked, recording images frame by frame onto 16 mm film stock at the speed at which the camera operator turned the crank. Similarly, film projectors were hand-cranked. To project the film at the correct speed to audiences, the projectionist had to exercise a meticulous judgment to crank the projector at the precise speed at which the camera operator had cranked the film camera. Audiences in the theater were acutely aware of any anomalies between the speeds at which the film was being screened and had been recorded. Although relatively passive, spectators would have been conscious that the film they were watching was hand-generated, of the intervention of the hand in film production.[9]

Thus, Gropius, who envisioned his Bauhaus traditional craft design displacing the entrenched industrial model, yet conceded they might have to coexist, and German filmmakers, who exploited a revolutionary new medium and art form that combined traditional storytelling with new photographic technology and mechanical reproduction were not as aesthetically dissimilar as might first appear. In fact, the Bauhaus, which Gropius conceived in the trenches of World War One, was the standard-bearer of Germany's cultural reconstruction. But the medium of film presented a bold new banner to the German public, the movie screen, a reflective image surface.

That art in any mode, medium, or discipline could be an efficacious means by which a defeated nation with a directionless culture and a runaway economy might be reconstructed was a revolutionary proposal indeed. In this respect, the Bauhaus emphasis on form and function both articulated the postwar *zeitgeist* in a tidy epigram and set a model for other art movements to probe the interstice between functionality and efficacy. Does art simply function as art, or might it also have the capacity to change the world, to achieve its desired effect, such as the effect on reintroducing such values as peace, stability, creativity, and happiness to a country intent on recovering from its defeat in the most atrocious and traumatic war in history? German art may have been efficacious in forging the *zeitgeist* of the Weimar Republic, but it could do nothing to prevent the Third Reich. The brief timeline of the republic was a catalog of political catastrophes and economic disasters, of ineluctable events that would absorb all personal artistic endeavors.

The Weimar Republic began under propitious circumstances, a de facto marriage of art and politics. After the November Revolution, which started on November 3, 1918, the abdication of Kaiser Wilhelm II and the establishment of the republic on November 9, and the Armistice to mark the end of the First World War two days later, César Klein and Max Pechstein started the November Group on December 3, a socialist association of Expressionist painters, architects, and musicians devoted to the ideal of political reform through artistic endeavors. In February 1919 the National Assembly convened in Weimar, and that April Walter Gropius founded the Bauhaus School of Art and Design there. Yet on February 24, 1920, Adolf Hitler addressed the inaugural meeting of the National Socialist German Workers' Party, in Munich, introducing a political rhetorical performative that, through the 1920s, would extend its cultural reach through Nazi paramilitary groups, as in the failed Beer Hall Putsch, in Munich, November 8–11, 1923; the publication of *Mein Kampf* in two volumes (1925–1926); and the Second Nazi Party Congress, July 3–4, 1926, in Weimar. Hyperinflation and massive unemployment, consequences of the war and the Allied Powers' imposition of German war reparations, according to the terms of the Treaty of Versailles on June 28, 1919, worsened through the 1920s and 1930s, culminating in the appointment of Hitler as chancellor on January 30, 1933, and the ratification of the Enabling Act on March 23, affirming him as a dictator. Paralleling this sequence of events, German artists articulated an antithetical message about reconstruction and reparation, not about political authority and power but about the cultural authority of creative endeavors and the power shared in executant-spectatorial collaborations about beauty, truth, imagination, mimesis, materials, methodology, data, and technology. These collaborations of filmmakers (directors and cinematographers) and film spectators were essentially phenomenological, about sympathetic perceptions and imaginations, about people discerning the same images and image sequences, without necessarily interpreting them or otherwise processing them in precisely the same way, in contradistinction to the coercive signals of propaganda. The power-authority differential of working relationships notwithstanding, what, if any, is the relation between the cultural production generated by film directors and cinematographers in collaborative partnerships and the production of Nazi political disinformation as the Weimar Republic came to an end, in reference to the construction of meaning within visual culture and on the postwar political scene?

First, the relation between film and propaganda as competing authoritative frameworks and systems of power in postwar Germany relies on two premises: (1) the theory that as a field of analysis film is linked to art history, specifically contemporaneous art of the Weimar Period; and (2) the theory that the distinction between images and words as signifying media is attributable to political ideologies and discourses. According to Roland Barthes, drawing on the theories of Ferdinand de Saussure in his *Cours de linguistique générale* (1918), images and words both signify as texts. Film and propaganda are related primarily as texts, and their differentiation as competing texts has to do with their relative degrees of truthfulness, in that film texts tend toward the maximally truthful and propaganda texts toward the minimally truthful. Fritz Lang's *Metropolis* (1927), an Expressionist text, is maximally truthful, whereas Leni Riefenstahl's *The Triumph of the Will* (1935), a propaganda text, is minimally truthful. Even though *Metropolis* currently occupies a more stable place in film history as a work of film art than *The Triumph of the Will*, the latter, along with other propagandistic works in various media, because it functioned within a German political paradigm in which images and texts were distinct and mutually exclusive categories, and binaries of information-disinformation and truth-falsehood carried arbitrary values, exerted the rhetorical power to persuade masses of people with state authority.

Second, Weimar art and politics are related in a social and iconographic hierarchy, a staircase with the police, the military, the government, and the Reich president on the top steps and with artists on the lower steps. Consider, for example, how the Odessa Steps function dramatically in the climactic scene of Sergei Eisenstein's *Battleship Potemkin* (1925), where they signify the social distinction between the Russian populace and the Czar's Cossacks and the inequity of power and authority. In the climax of *Metropolis* a massive staircase functions in a similar symbolic manner, to dramatize the factional distance between factory workers and the oppressive bosses who control the machines. In a discussion of Expressionism and set design, Jean Mitry observes, "There are countless examples. Among others, there is the staircase/steps symbolism, which is fairly constant in all the Expressionist directors' work, but in particular in Fritz Lang where the staircase (always rectangular) expresses an upward movement towards an ideal."[10] In the political model, where images and words are discrete, ideology is the ideal, the top step; in the artistic model, where images and words are conjoined as texts, aesthetics is the ideal, the top step. Where the two models are in conflict, and the political model has power and authority and ideology takes precedence over aesthetics, as in the Weimar Republic, the artistic model is dislodged from the top and forced to occupy a lower step. Thus, within the symbolic structure of the staircase, whether set design or nontheatrical architecture that incorporates steps, social movement is principally about corroboration through ascent and descent. Mitry considers this structure in Expressionist cinema as "symbolizing the accession to power, the desire for power,"[11] whereas J. E. Cirlot in *A Dictionary of Symbols* notes that the symbol of steps "embraces the following essential ideas: ascension, gradation, and communication between different, vertical levels" and "ascending . . . can be understood both in a material and in an evolutive and spiritual sense."[12] Thus, in the conflict between art and politics during the Weimar Republic (*Deutsche Reich*) and into the Third Reich (*Dritte Reich*), political associations desire power and ascend to it materially, biologically, and spiritually, degrade art (image) as a primary means of cultural production, relegating it to a lower step, and alter the public discourse (text), making propaganda a lingua franca to communicate throughout society and foster conformity.

These are two relational models, one model about words and images as media with the capacity to connect or disconnect, and the other model about power hierarchies, as symbolized by staircases. German artists faced an existential ethical choice, between (1) political collaboration (collusion) and artistic collaboration (cooperation), between consorting with the enemy, of government, the military, and the police, by complying with propaganda directives, and (2) working together with other artists on the massive cultural project of making art as a means of national reconstruction and collective free expression. The many collaborative partnerships of film directors and cinematographers in the Weimar Republic were the most prominent, noteworthy, and productive working relationships among practitioners in all the visual arts, excepting some other ensemble-based performing arts such as theater, dance, opera, and music. Thus, through creative partnerships, particularly in the context of an ensemble visual art form, directors and cinematographers found they could exercise considerable control over their own "ascension, gradation, and communication" in society and the German regime, as it evolved into an oppressive totalitarian political, military, and constabulary simulacrum. In addition to this kind of symbolic subversion of state control through a heterodox working relationship, film collaborations between directors and cinematographers express a new attitude toward art that could be termed *Neue Subjektivität* ("New Subjectivity"), corresponding to *Neue Sachlichkeit* in painting and the other visual arts. What was new in film aesthetics was the pairing of subjectivity and collaboration, as distinguished from the pairing of objectivity and solo work in painting. Members of the *filmemacher* ensemble, the director and the cinematographer, could exchange not just their film aesthetics, poetics, and techniques discursively but also their subjective formations and agencies regarding cinema as an art form, filmmaking as a process, and specific film productions. Film collaboration in the Weimar Republic, therefore, involved more than just a public exchange of theories, ideas, and practices; it involved more than just conventional cooperation in the workplace, such as by working together for the pragmatic effects of occupational productivity, financial security, personal convenience, and mutual benefits.

First, the collaborative relationship of the film director and cinematographer is distinctively intentional, about *wanting the same image and trying to realize it*, through direction and photography, frame by frame, scene by scene, through the entire filmmaking process, the project from its inception as an idea to its projection on screen, from an indefinite description to the precise definition of the final cut, on a spectrum where the intentional and representational conditions governing *wanting the same image* change significantly: "the difficulty here is the general one that arises when the object of wanting is not anything that exists or that the agent supposes to exist."[13] In other words, at one end of the spectrum, when the director and the cinematographer set out to make a film, one that does not yet exist, they cannot seek the desired image with certainty: "there are two features present in wanting; movement towards a thing and knowledge (or at least opinion) that the thing is there."[14] At this point in my argument about collaborative intention, I might propose, (1) that at the start of production the director presumes the image "is there" and the cinematographer has jurisdiction over the "movement toward" the image, and (2) that in desiring the same image they can be said to have the same intention. Yet at the start of production the image does not yet exist, except in the imagination of the agents or a facsimile of it like a scenario, a screenplay, or a shooting script. Thus, the theory of collaborative intention is not yet present, because the director cannot have knowledge of a thing that is not "there" and the cinematographer cannot approach a thing that is not "there." G. E. M. Anscombe notes, however, "where the thing wanted is not even supposed to exist, as when it is a future state of affairs, we have to speak of an idea, rather than of knowledge or opinion. And our two features become: some kind of action or movement which (the agent at least supposes) is of use towards something, and the idea of that thing."[15] Thus, at the start of production the film director has the concept of the image and the cinematographer has the means of attaining it. That each agent needs the other to move the camera toward the desired or targeted image is the principle initially of their shared intention and, as production continues, it becomes the foundation of their collaborative relationship. That directors and cinematographers should work closely together is hardly remarkable, given the ensemble nature of filmmaking since the initial period of actuality films, 1895–1903, and their custodial and executant roles over the filming process. That they should work together from a shared intention to procure an initial image, a series of frame-images, and the final cut of a film is extraordinary, however, because it implies a shared agency, which is the nature of collaboration. In other words, the essence of collaboration is not just quantitative, based on the principle that two people working together may be more productive than the same two people working individually at the same tasks, but also qualitative, about the common standard by which two artists can be assessed, their agencies together. In the Weimar Republic, therefore, directors and cinematographers working together in partnerships produced many avant-garde silent films of enduring merit because their shared intentions to attain images and their shared agencies in making original films enabled them to undertake monumental projects: "The mark of practical reasoning is that the thing wanted is *at a distance* from the immediate action, and the immediate action is calculated as the way of getting or doing or securing the thing wanted."[16] The shared image, both the film as it is envisioned collaboratively and the totality of camera shots executed, recorded, and edited frame by frame, and thus processed shared image by shared image, is "the immediate action" toward traversing any aesthetic distances between filmmakers "and securing the thing wanted," or the final cut.

During the Weimar period, however, this aesthetic distance was not simply a self-evident aspect of film composition and production, conforming to a typical Aristotelian design, with a beginning, a middle, and an end. The process of constructing films in Germany at this time was radically different from in other major filmmaking nations such as France, Russia, England, and America, all of which were relatively stable politically after World War One. This brings me to my second point about collaborative relationship in German film production. Although the Weimar Republic was characterized by extensive unfettered creativity and diverse and prolific multimedia and multidisciplinary artistic activity, it was also an ephemeral period of intense political, social, and cultural instability. German filmmakers and other artists knew how fragile and transitory their renaissance was, not because creativity, like inspiration, is fleeting, but because, post World War One and into the 1920s, it was clear Germany had not established an economy, a governance, or a sociopolitical infrastructure that would be able to protect, or even tolerate, the freedoms of expression and association that had inspired the German people to voice and discharge their radical new ideas about art, representation, gender, sexuality, class, and culture. With other artists, filmmakers suspected the German revival would be short-lived, but they continued to labor in it and to exercise creative license with their freedoms, and including the tenuous freedoms that instability and transitoriness yielded. Uncertainty was the defining characteristic of the Modern age in Europe, prompting artists to question established religious, scientific, political, social, and cultural traditions, but this was a skepticism about the past.

In the Weimar Republic uncertainty extended into the future as well as into the past, which complicated the positions of practicing artists, sealing them in the present moment of execution, yet protracting the aesthetic distance, so that calculating how to secure the desired object, in the case of filmmakers, the image, could be only speculative. German filmmakers dealt with this uncertainty by closing the ranks of their ensemble art and forging creative partnerships, most notably the collaborative relationships of directors and cinematographers. By sharing the image as the thing desired, they brought it into focus and made negotiating the spectrum between the immediate action of electing to make a film (the shared intention) and the final action of completing the film (achieving the thing desired) seem more practicable in an uncertain age than were they to work independently, thus eliding aesthetic distance somewhat. The collaborative relationships of directors and cinematographers in the Weimar Republic, therefore, were at once interpersonal, pragmatic, and activist means (1) of taking the fullest advantage of the new postwar societal freedoms and of opposing the political and military values of the previous regime as a model of society; (2) of undertaking new film projects with the greatest likelihood of completing them successfully, despite the economic insecurity and political uncertainty of the age; (3) of contributing to European Modernism in a distinctive way, by making art about the future as well as the past, and thus locating it in the ephemeral present moment of creative endeavor; and (4) of developing the new German film industry by branding it primarily in its production. The irony of these working relationships, in which directors and cinematographers were complete partners on an equal footing in production and with a shared vision, intention, and agency, is that the films of the Weimar period, some of the most technically and visually innovative in cinematic history, are remembered today mainly for their directors. Thus, in visual culture, the popular imagination, and even film history, German film directors are acknowledged as the great innovators and pioneers, credited for their films as works of art and artifacts, for formal and stylistic elements, for casting and costuming choices, and even for technical components like shot execution, lighting, and set design. For example, Ernst Lubitsch is universally remembered as a great director, whereas his collaborator on eighteen of his German films, 1916–1923, cinematographer Theodor Sparkuhl, is not nearly as well remembered, yet he too was a historically significant innovator and pioneer, and of course he was more responsible for film components like shot selection, design, and execution, and even for the distinctive look of Lubitsch films. After Lubitsch's departure to America in 1923, when Sparkuhl took on his next project, E. A. Dupont's first important film, *Das alte Gesetz* (1923), he was a well-established cinematographer recognized in the avant-garde of camera optics and shooting strategies because of his collaboration with Lubitsch but also because of his contributions to the art of cinematography, his industry reputation, and his distinctive style as a camera operator. Dupont secured the services of two more accomplished cinematographers, Karl Freund and Carl Hoffmann, on *Varieté* (1925), the signature film that led to his tenure at British International Pictures, 1926–1931. When he came to work with Dupont, Freund had shot major films with directors Fritz Lang, F. W. Murnau, Paul Wegener, and Carl Theodor Dreyer, and would be Lang's camera operator again on *Metropolis* (1927), one of the most highly regarded films in history. Hoffmann, another of Lang's favored cinematographers, along with Fritz Arno Wagner and Günther Rittau, had experience working on four feature films with Lang and one film by Murnau when he came to the set of *Varieté*. Collaborating with Dupont, Sparkuhl, Freund, and Hoffmann drew on their considerable cinematic experience and expertise, and the knowledge they had acquired working with Lang, Murnau, Wegener, and Dreyer, and passed it on to the younger and less experienced filmmaker, Dupont, thus emphasizing an important principle of collaborative relationships in the Weimar period, that of the free exchange of ideas and skills outside of the political, economic, and informational paradigm of the Second Reich. In imparting cinematic knowledge, this exchange was more than didactic: it was about reciprocal, blended knowledge, like two strips of film, spliced, and rendered whole and continuous, in which respect collaborations in film production were editorial relationships. If the working relationships of directors and editors were based on the exchange of ideas and skills, then they were essentially dialogic, both verbal and observational, in that in silent film dialogue is evident in the editing of dramatic pantomime and the interpolation of speech intertitles. Thus, the intellectual and artistic exchange of directors and cinematographers is like the splicing together of two autonomous yet incomplete strips of celluloid, of disconnected images, to form a continuous unit, an intentional shared image.

That cinematographers and directors were forging these relationships after Edwin S. Porter had introduced cross-cut techniques and while Sergei Eisenstein was exploiting montage, both through innovative editing, emphasizes that filmmaking was essentially a cultural practice: "Porter had demonstrated that the single shot, recording an incomplete piece of action, is the unit of which films must be constructed and thereby established a basic principle of editing."[17] The cinematographer who shot the film and the director who ordered the individual shots, by prescribing them in the shooting schedule, and typically editing them too, established the complete "piece of action" emblematic of human labor and technical production in German filmmaking. Thus, "Eisenstein, far from wanting a smoothly flowing series of images, deliberately set out to exploit the conflict implied at the junction of any two shots. Against this it must be said that the German film-makers of the late twenties, using a much more fluid camera technique, often made deliberate attempts to achieve smooth-flowing continuity."[18] In German film this kind of deliberation, or intentional image-making, designed to achieve continuous action, is attributable to the collaborations of directors and cinematographers. Notably, these relationships were fluid in nature, like the continuity, but also the discontinuity, of the films they produced. Thus, in the late 1910s and through the 1920s, whereas Lubitsch and Sparkuhl worked together exclusively on eighteen successive films over a period of eight years, Lang established several different cinematic partnerships of a similar kind, with Freund, Hoffmann, and Wagner, on nine films over fourteen years. The distinction between these two prototypes of collaborative partnerships, exclusive and inclusive, indicates they may have formed less because of any special personal compatibilities of directors and cinematographers, although this was likely true in the beginning of film, than because of a working model that these early collaborations established.

Thus, this model was the foundation of the concept of the *filmemacher*, describing the tandem, the equal partnership, of director and cinematographer, representative and characteristic of German film development and production in the formative silent era, and corresponding to the concept of *auteur* in contemporaneous films by Charles Chaplin, Buster Keaton, and others. As a cultural phenomenon, an articulation of the *zeitgeist*, the *filmemacher* model had counterparts in the other arts in Germany and in even in Weimar society and culture. For example, in German literature the "metropolitan miniature," a visual journalistic short prose form, a feuilleton, that represented modern urban experiences and metropolitan perceptions and imitated various aspects of the new media, such as in Walter Benjamin's *One-Way Street, and Other Writings* (1928), and in which "photographic and cinematic techniques such as quick cuts, close-ups, slow motion, and montage were not simply imitated in the feuilleton miniature: they were creatively digested and transformed into language. Photography and film were worked through both in their deficiencies and achievements as mirrors of urban life."[19] Through the device of focalization, the shared point of view of narrator and protagonist, the feuilleton functions as a kind of narratorial collaboration that evokes the mediatized metropolitan environment. Similarly, postwar urban life was characterized by a proliferation of same-sex couples and other nonheteronormative partnerships with shared perspectives on gender, sexuality, and society, that were collaborative relationships, people working together to change perceptions. German portrait photography and painting are remarkable for their paired subjects, such as Friedrich Seidenstücker and Heinz von Perckhammer's works, both *Untitled* (1930), depicting young lesbian women in love, Christian Schad's *Agosta, the Pigeon-Chested Man, and Rasha, the Black Dove* (1929), Heinrich Maria Davringhausen's *The Prostitute* (1921), and Rudolf Schlichter's *The Artist with Two Hanged Women* (1924). The association between collaborative couples in film production and the representation of nonstandard couples in the other arts is most explicitly evident in the gelatin-silver prints of Brassaï [Gyula Halász], such as *Female Couple* (1932) and *Homosexual Ball* (1933), and in the photomontages of Hannah Höch, such as *Training* (1925), *Vagabonds* (1926), and *The Strong Men* (1931): "Hannah Höch, one of the early exponents of Dada photomontage, cruised popular magazines in the 1920s, shattering the classically ordered, integrated bodies represented in the magazines into fragments, which she recombined into strange and exotic hybrid personae."[20] Höch's methodology in her photomontages, which were a form of *bricolage*, was effectively image editing, and she depicted her paired subjects, pieced together from repurposed fragments, in editorial procedures that were analogous to those of film directors and cinematographers, which also were socially and culturally heterodox, transgressive, albeit within the cinematic paradigm of class, intellectual endeavor, and physical labor, rather than the artistic paradigm of sexuality and gender. How, precisely, were collaborations in film production transgressive? First, they subverted the class hierarchy that had emerged in the feature-film industry after the actuality phase, in which the film director, as the title signified, was preeminent and proprietary in the ensemble of filmmakers. In the Weimar Republic, cinematographers and directors were equal partners in the recording and assembling of films and they, along with all other members of the crew, were equally *filmemacherin*. Second, these collaborations involved not just working together side by side but also work sharing: the director became a camera operator and the camera operator a director. Third, this model of collaborative film production made a lasting contribution to international film history, as continues to be evident today in several close film director and director of photography working relationships, notably American filmmaker Wes Anderson and his director of photography, Robert Yeoman, who have worked together on all eight of Anderson's feature films, 1996–2015, and who have constructed a distinctive visual grammar, with their own syntax of camera lenses, angles, ratios, shots, and color palettes, somewhat in the manner of collaborative partnerships in film production in Weimar. Table 1.1 lists the most significant collaborations of the era.

Of course, such collegial relationships in film production in the sound era are counterbalanced by many examples of autocratic directors like Cecil B. DeMille and Alfred Hitchcock. Yet DeMille, who rarely used the same camera operator twice, hired Victor Milner to shoot his *Cleopatra* (1934), for which he received the 1934 Academy Award in cinematography. DeMille worked with Milner on seven more films over the next decade, and together they designed the signature epic scale and visual spectacle of the DeMille historical dramatic film. Still, history has recognized this as the DeMille brand, not the DeMille-Milner brand, in part because, despite their success, DeMille and Milner had not an equal collaborative partnership but a conventional studio system working relationship, in which the camera operator, essentially subservient to the film director, obeyed his directions to achieve his shots, his distinctive look for the films. Alfred Hitchcock is another interesting case in point. He made his directorial debut in Berlin, with the feature films, coproductions of Gainsborough and Münchener Lichtspielkunst Emelka, *The Pleasure Garden* (1926) and *The Mountain Eagle* (1926), working with cinematographer Baron Ventimiglia, whom he hired again for the first film he directed back in England, *The Lodger: A Story of the London Fog* (1926). For the rest of his feature films in England, 1927–1939, until he moved to Hollywood, he directed the first two films

Table 1.1. Collaborations of Directors and Cinematographers in the Weimar Republic

Cinematographer	*Director*	*Film*	*Release Date*
Theodor Sparkuhl	Ernst Lubitsch	*Der G.m.b.H. Tenor*	Dec. 22, 1916
		Das fidele Gefängnis	Nov. 30, 1917
		Der Rodalkavalier	Mar. 1, 1918
		Das Mädel vom Ballet (lost)	Sept. 18, 1918
		Ich möchte kein Mann Sein	Oct. 1, 1918
		Meyer aus Berlin	Jan. 17, 1919
		Meine Frau, die Filmschauspielerin	Jan. 24, 1919
		Die Austernprinzessin	June 26, 1919
		Madame Dubarry	Sept. 18, 1919
		Rausch	Sept. 24, 1919
		Die Puppe	Dec. 5, 1919
		Kohlhiesels Töchter	Mar. 9, 1920
		Romeo und Juliet im Schnee	Mar. 12, 1920
		Sumurun	Sept. 1, 1920
		Anna Boleyn	Dec. 3, 1920
		Die Bergkatze	Apr. 14, 1921
		Das Weib des Pharoa	Feb. 22, 1922
		Die Flamme	Apr. 2, 1923
	E. A. Dupont	*Das alte Gesetz*	Oct. 29, 1923
Karl Freund	Fritz Lang	*Die Spinnen, 1 Teil: Der Goldene See*	Oct. 3, 1919
		Die Spinnen, 2 Teil: Das Brillantenschiff	Feb. 2, 1920
		Metropolis	Jan. 10, 1927
	Paul Wegener	*Der Golem: Wie er in die Welt kam*	Oct. 29, 1920
	F. W. Murnau	*Die Finanzen des Grossherzogs*	Jan. 7, 1924
		Der letzte Mann	Dec. 23, 1924
		Herr Tartüff	Nov. 16, 1925
	Carl Theodor Dreyer	*Mikaël*	Sept. 26, 1924
	E. A. Dupont	*Varieté*	Nov. 16, 1925
Carl Hoffmann	Fritz Lang	*Die Spinnen, 1 Teil: Der Goldene See*	Oct. 3, 1919
		Harakiri	Dec. 18, 1919
		Dr. Mabuse der Spieler	Apr. 27, 1922
		Die Nibelungen: Siegfried	Feb. 14, 1924
		Die Nibelungen: Kriemhilds Rache	Apr. 26, 1924
	E. A. Dupont	*Varieté*	Nov. 16, 1925

(continued)

Table 1.1. *(continued)*

Cinematographer	*Director*	*Film*	*Release Date*
	F. W. Murnau	*Desire*	Feb. 1921
		Faust: Eine deutsche Volkssage	Oct. 14, 1926
	Arthur Robison	*Die Todesschleife*	Sept. 15, 1928
Fritz Arno Wagner	F. W. Murnau	*Schloss Vogelöd*	Apr. 7, 1921
		Nosferatu, eine Symphonie des Grauens	Feb. 17, 1922
		Der brennende Acker	Mar. 3, 1922
	Fritz Lang	*Der müde Tod*	Oct. 6, 1921
		Spione	Mar. 22, 1928
		M	May 11, 1931
		Das Testament des Dr. Mabuse	Apr. 12, 1933
	Arthur Robison	*Schatten: Eine nächtliche Halluzination*	Oct. 16, 1923
	G. W. Pabst	*Die Liebe der Jeanne Ney*	Dec. 6, 1927
		Tagebuch einer Verlorenen	Sept. 27, 1929
		Westfront 1918: Vier von der Infanterie	May 23, 1930
		Skandal um Eva	June 13, 1930
		Die 3 Groschen-Oper	Feb. 19, 1931
		Kameradschaft	Nov. 17, 1931
Günther Rittau	Fritz Lang	*Die Nibelungen: Siegfried*	Feb. 14, 1924
		Die Nibelungen: Kriemhilds Rache	Apr. 26, 1924
		Metropolis	Jan. 10, 1927
	Joe May	*Asphalt*	March 12, 1929
	Josef von Sternberg	*Der blaue Engel*	Apr. 1, 1930
Günther Krampf	F. W. Murnau	*Nosferatu, eine Symphonie des Grauens*	Feb. 17, 1922
	Robert Wiene	*Orlacs Hände*	Sept. 24, 1924
	G. W. Pabst	*Die Büchse der Pandora*	Jan. 30, 1929
Guido Seeber	Fritz Lang	*Das wandernde Bild*	Dec. 25, 1920
	G. W. Pabst	*Die freudlose Gasse*	May 18, 1925
		Geheimnisse einer Seele	Mar. 24, 1926
		Man spielt nicht mit der Liebe (lost)	Nov. 10, 1926
Rudolph Maté	Carl Theodor Dreyer	*Mikaël*	Sept. 26, 1924
		La passion de Jeanne d'Arc	1928
		Vampyr	May 6, 1932

(continued)

Cinematographer	Director	Film	Release Date
Max Fassbender	Richard Oswald	*Anders al die Andern*	May 28, 1919
	Fritz Lang	*Harakiri*	Dec. 18, 1919
Willy Hameister	Robert Wiene	*Das Cabinet des Dr. Caligari*	Feb. 26, 1920
Max Lutze	F. W. Murnau	*Der Gang in der Nacht*	Jan. 21, 1921
Otto Kanturek	Fritz Lang	*Vier um die Frau*	Feb. 3, 1921
		Frau im Mond	Oct. 15, 1929
Karl Hasselman	Dimitri Buchowetski	*Othello*	Feb. 1922
Werner Brandes	E. A. Dupont	*Die grüne Manuela: Ein Film aus dem Süden*	Oct. 10, 1923
Helmar Lerski	Paul Leni	*Das Wachsfigurenkabinett*	Nov. 13, 1924
Gilbert Warrenton	Paul Leni	*The Cat and the Canary*	Sept. 3, 1927
		The Man Who Laughs	Apr. 27, 1928
Charles Rosher	F. W. Murnau	*Sunrise: A Song of Two Humans*	Sept. 23, 1927
	E. A. Dupont	*Atlantik*	Oct. 28, 1929
		Zwei Welten	Sept. 16, 1930
		Menschen im Käfig	Oct. 21, 1930

with cinematographer Claude L. McDonnell, and the next ten straight with John J. Cox, after which he started to rely on various camera operators. In America, this kind of ad hoc hiring pattern continued, until Hitchcock started working with Robert Burks on *Stranger on a Train* (1951), who became his cinematographer on twelve of his greatest films, including *Rear Window* (1954), *North by Northwest* (1959), and *The Birds* (1963). Given the very distinctive visual grammar that Hitchcock's major films have, was it attributable to a filmmaker partnership between Hitchcock and Burks? In one respect it was. Hitchcock had learned about collaborative partnerships during his tenure in Berlin in 1925–1926, initially as a scenarist, art director, and assistant director on *The Blackguard* (1925), and with Theodor Sparkuhl as cinematographer, yet "Sparkuhl knew as little English as Hitchcock knew German, so they communicated mainly via sketches and sign language."[21] In England, he invariably worked with Alma Reville, his wife, as assistant director or on continuity. At the start of his tenure in Hollywood, he twice worked with cinematographers he had met in Berlin, Rudolph Maté on *Foreign Correspondent* (1940) and Günther Krampf on the propaganda films *Bon Voyage* (1944) and *Adventure Malgache* (1944). In the end, Hitchcock's individualism as a director won out over his experience with cooperative filmmaking. His collaborative relationships with his camera operators were at best ambivalent: "Telling Burks he intended to shoot the film in black and white for a journalistic look, Hitchcock warned the cameraman that *The Wrong Box* might not be his kind of subject. But Burks stayed on, and once gain Hitchcock benefitted from his expressive camera work."[22] Burks did indeed contribute, as much as Hitchcock, and arguably more, to achieving the signature Hitchcock look on *The Wrong Box* and the other of his films he shot, but typically Hitchcock took all the credit for how they appeared screened in the cinema. The director did not acknowledge shared images.

That Hitchcock did not fully practice the teachings on collaborative filmmaking he had learned in Germany and England may be attributable (1) to his authoritative, domineering personality as an artist, (2) to the class trajectory of his film career, from title designer to one of the greatest directors in the world, and (3) to the studio and the star systems at Paramount, Warner Bros., MGM, and Universal, where individualism was the prototype. Even German directors and cinematographers who immigrated to the United States in the 1920s–1940s, from E. A. Dupont to Fritz Lang, Rudolph Maté to Günther Krampf, found they had to conform to American filmmaking conventions to stay gainfully employed. Dupont, who collaborated with cinematographer Karl Freund on *Varieté* (1925), was reduced to directing B pictures in Hollywood; Krampf, who along with cinematographer Fritz Arno Wagner had collaborated with F. W. Murnau on *Nosferatu* (1922), was reduced to shooting war propaganda films in Hollywood. The desperate political and economic times that forced German filmmakers to accept career compromises of this kind were the same forces that made filmmakers in Germany adopt and develop the collaborative principles of film production, not just for reasons of industrial efficiency, to make profound and popular visual art, the best in the world, but also to survive in politically and economically unstable times and to use visual art to effect meaningful social change through socialism and democratization, or, alternatively, to stave off personal and community destruction or the resignation of going into exile. The filmmaker collaboration was an expression of the Modernist art, utopian, and futurist collective movement prominent in Germany in the early 1920s, as typified by the Novembergruppe and the Bauhaus, which the Nazis appropriated later in the decade in political collectives like Nazi Youth groups, parades, rallies, and other public spectacles. For example, in *Metropolis* (1927), Fritz Lang documented this transition in the German collective ethos perspicaciously in his representation of an athletic youth society that degenerates into a dystopia. Neurologically, this transition from art to political collectives in the Weimar period, specifically from aesthetic knowledge to political knowledge or propaganda, is attributable to a "hidden" human condition: "The hidden state problem arises as a case of *perceptual aliasing*: the mapping between states of the world and sensations of the agent is not one-to-one. . . . If the agent's perceptual system produces the same outputs for two world states in which different actions are required, and if the agent's state representation consists only of its percepts, then the agent will fail to choose correct actions."[23] Thus, a "hidden state" arises when obstacles obstruct an agent's trajectory from the perceptual senses, in which case the agent can be said to be in a "hidden state" or be experiencing a hidden human condition. In the Weimar Republic, filmmakers and other artists discerned two world states requiring different courses of action, including career trajectories: an artistic state of social freedom and personal hope and a political state of economic uncertainty and increasing government control. Because Weimar was a period of unrestrained optimism, based on the collective belief that artwork, artistic practice, collectives, and movements could guide the postwar political system and the reconstruction of Germany, artists perceived art and the political state, their own sensations and the world, as having a one-to-one correspondence. They were relying only on their percepts, specifically their aesthetic perceptions of social and cultural infrastructures, their inputs, throughputs, and outputs, and naively assuming the same outputs for art and politics, which actually demanded different responses, different courses of action, as history has shown. In this regard the Weimar Republic was a period of *perceptual aliasing*. Just as the bourgeoisie were enjoying the new freedom of expression, the new social, class, gender, and sexual liberalism, they were hoping it would continue indefinitely. Persisting in acting freely and openly in society, as if they were completely free, was the people's way of immunizing themselves against impending disaster, not just the rise of fascism but also their own *perceptual aliasing* and hidden condition. Art, utopian, and futurist collectives were their principal means of resisting the state and of self-immunization. In the film industry, small collaborative partnerships, which were minimally collective, as the Novembergruppe and Bauhaus were maximally collective, functioned in the same fashion. Thus, by working together in teams and as equal partners, directors and cinematographers combined their perceptual systems by sharing images and agencies, augmenting their percepts, as it were. These collaborative associations were perceptual aliases, however, like Expressionism, designed to maximize production aesthetically. Generated by perceptual aliases, collaborations were pragmatic self-protective associations, linked arms against the ineluctable forces of the state.

They were also fundamentally a linking of the perceptions and percepts of two filmmakers with a shared experiential knowledge of film history. In contrast, the collaborative partnership of Salvador Dalí, a painter, and Luis Buñuel, a filmmaker, in making a contemporaneous film, *Un Chien andalou* (1929), was problematic, an alliance not based on common film knowledge and skills: "Studies of collaborations often amount to little more than considerations of paternity and motif hunting. *Un Chien andalou* had had its share of this treatment, to which Dalí and Buñuel have themselves contributed by assigning certain motifs to themselves as well as to one another."[24] The alliances of filmmakers and cinematographers, however, are more than opportunistic working relationships of this kind. They are epistemological collaborations based on optics, on a shared cinematic vision and a common knowledge of the optical capabilities of cameras, about practical matters like lenses, field depth, space compression, and image resolution. Given that in the formative silent era, in particular, filmmaking was largely about altering spectators' perceptions of film content and about film as a medium, or teaching the grammar and syntax of film, then directors and cinematographers that worked together closely as equal partners in the discipline and that even, I contend, shared film percepts and perceptions were especially well equipped to make efficacious films of this sort that made spectators part of the production. Therefore, the critical analysis of films for which directors and cinematographers receive equal credit as design partners tends not to raise questions of "paternity and motif hunting" as in the reception of *Un Chien andalou*. Each shot, and every frame, is directly attributable to the director and the cinematographer as a team.

How, precisely, were the percepts of filmmakers and spectators connected in the silent era? First, the connection between them had to do with attention, with the fact that directors and cinematographers attentive to the same image, to the same vision of the finished film, could eventually attract the attention of spectators in the theater, could engage and surprise spectators with their vision. With reference to filmmaking as a survival as well as an aesthetic practice in the unstable political and economic infrastructure of the Weimar Republic, two neurological principles must be noted here, (1) "attention plays an essential role in the survival of an organism" and (2) "there is an immediate connection between surprise and learning, or rather habituation."[25] Thus, by forging highly attentive working relationships German directors and cinematographers were increasing their own chances of prospering as filmmakers within the industry and surviving as members of the wider society, and they were helping their spectators also to survive, by securing their attention and allowing them to learn by being surprised, as historically spectators had been thoroughly surprised by the first actuality films and the new narrative films of Eisenstein and Porter. Second, according to the Bayesian theory of probability, named after eighteenth-century English statistician Thomas Bayes, "the amount of surprise in the data for a given observer can be measured by the change that has taken place in going from the prior to the posterior probabilities"[26] and "we can expect a form of habituation whereby, on average, surprise decreases after each iteration."[27] In film spectatorship, however, habituation was minimal, because each successive screening attracted a fresh audience. Thus, if according to Bayesian theory surprise decreases through habituation, after each iteration of data having prior and posterior distributions, it did not decrease this way in film, except for projectionists, ushers, and others with occasion to see films repeatedly, at least in the first phase of its development, when *in Kino gehen* ("to go to the pictures")—to take in the public space of the theater, the medium of film, and the protocol of viewing—was part of the surprise. Thus, even attending the pictures with great regularity, as most people did at the time, was not habituation diminishing surprise, yet it was a learning experience. This was the revolutionary paradox of early cinema, that it fostered in spectators habitual learning about cinema through nonhabitual surprises. Given that films only appear to be continuous entities but are actually projections with prior and posterior frame distributions, does the surprise inherent in watching a film diminish frame by frame at a particular frame rate through its duration? For example, Fritz Lang's *M* (1931) can be analyzed as a data set of information with a duration of 99 minutes, projected at 24 frames per second. This film can be calculated to contain 142,560 frames, each frame different from all the others.

> The concrete value of the images gives them a different meaning each time. They never repeat themselves. If we were to include only the 500,000 feature films produced in the world since 1912, there would be over 60 million images. And none of them bears the remotest resemblance to any other.[28]

Clearly, the first frame of *M* does not surprise maximally and the last frame does not surprise not at all, even though Bayesian theory would contend that each frame is an information set whose capacity to surprise diminishes through its own prior to posterior progression. In his "shortcut for attention," however, Pierre Baldi proposes that "the surprise can be defined as the 'distance' between the prior and posterior distributions: highly surprising data should correspond to substantive revaluation of the prior and, therefore, to larger distances."[29] Thus, in a screening of *M* projected at 24 FPS, spectators would perceive through the faculty termed *persistence of vision* 142,559 of these distances, corresponding to the bands between the film's frames. Neurologically, each of these distances, which contains no information, surprises because of the prior and posterior distributions of information in the frames around them. Experientially, spectators do not notice these bands, or any frames in isolation, excepting freeze frames, although "flicker appears on film as an uneven variation in exposure. This effect is a result of variations in exposure from frame to frame as a result of a mismatch in the output wave form of the light and the framing rate of the camera."[30] Experiential surprise comes directly from the moving images and sounds, the linear narrative content of film, although it too might be described as a distance between prior and posterior, as is apparent in sight gags and ironic tones.

Thus, in the Weimar period the percepts of filmmakers and spectators were connected through (1) nonhabituated surprise, the novelty of the film medium, and the visual and sonic narrative content of film, and 2) the habituation of regular public attendance at cinemas and of learning through their exposure to directors and cinematographers' shared images. Learning about film through its content and construction was more than a recreational benefit for spectators, for whom, as for filmmakers themselves, spectatorship was a form of *perceptual aliasing*, at once a celebration of the new social and cultural freedoms after the war and a kind of diversionary immunization against the collapse of the infrastructure. Whereas for directors and cinematographers, *perceptual aliasing* was a distinguishing feature of their industrial collaborations, for film spectators this condition was attributable to two factors: the public spectacle of film screenings, where the collective percepts of audiences established social relationships within visual culture; and spectators' exposure to the filmmakers' shared images, emblems of their collaborations, and their absorption of them into visual culture and knowledge.

Clearly, the Weimar Republic was a period of revolutionary sociopolitical change and radical new freedoms in the arts, gender and sexuality, and cultural identity and agency, and most notably the erosion of class and workplace hierarchies. In the film industry the emergence of the camera operator from the conventional hierarchy of the traditional filmmaking ensemble to assume the more powerful role of cinematographer or director of photography, and a higher-level creative status on par with that of the film director, was in one sense a by-product of this sociopolitical revolution, typical of other extreme changes in the arts and the workplace. But in another sense, the arrival of the cinematographer in this new prominent role as a collaborative visual artist was attributable to film itself, to the development of the new medium and its technology, which at the start of the Weimar Republic, were less than a quarter-century old, and to the establishment of a prosperous German film industry, with Berlin and Munich as the major centers, to rival film production in America, France, Denmark, and England, and to attract international contributors with the success of the film studios, but also with the environment of social and artistic freedom, directors such as G. W. Pabst (Austria-Hungary) and Carl Theodor Dreyer (Denmark), and cinematographers such as Otto Kanturek (Austro-Hungary), Rudolph Maté (Poland), and Charles Rosher (England). The attraction the German film industry had for Hitchcock is legendary: "Although he could be evasive about his influences, when pressed Hitchcock would mention *The Cabinet of Dr. Caligari*, Murnau, Lang, even Lubitsch. And when asked in general about stylistic mentors, his reply was unflinching. 'The Germans. The Germans.'"[31] For others the German film industry offered an aesthetic and professional freedom complicated by racial prejudice at home. Anna May Wong was the most prominent American movie star to appear in German films, *Schmutziges Geld* (1928), *Grosstadtschmetterling* (1929), and *der Weg zur Schande* (1930), all directed by Richard Eichberg. Racially stereotyped in exotic supporting roles in Hollywood, she was cast again as dancers in Eichberg's films. Nevertheless, her experience with Eichberg led to her first starring role, in E. A. Dupont's *Piccadilly* (1929).

> In 1928, after having played an Eskimo in *The Alaskan* (1924), Tiger Lily in *Peter Pan* (1924), a harem girl in *His Supreme Moment* (1925), a Chinese girl in *Old San Francisco* (1927), a barroom prostitute in *Across to Singapore* (1928), and other racially-profiled juvenile parts, she traveled to Germany with the expectation of landing non-stereotypical and better received Asian roles, stemming from her having made an acquaintance in Hollywood with Dr. Karl Vollmöller (1878–1948), a German playwright and a screenwriter, notably of Josef von Sternberg's *Der Blaue Engel* (1930), who, important for Wong, had connections to the film company Richard Eichberg Film GmbH.[32]

The historical irony here is not just that, despite her expectation that in relocating her career to Germany she would get better roles, Wong was cast in stereotypical dancer roles in all three of Eichberg's films, and even when she got the chance to play a romantic lead in Dupont's film, she was a scullery dishwasher who rose to become a featured nightclub dancer, exoticized as Asian, but also that Germany, which seemed a global center of unprecedented artistic and social freedom, acceptance, and tolerance in the 1920s, degenerated into an ineluctable force of brutal totalitarian control, hatred, cruelty, and racial, ethnic, gender, and religious bigotry in the 1930s.

The emergence of filmmaking partnerships among directors and cinematographers in the Weimar period is attributable to two main factors: (1) the artistic and social freedoms Germany experienced after World War One, which accommodated experimentation, subversion, mobility, and association, and thus inspired productivity; and (2) the knowledge among artists, intellects, and the general public that this fluid, adaptable culture was transitory, which inspired a sense of urgency among them. Collaboration in the film industry had to do with the greater productivity directors and cinematographers thought they might achieve by working together in an interdisciplinary manner, and it had to do with a pall of fear and despair that seemed to hang over the filmmaking industry because this revolutionary new medium was hyperlinked to nationalism.

NOTES

1. Jean Mitry, *Semiotics and the Analysis of Film*, trans. Christopher King (Bloomington and Indianapolis: Indiana University Press, 2000), 7.

2. Stephanie Barron, "New Objectivity: German Realism after Expressionism," in *New Objectivity: Modern German Art in the Weimar Republic 1919–1933*, ed. Barron and Sabine Eckmann, 15 (New York: Prestel, Los Angeles: Los Angeles County Museum of Art, 2015).

3. R. S. Furness, *Expressionism* (London: Methuen, 1973), 74.

4. Cited in Peter Kobel and the Library of Congress, *Silent Movies: The Birth of Film and the Triumph of Movie Culture* (New York: Little, Brown, 2007), 108.

5. Peter Kobel and the Library of Congress, *Silent Movies: The Birth of Film and the Triumph of Movie Culture* (New York: Little, Brown, 2007), 218.

6. Anne Rutherford, "Teaching Film and Mise-en-Scène," in *Teaching Film*, ed. Lucy Rischer and Patrice Petro, 301 (New York: Modern Language Association of America, 2012).

7. Raine Metzger, *Berlin: The Twenties*, trans. Clare Costa (2006; New York: Abrams, 2007), 124.

8. Philipp Stiasny, "Humanity Unleashed: Anti-Bolshevism as Popular Culture in Early Weimar Cinema," in *The Many Faces of Weimar Cinema: Rediscovering Germany's Filmic Legacy*, ed. Christian Rogowski, 63 (Rochester, NY: Camden House, 2010).

9. Paul Matthew St. Pierre, *Mediate! Digital Perspectives on Canadian Media History* (Dubuque, IA: Kendall Hunt, 2013), 45.

10. Mitry, *Semiotics and the Analysis of Film*, 189–90.

11. Ibid., 190.

12. J. E. Cirlot, *A Dictionary of Symbols*, trans. Jack Sage, 2nd ed. (London: Routledge & Kegan Paul, 1971), 312.

13. G. E. M. Anscombe, *Intention*, 2nd ed. (Cambridge, MA: Harvard University Press, 1963), 70.

14. Ibid., 68.

15. Ibid., 70.

16. Ibid., 79.

17. Karel Reisz and Gavin Millar, *The Technique of Film Editing* (1953; London and New York: Focal, 1968), 19.

18. Ibid., 48.

19. Andreas Huyssen, "Writing Photography," in *New Objectivity: Modern German Art in the Weimar Republic 1919–1933*, ed. Stephanie Barron and Sabine Eckmann, 116 (New York: Prestel, Los Angeles: Los Angeles County Museum of Art, 2015).

20. Jennifer Blessing, *Rrose Is a Rrose Is a Rrose: Gender Performance in Photography* (New York: Guggenheim Museum, 1997), 23.

21. Patrick McGilligan, *Alfred Hitchcock: A Life in Darkness and Light* (New York: HarperCollins, 2003), 62.

22. Ibid., 536–37.

23. R. Andrew McCallum, "Instance-Based State Identification for Reinforcement Learning," in *Advances in Neural Information Processing Systems 7*, ed. Gerald Tesauro, David Touretzky, and Todd Leen, 377 (Cambridge, MA, and London: MIT, 1995).

24. Haim Finkelstein, "Dalí and *Un Chien andalou*: The Nature of a Collaboration," in *Dada and Surrealist Film*, ed. Rudolf E. Kuenzli, 128 (Cambridge, MA, and London: MIT, 1996).

25. Pierre Baldi, "Surprise: A Shortcut for Attention?" in *Neurobiological of Attention*, ed. Laurent Itti, Geraint Rees, and Joh K. Tsotsos, 24, 26 (Amsterdam: Elsevier, 2005).

26. Ibid., 24.

27. Ibid., 26.

28. Mitry, *Semiotics and the Analysis of Film*, 28.

29. Baldi, "Surprise," 25.

30. Blain Brown, *Cinematography Theory and Practice: Image Making for Cinematographers, Directors, and Videographers* (Amsterdam: Elsevier, 2002), 261.

31. McGilligan, *Alfred Hitchcock*, 64.

32. Paul Matthew St. Pierre, *E. A. Dupont and His Contribution to British Film: Varieté, Moulin Rouge, Piccadilly, Atlantic, Two Worlds, Cape Forlorn* (Madison, NJ: Fairleigh Dickinson University Press, 2010), 82.

2

The Optical Convergence of Theodor Sparkuhl and Ernst Lubitsch

As a cinematographer, Theodor Sparkuhl (1894–1946) emerged on the Berlin film scene in the short film *Leutnant auf Befehl*, released in September 1916, directed by Danny Kaden and starring Ernst Lubitsch, Ossi Oswalda, and Harry Liedtke. Lubitsch was already an established silent-film actor, having appeared in twenty-four films, mostly comedies, but he had also directed seven films, 1914–1916, all but the first with his own film company, Matray-Lubitsch-Film, which he had established with his costar, the actor Ernst Matray. Lubitsch had yet to establish himself as a filmmaker of any significance. After his debut as cinematographer on *Leutnant auf Befehl*, Sparkuhl went on to shoot several of Lubitsch's short films over three years, the comedies *Der G.m.b.H. Tenor* (1916), *Das fidele Gefängnis* (1917), *Der Rodalkavalier* (1918), *Das Mädel vom Ballet* (1918), *Ich möchte kein Mann sein* (1918), *Meyer aus Berlin* (1919), *Meine Frau, die Filmschauspielerin* (1919), and two films that would mark the transition from their ad hoc working relationship to more of a collaborative partnership, *Die Austernprinzessin* (June 1919) and *Madame Dubarry* (September 1919). They further collaborated over the remainder of Lubitsch's career in Germany, on the masterworks *Die Puppe* (December 1919), *Sumurun* (September 1920), *Anna Boleyn* (December 1920), and *Die Bergkatze* (April 1921), until the director moved to Hollywood in 1922–1923. While working with Lubitsch initially, Sparkuhl also shot five films with a lesser director, the actor and World War One propaganda filmmaker Georg Jacoby (1883–1964): *Der Flieger von Georg* (1918); *Kaimendes Leben, Teil 1* (1918); *Kaimendes Leben, Teil 2* (1919); *Kreuzigt sie!* (1919); and *Vendetta* (1919). What distinguishes Sparkuhl's working relationship with Jacoby from his working relationship with Lubitsch? Did Sparkuhl simply take advantage of his opportunity to further his professional association with the more accomplished filmmaker, or did he and Lubitsch recognize some aesthetic and executional features in each other's artistry that might allow them to flourish together?

What distinguishes the visual grammar of Lubitsch's films is that it corresponds to the signifying system of Sparkuhl's cinematography, which is the distinguishing feature of the key films of Lubitsch's career in Germany. This arrangement that became an artistic partnership, the collaboration of a film director and cinematographer on the visual grammar and semiotic imprint of film, typical of filmmaking partnerships in the Weimar Republic, is a model of aesthetic poetics and practice.

Theodor Friedrich Franz Sparkuhl was born on October 7, 1894, in Hannover, Germany. He attended Georg August Universität Göttingen and Universität Bonn, but for financial reasons did not complete a degree. In 1911 he took a job in the projector sales department of L. Gaumont et Cie, La Villette, France, the photography and film equipment company of Léon Gaumont, who in 1902 had invented the chronophone, an experimental sound-on-disc recording apparatus for film. In 1912, Sparkuhl was promoted to the position of news cinematographer at its Cité Elgé studios, the film production and distribution division of the company, and the oldest film studio in the world, where filmmaker Louis Feuillade was artistic director. The experience Sparkuhl acquired shooting newsreel films and, from 1913, at his positions as a cinematographer first with Eiko-Film GmbH, Berlin, and then at Éclair, Paris, both film-production studios, prepared him for his military service in the First World War, shooting location war news footage for the German government, in Russia, France, Greece, Bulgaria, and Palestine, and also Turkey, where with the Red Cross he practiced as a surgeon in Constantinople. In 1918, he became a cinematographer at a new studio, Universum Film AG (Ufa), founded in 1917, in Potsdam, where he made eighteen feature films with Lubitsch, 1916–1923, and established a collaborative partnership. In November 1922, corporate economic instability forced Ufa to suspend production activities, although the studio compensated directors, including Lubitsch, with contracts to December 1923. As well as the comedies he shot with Lubitsch the actor, which were essential to their partnership because they introduced the camera operator to the director's "modern pantomime"[1] of postural, facial, and gestural displays in relation to the camera, Sparkuhl shot *Kreuzigt Sie!* (June 1919), directed by Georg Jacoby, starring Pola Negri, who would star also in Lubitsch's *Madame Dubarry* (September 1919) and *Sumurun* (September 1920). As he had done with Lubitsch, on *Kreuzigt Sie!* Sparkuhl committed to memory the image of Negri's "modern pantomime" for some future use, on her two films with Lubitsch.

The foundation of Sparkuhl's cinematographer-director partnership with Lubitsch was on *Ich möchte kein Mann Sein [I Don't Want to Be a Man]* (October 1918), a comedy about female-male (F-M) gender-crossing that draws on the theatrical conventions of *commedia dell'arte* but that also held a mirror up to film audiences, showing the kind of unrestrained experimentation in gender alterity and sexuality that would become common in the Weimar period. The plot is simple: Ossi (Ossi Oswalda), an exuberant *garçonne*, escapes from her overprotective guardian uncle (Ferry Sikla) by disguising herself as a gentleman and going out on an adventure, where she falls into a romantic relationship with Dr. Kersten (Curt Götz), meets the

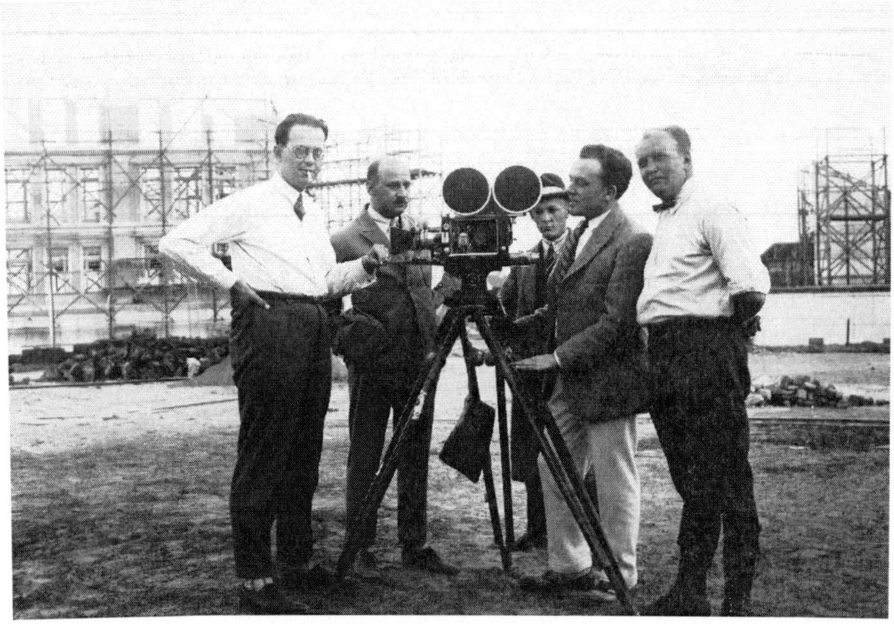

Figure 2.1. ***Left to right:*** **Theodor Sparkuhl, Ottmar Ostermayr, unknown, Charles Rosher, and Fritz Arno Wagner. Source: Deutsche Kinemathek.**

comic frustrations of many gender complications, and in the end resigns herself to her conventional role as a young woman. Specifically, *Ich möchte kein Mann Sein* is less about gender-crossing than about cross-dressing and gender impersonation, evident in that Ossi rejects her brief male experience.

> Still, plays that place issues of representation at the forefront—often by putting a character in cross-dressed disguise—remind us of the disarming possibility that our own guarded identities, even those that feel as intimate as skin, must be aggressively and institutionally enforced if they are to be sustained. Thus, through their mimetic apparatus, such plays denaturalize gender even as they may narratively represent patriarchal images of femininity and masculinity.[2]

Outside of the character's rationale in the context of the plot, Ossi's cross-dressing is indicative of the masculinization of women's fashions and grooming in the 1920s, which is apparent, for example, in Marlene Dietrich's tailored suits and in *Bubikopf* ("boy's head"), or Eton-crop and pageboy, hairstyles, a social trend that was represented in German films and portrait paintings.

> As seen in Rudolf Schlichter's *Margot* of 1924 . . . in [Otto] Dix's portrait of Sylvia von Harden [1926], and in [Christian] Schad's *Sonja* [1928], loose-fitting shirts or shifts that deemphasized the curves of the female body were common for both day and evening

> wear. The body type that looked best in such clothing was slim, flat chested, and small hipped—in a word *masculine*—and that in fact became the fashionable ideal for many women of the 1920s.[3]

Although tropes of cross-dressing and gender impersonation in the comic mode are conventional, apparent in Shakespeare's comedies as well as in *commedia dell'arte* pantomime, Lubitsch's allusion to gender-crossing in German women's fashion in the 1920s is bold and prescient. For Ossi Oswalda, playing a man was a matter of performance, particularly the subtle performance of the body, and also a matter of costuming, makeup, and grooming. Hers was a transparent gender-crossing performance, as in *commedia* tradition: the character Ossi must be recognizable as a woman in disguise, yet resemble a man enough to convince Dr. Kersten beyond suspicion, to persuade spectators that he is convinced. For Lubitsch, however, making Oswalda's gender-crossing performance persuasive on screen to spectators has to do not just with his directions to Oswalda and Curt Götz but also with his strategy in photographing the characters, particularly in their scenes together. It was precisely in addressing the special challenge of photographing Oswalda through an F-M lens, and framing the reaction shots of Götz, that Lubitsch and Sparkuhl established their collaborative partnership on the set of *Ich möchte kein Mann Sein*, albeit still an unofficial association, since Sparkuhl went unacknowledged in the film's credits.

In contrast to the visually innovative gender-crossing scenes in which Ossi disguises herself as a man and later passes as one in social situations, the opening scenes of the film, which serve to establish the characters as types, Ossi as a rebellious tomboy, her uncle as a halfhearted disciplinarian, her new guardian, Dr. Kersten, as an implacable disciplinarian, are conventional of early film, featuring theatrical sets in which characters walk on and walk off, filmed with a stationary camera, and iris-in and iris-out shots to mark scene changes. One exceptional early shot, however, shows Ossi's uncle, away on a business trip, in his ship's cabin, suffering from seasickness: Sparkuhl simulates the rocking of the ship on heavy seas by shooting the cabin in a tilt shot: with an extreme gesture that seems to call attention to the shot as a comic contrivance, more than to its mimesis of waves, he tilts the camera fully up and down repeatedly on its axis.

The second act, titled "I Want to Be a Man," features more innovative cinematography, starting with the first shot, showing Ossi in town, a modest pan shot that follows her a few steps along the sidewalk up to the entrance of a shop that turns out to be a men's tailors. Inside, a comic scene shows the tailors enamored with her and fighting over who is to take her measurements. In the next scene, in her bedroom, Sparkuhl films her in a stationary medium three-quarter angle profile shot, showing her partly dressed as a man, in trousers, shirt, and braces, and fumbling to tie her bow tie. Throughout, Oswalda gazes into a mirror, part of which is visible at the edge of the frame. The three-quarter angle shot, which tilts the set, strikes an intimate balance between spectators looking at Ossi not just in the privacy of her bedroom but also as she gazes at herself across the gender divide and in transformation, which makes the scene voyeuristically affective. She completes the transformation by putting on a man's wig, a tuxedo jacket, cape, top hat, gloves, walking stick, and monocle. A cross-cut to a companion bedroom scene in which Dr. Kersten also is getting dressed in preparation to go out for the evening establishes a new relationship between the two characters: they are no longer guardian and ward, but potential lovers. Sparkuhl shoots Kersten in profile, but the diagonal of a corner wardrobe in the background recalls the previous scene, its content, but more importantly its three-quarter camera angle. Thus, Lubitsch and Sparkuhl exploit a cross-cut to show two actions happening at the same time and to presage a romantic relationship, and to highlight their judicious use of camera angles. This marks the first collaborative decision of director and cinematographer.

At the ball, the characters' shared destination, Sparkuhl films the frenetic revelry on the dance floor in a passing wide shot, but, although the camera is stationary, he creates the illusion of extreme camera movement, analogous to the parallactic movement of stationary objects shot with a moving camera, through the choreography of the dancers, groups of whom waltz wildly around and around and sway back and forth horizontally from one to the other side of the floor, and move toward the camera. The effect is of the camera following the rhythm of the crowd. This swaying movement is important to the subsequent scene, where Ossi, as a man, first notices Dr. Kersten at the dance and goes over to confront him. An onlooker, Kersten is standing, swaying his hips to the music. Ossi stands next to him and, wishing to adopt a convincingly manly pose, sways her hips to the music. In implying two men are unwittingly dancing together, their coordinated gestures are funny, but, in recalling the swaying dancers in the previous scene, they also draw attention to the shot, the fixed camera, and illusion of camera mobility in the film.

The third act, "I Don't Want to Be a Man," focuses on Ossi and Kersten in commiserative friendship after the ball has ended, with no partner for either of them, commiserating with each other with champagne in abundance and cigars. Sparkuhl shoots them in profile, seated at a table, facing each other, across the gender divide, as it were. Adopting their perspective, tilt-down cross-cuts to the dance floor, which is still active with dancers, locate them on a mezzanine, but also in a male domain. Thus, when Ossi, already feeling ill from the cigar and downing the champagne too quickly, excuses herself from the table, she walks automatically to the women's washroom, until a servant intercepts her, corrects her mistake, and directs her to the men's. In the companion scenes in which she approaches the two washroom doors, Oswalda performs a wobbly drunken walk, a kind of dance in which she stumbles from side to side down the hallway and toward the camera, and in the following scene in which she walks back, away from the camera. As in the previous shots of the dancers, the actor's broad movements evoke revelry, but also indicate that, while Sparkuhl appears to have exploited pan shots, the camera has not moved.

When Ossi returns to the table, she and Kersten resume their drinking and toast "to brotherhood," linking their arms as they raise their glasses; she turns away, nauseated, to the camera, whereas he remains in profile. This combination frontal-profile shot recalls the two bedroom scenes earlier, she in three-quarter profile, facing the mirror, a proxy of the camera, he in full profile. This scene, along with the bedroom scenes and the stateroom scene earlier, call attention to shot selection and camera angles as aspects of the film aesthetics and visual content. As the scene continues, Kersten and Ossi, loosening up in their drunkenness, move in and out of profile and draw closer together, nearly kissing twice, foreshadowing a more passionate kissing scene in the back of the carriage home. Still, the homoerotic and incestuous overtones of the exchange and, alternatively, the suggestion either he may have seen through her disguise, or Ossi may have dropped her mask or simply forgotten she was wearing it, seem less important than how Sparkuhl has constructed the frame optically. Thus, when Kersten and Ossi start to leave the ballroom, stumbling arm in arm until, losing their balance, they grab each other and, trying to regain their form, carry out a pirouette before heading to the cloakroom, the scene shows their attraction to each other, reinforcing the gender-crossing theme, but it also contributes to the film's strongest motif of spinning, swaying, and tottering bodies and how they compose the shot. This is particularly evident at the end of the film, when Kersten sees Ossi at home and recognizes she was the man he spent the night with. In her bedroom, Sparkuhl films the characters in a series of cross-cuts, compartmentalizing them according to gender and social station, until she crosses into his frame and they now visually occupy the same scene, which confirms a romantic relationship has been established. More important, however, Sparkuhl uses cross-cuts correlatively, to show how, like frame lines and scenic boundaries, gender barriers can be crossed and, as the plot and the cinematography together suggest, transgressed. Conventionally, cross-cuts are narratological and therefore thematic, linking scenes and implying concurrent actions and discontinuous actions. But Sparkuhl's use of cross-cuts in *Ich möchte kein Mann Sein* is also metafilmic, or self-reflexive, encouraging spectators to examine the film's construction, and the relation between the ironies of a comic plot and the divisions among its individual frames and scenes, most evident in the disparity between a stationary camera and the motion of characters and objects it records. The metafilmic quality of *Ich möchte kein Mann Sein* cannot be ascribed to the director or cinematographer alone. Rather it is attributable to their collaborative action.

In *Die Austernprinzessin [The Oyster Princess]* (June 1919) Lubitsch and Sparkuhl developed their filmmaking partnership through more innovative photography, notably in the depiction of movement in dance. The first evidence of an enhanced working relationship is Sparkuhl's acknowledgment for "cinematography" in the opening credits. Like *Ich möchte kein Mann Sein, Die Austernprinzessin* is a comedy with a simple plot: Mr. Quaker (Victor Janson), an American oyster merchant prince, tries to arrange to marry his daughter, Oss (Ossi Oswalda), to actual royalty, Prince Nucki (Harry Liedtke). The film's opening cinematographic trick for comic purposes has more to do with frame composition than optical flair. The scene is a large office, where a pool of female typists and stenographers take dictation from Mr. Quaker, seated at a desk at the front of the room. That Sparkuhl uses an iris shot that opens to reveal four African American liveried servants standing around him and catering to his every need points to racial stereotyping in American film, slavery in American history, and racism in American culture; that he subsequently uses a tilt-up shot for him and a tilt-down for the women in the pool establishes the importance of his character, emphasizing his superiority and their subservience. The dexterous but conventional shot selection functions to initiate the comic mode. Similarly, when a servant calls Quaker away to attend to his daughter, who is "in a fit of raving madness," the camera follows his protracted course jogging through the huge mansion, followed by his four servants, to her bedroom. One remarkable scene shows him walking right to left along a mezzanine in the background, then down a staircase left to right, and finally across the room background to foreground in the direction of the camera. The great distance he has to traverse just to attend to his daughter's immediate need is comical in relation to the proximity of the servants who pamper him in the previous scene, but in its spatial symbolism his trajectory is cinematic, comprising the horizontal, diagonal, and vertical axes, and thus the entire field of view. Thus, while Quaker traverses the frame, Sparkuhl demonstrates (1) how a cinematographer can make full use of the action field, and (2) that the illusion of cinema is a three-dimensional one. Serving to cross from one scene to the next by conducting Quaker to his daughter's room, this connecting shot serves mainly a technical function. That Sparkuhl elected to encrypt a visual message about the nature of cinematography and filmic space into a simple shot, essentially a sight gag, is noteworthy, suggesting he and Lubitsch were starting to work together creatively.

The marriage plot and the comedy of *Die Austernprinzessin* center on mistaken identity. First, after learning his daughter's breakdown is due to her frustration with being unmarried, Quaker promises to "buy" her a husband. A professional matchmaker recommends Nucki, an impoverished prince, who sends his friend, Josef, to the mansion to inspect the prospective bride. Wearing the prince's clothes to look presentable as Nucki's "adjutant," the servants receive him and Quaker and Oss accept him as the prince, and Josef (Julius Falkenstein) does not correct them, instead offering them Prince Nucki's card from the wallet he extracts from his jacket pocket, with the equivocal explanation, "Take this one for now" (intertitle). While Quaker keeps him waiting, Josef takes his place in the drawing room. Sparkuhl shoots this scene in characteristic fashion, with presentative blocking: Josef enters the room though a door in the left background and, gazing in all directions around the high-ceilinged room with intricately decorated walls, then he walks a diagonal line to the center of the room, and from there he walks straight to the fourth wall, where he stops, nods his assent to all he has seen, glances toward the camera, and concludes, "They live well" (intertitle), and sits in a chair in the extreme left foreground. Whether he is acknowledging the camera or the audience of spectators is unclear, but he does occupy a space that Sparkuhl favors in his shot selection and frame composition, one evident in the earlier scene in which Quaker walks to Oss's bedroom, at the bottom extremity of the frame, immediately in front of the camera. In the previous scene, similarly, Quaker and Oss sit in this space, so close to the camera that their feet are out of frame, as a servant enters through a door in the background and walks to the foreground, and toward the camera, to deliver Prince Nucki's card. Sparkuhl established this spatial pattern in the earlier scene in which Quaker walks to Oss's room. Each of these framing motives takes a character to the space immediately in front of the camera. First, the progression from background to foreground, by generating motion within the frame, compensates for the fixity of the camera, and draws spectators' eyes to the focal point of the action, where it records with maximal definition. Second, the optical progression to this space acknowledges the intervention of the camera, the fact that the image has been constructed and, in the immediacy of the action, both the theatrical action on the set and the active participation of the spectator in the cinema, that it is being filmed. For Lubitsch and Sparkuhl to make this aesthetic statement is an extraordinary gesture that declares the consolidation of their collective partnership, their style, is one of their enduring contributions to German film history.

Technically, this space proximate to the camera is about camera angle, the position of the camera in connection with the theme of the image. Thematically, it is about the intimacy of spectatorship. Thus, in the scene in which Oss undertakes her prolonged preparation to meet with Prince Nucki, she stands directly in front of the camera while five of her servants remove her clothes and hold up her bathrobe, shielding her body from the camera and as if from onlookers in the cinema. It is a moment of beautiful intimacy that endears spectators to the character in a marriage plot. The scene ends as she walks center-frame through a vanishing point of more servants lined up and each side of the trajectory to her bath in the background. But because of Lubitsch and Sparkuhl's manipulation of cinematic space, in this scene and many other scenes throughout *Die Austernprinzessin*, spectators develop at least intuitive awareness of the technical role of the camera in invoking intimacy through the relation between field of action and field size, how camera lens focal length determines the distance between the subject and the camera. For example, when Josef as Prince Nucki and Oss finally meet, she enters the drawing room through the door at the back and walks directly to him, but because he is already in the action field, they have their encounter in the field size space, in a mid shot with a short focal length. The visual effect of watching the characters close up is less of sitting in the front row at the theater than of looking over the shoulder of the camera operator, Theodor Sparkuhl, into the lens. He films Josef and Oss in mid shots standing opposite each other, in profile, and individually in close-up iris shots that encapsulate the bad impressions they form after inspecting each other.

Lubitsch and Sparkuhl make light of their preoccupation with field size space when Oss and Josef return home after eloping to get married, while her father takes a nap, and she now makes him ride in the back of the horse-drawn carriage, not in front with her as on their way to the minister. In an intertitle, Josef complains, "I was in front before," and Oss replies, "Yes, we weren't married then." In this metafilmic moment, Lubitsch and Sparkuhl parody their own methodology, subverting the field size space and the visual trope of intimacy for comic purposes.

They exploit their frame composition design of background-to-foreground horizontal, diagonal, and vertical trajectories to greatest effect in the dinner and reception Mr. Quaker hosts for the many wedding guests, specifically when they dance the fox-trot, entering the room at the back and advancing in couples in a diagonal to the foreground and passing in front of the camera, before scattering into several linear group configurations on the floor, along the horizontal, diagonal, and vertical axes. Sparkuhl films the dance floor mainly in a tilt-down shot that allows full view of the mass movement of people below, a trope he developed earlier in his shots of dozens of servants moving in unison throughout the Quaker mansion. The tilt-down high-angle shot is conventional, likely improvised on a mezzanine above the dance floor, but the depiction of quickly moving subjects, the evocation of a moving image, and the illusion that the camera is moving create a complex visual effect, and a signature of Sparkuhl's cinematography. The dance sequence features several novelty shots. In one intercut scene, for example, Oss and a servant fox-trot together down a staircase, a vertical diagonal. In another, the cooks dance around the perimeter of the kitchen. Yet another shot comprises a multiple-image frame: three close-up images of dancers' feet, of the dancers in the ballroom, of Oss and the servant in the drawing room, and of the staff in the kitchen, compartmentalized vertically. The multiple image was then still a new visual composition device, recently introduced by D. W. Griffith in *The Birth of a Nation* (1915), and others. Lubitsch and Sparkuhl use the device to depict three simultaneous actions, specifically the fact that the mansion is filled with dance and that dance crosses all class barriers. Another distinctive shot features Josef, who has lingered in the dining hall rather than accompanying his wife to the reception, sitting in a corner in the background, with dozens of wine bottles at his feet, excluded from the field size space and the intimacy of love and dance. Later Sparkuhl exploits a keyhole iris shot to show the drunken Josef, when Oss has been banished to another bedroom across the hall, spying on her in her own chamber, where a servant is helping to undress her, unraveling her stocking to reveal a bare calf and foot. The keyhole iris shot captures his point of view and is comic, an optical gag, but as a mask shot it is a voyeuristic corruption of the short focal length of shots of intimate spaces in front of the camera, as well as an erotic perversion, albeit within a comical mode, of the consummation of a marriage. Typically, the wedding-night shots show a long staircase in the background and a long hallway with the bedrooms on either side, in the foreground. When a servant comes twice to direct Josef from Oss's to his own bedroom and when Mr. Quaker comes later to check in on his daughter, spying on her in a keyhole iris shot that captures his point of view, revealing her as a virginal little girl fast asleep, hugging her *teddybär*, spectators witness characters' gradual progression from a distant vanishing point at the top of the stairs and along diagonal and horizontal axes in the direction of the camera and into clear focus in the field size space outside of the bedrooms. Similarly, when the real Prince Nucki returns from a night on the town with five of his friends, Sparkuhl shoots them in reverse vanishing-point perspective, from background to foreground, walking, arms linked, side-by-side, up a tree and bench-lined pathway through the park: drunk, they sway from one to the other side of the path, and one after another the men on the ends of the line drop off onto the park benches, until only Prince Nucki remains standing, occupying center frame in the field space, which signifies he has arrived to resolve the case of mistaken identity.

Of course, in a comedy, resolution has many complications. Picked up for public drunkenness, Prince Nucki is taken to sober up at the Association Against Dipsomania, where, as it happens, Oss is a volunteer. She and the other women volunteers see Prince Nucki at his worst. Nevertheless, Nucki and Oss have an instant romantic attraction for each other, and she brings him home with her, where Josef eventually informs them they are already married, explaining, "I got married in your name." Truly in love, they excuse themselves from their wedding dinner with Mr. Quaker and head to their bedroom to consummate the marriage, down the long staircase and along the hallway into the field space of intimacy. When he realizes they have gone, Quaker leaves the table and goes to check in on them, following the same optical trajectories. In a masking iris shot, he peers through the keyhole to reveal them, wife and husband, newlyweds embracing and kissing in bed. Pleased with what he has seen, Mr. Quaker turns directly to the camera and concludes, "Now I'm impressed?" Through his gesture transgressing the fourth wall, an instance of presentative blocking, Lubitsch and Sparkuhl state that whereas masking shots are conventional, comical, and illusory, the film camera is an instrument of verisimilitude, bringing into focus the intimate relationships of characters and the discoveries of two new partners in film optics: In *Die Austernprinzessin* Lubitsch and Sparkuhl claim the foreground as their field space.

Released on September 18, 1919, fewer than three months after the release of *Die Austernprinzessin*, *Madame Dubarry* was their next collaboration, in an expanded working relationship, with Kurt Waschneck as technical director and Fritz Arno Wagner as assistant camera operator. The film, a historical costume drama, set in eighteenth-century pre-Revolutionary France, features Pola Negri (Jeanne Vaubernier/Madame Dubarry), Emil Jannings (King Louis XV), and Harry Liedtke (Armand de Foix) in the leading roles. Like *Die Austernprinzessin*, the film comprises three principal shots: mid shots in which characters occupy the field space immediately in front of the camera; wide shots in which characters and vehicles move from the background to the foreground, marking out the frame space; and standard masking shots and cross-cuts as transitional and continuity devices. The novelty of the shot list in *Madame Dubarry* is that shots Lubitsch and Sparkuhl designed to enhance the comic mode in *Die Austernprinzessin* they now adjust to the romantic melodrama. For example, they similarly exploit the field space to evoke an intimate space and intimacy between characters, as is first evident at the meeting of Jeanne Vaubernier, a milliner, and the Comte Jean Dubarry.

Jeanne Vaubernier is enjoying a romantic luncheon at the home of Don Diego (Magnus Stifter), the Spanish envoy, when the Comte (Eduard von Winterstein) pays an unexpected visit. Before receiving him, Don Diego makes Jeanne conceal herself behind a screen in the dining room. Their intimacy has been disrupted, and the space in front of the camera has been reassigned for a dull lunch between Dubarry and Diego. But knowing the Comte's back is to her, capricious Jeanne cannot resist peering over the top of the screen to tease Don Diego. Seeing her reflection in a mirror, the Comte blows her a kiss and then turns around to expose her and Diego's *affaire de coeur*, but clearly he has fallen in love with her (although she eventually enters into a marriage of convenience with his brother, William Dubarry, to legitimize her role as the king's mistress). Even after it has been disrupted, the intimacy of the field space is restored under the Lubitsch-Sparkuhl collaboration. This space functions like the proscenium of the theatrical stage. When Don Diego and Jeanne meet again, at the Opera Ball, they film the public dance sequence much as in *Die Austernprinzessin*, in a wide shot in which the dancers fabricate the motion picture motion recorded with a stationary camera, and circulate in mesmeric patterns to the foreground and in front of the camera, effectively turning the wide shot into a mid close-up. When Armand shows up at the ball to take Jeanne back from Diego, and ends up killing him in a duel, the Comte Dubarry intervenes to spirit her away from the trouble. His action of taking her in his arms to carry her off, like all key romantic moments in the film, occurs in the intimate space closest to the camera. Here the camera reveals all; the mid close-up is the antithesis of the mask shot, since the short focal length exposes every emotion. This space is also a starting point for other emotional encounters, of lovers and adversaries, such as when, acting as Dubarry's emissary, Jeanne becomes King Louis's lover. Even the mask shot, the static iris, as distinguished from the iris-in and iris-out, which are conventionally transitional, can function to focus on emotion. For example, when Jeanne, hugging him from behind, happens to notice he is reading the judicial document condemning Armand de Foix to death for murder, an iris shot heightens the dramatic effect and subjective point of view in a close-up of her facial expressions. Although the camera does not pull in for the close-up—movie cameras did not become demonstrably mobile in German cinema until the mid-1920s, initially in the films of G. W. Pabst and F. W. Murnau—the iris shot gives the illusion of zooming in, and masks that the camera is immobile. Reaching over his shoulder to disrupt the intimate space in which the king is to sign the order of execution, directly in front of the camera, Jeanne manages to intercede for a pardon for Armand. Yet even his prison cell, where we see Armand when he learns of his reprieve, is this intimate space, albeit an adversarial one. Armand sits on a bench, his back against the wall, along a diagonal line, in the extreme right foreground. Sparkuhl shoots him in a mid close-up, from the knees up. With two prison officials looming over him and the wall behind him, he is masked in a corner of the frame. Sparkuhl achieves this optical effect not by covering the lens with a blocking device, masking it in an iris shot, for example, but by making the details of his shot construction conspicuous to spectators: the camera angle, the lighting and shading, and the frame composition, most remarkably the horizontal, diagonal, and vertical axes of all the set properties.

Sparkuhl's dexterity in frame composition is particularly evident in the scene in which Armand and Jeanne are reunited. In gratitude to Louis XV for commuting his sentence, he joined the king's army. When he and Jeanne meet again, he is in command at a strategy meeting of French citizens, insurgents plotting to murder Madame Dubarry on the charge she has corrupted the king and the kingdom, when in fact she is present there, disguised as a male insurgent, determined to uncover the plot against her. When the meeting is adjourned, they come face to face to experience a moment of painful recognition. Sparkuhl films them in a tight mid shot, from the waist up, standing very close together at the door, in a back corner of the room. He looks terrified and guilt-ridden, leaning back against the wall, she ecstatic and relieved, leaning in to him. When, overwhelmed by emotion, she drops to her knees and grabs his coat imploringly, the composition of the shot changes entirely: the contours of their bodies now form a diagonal line, like a wipe, across the frame. That Sparkuhl could change the composition of such a dense frame, with no free space, so radically, intensifying the poignancy of the confrontation, points to the sophistication of his film aesthetics. When Armand raises Jeanne from her knees, the frame composition of forms and axes shifts again, and the mood changes accordingly, to one of conditional reconciliation. She moves toward him twice, to embrace him, but he pushes her away each time and then exits through the door, leaving her standing there alone, thus opening up the heavily blocked spatial configuration. Sparkuhl then cuts to a shot of Armand outside the door, in similar spatial configuration to hers. When she joins him outside to ask, "Cannot you find it in your heart to forgive?" (intertitle), their bodies form a pyramid that fills most of the frame, symbolizing their desire for reconciliation. After he responds, "The forgiving is easy. It is the forgetting I cannot do!" she falls away from him, devastated, leaning back against the wall. The pyramid dissolves, and now the gap between them forms an inverted V, another pyramid, this one symbolizing the fragility of their desire. As Armand turns away from her, the pyramidal space between them grows wider, until he walks out of frame, destroying its configuration. This formlessness anticipates their fates: Armand is murdered as a traitor for trying to free Jeanne from prison; she awaits execution. The film ends with her at the guillotine.

The climax of *Madame Dubarry* counterbalances these very private and intimate conciliatory scenes with street scenes of the Reign of Terror, of the public outrage and rebellion, the storming of the Bastille followed by the accession of Louis XVI with his consort, Marie Antoinette, the start of the French Revolution. Sparkuhl films these scenes with hundreds of extras portraying a mob engaged in the frenetic activity of insurrection, using some of the camera techniques he used to film the ballroom scenes in *Ich möchte kein Mann Sein* and *Die Austernprinzessin*, except that here the rhythm of crowd activity is unruly, the ultimate cinematic motion, highly choreographed, carefully composed like every frame of Lubitsch-Sparkuhl films.

But *Madame Dubarry* is a problematic film in the history of cinema, both mimetically and narratologically, because of its casual representation of eighteenth-century French political and social history. Mimetically, the film is primarily a costume drama, in which the semiotics of garments is a signifying system that shrouds the historicity of the narrative. Thomas Elsaesser observes, "The gender issue in *Madame*

Dubarry subtly undercuts the class discourse of social mobility in the fantastic genre, ironizing it via its operetta subtext, where power appears a charade of costumes and a matter of imposture and disguise."[4] Narratologically, the film distorts by dramatizing French revolutionary history, fictionalizing it in the heroine, in contradistinction to Jeanne Bécu, the historical person on whom the character of Jeanne de Vaubernier is based. Other Lubitsch-Sparkuhl collaborative films also are quite controversial historiographically, such as *Sumurun* (September 1, 1920), for its orientalist stereotypes, and *Anna Boleyn* (December 3, 1920), for its highly romanticized and oversimplified interpretation of British monarchic history. The representational problems of *Madam Dubarry*, *Sumurun*, and *Anna Boleyn* have two main sources. First, Ernst Lubitsch was an accomplished comic actor with a profound theatrical sensibility, not a political historian: his political historical films masquerade as costume dramas. Second, all three films were made in Germany but also for the American market, and rebranded, *Madame Dubarry* retitled as *Passion*, *Sumurun* as *One Arabian Night*, and *Anna Boleyn* as *Deception*: film historians have credited these films along with *Sumurun* as the foundation of Lubitsch's successful filmmaking career in Hollywood. Richard W. McCormick explains: "In 1919 his career really took off with comedies such as *Die Austernprinzessin* (The Oyster Princess) and *Die Puppe* (The Doll) and the big-budget historical epic *Madame Dubarry* (Passion), which not only made him internationally famous but also led ultimately to the offer from Hollywood that lured him to America in 1922, where he would remain until his death in 1947."[5] Despite their representational flaws, however, *Sumurun* and *Anna Boleyn*, like *Madame Dubarry*, feature some remarkable cinematography typical of the Lubitsch-Sparkuhl partnership.

Based on a pantomime by Friedrich Feska, *Sumurun* opens with an establishing shot of a desert scene, showing two cars, one donkey-drawn, the other horse-drawn, as they emerge from between the sand dunes into the center of the frame and then cross on a diagonal line into the left corner of the foreground and out of the frame. This shot establishes the setting, but more importantly it establishes how Sparkuhl will delineate and configure cinematic space in this film. Lubitsch cuts to an interior shot of the horse-drawn cart to show the occupants, a band of itinerant performers, including Yannaia (Pola Negri) and Yeggar the Hunchback (Ernst Lubitsch), who after a scuffle with a rival for her affection spectators witness thrown off the cart, the film's first action. Lubitsch's performance in the supporting role of an abject grotesque, albeit a caricature, is entrancing in the film. Part of his attraction, however, derives from their knowledge he is also directing the film spectators are watching, more than about how he is managing to direct himself. In some respects, Sparkuhl's shot repertoire is similarly self-reflexive. For example, the film features an unusually large number of mask shots, particularly conventional close-up reaction iris shots of characters engaging in conversations across class lines, but also mid shots of characters naturally framed in windows, arches, apertures, and other architectural structures. The latter are of greater interest because they parody an optical convention and because they are perspectival, involving looking out of the frame structure at something in the field of action, and thus across the frame of film. In another scene Yeggar asks Yannaia to intercede with the Young Sheikh on behalf of the band of performers. Sparkuhl films her in a tilt-down shot that evokes the perspective of the sheikh, who, mounted on his horse, is looking down at her. But imploring the sheikh for his favor, Pola Negri performs a highly seductive dance that she begins standing and ends writhing on the ground. Extending the distance between the camera and the subject, it seems she is performing her dance primarily for the camera, not for the Young Sheikh, aware the camera is watching her, and it seems the shot has been constructed as self-referential. The self-referential camera is powerfully evident in the scene in which Yeggar, despondent because Yannaia is going to leave the troupe, commits suicide by swallowing poisoned pills. Death comes upon him gradually, which allows Lubitsch to deliver a virtuoso performance in Sparkuhl's unrelenting close-up shot. Yet, whereas the experience of knowing he is dying is a clearly self-reflexive one for the character, as is apparent in his repertoire of highly stylized facial displays, for the actor Lubitsch the performance seems to be expressly for the camera, for this shot. The follow-up medium and mid close-up shots of Yeggar stumbling onto the stage, holding one of Yannaia's scarves to his lips, and acting out the consummation of his unrequited love for her are similarly self-referential: Lubitsch's performance is amazing because it is conspicuously for the camera, as well as because of the pathos of the character's death scene. As McCormick concludes, "it is Lubitsch's hunchback clown who is the hero of the narrative."[6]

Like *Madame Dubarry* and *Sumurun*, *Anna Boleyn* is a historical drama clad in costumes, about King Henry VIII (Emil Jannings) and Anna Boleyn (Henny Porten), his second wife, and in this film too the cinematography is more distinctive than the screenplay and characterization. The establishing shot is of the open sea, and then of the ship bringing Anna Boleyn from France to England, where she is to become Lady in Waiting to Queen Catherine, Henry's wife. As a shot reveals the ship entering the frame from the right, spectators realize its progress is simulated by camera mobility, a pan shot devised by swinging the stationary camera on its horizontal plane. The shot sequence that records the first meeting of Catherine and Henry is equally basic. After showing Henry following Anna into a room, Sparkuhl films each of them greeting the other in alternating mid shots of them standing, first looking at each other, then smiling and laughing, and then in another mid shot of the two of them together, affably, until he starts to flirt by leaning his body into hers provocatively, her body upright, his on the diagonal. Thus, through a basic shot sequence, and transverse frame lines, Sparkuhl establishes their relationship. Most of the rest of the shot repertoire for the film comprises tableaux shots of formal regal, military, and aristocratic social gatherings, characterized by protocol more the kind of free human movement one sees in Lubitsch's earlier films, in which Sparkuhl films the entire field of action, tracing movement along horizontal, diagonal, and vertical axes and even into the corners. Nevertheless, some of these standard shots are inventive. For instance, Sparkuhl takes a complex tilt-down shot of Sir Henry Norris (Paul Hartmann), Anna's uncle, in conference with sixteen of his soldiers, who gather around him in a tight oval. Because of the steep angle of the shot and the focus on Norris in the center, the three soldiers in the foreground, with their backs to the camera, appear formally nondescript, whereas the others can be seen clearly, their facial displays, the details of their uniforms. In its composition the shot signifies the urgency of Norris's message, issuing an order that the army cheer for Henry and Anna, and show no favor for the former queen, Catherine, whereas as a pictorial image or tableau, an arrangement of forms, lines, and spaces in the action field, the shot is aesthetically significant. There is a comparable scene in the climax of the film, before her execution, when Sparkuhl shoots Anna along with her two hooded executioners in a still tableau as they pause for a moment before heading out to the gallows. Anna, dressed in white, stands reflectively between the phlegmatic hangmen all in black; the profile of the group forms a distinct diagonal line across the action field, like a beautiful brushstroke across a canvas.

Otherwise, however, *Anna Boleyn* is a rather tedious chronology of reconstructed events, which Thomas Elsaesser categorizes as "historical imaginary" and Christian Rogowski describes as "reinvented moments from European history."[7] Nevertheless, the film does feature several intriguing action sequences, most notably Sparkuhl's footage of the Spring Festival, including scenes of feasting and dancing, with crowds of merry courtiers moving about in all directions, initially boaters on the Thames, their craft positioned in every trajectory and filling up the frame, and later intercut shots of onlookers standing on steep hillsides, complete diagonal action fields. In contrast, an iris shot of Henry, who has slipped away from the festivities to a secluded bower, where he is shamelessly flirting with a young woman in the costume of a sprite: the choice of an iris shot for this event is uninspired, because it is conventional, but also because, regrettably, Jannings portrays Henry as a caricature of a compulsively lusty king who flirts throughout the film, and the iris isolates him in his single dimension. To Sparkuhl, the iris shot is utilitarian, masking the frame; it is the antithesis of the intimate field spaces he opens directly in front of the camera, which is a visual signature of his cinematography in his less historically burdened films.

After *Madame Dubarry*, Lubitsch directed *Rausch*, with Sparkuhl and Karl Freund codirecting the cinematography. The moral and cautionary narrative is about Gaston, a struggling playwright who, finding success, abandons his wife and child for another woman. When the child dies, he is implicated, with disastrous consequences. Unlike Madame Dubarry, who prospers though her opportunistic sexual adventures with multiple partners and does not face judgment until the end of the film, Gaston experiences a protracted fall and judgment, which are the focus of the screenplay, based on the play *Brott och brott* (1900) by August Strindberg. *Rausch* is a small film, a side project made with Argus Films, in Berlin, and released just six days after *Madame Dubarry*. Working with two accomplished cinematographers, Lubitsch sped up the production, double-tracking it with *Madame Dubarry*, and adding Pola Negri to the cast.

Lubitsch returned to form in *Die Puppe*, released December 5, 1919, with Sparkuhl as cinematographer, and assisted again by Kurt Waschneck, who worked as the technical director on *Madame Dubarry*, *Sumurun*, and *Anna Boleyn*. Based on an eighteenth-century dark romantic story by E. T. A. Hoffmann, and *La Poupée* (1896), an *opéra comique* by Edmond Audran,[8] *Die Puppe* is a fairy tale epithalamium with a subversive fetishistic subtext, and as such it is Lubitsch's darkest film. *Die Puppe [The Doll]* stars Lubitsch regular Ossi Oswalda in a double role, as the lifelike puppet, essentially an automaton that Lancelot (Hermann Thimig), a fastidious young man, elects to marry to secure his inheritance, and as the doll maker Hilarius's daughter, with whom, in the end, the young man falls in love and marries. The fairy tale archetype is of a dead lover who comes back to life. The techno-fetish is about an androgyne who prefers playing with a mechanical doll, a sex doll, to being intimate with a human partner.

Described in the front matter as "four amusing acts from a toy box," the film is prefaced with two shots of Ernst Lubitsch as a puppeteer removing the contents of a toy box and using them to assemble a diorama of the doll maker's house on a tree-lined cardboard property: in mid shot he empties the box and puts together the set, and in a mid close-up he displays the figurines of Hilarius and his wife and then places them carefully inside the house. Then Sparkuhl cuts to a close-up of what appears to be the diorama but which is actually a full-size movie-set replica of it: it shows the doll maker and his wife emerging from the house and scurrying down the winding sidewalk in the direction of the camera; losing his footing, Hilarius tumbles the rest of the way down the slope, into a pond, from which his wife manages to extract him with the aid of her umbrella. Soaking wet, he cries, "Kind sun, please shine so that I don't catch cold" (intertitle), when Sparkuhl cuts to a bas-relief papier-mâché animated model of the sky, in which the clouds draw back to reveal a pencil drawing of a smiling sun, and then cuts back to the previous scene to show, disaster averted, steam rising from Hilarius's drying clothes. This front-matter montage, a visual overture, introduces the fairy tale theme of the storytelling and some features of Sparkuhl's cinematography in this film, which combines natural with fantasy characters and settings in the manner of the films of Georges Méliès. Lubitsch and Sparkuhl's use of the diorama as a storytelling device here also anticipates how, almost a century later, American director Wes Anderson and his cinematographer Robert D. Yeoman exploit dioramas, books, pages, and other frame and storytelling properties in the films they have made together.

Die Puppe begins with a scene in the village square, with the crier ringing his bell and, when the villagers are assembled, reading a proclamation that Baron von Chanterelle, Lancelot's uncle, "does not wish for his lineage to die out . . . and invites all maidens of the region to gather in the marketplace so that his nephew, the sole heir, may choose a fitting wife for himself" (intertitle). Sparkuhl's repertoire of shots here is similar to in his previous films with Lubitsch, combining mainly mid close-ups of actors performing directly in front of the camera, and mid and wide shots of actors moving through three-dimensional space, along horizontal, diagonal, and vertical axes, from background to foreground. For example, one early mid shot shows a gathering of forty eligible young women at the village hall, getting ready to go not to the marketplace but directly to Baron von Chanterelle's mansion: in the hall they queue up in pairs in a diagonal line that extends from the back to the front of the frame, and when the line advances they disappear into the left corner frame two by two. This is an establishing shot and a connecting scene, but the cinematography is immediately recognizable as Sparkuhl's. Lubitsch is traditionally credited with "the Lubitsch touch," referring to his style of light comedy, but the Lubitsch-Sparkuhl collaborations also have a distinctive cinematographic style, a look, a visual grammar, and an attention to perspectival motion that could be termed *the Sparkuhl touch*. For example, Thomas Elsaesser categorically observes, "The lighting of Fritz Arno Wagner, Theodor Sparkuhl, Günther Krampf and others practically defines the German look."[9] But Sparkuhl's look is idiosyncratic, and it is not restricted to light: it is a total cinematographic vision of reality.

It is impressively evident in the first extended shot in *Die Puppe*, of a chase that ensues when, to escape from his uncle's peremptory lecture to him on the necessity that he marry, particularly after a servant arrives to announce "40 women at the door" (intertitle), Lancelot in a panic attack leaps out the window only to land into the midst of a crowd of prospective brides eager for his hand. Although he is a fragile invalid, the Baron von Chanterelle, accompanied by his servant, immediately runs after him, also jumping out the window. The stream of forty women with the baron and his servant following not far behind pursue Lancelot in a long queue through the circuitous streets of the village, which Sparkuhl films in three inventive shots from a stationary camera. One characteristic shot, typical of his style, shows the women running diagonally across the frame into the left foreground and out of the camera's field of view. The next shot is a tour de force, a continuous shot with a duration of sixty-five seconds, filmed at a slower than usual camera speed for comic effect of slightly accelerated motion, that shows the participants in the pursuit running back and forth along the main street toward and away from, and laterally across the camera and, most remarkably, up and down stairways and through building arches, and slipping into and out of the camera's field of action. Finally, Sparkuhl picks up the chase outside the village gates, in a country scene with a narrow path that extends from a painted backdrop depicting it in vanishing-point perspective, across the gully, and into the foreground. In this shot, Lancelot quickly hides in a gully to evade the women, who in single file pass through the action field from center left to the center of the frame, and diagonally to the left foreground corner and, one by one, out of view. The entire chase scene, comprising three shots with a cumulative duration of 2:08, from the servant's announcement the women have arrived to the moment the last of the runners, the baron and his servant, pass out of frame, functions as an elaborate establishing shot, stating that in this film flight is the main obstacle to plot resolution through marriage within the comic mode. More remarkably, the chase sequence draws attention to how it was filmed, to the distinctive tropes of Sparkuhl's cinematography, its visual design and balance, exploiting character movement through all the spatial axes, and taking advantage even of the frame periphery and the corners of the field of view. In this respect, I would like to propose, Sparkuhl's visual design is a correlative of how spectators process diverse film images.

> Good composition reinforces the way in which the mind organizes information. In some cases it may deliberately run counter to how the eye/brain combination works in order to add a new layer of meaning or ironic comment. Composition selects and emphasizes elements such as size, shape, order, dominance, hierarchy, pattern, resonance and discordance in ways which give meaning to the things being photographed that goes beyond the simple: "here they are."[10]

Thus, the chase sequence engages spectators not just because of the kinesis on the screen, like the movement of the mob in *Madame Dubarry*, the dancers in *Ich möchte kein Mann Sein*, and the dancers and servants in *Die Austernprinzessin*, but also because it confirms something of their experience of spectatorship, which may include discerning elements of the cinematography that contribute to the visual design or style, and attributing them to the camera and its operator. This cinematic information is a "new layer of meaning" that Lubitsch-Sparkuhl encode into film.

Notwithstanding aesthetics, the trope of flight remains the principal means of advancing the plot of *Die Puppe* to resolution. Flight takes Lancelot to the refuge of a monastery, where after several days the abbot learns Baron von Chanterelle has offered his nephew an incentive of a 300,000-franc dowry, which the abbot covets for his impoverished community. When Lancelot vows never to marry a woman, the abbot informs him, "you don't need to marry a woman; you can marry a doll!" (intertitle). The monks persuade him to buy a mechanical, button-operated, doll, marry it, and give them the dowry. When the plot shifts from the monastery to Hilarius the doll maker's dollhouse-like studio, the film enters a fairy tale mode, and its mimesis becomes that of a diorama. In this fantasy section Sparkuhl's shot repertoire consists mainly of mid shots in the short field space directly in front of the camera, as distinguished from the longer shots of subjects darting around the field of action, as in the chase scene. This is an intimate camera appropriate to a love story, even a heterodox story about the love between a man and a doll. The subjective camera also allows Sparkuhl to humanize the doll maker's puppet (Ossi Oswalda) as well as lending her mechanical movements to close scrutiny, which is necessary because she essentially plays a triple role: Oss, the doll maker's daughter; the mechanical doll for which she was the model; and, after the apprentice accidentally breaks the doll's arm, Oss, who agrees to impersonate the doll until he can repair it. But before he has a chance to repair it, Lancelot purchases the doll, believing it to be the real one, when it is actually the performative replica, Oss, pretending to be the doll. The fantasy mode persists in the film's properties and cinematography even when Lancelot leaves the doll maker's studio to venture home with his doll fiancée, in a carriage drawn by two-man costume horses, to discover his father's mansion has come to resemble a diorama. The link between the doll maker's studio and Chanterelle's mansion is confirmed symbolically when the apprentice, in a desperate attempt to escape the doll maker's wrath, leaps out the window, recalling when Lancelot, the baron, and his servant do earlier, and on their wedding night when Lancelot and Oss observe both a paper moon and a paper rooster.

Among the most innovative mid close-up shots is the reaction shot of Hilarius when he discovers his daughter has gone off with Lancelot, in place of the doll his apprentice broke. After hearing the apprentice's confession, he observes, "That is truly hair-raising." The intertitle is followed by a mid close-up of Hilarius, whose unruly hair appears to change radically through multiple exposures: in the first sequence it stands upright, in the second it turns white. Later, Sparkuhl films Hilarius in two double-exposure animated fantasy shots, as the apprentice witnesses him sleepwalking across the rooftops and, later, floating through the air on a bunch of helium balloons. Another innovative shot is the mid close-up of Lancelot and Oss at their wedding reception: seated by her side, he informs the servers his wife is not hungry, whereas she, famished, attempts to eat and drink whenever he is not looking, and she also threatens to break out of character. They occupy the intimate space in the camera's immediate field of action, but here the mood of intimacy is more complex than in Lubitsch and Sparkuhl's earlier collaborations, because it is about the non-heteronormative love of a human being and an automaton. The heterodoxy of love is apparent also in later scenes at the monastery, where on his fake honeymoon Lancelot has gone to deliver the money he has promised the monks, when Oss flirts with the monks and then engages them all in a dance, and when Lancelot and Oss spend their wedding night together and he is delighted to discover she is a "real girl." The confirmation of his acceptance of Oss comes when the apprentice shoots all his balloons and Hilarius drops from the sky right at the newlyweds' feet. Once he knows his daughter is safe and she is married to Lancelot, his hair, in another special-effects shot sequence, changes color again, back to dark and unruly. What makes *Die Puppe* one of Lubitsch and Sparkuhl's most visually complex films is the unusual combination of aesthetic and action shots and special-effects shots, including mask shots, and the strange story of a man's love for a signifying machine, for "man's inert extensions, such as automata, computers, or robots."[11] For Lubitsch and Sparkuhl romantic love and comedy naturally happen in proximity to new machines and also right in front of the mechanized camera.

His filmmaking style changed not so much when Lubitsch turned to screenplays with epic scopes and infrastructures like *Madame Dubarry*, *Sumurun*, and *Anna Boleyn* as when he modified his film content to attract a new spectatorship through the release in the United States with the opportunity to relocate his career to Hollywood. What is remarkable about the Lubitsch-Sparkuhl filmmaking partnership is that the stylistic compromises Lubitsch made to his film content did not extend significantly to the strategies and techniques Sparkuhl used to photograph them. Both of them could preserve the Lubitsch-Sparkuhl touch, as it were, because, structurally, their films were partly metafilmic, about the construction of their own visual grammar, in which respect their brand was intrinsically cinematographic, and not just in the obvious sense that a camera was used to record images on film stock. In their films cinematography is content as well as technique. For example, the visual trope of an action field defined by a short focal length, with human subjects and set properties positioned proximate to the camera lens, is recurrent and distinctive in all their films. Another of their characteristic visual tropes is the kinetic field of view, in which human subjects move about on all three spatial axes and more often move toward the camera than away from it. According to Daniel Arijon, "the distances from which we record the event" and "the motion of the subjects performing that event"[12] are essential elements of film grammar, the set of rules—shot breakdown plus shooting schedule—governing film development from screenplay to finished movie. Lubitsch and Sparkuhl preserve this grammar throughout their body of films, regardless of whether they are light comedies or historical epics. They exploit this grammar eloquently in their light comedies, their films with the lightest touch, *Die Puppe* and, their most ambitious film cinematographically, *Die Bergkatze [The Wildcat]*, released April 14, 1921, and with no plan for American distribution.

Die Bergkatze starred Lubitsch regulars Pola Negri, Victor Janson, and Hermann Thimig and is the most contemporary of his German films: its theme on the power imbalance between military systems and renegade social movements and communities addresses the role of cinema and other arts in the Weimar period as putatively efficacious antiauthoritarian creative projects. For instance, the army and the rebel bandits battle in the mountains in *Bergkatze*, the former armed with rifles, the latter with snowballs. After her snowball strikes a soldier in the head and he admonishes her not to play rough, Rischka (Pola Negri) defies him, "War is war" (intertitle).

Die Bergkatze, which the front credits describe as "a grotesque in four acts" set "not far from Piffkaneiro," begins with an iris-out shot of wooden gates that open into the courtyard of a military border fortress, a diorama setting where, center frame, a soldier is playing reveille on his bugle. Sparkuhl cuts to his second shot, a rectangular masked shot of a meticulously organized dormitory, where in two tiers of beds eight soldiers awaken from their sleep. The ensuing shot sequence, which reveals the soldiers performing their ablutions and their Kommandant (Victor Janson) barking orders at them, comprises an array of masking shots: circles, ovals, squares, and rectangles. Some of these function to enhance the closeness of close-ups, as when the commander screams and twirls his enormous handlebar mustache, others to provide novelty perspectives, such as the head-on mid shots of the men washing at the sinks, taken as if through the wall next to which they are mounted. But these initial masking shots serve a more important function: they give notice that Lubitsch and Sparkuhl intend to vary the aspect ratio over the course of this film, to alter the parameters of the horizontal, vertical, and diagonal axes, and make an aesthetic statement about the instability of spectatorship and arbitrary perceptions of the action field. For instance, each of the four acts begins with an iris-in and ends with an iris-out. Each masking shot is a plane of critical focus. Nevertheless, Lubitsch and Sparkuhl provide relief from the tedium of a constantly reduced and reconfigured aspect ratio by using some sustained letterbox masking that is only slightly smaller than and in exact proportion to the film's actual aspect ratio. Lubitsch and Sparkuhl have fun with the film medium itself, transforming it, like the set, into a diorama, which is evident when they film the wedding ceremony of Rischka and her man, set on a snowy mountainside, using a mask in the form of a pointed arch, thus turning a wilderness into a church. Their experiments in cinematography, in the physical properties of film and spectatorship, sight gags and filmic space and time, modernist set design, and the metafilmic deconstruction of the film medium, anticipate later European filmmakers, notably Jacques Tati in *Mon Oncle* (1958) and *Playtime* (1967). As Fred Gehler observes, "Lubitschs Lachen ist in der *Bergkatze* ein Lachen ohne Illusionen"[13] ["In *Die Bergkatze* Lubitsch's laugh is a laugh without illusions" (St. Pierre's translation)]. Lubitsch's "laugh without illusions," however, wears a mask.

The repertoire of mask shots is diverse, with little variation in size but an excessive variety of shapes, a chef's cookie-cutter drawer of squares, rectangles, circles, ovals, diamonds, and polygons. Lubitsch and Sparkuhl use these shots to frame some of the heterodox business of comedy, which masking turns into sight gags. The first example of this is a polygonal mask shot of the Kommandant at his private quarters. The scene is the bedroom, where his wife is seated before the mirror, doing her hair. Their dramatic pantomime shows her asking him to pin a postiche in her hair, and he, still clad in his flamboyant and period uniform, immediately obeys her and pins her hair with the delicacy of a professional hairdresser. The contrast between his refinement with his wife and his vulgar bombast with the soldiers in the dormitory is funny. More importantly, the humor is masked in the paraphernalia of the filming. The diagonal-shaped masking shots also perform a technical cinematographic function, in accommodating how Sparkuhl typically films human movement, traversing the action field from the background through a frame corner in the foreground. For example, he shoots thousands of young women who riot across the frame diagonally toward the camera after they learn Lieutenant Alexis (Paul Heidemann) is to be transferred to the border fortress because of his indiscretions, which another shot reveals have yielded hundreds of children. Sparkuhl uses a similar diagonal masking shot to film the lieutenant's sleigh, on which he is being conducted through the snowy mountains to the border fortress, when Rischka, the daughter of the leader of a gang of bandits, intercepts the sleigh and Alexis is taken prisoner. They are clearly attracted to each other, despite their obvious class difference: he is an effete gentleman and a narcissist, she the mountain cat of the title. Yet because of her feelings for him she allows him to escape, to hike the rest of the way to the fortress. Alexis then leads a force back into the mountains to engage the rebels in battle. The German soldiers prove themselves slapstick clowns, inept in every aspect of military strategy and execution, more concerned with performing in the brass band, which Alexis conducts, than in the theater of war. They return victorious, but only because they managed to avoid engagement with the enemy entirely. To reward Alexis for his victory, the Kommandant offers him his daughter's hand in marriage. That Alexis must choose between his feelings of obligation to marry the Kommandant's daughter and his fascination with Rischka provides the main impetus to the plot. But in the end experimentation with aspect ratios takes precedence over any plot complication. For example, during the Kommandant's massive victory celebration for the soldiers,

Rischka and six of the men wage a guerrilla attack at dusk. Sparkuhl films them in a diagonal trapezoidal masking shot as they devise a way to storm the wall. Kneeling, the men link bodies, one on top of the other, to fashion a human ladder up the wall; Rischka uses their backs as steps. The physical comedy is clever, but the vectorization makes an unforgettable sight gag, as the angle of the human ladder and the angle of the masking shot are identical, as if the characters are aware, in the manner of the actors who portray them, that they have to meet the demands of the camera. This may correspond to film spectators' awareness of shot construction and to the phenomenal experience of film spectatorship, which too can be seen as meeting the demands of the camera.

> Experimental masking can still be found in artistically ambitious film—Lubitsch's *Die Puppe* (1919, The doll), *Die Austernprinzessin* (1919, The oyster princess), and *Die Bergkatze* (1921, The mountain cat) offer a virtual catalog of shapes—but masking as a whole becomes more and more standardized. Not surprisingly the excessive use of masks in *The mountain cat* becomes a function of its Expressionist set design. Framing assumes some of the self-referential functions of masking, as is evidenced by the imaginative use of doors, windows, and other devices that, by introducing alternative formats and divisions into the frame, draw attention to the cinematic mise-en-scène as a constructed space.[14]

Dietrich Scheunemann concurs with Sabine Hake about the "Expressionist set design" in *Die Bergkatze*, stating, "Yet a remark Lubitsch made to Rudolf Kurtz [in *Expressionismus und Film* (1928)] indicating that he intended to direct his comedy *Die Bergkatze* (The Mountain Cat, 1921) in a manner 'far from everyday life' as a 'grotesque' parody of militaristic habits on the Balkans was enough to secure him a place among the directors as using 'expressionist elements' in their films."[15] Lubitsch's set design is not Expressionist, however, primarily because it lacks the strong contrast of light and shade characteristic of Expressionist film. In fact, the sets in *Die Bergkatze* are intensely lit, with no dramatic use of shading; they consist of brightly lit location shots in snow-laden mountains and brightly lit interior shots in the fortress. As a set, the fortress is in the Art Deco style, which flourished in Germany in the 1920s, a dominant example of the visual design of the *Neue Sachlichkeit* movement. More specifically, the set is a diorama, in the manner of the set design in *Die Puppe*, where it functions to evoke fantasy and romance. *Die Bergkatze* also is a romantic fantasy, as well as a comic satire on military systems and war, turning the theater of war into a film-set toy shop. The fourth act of the film, for example, begins with an elaborate fantasy sequence, in which Rischka dreams of her romantic encounter with Alexis earlier at the fortress. Alexis appears in her dream, and she appears to rise from her sleeping body to interact with him in conventional double-exposure dream images. Lubitsch exploits the diorama set design fundamentally to deconstruct the military machine: the Kommandant, Lieutenant Alexis, and the other soldiers at the fortress are toy figurines, and Alexis, despite his scandalous notoriety as a womanizer, is actually quite fastidious, in the manner of Lancelot, in courting both the Kommandant's daughter and Rischka. *Die Bergkatze* is "constructed" only as a fantasy diorama set and as a diorama of mask shots. For example, when Rischka awakes from her dream, her father, having witnessed her thrashing around in bed, and sensed her desires, decides to marry her off to one of the rebels, who, despite her protestations, claims her anyway by knocking her down, grabbing her ankles, and dragging her away. In a diagonal mask shot, Sparkuhl films him trailing her body down a snowy hillside, from the top left to the bottom right corner of the frame, through the chute of the mask window. This sight gag is also metafilmic, referring to the inverse diagonal mask shot—its vector from the bottom left to the top right of the frame—of Rischka climbing the human ladder at the fortress. Both shots also make reference to other dense shots in Lubitsch-Sparkuhl films, such as the tableaux of Anna Boleyn and the hangmen in an oblique formation and Sir Henry Norris in conference with his soldiers in an elliptical formation. These rich shots, packed with visual information, whether they are in the comical or the pathetic mode, are of the kind that is traditionally attributed to Lubitsch's directorial style, and termed "the Lubitsch touch." And indeed his films do lend themselves to shot analysis. Their shot-by-shot configurations are arresting, the most insistent structural and compositional feature of this style. *Die Bergkatze* may be the strongest example of a Lubitsch film from this period in which literally every shot counts. Indeed, much of the comedy of a film structured entirely of mask shots that keep changing the aspect ratio arises from the fact that Lubitsch seems to be parodying his own visual style by carrying it to the extreme.

Nevertheless, in a long, successful collaborative partnership like that of Lubitsch and Sparkuhl, it would seem the cinematographer is as much responsible as the director for shot selection. After all, the director only calls for the shot; the cinematographer actually sets it up, takes it, and secures it. It is the cinematographer who selects the mask and puts it over the lens, who determines how much of the camera's field of view is cut off, how big the window is to be. That the cinematographer adjusts the mask to fit the subject is apparent when the diagonal mask shot of her suitor dragging Rischka across the landscape changes to a circular mask shot of him getting to the bottom of the hill and pulling her around in circles, and then to a rhythmic circular mask shot of him hauling her to the foot of another hill, where he finally lets her go and, rising to embrace and kiss him, she appears to submit to his overwhelming marriage proposal. This final mask, which I have described as *rhythmic*, has an irregular shape that resembles a flower petal, or an animal track, a circular shape with a rippled border. This mask is rhythmic because "*pure, rhythmic images* (such as signs for animals deriving from their tracks) . . . are not representations of physical shapes but rhythmic lines determined by the animals' movements."[16] Thus, the suitor, like an animal, drags off his prey, a mountain cat, leaving their tracks in the snow. Thus, the irregularly shaped mask that Sparkuhl uses to film them is appropriate to their actions, since its rippled edge comprises "rhythmic lines determined by the animals' movements." The next shots in this abduction sequence are (1) a conventional iris shot, a circle symbolizing the characters' betrothal or marital union, which establishes the romantic rivalry between Rischka's new fiancé and Alexis, for whose love Rischka and the Kommandant's daughter are rivals, and (2) another rhythmic mask shot, which calls into question Rischka and the rebel's betrothal, destabilizing it by suggesting it is animal attraction. By establishing and qualifying Rischka's engagement, these two shots drive the remainder of the romantic plot to resolution in *Die Bergkatze*. All the shots making up Rischka's wedding scenes, for example, are rhythmic masks, the animal associations of which are apparent in her wedding dress, made of a mountain cat print hide. But when Rischka and Alexis, now having both run away from their wedding receptions, happen to stumble into each other on a mountainside and they both realize they are meant to be together, Sparkuhl shoots them not in a rhythmic mask but in a round iris, symbolizing their unity, though it is a coming together of the opposites of civilization and wilderness, evident in that Rischka has not yet changed out of her animal-skin wedding dress. At the fortress, she clings to it, and uses it functionally, waving it to disperse smoke from the fireplace and later to comfort Alexis's new wife in her sadness, using it to wipe her tears and blow her nose into. Offering her animal succor, Rischka has so much sympathy for her that she decides to back away from Alexis, which she does by acting in a decidedly uncivilized manner at dinner with him until, exasperated by her sudden change of heart, he expels her from the fortress. Still wearing her animal skin, Rischka returns to the rebel camp to reunite with her new husband, an event that Sparkuhl signifies with an iris shot. The film that in its shot-list infrastructure is essentially a parody of silent-film cinematography, in which the use of masks was formulaic, concludes appropriately, with an iris-out shot that is standard but that also functions to remove the mask.

Thus, in a film whose shot repertoire is determined entirely by masking, how the cinematographer selects appropriate masks for individual scenes, how he places them on the camera to obscure some of its field of view, and how he looks through the mask window to focus on subjects in the action field determine how the plot unfolds, and also how themes like the military satire and the metafilmic parody develop. It is the cinematographer who executes the shot the director calls for and makes it significant. In their films' two dominant diagonal mask shots, of Anna Boleyn ascending to the gallows and Rischka mounting a fortress wall, the cinematographer aligns the window with the subject, vectorizes the field of action, and thereby evokes the exact mood of poignancy or slapstick these scenes and the films as a whole require.

Therefore, it would seem that through their liberal use of a masking-shot schedule Lubitsch and Sparkuhl do indeed shake up the aspect ratio in *Die Bergkatze* to take full advantage the spatial parameters of the frame, of the horizontal, vertical, and diagonal axes, and to make an aesthetic statement about the instability of spectatorship and arbitrariness of spectators' perceptions of the action field. So how precisely did they accomplish this? First, they made *Die Bergkatze,* and to varying degrees the other films they made as a team, partly about the viewing experience, about how viewers process cinematic information. Thus, in *Die Bergkatze* they made spectators think about their own spectatorship, fundamentally by varying the aspect ratio to destabilize the viewing experience and make spectators more aware of the dimensionality of the projected film. Second, and consequently, they made spectators aware that film content may be hierarchical, the most important centered in the frame or focused in some part, and the less important scattered around the center and to the borders and into the corners. Rather, Lubitsch and Sparkuhl demonstrate that film information, as distinguished from film content, is nonhierarchical and is to be found throughout the frame, not just at the center. Obviously, they conveyed this message to spectators precisely because in *Die Bergkatze* they tried to make full use of the frame space, signifying visual information out to the boundaries as well as in the center. Because the action field has four corners but only one center, three spatial axes but only one focus, Lubitsch and Sparkuhl engage the entire field. By changing the focus plane (1) through conspicuous shot-by-shot film structure, (2) through a system of masks, and (3) through character movement along all three axes, including into the corners and of the frame, they forced spectators to venture out from the center into the surrounding spaces and to realize that significant visual information can arise anywhere on the screen. The cinema of Lubitsch and Sparkuhl can be seen as an expansive three-dimensional space capable of surprising the audience in original and provocative ways. They enhanced spectators' perceptions of cinema, as if by blocking one eye with a covering, a mask. They emphasized that spectators' perceptions of the action field are arbitrary because the field itself is fluid, but arbitrary perceptions are preferable to perceptions that have been fixed by someone else. To Lubitsch and Sparkuhl, centering and focusing are fixing strategies, whereas masking is a parody of fixing strategies, and axial subject motion is liberating. Masking in *Die Bergkatze* also is liberating, however, in the sense that masks are part of the set design, in which respect they are part of the diorama. Like the fortress that resembles a dollhouse, the mask shot recalls an earlier period of silent-film history when the mask was still novel. The traditional diorama, Louis Daguerre's "mode of presenting scenes in which a series of paintings (some opaque, some translucent) are seen at a distance through a sequence of openings controlled by screens and shutters,"[17] consists of an image the spectator looks at through a peephole. In *Die Bergkatze*, the mask window is the peephole, the action field, the image. By giving spectators this masked, proxy access to the action field, Lubitsch and Sparkuhl were actually inviting them to look at films as if through the viewfinder of the camera, in the manner of the cinematographer. This was their chief contribution to German film theory.

NOTES

1. Walter A. Koch, "Ecogenesis and Echogenesis: Some Problems for Biosemiotics," in *Biosemiotics: The Semiotic Web 1991*, ed. Thomas A. Sebeok and Jean Umiker-Sebeok, 195 (Berlin and New York: Mouton de Gruyter, 1992).

2. Alisa Solomon, *Re-Dressing the Canon: Essays on Theater and Gender* (London and New York: Routledge, 1997), 17–18.

3. Maria Makela, "New Women, New Men, New Objectivity," *New Objectivity: Modern German Art in the Weimar Republic 1919–1933*, ed. Stephanie Barron and Sabine Eckmann, 52–53 (New York: Prestel, Los Angeles: Los Angeles County Museum of Art, 2015).

4. Thomas Elsaesser, *Weimar Cinema and After: Germany's Historical Imaginary* (London and New York: Routledge, 2000), 10.

5. Richard W. McCormick, "Desire versus Despotism: The Politics of *Sumurun* (1920), Ernst Lubitsch's 'Oriental' Fantasy," in *The Many Faces of Weimar Cinema: Rediscovering Germany's Filmic Legacy*, ed. Christian Rogowski, 68 (Rochester, NY: Camden House, 2010).

6. McCormick, "Desire versus Despotism," 73.

7. Christian Rogowski, "Introduction: Images and Imaginaries," in *The Many Faces of Weimar Cinema: Rediscovering Germany's Filmic Legacy*, ed. Rogowski, 10 (Rochester, NY: Camden House, 2010).

8. Elsaesser, *Weimar Cinema*, 198.

9. Ibid., 37.

10. Blain Brown, *Cinematography Theory and Practice: Imagemaking for Cinematographers, Directors, and Videographers* (Amsterdam: Elsevier, 2002), 30.

11. Thomas A. Sebeok, *Global Semiotics* (Bloomington and Indianapolis: Indiana University Press, 2001), 38.

12. Daniel Arijon, *Grammar of the Film Language* (Beverly Hills, CA: Silman-James, 1976), 15.

13. Fred Gehler, "Die Bergkatze," in *Deutsche Spielfilme von den Anfängen bis 1933: Ein Film Führer*, ed. Günther Dahlke and Günter Karl, 52 (Berlin: Henschelverlag Kunst und Gesellschaft, 1988).

14. Sabine Hake, "Self-Referentiality in Early German Cinema," *Cinema Journal* 31 (Spring 1992): 40.

15. Dietrich Scheunemann, "Activating the Differences: Expressionist Film and Early Weimar Cinema," in *Expressionist Film*, ed. Scheunemann, 8 (Rochester, NY: Camden House, 2003).

16. J. E. Cirlot, *A Dictionary of Symbols*, trans. Jack Sage, 2nd ed. (London: Routledge & Kegan Paul, 1971), 129.

17. Don Gifford, *The Farther Shore: A Natural History of Perception, 1798–1984* (New York: Random House, 1990), 30.

3

Karl Freund's Signature Visual Designs in Manifold Collaborations

Like E. A. Dupont, whose film *Varieté* (1925) he shot, Karl Freund (1890–1969), sensing the rise of fascism and anti-Semitism, emigrated from Germany to America in 1929 to work in Hollywood. Though he went on to win the 1938 Academy Award for best cinematography for *The Good Earth* (1937), his most inventive cinematography is apparent in his silent films in Germany and his multiple aesthetic partnerships, with directors Fritz Lang, Paul Wegener, Richard Oswald, F. W. Murnau, Carl Theodor Dreyer, and Dupont. Freund served his apprenticeship as a cinematographer on forty-nine short and feature films, 1911–1919, notably F. W. Murnau's *Der Knabe in Blau* (1919), Robert Wiene's *Die Arche* (1919), *Gräfin Küchenfee* (1918), *Der Liebensbrief der Königin* (1917), and *Dei Räuberbraut* (1916), and twenty films under Rudolph Biebrach's direction, 1916–1919. His first collaboration based on a cinematographic coauthorship was with Fritz Lang (1890–1969), on his third film *Die Spinnen, 1 Teil: Der Goldene See* (1919), and its sequel, *Die Spinnen, 2 Teil: Das Brillantenschiff* (1920), and their working partnership culminated with the masterwork *Metropolis* (1927), in which they fabricated an indelible model of a dystopian future. Concurrently, Freund collaborated with other directors to give their films distinctive looks and new visual arcs, futuristic, anticipating the future of film, as well as Expressionistic, and horror genre arcs, notably Paul Wegener in *Der Golem: Wie er in die Welt kam* (1920), Carl Theodor Dreyer in *Mikaël* (1924), and most remarkably F. W. Murnau in *Die Finanzen des Grossherzogs* (1924), *Herr Tartüff* (1924), and *Der letzte Mann* (1924). An actor and screenwriter, Wegener had written, codirected, and starred in two earlier films about the Golem (1915 and 1917), but only his third attempt, *Der Golem: Wie er in die Welt kam* (1920), codirected with Carl Boese, is arresting cinematographically with Freund's imprint. Having shot the director's first film, *Der Knabe in Blau*, Freund worked with Murnau again on three films in 1924, at a crossroads in his career, to assign them a distinctive new visual grammar after Murnau's collaborations with cinematographer Fritz Arno Wagner in 1921–1922 on *Schloss Vogelöd* and *Nosferatu, eine Symphonie des Grauens*. Similarly, he gave Carl Theodor Dreyer's *Mikaël* (1924) a signature visual design when he worked with his cinematographer Rudolph Maté, and in which he made his acting debut; and in *Varieté* (1925) he executed many innovative shots, notably of trapeze performance, which distinguished Dupont's directorial style:

> In their expressionistic nature the shots also allow Dupont and Freund to experiment with the visual language of the silent film camera, in particular by emphasizing the illusory nature of the ambulatory camera, not only in the traveling shot produced by a camera mounted on a trapeze swing but also in the movement of the photographed body across the frame.[1]

During his tenure at British International Pictures, 1925–1931, Dupont met Freund again, who went to work there in 1928, after he had finished shooting *Metropolis*, and stayed till 1930. When Dupont returned to Germany in 1931 he made his second film on circus themes, *Salto Mortale* (1931), in which he tried to incorporate some of Freund's camera techniques. Because of the diversity of his professional engagements, with Dupont and many other directors, Freund developed an experimental technique that was both avant-garde and versatile: his was an ambulatory camera not only because he devised so many inventive ways of creating the illusion of extreme camera movement but also because he could adapt his camera to any shooting script. His innovations into camera mobility and camera movement were instrumental in the evolution in German filmmaking from the stationary camera of Theodor Sparkuhl to the movable camera.

Karl Freund was born on January 16, 1890, in Königsdorf, Bohemia, Austria-Hungary, now Dvur-Králové, Czech Republic. In 1901, his family relocated to Berlin to take advantage of business opportunities for his father, an entrepreneur. At the age of sixteen Freund entered the film industry, and in the next few years he rose through the ranks at a meteoric pace. In 1906, he became an apprentice projectionist at Spezial Fabrik für Kinematographen und Films Alfred Duskes, Berlin, where he also acquired his first experience as a camera operator, as an assistant to cinematographer Charles Paulus on the film *Der Hauptmann von Köpenick* (1906), directed by Heinrich Bolten-Baeckers; in 1907, an assistant camera operator at Internationale Kinematographen und Licht Effekt Gesellschaft [IKLG], Berlin; in 1908, a newsreel camera operator at Pathé Frères, Vincennes, France, the same year they invented the newsreel, where he built his own camera and undertook his first experiments with sound-on-film; in 1910, a camera operator at Sascha Film, Vienna; in 1911, a film laboratory designer at Brothers Savic, Belgrade; in 1912, chief camera operator at Projektions-AG Union [PAGU], Tempelhof Studio, Berlin; in 1913, director of photography at Gad/Nielsen-Filme, Neubabelsberg; in 1914, a film production researcher with film camera pioneer Oskar Messter's Projection GmbH, Berlin, where he experimented with sound-on-film, including recording opera singer Enrico Caruso; and in 1919, a freelance cinematographer in great demand and with the freedom to exercise control over his career. After making major feature films with Dupont, Lang, Wegener, Murnau, and Dreyer over the period 1919–1925, Freund became production head at FoxEuropa-Film from 1926–1929, and in 1929 he immigrated to the United States, where he had a productive career as a cinematographer in Hollywood. He won the 1938 Academy Award for best cinematography for *The Good Earth* (1937) and, in 1944, founded the Photo Research Corporation of Burbank, which specialized in television cameras and the Norwood Director handheld exposure meter, a 3D light meter that Freund invented with Donald W. Norwood. In 1950, he shifted from film to the new medium of television to become the chief cinematographer at the recently formed Desilu Productions, after he had been the cinematographer on *Du Barry Was a Lady* (1943), which costarred Lucille Ball. Is it possible that the cinematographer on 150 episodes of *I Love Lucy* on television, 1951–1956, also filmed Lang's *Metropolis*? Is it possible that a sixteen-year-old apprentice projectionist who got hired as a camera operator on *Der Hauptmann von Köpenick* would later film *Metropolis*? The trajectory of his career monumental, Freund was among the greatest of German visual artists.

Years before making *Metropolis* in 1927, however, Freund, with Emil Schünemann, shot two feature films with Lang at the beginning of his career as a director, *Die Spinnen, 1 Teil: Der Goldene See [The Spiders, Episode 1: The Golden Sea]* (October 1919) and *Die Spinnen, 2 Teil: Das Brillantenschiff [The Spiders, Episode 2: The Diamond Ship]* (February 1920), an Orientalist fantasy that traces adventurer Kay Hoog (Carl de Vogt), in quest of rare treasure, Inca gold, and the Buddha's Head diamond, as he is pursued by The Spiders, a criminal gang of spies.

The Golden Sea begins with a prologue that shows the film's antecedent action: a marooned sailor who, just before an Inca warrior pursuing him kills him, impaling him with an arrow, manages to cast a message in a bottle into the sea. The first scene, consisting of establishing long and mid shots introducing characters and themes as well as the setting, an adventurers' club, centers on an aristocratic dinner party at which some of the guests, and specifically Lio Sha (Ressel Orla), discuss the unexpected absence of Kay Hoog, who later arrives with his story of having found the bottle containing the message when he was out on his yacht. Thus Lang establishes the plot. Notably, the establishing shots include several subtle pans, merely the suggestion and promise of camera movement, showing characters interacting at the table and socializing around the room. But when Hoog extracts the message from the bottle, Freund films him in a mid shot that by tilting down and then panning right follows him as he sits down and places the message on a desk. This may seem insignificant camera movement, this actually complex combination of a tilt and pan, but compare it to the illusion of camera movement in a contemporaneous film, Lubitsch's *Die Puppe*, released just two months after *The Golden Sea*, in which the character would extract the message in the center of the room and then bring it to a desk positioned directly in front of the camera. On the whole, *Die Puppe* is a much better film than *The Golden Sea*, even though its camera technique is less sophisticated. In other words, a cinematographer may do more with a stationary camera than with a mobile one, just as post-1927 directors and cinematographers such as Charles Chaplin, who continued to make silent films even after the introduction of synchronized sound and dialogue, show they could do more in silents than in the new talkies. The introduction of synchronized sound and dialogue, universally recognized as a landmark in film history, was proceeded by an equally momentous change in filming technique, the introduction of the mobile camera, of which the scene in *The Golden Sea* yields an example. Freund's opening shot sequence identifies the location of the adventurers' club, establishes the confessional mood through gossip and a cryptic message in the bottle, and provides information about the chronology of events, that Hoog reports he has just received a telegram in response to his inquiry to Harvard University about the message, which accounts for his late arrival for dinner. But Freund establishes much more than the opening shots as antecedent action and pieces for solving the puzzle of the plot. He establishes that his camera will be a mobile camera, not fixed, and by extension that his technique of using tilts and pans as transitional devices, as distinguished from a system of rapid cuts to convey continuous action, in the manner of Theodor Sparkuhl in the films he made with Ernst Lubitsch, is not just a facet of his cinematic style: Freund's innovations in camera mobility were also indicative of a revolution in filmmaking procedures then under way in Germany, France, Denmark, England, and America.

Freund's tilts and pans are typically subtle in *The Golden Sea*. For example, throughout Hoog's account of his research into the message, Freund cuts to close-up shots of Lio Sha, whose anxious expressions suggest she may have a special personal interest in the content of the story. Then in a mid shot of Hoog standing to explain what he has discovered so far about the mystery of the message, he holds the message near the bottom of the frame, Freund tilts down to focus on his hands, and the camera movement reveals Lio Sha, who is seated next to him, as she tilts her head up to steal a glance at the document. The camera tilts down to reveal a character tilting up: this clever shot is characteristic of the precision and subtlety of Freund's camera movements in this film, and it might also imply, synecdochically, that the human head signifies the film camera. Freund completes this camera-movement sequence by tilting back to the medium shot of Hoog.

The film's next scene, at Hoog's house later on the evening of the party, serves to advance the plot: relaxing at the hearth, Hoog contemplates the mystery of the message, when a Spider intruder disables him and steals the document. Having earlier seen an intercut shot of the message, which contains the geographical coordinates to the sailor's position, spectators now comprehend the contest between good and evil: both Hoog and the Spiders know the location of the treasure. But this scene is more important for its cinematography than for plot development. Freund shows Hoog, accompanied by his servant, walking along an open mezzanine that resembles a clerestory in ecclesiastical architecture, which, like the study below, consists of large rectangular openings, like windows, with passageways behind them. Because the room is totally dark and the passages upstairs and down are backlit in an Expressionist fashion, the windows and back walls of the mezzanine and the study look like two rolls of film. As Hoog and the servant walk along the mezzanine, they appear to move frame by frame as they pass behind the breaks between the windows. The cinematography here builds up tension for the dramatic confrontation that is to happen downstairs. But more remarkably, Freund uses it to direct spectators' attention to the construction of the set and the shot, to the fact that they and the cinematography are constructed. This was an important statement for him to make, because *Die Spinnen* is not an art film but a serial adventure thriller that does not accommodate much cinematic experimentation, and also because he was conscious that he was riding the *nouvelle vague* of an optical revolution, which becomes more apparent in the following scene, which shows Hoog "on an observation car on the South-Mexico Railway" (intertitle), the last car on the train, which Freund films in a wide shot to the back wall that comprises three large windows through which the receding landscape is apparent. The row of windows, recalling the clerestory windows in the previous scene, with the landscape changing behind them in a live-action shot, also evokes a projected film, which Lotte H. Eisner describes as "the scenes actually filmed in a train without back projection."[2] When Hoog walks into the car from the right side of the frame, he is also entering a scene in a movie. The scene is visually arresting, in part because it is so cleverly metafilmic: the twenty-second shot is stationary, with no camera movement, but the shot content is kinetic, all because Freund elected to shoot it as live action, rather than in a train car set on a sound stage and using the traveling matte process to add background footage later. Although Lang would have made the decision to shoot the scene on location, he would have relied on Freund to get the shot, which he most decidedly did: it is the shot that makes *Die Spinnen* a work of art, even though most of the film comprises standard adventure-film shots, such as stationary shots of long duration, in which "everything continuously falls into rapid movement. Everything constantly collides: avarice and exotic cultures, spirit of adventure and strange mechanical worlds, morals and bound desires."[3] Yet the receding landscape of a rapidly moving train as it appears in a live-action stationary location shot seems to have nothing to do with adventure, other than that the hero walks into it. Freund got this shot in part because of his ambition, as well as his proficiency, as a camera innovator. On this film he was the camera operator, ascribed in the front credits, along with Emil Schünemann, with "Photography," not cinematography. But by distinguishing himself in a revolutionary spirit with this live-action shot, with some subtle tilt and pan shots, with one amazing traveling shot, and with all the standard shots and continuity and cross-cuts that evoked the adventure genre to the director's satisfaction, Freund established a productive working relationship with Lang, which became a true artistic collaboration on the set of *Metropolis*.

Most of the camera movement in the two episodes of *Die Spinnen* is of this kind, elementary investigative tilts and pans, but the film also presents several more daring examples of mobility, such as one long, slow shot from the base to the observation basket of the main mast of the tall sailing ship, from which the sailors spot Hoog and Naela (Lil Dagover), an Incan sun priestess whom he rescues after she refuses to execute Lio Sha, who has been taken prisoner, in a ritual sacrifice, drifting on the raft he devised for their escape from the Spiders, who, like the prospectors in John Huston's *The Treasure of the Sierra Madre* (1948), are eliminating one another for a greater share of the treasure. What at first looks like an amazing tilt-up shot of the mast closer analysis reveals to be a traveling shot, a crane shot that Freund probably improvised by securing the camera to a rope and pulley system on one of the ship's other masts. Freund used this shot again when he filmed the imagined murder of the trapeze artist Artinelli in *Varieté*:

> Dupont represents this fatal fall from Artinelli's point of view in a short-duration follow shot resembling a zoom-in, which Freund probably executed by suspending the camera from a rope and pulley and lowering it to the floor, stopping it just before impact, and then cutting to a reaction shot of the horrified audience.[4]

Throughout, Freund exploits cross-cuts liberally to move back and forth between the two independent but concurrent narratives of Kay Hoog and of Lio Sha and the Spiders as they search for the treasures. Special optical-effects shots enhance the air of mystery in both narratives, such as the matte shot of a mirror Lio Sha looks in, whose display she converts, by flipping a switch, into a monitor, like a miniature movie screen, on which she can observe the proceedings of a closed meeting of the Spiders leadership, from which she has been excluded. Still, the shot repertoire is a mix of the old and new. Freund films Hoog and Naela's retrieval from the sea in an iris shot, yet films the rescue rowboat approaching the ship with a pan shot.

After he returns to San Francisco with Naela, they become lovers. In a fit of jealous defiance, Lio Sha, who also loves Hoog after he saved her from ritual sacrifice, now declares, "When Lio Sha's love is rejected, it turns to hate" (intertitle), which is the impetus for the next adventure, in *The Diamond Ship*, till Lio Sha murders Naela and Hoog vows to avenge her death.

The opening of episode 2, *The Diamond Ship*, consists mainly of cross-cuts showing the preparatory activities of the Spiders to recover the diamond and of Kay Hoog to smash their crime network and take his revenge. Freund's establishing shot repertoire is fairly standard. For example, he shows a Spiders conference call in a multi-image composition consisting of five people, one person in the middle, at a switchboard, four persons in the corners of the frame, all talking at once on the telephone. The previous scene shows Hoog in a negotiation with the police to undertake a raid later that evening on Spiders headquarters in the underground city in Chinatown. When the inspector inquires about whether he has any personal involvement in this affair, Hoog says only, "I have an old score to settle" (intertitle). Freund then cuts to a close-up of Hoog for presence, this facial expression showing his resolve for vengeance, then fades to archive footage from the previous episode, signifying his act of remembering, one scene showing him informing Lio Sha that he loves another woman, Naela, and another showing him discovering Naela's dead body, and then finally returns to the close-up of Hoog for presence, indicating he has remembered. Although the phone call and flashback provide essential information for the plot, Freund's devices to represent these events, the multi-image and close-up, are conventional in film. Elsewhere his camera technique in this episode is not much more inventive, remarkable more for its rapid cuts and cross-cuts, its static shots in which characters come and go, and its seemingly random mid shots and close-ups of characters in public settings.

Most of the action-shot sequences in *The Diamond Ship* are tinted, such as sepia for the underground city in Chinatown and for the coastline and cliffside, blue for city streets at night, red for the diamond cavern, and deep red for the poisonous crater. These colors serve to evoke the atmosphere of the settings, and the mood of the activities undertaken in them, mostly activities having to do with surveillance, subterfuge, discovery, and violence. Tinting was a common practice in film processing in the silent era for these and for other reasons, such as to evoke large-scale events like warfare or mass migration or the temperaments of characters. In these respects, tinting functioned much like light and shade, silhouettes, irises, and fades, to evoke dominant aspects of settings, characters, plots, and events. Freund may have shot these scenes on tinted film, that is, film stock the base of which had been dyed in specific colors. Otherwise after filming the print base could have been dyed or it could have been tinted by hand.

After Hoog finds the Buddha's Head diamond in the cavern, he takes advantage of his knowledge that one crater emits poisonous gas every evening, to evade his captors Lio Sha and the Spiders, all of whom perish there. They succumb to gas poisoning, but in a sense they are overwhelmed by the tinting too. Hoog is the sole survivor because he is the hero and he exacts revenge against his enemy, Lio Sha. Then he squeezes through a fissure into a nontinted print.

Despite his great achievements on *Die Spinnen*, Freund would not work with Lang again for six years, when he became the cinematographer on *Metropolis*, which was released January 3, 1927. In the six-year interim, Freund shot twenty-seven films with some of Germany's leading directors, including eight with F. W. Murnau, two each with Paul Wegener and E. A. Dupont, and one each with Carl Theodor Dreyer and Arthur Robison, and he was cinematographer on two feature films he also directed: *Der Tote Gast* (1921) and *Der Grosse Sensationsprozess* (1923). The ambitious camera operator who had impressed Lang on the set of *Die Spinnen* now came to *Metropolis* an accomplished cinematographer and his collaborator on an original masterwork, on which he had working relationships with cinematographers Günther Rittau, who had shot Lang's *Die Nibelungen: Siegfried* and *Die Nibelungen: Kriemhilds Rache* (1924), and Walter Ruttman.

After the opening multi-image animated and location footage of industrial machines in operation, the first shot in *Metropolis* is of the shift change, a wide vanishing-point perspective shot of a tunnel with two phalanxes of men dressed in dark overalls and skullcaps, one group ending their shift, on one side, the other starting, on the other side, marching in unison, in identical postural, facial, and gestural (PFG) dramatic pantomime displays. Pictorially, the shot is perfect, like the shot of the train in *Die Spinnen, 2 Teil: Das Brillantenschiff*, Freund's signature. Freund follows the workers who are beginning their shift onto an open industrial elevator that

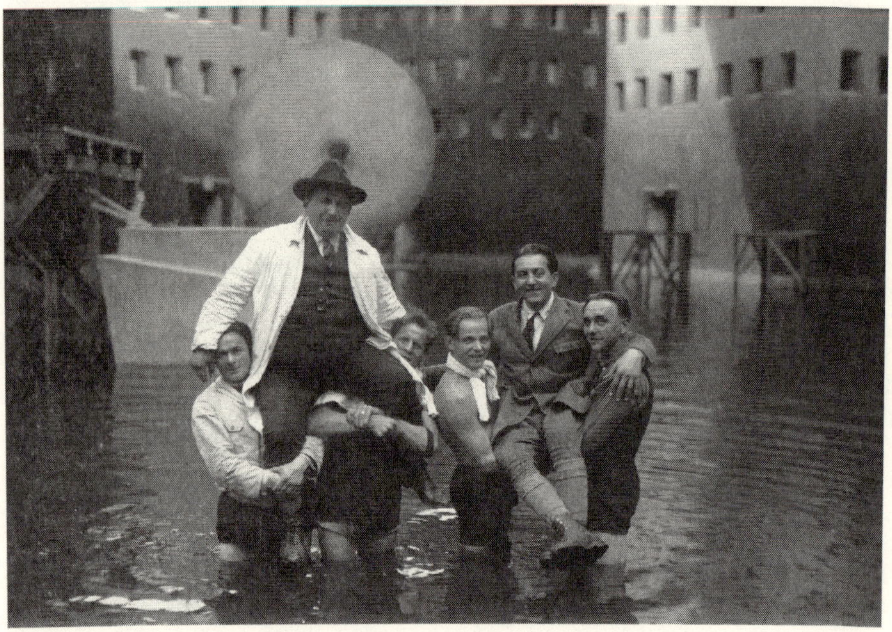

Figure 3.1. Karl Freund (left) and Fritz Lang, 1925–1926, on the set of *Metropolis* (1927). Copyright: Horst von Harbou–Deutsche Kinemathek.

descends to the workers city deep underground. That standing outside the elevator he is able to shoot the men on the descent of the elevator as the architecture of the city rises on the other side of it suggests that the shot is achieved through the elevation of the artificially constructed set, the miniature model of the city, designed by Otto Hunte, Erich Kettelhut, and Karl Vollbrecht, not the descent of the elevator. The shot seems to ask spectators to consider how it was attained.

> To describe the mass of inhabitants in the underground town in *Metropolis* Lang used Expressionistic stylization to great effect: impersonal, hunched, servile, spiritless, slavish beings dressed in costumes of no known historical period. The stylization is extreme during the change of shift when the two columns meet, marching with rhythmic, jerky steps, and when the solid block of workers is heaped into the lifts, heads bowed, completely lacking individual existence.[5]

The opening image of the workers is a motif throughout *Metropolis*, notably in scenes that depict machine operators performing a techno-fetishistic choreography, but also as a mnemonic, for example later in the film when Freder appeals directly on behalf of the workers to his father, Joh Fredersen (Alfred Abel), the architect of the metropolis, after he has witnessed a breakdown in the machine hall, in which some workers suffer severe burns from a massive escape of steam and others are ritualistically sacrificed afterward for the malfunction, to appease the machine, marching "with rhythmic, jerky steps" up a huge staircase and to their deaths into the mouth of the machine "Moloch." When his father tells him the workers are "where they belong," Freder responds, "where they belong?" (intertitles). Here Freund intercuts a brief shot of the workers, with their backs to the camera, standing at the elevator, reintroducing the visual trope from the beginning of the film. This is a perceptual shot, which Freder would seem to focalize, because it appears immediately after he poses his question. Yet Freder was not present at the opening scene, and has only recently seen workers for the first time, when he witnessed the mishap in the machinists' hall. Who, therefore, is responsible for this memory, for this image? Spectators remember the opening scene, and they recognize the image, even though the shot of the workers here is a mid shot and from a different angle. Spectators make the connection between the two images mnemonically; they identify the motif *workers descending* and how its introduction into the scene between Freder and Joh functions thematically. Thus, this is a moment when spectators connect with the cinematographer, who is responsible for the shot, in which respect they contribute to the construction of the film through their spectatorship. Freund gets (takes) the intercut shot of the workers at the elevator, and spectators also get the shot by understanding it.

Corresponding to the subterranean City of Workers is the terrestrial urban complex "Club of the Sons," the first shot of which is of a field where young athletes are moving spontaneously, exercising and practicing, though Lang hints at some regulation here too in the oval track some are running around, in their all-white outfits, and the uniformity of their PFG displays of elation. Even the brief mid close-up shot of Master Freder (Gustav Frölich) with two other athletes, the first of the protagonist, is just an anonymous face in the crowd at this early point in the film. Freund's first outstanding shot of continuous action shows ten sprinters racing on the track, and comprises two three-second mid close-up tilt-down traveling shots for presence (power, kinetic energy, freedom) in which Freund keeps the retreating camera equidistant from the frontrunners. He takes a similar retreating traveling shot later in the film, when Freder and Maria (Brigitte Helm) meet in the catacombs for the first time: as she approaches him, Freund films her in a seven-second continuous shot, a medium shot that, as he draws back the camera, at a slower pace than her walking pace, and tilts it up slightly, becomes a close-up. It is one of the most complex, resourceful, and beautiful shots of the film. He takes a counterpart of this shot in an earlier scene at the Eternal Gardens, when Freder, who is flirting with one of the young actresses, is interrupted by the first appearance of Maria, accompanied by her group of young children from the City of Workers. Spectators see her in a medium shot with toning to shroud the children around her in an ethereal mist, an effect that could be achieved by dyeing silver particles in the emulsion, the layer of silver salts in gelatin on the base of the film. She tells the children, "Look! These are your brothers!" (intertitle), and repeats her words as a political statement, directing it to Freder. Freund establishes the bond between Freder and Maria by cutting between close-ups and then mid shots of them, signifying they are looking at each other. Then he cuts to a wide shot of her and the children in the distance, as authorities arrive to expel them from the garden, where it is clear they are forbidden because they are working class. This wide shot for absence is the counterpart of the mid close-up for presence of the sprinters earlier. By matching the shots Lang emphasizes the class binary and the perceptual distance between them. But the scene between Freder and Maria also establishes that he is in love with her, and it sets up the Dantesque quest that he will now undertake in the rest of the film, to descend, like the workers on the elevator starting their shift in the opening scene, into the underworld to find her, like Beatrice, which becomes clear when he breaks through the garden doors to start his journey, both to find Maria and his brothers and sisters and to subvert a supersystem based on social division. Lang and Freund exploit their motif of matched shots to evoke this class dichotomy. *Metropolis* is replete with thematic as well as shot dichotomies, fundamentally, terrestrial and subterranean cities and anthropomorphized machines and dehumanized designers and operators. Visual contrasts abound in the film. For example, when Freder questions his father about the injustices of the system, Lang and Freund signify their opposition in a meticulously constructed over-the-shoulder mid shot of them, Joh, dressed in dark colors, his back to the camera, his large form dominating the frame, and Freder, dressed in white, facing the camera in three-quarter profile.

Contrasts are prominent in the theme of surveillance, such as the pure form-shadow relationship of Freder with the Thin Man (Fritz Rasp), whom Joh enlists to shadow his son in the underworld.[6] Antithetically, the similitude of characters becomes apparent when, after abandoning his father, Freder finally enters the steamy underworld, where his first encounter is with a distressed worker named 11811 Georgy (Erwin Biswangea), who is struggling to operate a clockwork machine whose three arms he manipulates to maintain the macro mechanism of the City of Workers. When 11811 Georgy, suffering an emotional breakdown, is unable to continue, Freder intervenes to take up his duties, assuring him, "Listen to me . . . I want to trade lives with you!" (intertitle), and then changing clothes with him and instructing him to take his own place in the upper city. (Later, when the Thin Man apprehends 11811 Georgy, he demands, "Where is the one whose clothes you are wearing?" [intertitle].) The dominant character similitudes in *Metropolis*, of course, are (1) Hel, Joh Fredersen's dead wife, and Hel, the "Machine-Man" Rotwang the Inventor (Rudolf Klein-Rogge) fabricates in her image, (2) Maria and the robot Hel, both of whom Brigitte Helm portrays, and (3) Freder and 11811 Georgy, who exchange roles and identities to subvert the class system. These character pairings are thematic. That Lang and Freund reflect character pairings in camera-shot pairings is highly innovative, such as the sequence consisting of a shot of Freder operating the clockwork arms and a cross-cut to Joh with Rotwang manipulating the arms of a compass as he reviews his design plans for Hel. In his role as the Mediator, Freder attempts to reconcile all such pairings, whether they are traded and replicated identities like Freder's and Hel's or entrenched binaries that essentialize workers. In contrast, after spying on Freder and Maria kissing in the catacombs, Joh Fredersen instructs Rotwang, "give the Machine-Man the likeness of that girl" (intertitle). In other words, as a social architect, Joh Fredersen makes likenesses, replicates images, just as Rotwang appropriates Maria's face for his Machine-Man, whereas, subversives within the supersystem, Freder and Maria make original images, like frames of film in original shots, this image one of them kissing for the first time, and the following image one of them kissing again, the latter an ingeniously composed extreme close-up in which the outlines of their profiles effectively intersect the frame.

When Rotwang chases down Maria in the catacombs to steal her face, Freder hears her cries for help. Freund's sequence of shots for the abduction-rescue scene is ambitious. When Maria desperately tries to escape from Rotwang's grasp through a grilled window in the roof, Freund films her in two overhead shots, one through the grill, in which the two figures are severely foreshortened, the other a close-up, as if through a gap in the grill, showing only her face. He represents Freder outside trying to ascertain the source of the cries, in a series of alternating tilt-up, tilt-down shots that evoke his head movement, his looking in all directions. Searching for her through a line of interlocking rooms with doors that close and lock behind him, Freder notices a scarf protruding from under a door and recognizes it as belonging to Maria. (Freund provides a glimpse of the scarf in the previous shot, a wide pan past several closed doors, evoking Freder's perspective surveying them.) When he reaches to retrieve the scarf, Freund films him in an extreme over-the-shoulder forward traveling shot that looks down his arm and moves with his hand. With a duration of just two seconds, this shot provides an original point of view, and it also contributes to the growing repertoire of camera moves in German film.

Meanwhile, Rotwang is in his laboratory already conducting the electrical procedure to copy Maria's facial features to the Machine-Man, turning it into a decoy of Maria. Freund effects the changeover in a special-effects rapid lap (overlap) dissolve close-up from one image, the robotic facial display, to the other, the human. Lap dissolves were rare in silent film, because they had to be executed in the film camera, as distinguished from with an optical printer, a projector connected to the camera, which came into use in German film in the mid-1930s. Even though the face-to-face image transition is blatant, Freund's dissolve does impress as a visual effect attained by unusual technical means and also as a scientific simulacrum in the context of an apocalyptic fantasy. When Freder sees the counterfeit Maria for the first time, in the company of his father, and, clearly sensing something is wrong with her, he experiences an emotional breakdown, which Freund represents in a montage of strident special effects, such as rapid cross-cuts, flashing lights in the form of globes and starbursts, soft focus, superimposures, and various distorted images, all culminating in a traveling matte shot of Freder falling through black space.

The German film industry during the silent period achieved a high degree of sophistication in special effects, especially in both parts of Fritz Lang's *Die Nibelungen* (1924) and in his *Metropolis* (1927)—animation, miniatures, glass shots, and stationary and traveling mattes were among the techniques used. Eugene Schüfftan developed the "Schüfftan process," which shot live-action through the clear portion of a mirror placed at a forty-five degree angle in front of the camera and combined it on the negative with the image of a miniature setting, which was reflected off the silvered part of the mirror into the camera; or the process combined live action reflected off the silvered part with a miniature or painting shot through the glass—this type of "mirror shot" achieved some convincing and powerful effects in Lang's *Metropolis*.[7]

Freund's wide shots of the miniaturized model of the city and of animated and miniaturized model automobile and airplane movement establish the metropolis as a futuristic supersystem and provide a credible setting for the imagination and an intellectual context for the internal narratives, both terrestrial and subterranean, and particularly for the film's climactic scenes of destruction, flooding, sacrifice, and reconciliation. In relying on special effects, most of them invented specifically for *Metropolis*, Lang and Freund also drew on two other conventions. The first convention was that of miniaturization in recent German film, most notably Ernst Lubitsch and Theodor Sparkuhl's diorama settings in *Die Puppe* (1919) and *Die Bergkatze* (1921), which at the films' release were avant-garde effects. The second convention was that of mechanization in German painting in the *Neue Sachlichkeit* movement: "More than Verism, Magic Realism, and Post-Expressionism, the term *New Objectivity* evokes the machine. As early as 1902, architect and theorist Hermann Muthesius described *Sachlichkeit*, roughly translated as 'objectivity,' as a machine aesthetic stripped of ornament and appropriate for industrial society."[8] For example, an untitled photocollage (c. 1920s) by Alice Lex-Nerlinger depicting an androgynous cyborg bears a close resemblance to the Machine-Man in *Metropolis*: "Here the body is replaced with the machine rather than enhanced by it, thereby announcing a new kind of human existence in which the boundaries between natural and artificial are blurred."[9] Other works in this style, such as paintings and photographs of industrial machinery, including still lifes of machine parts, and of factories, shipyards, train stations, and oil refineries, were inspirations for *Metropolis*'s art directors, Otto Hunte, Karl Vollbrecht, and especially Erich Kettelhut, who also worked with Eugen Schüfften and others on the film's special visual effects. The most likely inspiration for the industrial design of Lang's metropolis was Karl Völker's painting *Picture of Industry* (1924), which represents workers outside a factory: a foreground figure in an over-the-shoulder position looks askance from a group of essentialized workers, including a child, insignificant in the mid ground, diminished in scale less perspectively than by the industrial complex that envelops them.

The industrial complex in *Metropolis* is similarly dehumanizing, but thematically it is also a moral construct, in which some characters have the propensity to recover their humanity, to differentiate the genuine from the counterfeit self, much in the manner of the figure in the foreground of *Picture of Industry*. The counterfeit Maria is the vamp to the genuine Maria's virginity, a contrast that becomes evident universally when the former makes her first public appearance at Yoshiwara nightclub, a performance that Fredersen has organized to turn Freder against Maria and that Rotwang is using to destroy the father and son. Rotwang has programmed his Machine-Man, and therefore the counterfeit Maria, to do his will only. The spectacular dance performance is sensual, erotic, and profane. As *die grosse Babylon*, the apocalyptic archetype from Revelation, Maria performs to a shocked but fascinated all-male-gaze audience, which Freund films in mid and close-up intercut reaction shots, including intercut shots of Freder, in his sickbed, imagining the counterfeit Maria's performance and a macabre dance of the Seven Deadly Sins human statuary and a Death skeleton he saw earlier, all experienced in his delirious hallucinations and in his heart. The special effects and ambitious stage properties that accompany the counterfeit Maria's dance are effective, and Brigitte Helm's dance performance is momentous, particularly as footage of her subsequent appearances at Yoshiwara indicate how she is sowing violent discord within the terrestrial community, just as expectation of a Mediator is causing civil unrest and impeding production among the subterranean workers. Yet his first impression of the counterfeit Maria is confirmed when Freder exposes her at a rally where she is counseling workers to destroy the machinery. "You are not Maria!" (intertitle), he cries twice. And later, amid the destruction and flooding of the workers city, he is reunited with the genuine Maria, and as he tells her, "Yes, you are Maria!" he completes the film's climactic pairing, at least until the climax, when he briefly mistakes the counterfeit Maria for the genuine, and Rotwang mistakes the genuine Maria for the Machine-Man. Freder and Maria are united forever in the heart, which in *Metropolis* mediates between the director's brain and the cinematographer's hand.

The *filmemacher* collaboration that developed between Lang and Freund on this film is directly attributable to the complex optical experiments they conducted together with their art and special-effects directors, but what prepared Freund for this kind of avant-garde deliberation was his learning experience with directors Paul Wegener, F. W. Murnau, and Carl Theodor Dreyer over the six years between Freund's engagements on Lang's *Die Spinnen* and *Metropolis*.

In *Der Golem: Wie er in die Welt kam [The Golem: How He Came into the World]* (October 1920), codirected by Wegener and Carl Boese, Freund worked with cinematographer Guido Seeber (uncredited), who was also shooting Lang's *Das wandernde Bild* (December 1920), and on which he applied the talents for filming properties and special effects in fantasy he had acquired working with Fritz Lang on *Die Spinnen*. These served him well, specifically in addressing the challenge of filming the folktale narrative, set in the sixteenth century, about Rabbi Löw (Albert Steinrück), who, to shield the Jewish community of Prague from persecution, makes a gigantic clay figure, the Golem, which he magically instills with life, in a manner that anticipates how, in *Metropolis*, Rotwang animates the Machine-Man Maria in his laboratory. Like the shot transition from Hel's face to Maria's, the transition in *Der Golem* is from a shot in which Rabbi Löw is modeling the Golem figure in clay to a later shot in which the Golem figure appears to be finished, and it now has a human face, that of Paul Wegener. Because Wegener himself played the part of the Golem, Freund and Seeber worked especially closely with him on the technical issues of representation within the fantasy mode, such as shot selection, camera angles, camera movement, light and shade, and the use of life-size models and blue and green tinting and other special effects. The opening blue-tinted wide shot of Rabbi Löw at his nighttime observatory is part of a blue-tinted sequence, which includes a wide shot of the sky in isolation and then a close-up iris shot of the animated stars in which the mask simulates the aperture of his telescope. The blue tinting functions to evoke the sign he discerns in the night, that "The stars foretell disaster!" (intertitle) to the Jews of Prague. This scene is followed by a green-tinted shot sequence set in Rabbi Löw's house to establish the characters of his daughter, Miriam (Lyda Salmonova, Wegener's wife), and the rabbi's *famulus*, or attendant (Ernst Deutsch). When Löw enters the house, he simply comes in from the night, but, to spectators, he crosses another kind of threshold by making an optical transition from blue to green tints. The remainder of *Der Golem* is a series of such transitions between blue and green tints, and to a sepia tint, which is the predominant, and also a red tint. Most remarkable are the symbolic transitions, each phase executed with green tinting, from a mid shot of the stars in the sky, to a close-up of the Star of David, to a first close-up of the face of the Golem, and (2) the scene in which with his *famulus* assistant Rabbi Löw invokes the sacred word, which features an array of illuminated multi-image special effects, and the next scene, in which Löw instills the Golem with life not through the intervention of special effects, but just by pinning a magic star to his breast.

S. S. Prawer describes the special-effects invocation in more poetic, less cinematic terms:

> We now approach the only conjuration scene in the German "silent" cinema which can stand comparison with that in Murnau's *Faust*. In my view it is even better. The waving of a wand in invocation to "Astarte" brings a ring of fire—which involved building the whole set on a platform beneath which fire and smoke could be sent upwards. There follow electrically generated lightning flashes of an intensity never seen on screen before, and the gradual emergence of a terrifying head with smoke issuing from its lips. This smoke forms itself into the magic word AEMAET needed to animate the Golem.[10]

Cinematically, by counterbalancing Freund's spectacular visual effects and Rabbi Löw's rather ordinary gesture of giving the statue a symbol, in the manner of Fritz Lang's symbolic epigraph to *Metropolis*, "the mediator between brain and hands must be the heart," Wegener and Freund effectively show that every action performed well in front of the camera has a special effect, like Rabbi Löw's action of deactivating the Golem simply by removing the magic star from his chest, and in a later scene when the Golem stops the rabbi from taking the star and threatens to kill him. The Golem wields superhuman strength as a bodyguard, but here he expresses the will of a man. Rabbi Löw deactivates the Golem permanently, but the *famulus* later reactivates him to dispose of a rival, Knight Florian (Lothar Müthel), who is having an affair with Miriam. The Golem ends up killing Florian, by hurling his body from the top of a turret, and, after refusing to surrender his star to the *famulus*, in another show of free will, he accidentally sets Rabbi Löw's house on fire, which Freund films in a red tint, and carries away Miriam, dragging her body by her long braids, but only to take her to a safe place away from the fire, where her father finds her. Eventually, his human impulses get the better of him: when he picks up a little girl in the playground to hold her in his arms, she is attracted to his star and pulls it off, deactivating him.

Der Golem features little camera movement but is distinguished by its tilt-up shots, most of them of the Golem, to accentuate the height of a giant,[11] but also, numerous tilt-up shots of crowds gathered on the long staircases in the village. These are beautifully designed shots because they are integrated with the on-location village architecture, which comprises steep buildings on narrow brick roads. They also function in foreshadowing the climax, where the Golem commits murder atop the turret, the village's highest structure. In the end the tilt-up shot is the signature of Freund's visual syntax in *Der Golem*, more than blue, green, sepia, and red tinting, the special effects that complement Rabbi Löw's magic, or the animated constellations and iris shots of his observatory. Like Theodor Sparkuhl, in his tenure with Ernst Lubitsch, an actor turned director, Karl Freund fixed his camera on Paul Wegener, an actor still finding his *métier* as a director, and his larger-than-life portrayal of the eponymous character. *Der Golem: Wie er in die Welt kam*, codirected with Carl Boese, was, with *Der Golem* (1915), codirected with Henrik Galeen, and *Der Golem und die Tanzerin* (1917), codirected with Rochus Gliese, his third film about the folk hero, and only his tenth directorial effort, 1915–1920, of the nineteen films in total he directed to 1937, after which he concentrated on acting. In contrast, he appeared in seventy-one films as an actor, 1913–1951. Clearly, in *Der Golem: Wie er in die Welt kam* Wegener was still in his apprenticeship as a director and his filmmaking concentrated on acting, traditional storytelling, and visual effects, which are largely the focus of Freund's camera also in the film, particularly the special-effects shots that convincingly evoke the film's premise of sorcery, so that when the villagers call on Rabbi Löw to extinguish the fire that threatens to consume the village, they seem credible in making their entreaty, as he is believable as a man with this magic power.

Special-effects cinematography, popularly known as trick photography, points to another kind of trickery in camera operation in the silent era of film history, another aspect of magic, that of the tricks of the trade, the skills and techniques that the best of the German cinematographers were able to bring to their projects. This kind of trickery, the innovative, revealing, or original shot, not necessarily executed through special effects, that prompts spectators to take notice and to question how it works and how it is done, Karl Freund had more occasions for trickery on the three films he made with F. W. Murnau 1924–1925, than he had on *Der Golem: Wie er in die Welt kam*. In *Die Finanzen des Grossherzogs* (January 7, 1924), *Der letzte Mann* (December 23, 1924), and *Herr Tartüff* (November 16, 1925), Freund worked some of his most attractive cinematic magic.

On the cinematography of *Die Finanzen des Grossherzogs [The Finances of the Grand Duke]* he was assisted in an uncredited capacity by Franz Planer, a fellow Austro-Hungarian, who had shot eleven films with minor directors. A comedy, the film centers on the character of Ramon XII (Harry Liedtke), the Grand Duke of

Abacco, a fictional island in the Mediterranean Sea, burdened by the national debt, assailed by four conspirators, and inhabited by *Dummköpfe*.

The establishing shot identifies the setting, a standard iris-out showing the island of Abacco, and this fades into a shot sequence establishing the character of the Duke, who, rather than attending to his government duties, is sitting high on a perimeter retaining wall of the castle grounds, throwing down coins to some young swimmers to dive for. The first in this sequence is an overhead shot of waves rippling in the sunlight, as seven boys enter the frame, diving headfirst into the sea. The next are a mid shot of the Duke tossing coins, a mid shot of the boys diving for them, and a wide shot for context, showing him sitting on the wall and the swimmers below. In a few transitional shots Freund establishes Abacco as picturesque idyll, and the Duke as a carefree leader, but the ensuing scenes inside the castle, which indicate he is neglecting his responsibilities, ironize these opening shots. After a servant reports he has been unable to find the Duke, the finance minister, Don Esteban Paqueno (Adolphe Engers), tries to cover for him by explaining to Semjon Markowitz (Guido Herzfeld), a moneylender who has been kept waiting a long time for his appointed meeting about the Duke's overdue loans: "but His Highness is still sleeping" (intertitle). Freund intercuts another shot of the Duke amusing himself with the swimmers, before cutting back to the dignitary, who replies, "Then I shall wait until he is awake." His line is funny, but it also emphasizes the determination of a creditor and the extent of Abacco's economic crisis. When he finally finds the Duke, still diverting himself with the divers, Don Esteban chides him, "As you wish, Your Highness. Throw the rest of your fortune in the water" (intertitle). The initial images of a quaint idyll and insouciant ruler are now thoroughly shattered, like the image of the waves earlier when the boys knife through the frame. Freund's opening shot sequence establishes the setting and the financial premise of the plot, but it also facilitates the comedy through its ironic transitions among images of diversion and distraction. In theory all cross-cuts are ironic, because they demonstrate the relation, and thus the disparities, between independent actions. But Freund's cross-cuts in the opening scenes of *Die Finanzen des Grossherzogs* do not simply construct irony, specifically the irony of a debtor throwing money away while his creditor awaits payment. The camera movements, including the work of editing, implicit in the cross-cuts are ironic and contribute to the comedy of the characters, the setting, and the plot, as distinguished from just facilitating it technically. Thus, when Freund first cuts from the Duke to Markowitz with the finance minister, he establishes the comic irony, but when he cuts back to the Duke again and again, the camera movement itself is funny, part of the comic framework. Thus, it seems, in *Die Finanzen des Grossherzogs* Freund exploits an ironic camera, which was quite uncharacteristic of the cinematography in German films of the Weimar period. Thus, after Don Esteban goes out to summon him back into the castle and the Duke petulantly stomps his foot and flings the rest of his coins into the water, like a child ordered to come in from play, the comic business is clear, but the cross-cut to an action so trivial and predictable also is funny, because the previous shots have indicated the Duke is an immature and distracted person.

In the perceptual context of Freund's ironic camera, Murnau consolidates the film's comic premise: in the face of Mr. Markowitz's threat to foreclose on the loan in three days and take possession of Abacco, the Duke has two options to raise money: accept a business offer of ten million francs from Mr. Becker to mine asbestos on the island or accept a marriage proposal from Princess Olga of Russia. After the Duke rejects his offer, Mr. Becker, in revenge, commissions four vagabond conspirators, including one particularly frightening conspirator, played by Max Schreck, who had starred in Murnau's *Nosferatu, eine Symphonie des Grauens* (1922), to incite a revolution to destroy the Duke. Freund overemphasizes the gravity of this political threat by cross-cutting between shots of Becker and the conspirators plotting insurrection and of the Duke, having dealt with Markowitz's demand, rejected Becker's offer, and entertained Princess Olga's proposal, sunning himself on his chaise-longue, carefree again.

Freund also uses cross-cuts analeptically, to show the relation between actions that are not concurrent. Thus, when Don Esteban confesses to the Duke that he stole the letter in which Princess Olga proposes to him because he wanted to submit it to Markowitz in hopes of persuading him to extend the deadline on foreclosure, Freund uses cross-cuts, as distinguished from a more conventional device like a fade-out, fade-in, or an iris-in, iris-out, to flash back to scenes of these events, and transition to the visualization of Don Esteban's recollected narrative. His use of cross-cutting to show actions that are not happening at the same time, or parallel cutting, was still progressive in German film of the period, although the invention of the device is attributable to American filmmakers such as Edwin S. Porter and D. W. Griffith in the 1910s.

Freund radicalizes another conventional shot, the stationary shot in which human or mechanized subjects move either toward or away from the camera. One wide shot features Markowitz in his office: the set consists of his desk in the left foreground, the door in the left-center background, and an open space, the floorboards running diagonally from the right front corner to back left corner, toward the door, which is narrow and has a large window in it. Sitting at the desk, Markowitz reads a letter from Philipp Collin about an incriminating letter in his possession and decides to meet him. He stands up, puts on his hat, and walks out the door. But as the set and the shot are constructed, perspectivally, in his walk from the desk to the door, foreground to background along the parallel lines of the floor, Freund makes Markowitz appear as if he is moving into a vanishing point, an effect that is most powerfully apparent (1) when he descends a few steps to the entry and (2) when he pauses on the other side of the door, where he is visible, in miniature, through the window, which functions like the aperture of a camera. This filming technique, involving subjects moving toward and away from a stationary camera, is a trademark of cinematographer Theodor Sparkuhl in the early films of Ernst Lubitsch. But Freund takes the technique to an extreme, by exploiting set construction in conjunction with the subjective movement, to create an extraordinary cinematic effect, in which he projects the camera's depth of field into the field of action, a setting constructed for depth, but also in the field of perception of spectators. He creates the illusion of three dimensions in a two-dimensional field, but this shot has a genuine perceptual three dimensionality, a cinematographer's depth of field. That Freund executed it for an ostensibly basic transitional scene makes it especially remarkable.

But it is a surprise scene too when, moments after Markowitz's departure, Philipp Collin (Alfred Abel), disguised as a chimney sweep, emerges from his hiding place, in the fireplace. Although he enters the same shot Markowitz exits, Freund films him in a mid shot, changing the perceptual configuration of the elongated space: rifling through his safe for a document, which he steals, he chances upon Princess Olga's letter to the Duke, reads it, and elects to take it too. Sitting at the desk, like Markowitz earlier, but in the foreshortened space of a mid shot, he forges a copy of the letter, places it strategically it in the safe, and then escapes up the chimney. When Markowitz returns to the office, after learning the meeting was a ruse, Freund films him in a wide shot, entering through the door, climbing the stairs, and walking across the floor into the foreground. Because he negotiates the vanishing-point space in reverse, the shot too is reversed, at least in how spectators familiar with the original office shot perceive the subject's movements.

While the Duke is away on the mainland, Abacco experiences a coup d'état. Philipp Collin, also on the mainland, encounters Princess Olga (Mady Christians), fleeing from her brother, who is trying to prevent her from contacting the Duke. Masquerading as his wife, she and Collin secure passage on the Duke's yacht back to Abacco, where the Duke, with the help of Collin, Princess Olga, her brother, and the Russian Navy, eventually manages to apprehend Becker and his coconspirators and to restore order. Freund films the counterinsurgence and restoration-to-order with a standard shot repertoire, but one shot does stand out for its inventiveness. With a camera mounted in the stern, he shoots a boatload of sailors as they dock and disembark: the camera moves in with the boat, and as the stern swings parallel to the dock, Freund pans right to show in close-up the sailors springing out of the boat, their torsos, heads, and arms passing through the field of view, quickly, as pure forms. Here his camera is not ironic but *vérité*. By paralleling the opening transitional shot in which the young swimmers dive into the frame and cut across the field of view like an organic diagonal wipe to disrupt the image of light rippling on the water, thus setting the story in motion, this shot functions transitionally as well as imagistically. Transitionally, it ushers in the resolution of the film's plot, in which (1) the Russian sailors apprehend Becker and his coconspirators, (2) Philipp Collin produces the original letter from Princess Olga, which he stole from Markowitz's safe, proving that the Duke did not use it as collateral in an attempt to renegotiate the national debt, and thus removing the final impediment to their union, and (3) the Duke is restored as the rightful, and now conscientious, leader of Abacco, no longer distracted by children's play. Imagistically, the shot of the sailors leaving the water, by recalling and complementing the shot of the divers entering the water, rounds off the visual syntax of *Die Finanzen des Grossherzogs* as a rare German comic film and as a showcase for several good examples of Freund's original shot compositions and executions.

In the second film they made together, *Der letzte Mann [The Last Laugh]* (December 23, 1924), Murnau and Freund, drawing on the latter's success with camera movement in *Die Finanzen des Grossherzogs*, established a collaborative relationship based on their belief in the capacity of the mobile camera[12] to achieve the avant-garde visual effects of *Neue Sachlichkeit*.

> Not unexpectedly, Murnau uses aesthetic categories detrimental to any programmatical manifestation of expressionism. The realization of the proclaimed concept in *The Last Laugh*, imaginatively supported by the cameraman Karl Freund, has made this film one of the outstanding documents of early Weimar cinema.[13]

In the opening shot, Freund declares his intention to exploit a dramatically kinetic camera in *Der letzte Mann*: a ten-second fluid high-angle wide shot of a hotel lobby, filmed though the door grating of an elevator descending four floors to the ground level, a kind of infrastructural trucking shot. In contradistinction to a conventional title shot, in which the camera is in a fixed position, Freund's shot acquires its acute vertical axis from the four-story height of the elevator at the start, and the camera angle diminishes at a constant pace with the descent until it becomes eye level at the ground floor. This imaginative shot is notable partly because it clearly shows how the camera operator executed it. It concludes when the elevator operator, stepping into the field of view, draws open the door to allow passengers out and also to enter the field size space immediately in front of the camera. The next shot shows a bellhop whose job is to keep a revolving door turning for guests departing and arriving for the evening: in a forward tracking shot of the door, Freund films the guests already outside through the glass as he moves the camera to a close-up of the revolving doors, as the bellboy continues to turn them. The flickering effect of the glass panels passing in front of the camera is reminiscent of the progression of frames in the camera, or of film passing through a projector in a screening. Thus, in this shot, as in the first, Freund has drawn attention to his own camera operation, which is a most inventive articulation of *Neue Sachlichkeit*, the new objectivity of his film aesthetics, focusing on the phenomenological responses of spectators as well as the optics of shot construction. In the film's establishing shots he takes spectators down four floors on an elevator, across a hotel lobby, and through the revolving doors onto the pavement: thus, he establishes his spectatorship by showing spectators how to perceive film and shot sequences and repertoires as constructs.

These shots function also to take spectators out onto the pavement, where they encounter the Hotel Atlantic porter (Emil Jannings) doing his job, including struggling to carry in a heavy trunk on his shoulder. Overwhelmed by the task—he is an old man—he sits down to collect himself in the lobby, and a bellhop comes to give him a dram of spirits to help revive him. Freund then cross-cuts to show a hotel manager who, having witnessed the porter drinking on the job, makes an entry in his notebook. Later shots show the porter at home. Freund uses a tilt-up shot to disclose the inner courtyard of an apartment complex and various residents doing housework on their inner balconies. He focuses on one resident, who is brushing a uniform like the porter's. Next he takes spectators into the apartment to see the Hotel Atlantic porter and his niece (Maly Delschaft), and to learn about their routine, and about the working-class community. Next, Freund shows the porter going to work in the morning, revealing him in an expansive pan shot, walking from one end of a long street, directly in front of the camera, to the other end. The next shot, taken from inside the hotel, of him approaching the door from outside, could easily have made the transition from his home to work. In other words, the panoramic street shot of him was extraneous to continuity. Freund seems to have taken the street shot mainly to demonstrate his camera mobility, to draw attention to how he executed the pan. Therefore, the panorama, like the elevator trucking shot and the tracking shot of the revolving doors earlier, is discontinuous not so much because it is extraneous to continuity as because it makes spectators aware of how the camera manipulates their responses to images. Thus, to Freund, the cross-cut from the balcony to the interior of the porter's apartment is continuous, the panorama of the porter in the street is discontinuous, but Freund constructs both to be conspicuous in how the camera controls images. He takes a similarly superfluous shot later in the film, when from a simple wide shot of the facade of the Hotel Atlantic, Freund tracks back rapidly into an extreme wide shot merely to set up the next shot, of the porter inside the hotel. The simple wide shot would have been enough to establish the setting. The extreme track-out functions for Murnau and Freund to demonstrate to spectators the capability of the fluid camera of their collaborative partnership. Thus, in *Der letzte Mann* Murnau and Freund exploit camera mobility for perceptual as well as for technical reasons: to engage spectators in perceptual film analysis but also in production, in their collaboration. Christiane Mückenberger observes, "*Der letzte Mann* gilt als Höhepunkt des deutschen Stummfilms, als Prototyp des Kammerspielfilms und als Premiere der 'entfesselten Kamera'"[14] ("*Der letzte Mann* is regarded as the high point of German silent films, as the prototype of the *kammerspielfilms* and as the debut of the 'mobile camera'" [St. Pierre's translation]). Freund's mobile camera is indeed *entfesselten*: it is "unfettered" and "wild."

This strategy of linking technical with nontechnical camera movement is most evident when the porter enters the hotel to start his shift in the morning. From the pavement outside, he engages the revolving door precisely as another man, his double, dressed in a porter's uniform identical to his, a military-style greatcoat with a peaked cap, engages it from the inside: with his camera positioned inside the door, Freund shoots the porter from the front and the *doppelgänger* from behind, initially in a mid shot, and then in two close-ups, one a reaction shot of the porter to the other man, the other a double profile shot of the proxy, his image reflected in the glass in front of him, who looks young and capable. With his camera positioned within one of the compartments and moving with the revolving door, Freund follows both men until the new porter takes his position on the pavement and the old porter watches through the door and then passes through it to inspect closer from the pavement, in astonishment as—he realizes—his replacement is walking to the curb to attend to his first arrival. His realization he has been replaced is apparent in his reaction, his facial expression, posture, and gestures only, and is not articulated in an intertitle, which is typical of the *kammerspielfilms* (literally, "chamber talk films") that derived stylistically from Max Reinhardt's *Kammerspiel* theater, and, as Murnau and Freund adapt the theatrical style, the *Neue Sachlichkeit* reaction against Expressionist cinema. Characteristic of a *kammerspielfilm*, *Der letzte Mann* features no intertitles, which facilitates narrative continuity and visual flow and the chance for spectators to engage the film analytically; it features significant settings, which materialize the psychological states of principal characters; it relies on naturalistic visual displays as opposed to the standard spectacle of Expressionism.[15]

When the hotel manager formally dismisses the porter, Freund films them in a wide shot from outside his office through the leaded-glass double doors, each framed by one door. After the manager presents the porter with his letter of dismissal, turns his back on him, and resumes his work at the desk, Freund shows the porter in a mid wide shot, reading the letter, then advances in a tracking shot toward his glass door and right up to a pane of glass. Here the camera's lens focus blurs to simulate the spectator peering through the unframed glass, and specifically the camera passing through it, transcending its materiality, as Freund match cuts to an interior close-up high-angle shot of the porter now on the other side of the glass, still studying the fateful letter, an intercut shot of which clarifies he has been demoted to the position of a toilet attendant. Even this shot, a close-up of a kind of intertitle, involves a back-and-forth camera movement that mimics the porter's act of reading, and an extreme close-up of the words *age and frailty*, the reasons cited for his demotion, which slip out of focus to evoke the porter's emotional reaction. Obviously, spectators are reading the words of the letter shot exactly as the porter is. Less obvious, however, is that, because of the dramatic camera work in the film, they might be conscious of this perceptual link. Similarly, when the hotel manager's secretary ushers the traumatized porter out of the office and they pass through the glass double doors, spectators are aware they peered through these doors when he was dismissed recently. They recall that crossing of this threshold, but they also may be conscious of how different that shot construction was from this one, that the camera moved forward unusually then, whereas now it pans horizontally.

The night after his dismissal, he returns surreptitiously to the Hotel Atlantic and uses a key he stole earlier to enter the manager's office and remove the uniform that was confiscated from him. As the porter attempts to get back out of the hotel undetected, Freund uses a camera move characteristic in this film, a rapid track-in that travels from behind the subject to far ahead of him, to simulate his looking into the distance, in this case to the front desk, where the night clerk and two bellhops are asleep, confirming he will be able to sneak past them. He emerges from the front door of the hotel and into an extreme wide shot of the hotel facade, a shot that Freund used earlier to show the porter arriving for work that morning. Then, the shot, a rapid track-out to this extreme wide shot, seemed superfluous, merely a show of the capacity of the *Neue Sachlichkeit* camera to move. Now, however, the wide track-out shot functions also as an intrafilmic reference to the earlier wide track-out shot, and hints it functioned to set up this shot.

Track-in and track-out shots are most typical of Freund's camera movement in *Der letzte Mann*. For example, when the porter returns home after breaking into the hotel manager's office, he encounters his niece's exuberant wedding celebration under way in his apartment building, which he joins. The morning after, two drunken revelers are lingering in the courtyard, one of them insisting on playing the flugelhorn, which Freund films in part in an extreme close-up shot of the elevated flugelhorn bell that moves into a swift high-angle track-out shot of the men, as if from a second-story window. Then he shows the porter in his apartment, where he is still happily intoxicated, the room spinning around him, which Freund represents first in a mid trucking shot of him, his body oscillating, probably executed with both subject and camera positioned on a rotating platform, and second, in a montage of oscillating forward, backward, and horizontal mid shots to evoke the room turning around him, as the porter is experiencing it, the montage culminating in a double-exposure shot of the flugelhorn bell, as he hears its sounds. Later he executes the same kind of shot to emphasize how gossip of the porter's demotion is spreading through the community, cried from balcony to balcony in the apartment complex: a track-in to an extreme close-up of one gossiper's ear, signifying she has received information.

With its ingenious and extensive camera movement, comprising traveling, tracking, and trucking shots, tilts up and down, and pans left and right, and its dramatic *kammerspielfilm* camera, *Der letzte Mann* is arguably the first modern feature film in which the phenomenon of camera mobility is inherent both in the narrative and in spectatorship. It is also one of the great films set in hotels that are signifying environments or microcosms, along with Edmund Goulding's *Grand Hotel* (1932) and Wes Anderson's *The Grand Budapest Hotel* (2014).

In the third and final film they made together, *Herr Tartüff* (November 1925), based on Molière's *Tartuffe* (1664), Murnau and Freund visualize the classic play as a contemporary melodrama, about a young man, an actor, who, in an attempt to convince his grandfather that his housekeeper is robbing him, specifically by persuading him to write his grandson out of his will and bequeath his estate to her, mounts a touring show in which he screens his film adaptation of Molière's *Tartuffe*. The transposition of Molière's Tartuffe and the housekeeper as the villain is dubious characterization, but the film-within-the-film adaptation of Tartüff does have currency.

> *Tartuffe* appears to have been a reluctant commission for Murnau. Since UFA had [Emil] Jannings under contract, [Erich] Pommer, after the success of *The Last Laugh*, wanted to exploit the box-office potential of this winning team. Murnau, from his point of view, was keen to be given *Faust*, which had initially been promised to Ludwig Berger, UFA's third star director, and who is still credited with the original manuscript, called "The Lost Paradise." A deal was struck, and Murnau agreed to shoot *Tartuffe*.[16]

This "winning team" of Murnau and Jannings, of course, also included Karl Freund, who puts his stamp on *Herr Tartüff* from the opening scenes, which depict the housekeeper (Rosa Valetti) awaking, summoned by the master's bell, and looking for her shoes. Freund films her in a floor-level wide shot at the far end of a vanishing-point perspective hallway, her master's shoes in the foreground, in extreme close-up in the proximate field size. The action shot reveals where she is going: she walks to the camera, out of the field of view, and kicks the shoes, contemptuously. The shot establishes the housekeeper's hatred for her master, but, in one of his characteristic capability shots, Freund demonstrates a curious way to film and to scrutinize cinematic space. When the grandson (André Mattoni) arrives to visit his grandfather, he picks up the shoes in the hallway and puts them tidily away. His antagonism toward the housekeeper is established, but the simple mid shot of him doing this also cross-references the optically adventurous shot earlier. Despite its innovative camera work, however, *Herr Tartüff* is not a *kammerspielfilm* or a *Neue Sachlichkeit* film in the style of *Der letzte Mann*. For instance, whereas *Der letzte Mann* has no dialogue intertitles, *Tartüff* uses them liberally, within the conventions of silent-film dramaturgy. When his grandfather refuses to receive him and the housekeeper ushers him out of the house, the grandson takes a few steps into the street directly into the foreground and, directly addressing the camera, and by extension the spectator-narratee, says, "You, who witnessed this scene, may rest assured I shall not give in without a struggle" (intertitle). How does this scene function within the Murnau-Freund partnership in *Herr Tartüff*? First, it operates within the comic mode. Second, it is theatrical, deriving from the role of the narrator who addresses the audience. Third, it is a distinguishing feature of silent cinema, a performative remnant of the first actuality films. "The spectator-narratee in a film may be either the receiver of the narrative, usually a character within the narrative, or the receiver of the gaze, the implied receiver of the moving pictures as signified by the camera."[17] In these respects the grandson's direct recognition of the camera in presentative blocking is an extreme example of how Murnau and Freund acknowledge the spectator or implied receiver, indirectly, not through intertitles or breaches of the fourth wall, but through subtle innovative camera movement, shot construction, and intrafilmic cross-references.

The film-within-the-film, the disguised grandson's traveling cinema feature of *Tartuffe* he manages to screen to his grandfather and the housekeeper, in the manner of Hamlet staging the Mousetrap play in front of Claudius and Gertrude to expose them, is more metafilmic than intrafilmic: it operates self-reflexively, as a parody of silent-filmmaking and acting conventions, in its sepia toning, stationary camera, preponderance of mid shots, and mannered performances, and is notable for its absence of camera movement and of experimentation in shot construction.

Three months before the release of *Der letzte Mann*, Danish director Carl Theodor Dreyer launched *Mikaël* (September 26, 1924), his sixth film as director, his first produced in Germany, at Ufa studios, and his first to rely on two cinematographers, Karl Freund and Rudolph Maté.[18] Maté was the second unit camera operator on *Mikaël*, and took over for Freund when he was required to work on *Der letzte Mann*. The opening shots serve to establish the setting, the mansion of artist Claude Zoret (Benjamin Christensen), and to introduce characters, notably Mikaël (Walter Slezak), his principal model, Charles Switt (Robert Garrison), a journalist who is writing a biography of Zoret, the Duke de Monthieu (Didier Aslan), a friend, and

Countess Lucia Zamikow (Nora Gregor), a visitor who would like her portrait painted. These are standard establishing shots from a stationary camera linked by standard cuts to different corners of the salon. The shot repertoire changes slightly when the Duke asks Mikaël how he became Zoret's model, which introduces a brief flashback to four years ago, which Freund and Maté signal with an indistinct iris-out, a fading device they exploit to designate room changes and time changes within the mansion, such as from the salon to the dining room, and also to fade from the moment when Mikaël and Countess Zamikow first kiss. Freund and Maté also use iris-out and fade-outs to signal transitions to scenes in other locations, such as the opera, where Mikaël and Countess Zamikow attend *Swan Lake*. Camera movement is modest early in the film, for example, when at dinner a guest hands a photograph to Switt, sitting beside him, and the camera pans along with it, and later that evening when Zoret shows Countess Lucia some art on the walls, and the camera pans with them as they move across the room from one painting to another. Other examples of modest camera movement include a tilt-down shot of Mikaël when he kneels to address Countess Zamikow, who is seated, and a wide pan shot of them walking through a park. Otherwise, the shot repertoire comprises stationary wide shots of spacious rooms with guests socializing and mid shots for more intimate presence, such as of the Duke and Mrs. Adelsskjold (Grete Mosheim) engaged in a private conversation after dinner, which will lead to a fatal affair.

The plot of *Mikaël* is progressive but simple, that of an unconventional love triangle in which Mikaël is torn by his affection for Zoret, with whom he has a homosexual and filial relationship, and for Countess Zamikow, for whom he feels a romantic heterosexual attraction. This *ménage* is complicated by the fact that Zoret relied on Mikaël to paint the eyes in his portrait of the countess, which symbolizes the fading talents of an older artist and his feelings that he is losing his companion and lover, and, mainly, the young man he has regarded as his son. Claude Zoret's dying words, "I can now die in peace because I have seen true love," are ambiguous, referring to his love with Mikaël, and to Mikaël's love with Countess Zamikow.

Mikaël is a great film because of its screenplay, cowritten by Dreyer and Thea von Harbou, based on the novel *Mikaël* (1902) by Herman Bang, with its progressive love story. But in its cinematography it is quite conservative, consisting of minimal and moderate camera movement and relying mainly on fade-outs, rather than edited cuts, to effect scene changes. In fact, Freund discouraged Dreyer from attempting mobile shots, because, working concurrently with Murnau, the more experienced director, he wanted to save all his best camera moves for *Der letzte Mann*.[19] That, in contrast, the cinematography of *Der letzte Mann*, a contemporaneous film, is so avant-garde, with a dramatically mobile camera, an array of complex tilt, pan, and trucking shots, multiple exposures, and experimental shots, suggests that Freund and Murnau's collaborative partnership was a commitment to a radical adventure in the *Neue Sachlichkeit* of modern cinematography, which included the exploit of strapping a camera to his chest for greater mobility, like the Night Watchman (Georg John) in the film, who inspects the corridors of the Hotel Atlantic with a flashlight strapped to his chest and who in the climax and the epilogue proves to be the porter's only faithful friend. The Night Watchman functions symbolically in two key scenes in the film as a proxy of the cinematographer, much as Freund appears in his own field of view, the implied cinematographer, in the character of LeBlanc the art dealer, in *Mikaël*. In the first scene, the porter, who has returned to the hotel at night to steal his uniform from the manager's office, must evade the Night Watchman. In the second, in the climax of the film, the Night Watchman shines his light, like a theatrical spotlight, on the porter as he sits, defeated, in the men's toilet, which, notwithstanding the fantasy epilogue, is where the film leaves him, a tragic figure. With his camera strapped to his chest, Karl Freund shined a light on modernism.

NOTES

1. Paul Matthew St. Pierre, *E. A. Dupont and His Contribution to British Film:* Varieté, Moulin Rouge, Piccadilly, Atlantic, Two Worlds, Cape Forlorn (Madison, NJ: Fairleigh Dickinson University Press, 2010), 38.
2. Lotte H. Eisner, *The Haunted Screen: Expressionism in the German Cinema and the Influence of Max Reinhardt*, trans. Roger Grieves, rev. ed. (1952; Berkeley and Los Angeles: University of California Press, 1969), 237.
3. Norbert Grob, "'Bringing the Ghostly to Life': Fritz Lang and His Early Dr. Mabuse Films," in *Expressionist Film: New Perspectives*, ed. Dietrich Schuenemann, 90 (Rochester, NY: Camden House, 2003).
4. St. Pierre, *E. A. Dupont*, 49.
5. Eisner, *The Haunted Screen*, 225.
6. Fritz Rasp in the role of the Thin Man appears within the twenty-five minutes of rediscovered footage in the 2010 restoration of *Metropolis*.
7. Ira Konigsberg, *The Complete Film Dictionary* (New York: New American Library, 1987), 339.
8. Pepper Stetler, "Man and Machine," in *New Objectivity: Modern German Art in the Weimar Republic 1919–1933*, ed. Stephanie Barron and Sabine Eckmann, 203 (New York: Prestel, Los Angeles: Los Angeles County Museum of Art, 2015).
9. Ibid., 205.
10. S. S. Prawer, *Between Two Worlds: The Jewish Presence in German and Austrian Film, 1910–1933* (New York and Oxford: Berghahn, 2005), 38.
11. Paul Wegener was 6'6". In *Der Golem* his massive "clay" wig and his platform-soled shoes made him look taller.
12. Dietrich Scheunemann, "Expressionist Film and Early Weimar Cinema," in *Expressionist Film: New Perspectives*, ed. Scheunemann, 15 (Rochester, NY: Camden House, 2003).
13. Ibid., 15–16.
14. Christiane Mückenberger,"Der letzte Mann," in *Deutsche Spielfilme von den Anfängen bis 1933: Ein Film Führer*, ed. Günther Dahlke and Günter Karl, 110–11 (Berlin: Henschelverlag Kunst und Gesellschaft, 1988).
15. *Der letze Mann*, however, is not entirely without Expressionist aesthetics. For example, after the porter steals his old uniform from the manager's office, he looks back at the Hotel Atlantic and envisions the building toppling over onto him, which is represented in an

intercut animated shot. Subsequently, Freund presages the porter's ascent of the stairs to his apartment with a shot of the ominous distended silhouette he casts on the wall ahead of him. He also shows the porter, disguised in his uniform, returning from his first day as a washroom attendant, hiding from detection in a passageway, his shadow projected grotesquely on the wall. Freund and Murnau may have executed these Expressionist shots parodically.

16. Thomas Elsaesser, *Weimar Cinema and After: German's Historical Imaginary* (London and New York: Routledge, 2000), 240.

17. Paul Matthew St. Pierre, *Music Hall Mimesis in British Film, 1895–1960: On the Halls on the Screen* (Madison, NJ: Fairleigh Dickinson University Press, 2009), 137.

18. Karl Freund also appears in *Mikaël* as an actor, in the supporting role of LeBlanc, an art dealer.

19. Jean Drum and Dale D. Drum, *My Only Great Passion: The Life and Films of Carl Th. Dreyer* (Lanham, MD: Scarecrow, 2000), 111.

4

Carl Hoffmann and the New Visual Discourse of German Silent Film

Carl Hoffmann (1885–1947) had already established himself professionally as the cinematographer on thirty-two minor films, 1913–1919, when he began to work with some of Germany's leading young directors: as the assistant cinematographer, under Karl Freund, on F. W. Murnau's *Der Knabe in Blau* (1919) and *Der Januskopf* (1920), Fritz Lang's *Die Spinnen, 1 Teil: Der Goldene See* (1919), and E. A. Dupont's *Varieté* (1925), and as chief cinematographer on Paul Leni's *Prince Kuckkuck: Die Höllenfahrt eines Wollüstlings* (1919), *Patience* (1920), and *Die Verschwörung zu Genua* (1921), and Lang's *Halbblut* (1919). Hoffmann went on to distinguish himself artistically as the principal cinematographer on some of the most visually spectacular German films of the 1920s: Lang's *Harakiri* (1919), *Dr. Mabuse der Spieler* (1922), *Die Nibelungen: Siegfried* (1924), and *Die Nibelungen: Kriemhilds Rache* (1924), Murnau's *Desire* (1921) and *Faust: Eine deutsche Volkssage* (1926), and Arthur Robison's *Die Todesschleife* (1928). In his collaborations with Lang, Murnau, Dupont, and Robison in the 1920s, Hoffmann developed a capacious visual grammar, ranging from panoramic establishing shots to intense close-ups of partial facial displays, from Expressionistic to Impressionistic lighting, and from stationary camera shots of movement to tracking shots of stationary objects. He contributed his original repertoire of camera shots, angles, properties, and mechanics to the visual discourse of Lang and Murnau's grand operatic stories, settings, and characters, Dupont and Robison's spectacular evocations of the radiance, motion, and illusion of circus performance, and, most notably, the social decadence and revelatory montages of Lang's crime thriller. To make these ambitious films Lang, Murnau, Dupont, and Robison relied principally on Hoffmann as cinematographer, trusting his singular ability to design the nonstandard shots they most needed to recount their narratives effectively but also to distinguish their filmmaking styles. These collaborations were midcareer for Hoffmann and the directors whose films he shot. When he came to work with them in the 1920s, Hoffmann was already secure in his filmmaking career: he had mastered his signature techniques and photographic style as a camera operator. But his extraordinary opportunities in the years 1922–1928 to work on avant-garde projects with leading directors necessitated he make his techniques and style adaptable and versatile, capable of framing the facial and body displays of characters as diverse as Mabuse, Siegfried, and Faust. His collaborations with experimental directors were the cutting edge of silent-era German film.

Carl Hoffmann was born June 9, 1885, in Neisse, in Silesia, Germany, now Poland. An active photographer from the age of thirteen, he maintained his own photography studio in Freiburg until 1908, when he joined the Welt Kino film company as a laboratory technician and projectionist, where he was soon promoted to camera and landscape photographer. In 1912, he was appointed as a camera operator at Filmindustrie Heidelberg GmbH, where he shot short films based on German literature, such as *Fiesko* (1913), an adaptation of Friedrich Schiller's play *Die Verschwörung des Fiesco zur Genoa* (1783), which he also codirected with Phil Jutzi, and also *Macbeth* (1913), with the English director Arthur Bourchier. After his plan to found his own film production studio in Munich was disrupted by the outbreak of the First World War, he worked at Deutsche Mutuscop & Biograph, Berlin, in 1915, before accepting the position of chief camera operator at Decla Bioscop, where the head of production, Erich Pommer, having become aware of his technological versatility with the film camera, enlisted him to shoot the six films in the *Homunculus* series (1916), which, in its representation of a humanoid creature, was a precursor of both Wegener's *Der Golem* (1920) and Lang's *Metropolis*.

In 1920 Hoffmann became a freelance filmmaker (that is, cinematographer, film developer, and film editor) and, with fellow cinematographer Gotthardt Wolf (1887–1947), established a film copying laboratory in Berlin, Hoffmann & Wolf GmbH, Film Kopierwerk, which they designed to meet the needs of German film-production companies and to network with directors. Whereas Wolf secured positions with minor directors such as Ernst Wendt, Lupu Pick, and Henrik Galeen, Hoffmann managed to forge collaborative partnerships with well-established directors like Fritz Lang, E. A. Dupont, F. W. Murnau, and Arthur Robison. After serving an apprenticeship to Lang as assistant camera operator to Karl Freund on *Die Spinnen, 1 Teil: Der Goldene See* (October 1919) and to Max Fassbender on *Harakiri* (December 1919), Hoffmann was promoted to Lang's principal cinematographer on *Dr. Mabuse der Spieler* (1922).

Along with *The Cabinet of Dr. Caligari* (1919) and *Nosferatu, eine Symphonie des Grauens* (1922), *Dr. Mabuse der Spieler [Dr. Mabuse, the Gambler]*, starring Rudolf Klein-Rogge (C. A. Rotwang, the inventor in *Metropolis*) as the antiheroic protagonist, is a prototypical German film noir, and also an action film and a chase film. The establishing shots show Dr. Mabuse, along with his cocaine-addled makeup artist, Spoerri (Robert Forster-Larrinaga), as one by one he picks up various photographs of himself from a deck of cards and fans them out in one hand as casually as if he were deciding what to wear for the night. In each image he is in disguise, and Spoerri's job

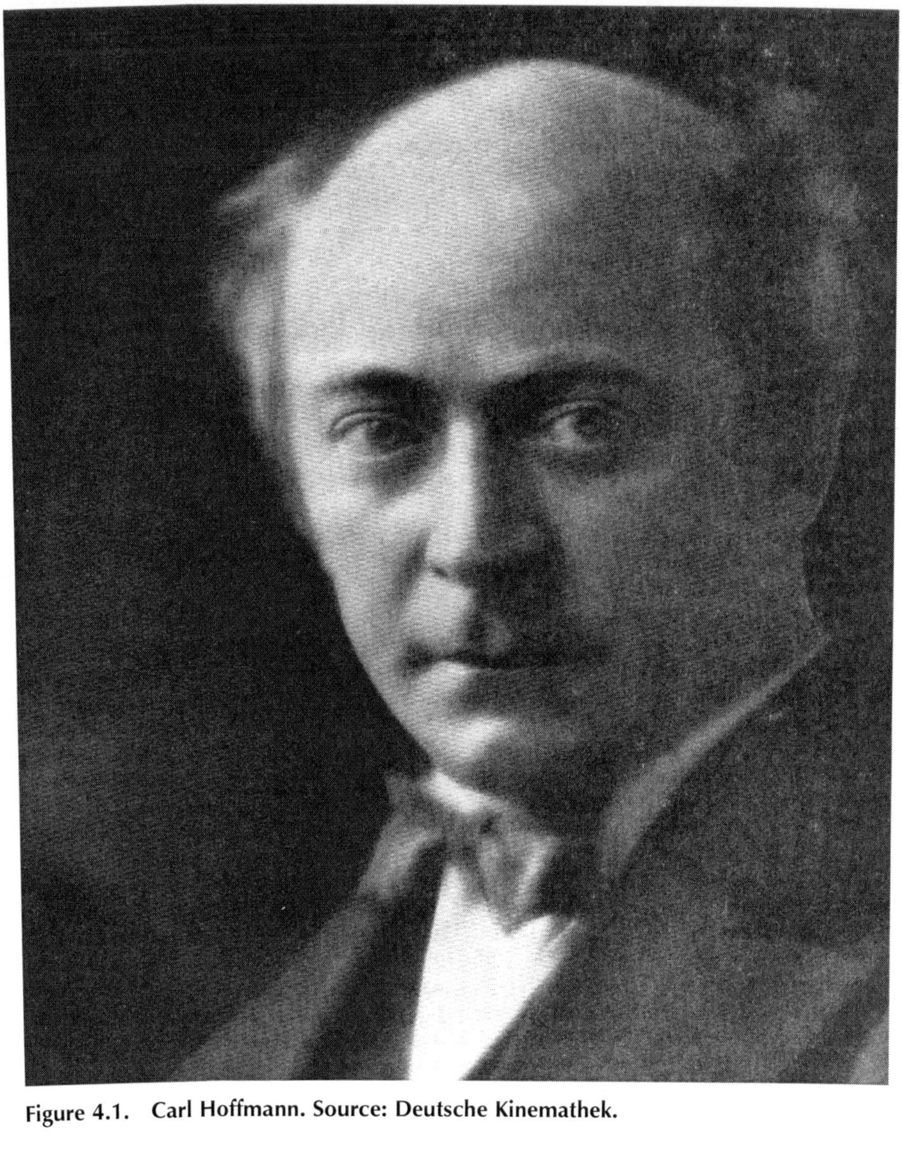

Figure 4.1. Carl Hoffmann. Source: Deutsche Kinemathek.

is to transform the appearance of Mabuse so he can circulate undetected through his criminal network. Hoffmann offers some intimations of how this system works in a sequence of cross-cut shots that show (1) a man who steals a briefcase he has targeted on a train passenger and, as the train is crossing an overpass, hurls it out the window into a car that at that precise moment is passing under; (2) the car driver blows a horn as a signal to a nearby man who has climbed a telephone pole to intercept a line; and (3) Dr. Mabuse receives a phone call from the man on the pole confirming the criminal act has been performed according to plan. The fast-paced establishing shots determine Dr. Mabuse is a master of disguise, he has many accomplices in the field, and he executes his criminal activities like clockwork, as is signified in intercut close-ups of their pocket watches when the thief and Mabuse verify the time. Subsequent scenes reveal Dr. Mabuse, an underworld figure intent on running the city, is involved in international smuggling, stock market fraud, counterfeiting, and many other crimes. For example, the briefcase stolen from a Dutch emissary traveling to Geneva contained the contract of a secret Dutch-Swiss trade deal. Reacting to the theft, the Swiss threaten to pull out of the deal, which causes stock in Dutch cocoa to fall drastically on the exchange. At the stock exchange, Dr. Mabuse buys all the Dutch stocks others are unloading, and only then, again at the appointed time, has he instructed one of his accomplices to publicize that the briefcase has been found by a railway attendant. When the rising price of Dutch cocoa peaks, just before closing time, Mabuse sells all his stocks. Hoffmann films the activity on the stock-exchange floor in wide shots and rapidly paced cross-cuts to mid and close-up shots of Mabuse and individual investors. The sequence ends with two double-exposure shots of Mabuse's head superimposed onto the image of the vacated stock exchange, signifying his dominance over the transactions. While the symbolism is strong, the shot selection evokes only the conventional cinematography of the era. *Dr. Mabuse* is plot driven, scattered with visual cues such as multiple character disguises, liberal uses of narrative as well as dialogue intertitles, and frequently executed iris shots and fades, which sustain the pace of disclosure by facilitating character development and scene transitions. Nevertheless, the film is notable for several experimental shots and instances of camera mobility.

For example, one shot sequence, set at a performance of the *Folies Bergère*, comprises wide shots of the stage and the audience, mid shots of small groups of performers and spectators, low-angle shots of the chairman or master of ceremonies, high-angle shots of the pianist, close-ups of the top of the bill, dancer Cara Carozza (Aud Egede-Nissen), and gender-specific reaction shots. The shot sequence serves to establish the *Folies Bergère* as a site for the arrival of Dr. Mabuse, in disguise as Mr. Balling, precisely to stage an encounter with Edgar Hull (Paul Richter), a millionaire vulnerable to his mind-control strategy, which is based on psychoanalysis free from third-party intervention. Later, Mabuse and Hull play cards at the Pontoon Club. When Mabuse introduces himself to others as Mr. Balling, Hoffmann tracks in to the group for presence. When the *maître d'hôtel* leads him and Hull to their table, Hoffmann follows them across the room in a horizontal pan, a subtle one, almost imperceptible. These brief actions, both involving modest camera movement, serving to establish their situation, conclude with an iris-out shot. Hoffmann's combination of moderate camera movement and traditional transitions is characteristic of his cinematography in this film. In this scene the camera movement establishes the situation in which, by exercising control over his mental state, Mabuse beats Hull at *va banque* and secures twenty thousand marks of his fortune. In a later scene, after Mabuse has had one of his men, posing as a guard, deliver poison to Cara Carozza in her prison cell, a directive for her to commit suicide, Hoffmann films her in a pan shot as she walks from the wall across the frame to sit on the bed, where she swallows the lethal potion. The camera movement is discreet, yet the character's motion across the action field invokes Mabuse's control over life and death.

Dr. Mabuse consists of parts, essentially two feature-length films. The first part concerns encounters like that of Mabuse and Hull, at a series of gambling rooms, at each one of which Mabuse appears in the new disguise and, through his psychological advantage, wins at cards. Throughout, he is pursued by Staatsanwalt ("state prosecutor") Norbert von Wenk (Bernhard Goetzke), who often wears a disguise, going undercover by posing as a target at gambling establishments, in hopes of exposing Dr. Mabuse, and to enhance the film's theme of appearance and reality. When they first meet at a card table, at the Palais Andalusia, Hoffmann represents the profound hypnotic perceptual influence Mabuse extends over Wenk through the use of lens masks and double exposures, notably a superimposed image of Mabuse's disemboded head in a severe track-in shot and a track-in of the intertitles of his commands to Wenk, "Take it" and "You take." The theme of appearance and reality focuses on concealment and exposure: when the prosector commits to tracking down, exposing, and apprehending Dr. Mabuse, once the pursuit is on, Hoffmann structures the film on cross-cuts showing concurrent actions in separate locations; these have a special urgency because the locations are so close, with Wenk always one step behind Mabuse. Because both are protagonists, both antiheroic, the antithesis of each other, the cross-cuts effectively negotiate between two autonomous but interrelated narratives. In such a fast-paced *policier*, parallel cuts, along with iris masks and other transitional devices, correspond to narrative actions like those of Mabuse and Wenk when they put on and remove their disguises.

> Lang's films function like a spiral. After a while, an image, a motif or a situation recurs, only in a slightly different form. The unexpected emerges from the obvious. The small changes drive events onwards. With every turn one penetrates deeper, below the unambiguity of superficial attraction. The films are images to correct and transform other images.[1]

Hoffmann's greatest cinematic achievement in *Dr. Mabuse der Spieler* is apparent in the novel performative parallel he draws between action cross-cuts and character disguises as transitional actions. Like *Metropolis, Dr. Mabuse der Spieler* is a veiled commentary on Weimar Republic Germany, its excesses and corruption. Cara Carozza's description of Mabuse to Countess Dusy Told (Gertrude Welcker), when they share a prison cell, Cara for her part in the murder of Hull, Dusy planted there by Wenk to interrogate Cara about Mabuse's involvement—"No one knows who he is! But he is there! Alive! He lives above the city—big as a tower! He is the damnation and the salvation!" (intertitle)—anticipates the moral dichotomy of Freder and Fredersen, Mediator and Master, in *Metropolis* and also the archetype of the monster in the emergence of Hitler as a ruthless dictator. In the climax, when Mabuse suffers a hallucinatory breakdown, he envisions a wall clock and other objects transformed into menacing robots, in the manner of *Metropolis*. Lang reinforces the political parallel through the reported dialogue in intertitles. When Count Told (Alfred Abel) asks his views on Expressionism, Mabuse replies, "Expressionism is just playing about. But—why not? Everything is 'playing about'!" He informs Countess Told, "There's no such thing as love—there is only passion! No such thing as luck—only the will to gain power!" Mabuse tells his gang, "Only now, shall the world know who I am—I—Mabuse! I want to become a giant—a titan, churning up laws and gods like withered leaves!!" And, defiant in her prison cell, Cara Carozza refuses to cut a deal with Inspector von Wenk, boasting, "He's stronger than all of you! He exterminates whomever he wants! And he will exterminate you, if you stand in his way!" Finally, when Inspector von Wenk, having cornered Mabuse and his gang, phones him to demand his surrender, Mabuse replies, "I feel as a state within a state with which I have always been at war." These remarks form an armature on which Lang and Hoffmann build the *zeitgenosse*, their "contemporary" gallery of images and archetypes, and the *zeitgeist*, their allusions to representative personages of the Weimar Republic.

> Even now, Mabuse's several disguises seem taken out of a catalogue of Weimar types, familiar from the drawings of Otto Dix and George Grosz: stock-broker in top hat, derelict drunk in a housing tenement, Jewish peddler at the street corner, bearded *rentier* in flashy limousine, industrialist with monocle and moustache, pimp, psychiatrist, hypnotist and opium-smoking Tsi-Nan-Fu in a gambling den.[2]

In its references to Weimar types in art and a totalitarian archetype and its link between changing costumes and identities and film cross-cuts, *Dr. Mabuse der Spieler* was Lang's most topical film. For example, when Mabuse's henchman Pesch (Georg John), having posed as an electrician to sabotage Wenk's office, has to escape quickly when Wenk returns unexpectedly, he detonates a small bomb as a distraction and jumps out the window. Hoffmann cuts to a wide shot of the street below, where a group of pedestrians, alerted by the explosion, immediately swarm Pesch and arrest him. This scene alludes to the political unrest in Berlin and other German cities in the early 1920s and to citizens' awareness of the potential for acts of sabotage and of civic responsibilities. In a later scene, Mabuse, disguised as a social activist, incites a crowd of working-class bar patrons to free Johannes Gutter, his alias for his own henchman Pesch, who has been arrested. Granted the scene is designed to demonstrate Mabuse's overwhelming willpower, Lang and Hoffmann show how volatile the German proletariat is on issues of social justice. When the mob intercepts the police van to demand the release of Johannes Gutter, the guard, displaying Pesch at the door as proof that Gutter is not the prisoner in transit, Mabuse's sniper, his gun barrel visible through window overlooking the scene, takes the confusion as his opening to assassinate Pesch.

Part 2 of *Dr. Mabuse der Spieler* begins with a daring shot from a stationary camera. Inspector von Wenk is in the office at his desk when he hears a shout from outside. In a mid shot he walks to the windows and opens them. The next is a high-angle iris shot of Count Told standing in the road, drenched with rain. Then Hoffmann returns to the previous scene in a wider shot, which shows Wenk running from the windows across the office and out the door, presumably to get Told, which is indeed what he does. He also runs out of the camera's field of view. What makes this conventional shot sequence daring is that in Wenk's absence, Hoffmann simply continues to film the office in a wide shot from his stationary camera, for a full eighteen seconds, in which the only action is the movement of the curtains in the wind. In a film that maintains the continuity of its intricate plot through cross-cuts, and has already used an intercut iris shot to indicate simultaneous action in another location, Told shouting in the street, and might easily have introduced another cut to show Wenk after he leaves the office, running down the stairs or out into the street, or coming back to the office with Told, a shot of long duration of a virtually static scene calls attention to itself. How does it function in this film? First, it feeds expectations and builds suspense. Spectators know Inspector Wenk has rushed downstairs to assist Count Told and will bring him back to his office. They draw this inference based on the iris shot of Told, obviously in peril, and how it seems to inform the static shot. Second, the static shot draws attention to the camera, to the fact that the camera is continuing to run and that it is on the set, in the office as it were. Spectators might imagine they are in the office waiting for Wenk and Told to return. But the shot informs them they are only place holders, like the rustling curtains, which evoke the action happening outside the camera's field of view. It reminds them of the presence of the camera. Third, the shot speaks to the nature of action in the action field: action can be minimal, a rustling curtain, or it can even be static, zero-degree action. When spectators watch the empty office, an anticipatory setup with a duration of eighteen seconds, they know Wenk and Count Told are outside the field and they speculate on what they are doing, which the succeeding shot of them entering the office confirms. Absent, the characters act on the nonevent of the frame, while the rustling drapes are *bruits* confirming all speculation.

At the film's climax, when Mabuse, having escaped through the city's underground sewer system and up through a trap door into his counterfeiting shop, only to discover he is trapped there, in a counterfeit prison, Hoffmann exploits another static shot, leaving Mabuse as the only moving subject, struggling desperately to reopen the trap door and unlock the main door, and confronted by double-exposure images of the ghosts of Hull, Pesch, Told, and Cara, whom he murdered. When the blind men who work at the shop confront Mabuse, Hoffmann uses double exposure again to transform them into the ghosts, who do not appear unfocused and ethereal, as before, but now resemble the characters when they were alive, with the same sharp definition: they challenge Mabuse to a game of cards, in which they quickly expose him as a cheater. When Inspector von Wenk and his men arrive to arrest Mabuse, he is effectively alone in a static set, the object of the shot, a stage property moving, like the curtains in the breeze. Hoffmann holds this closing shot, like the shot of his office earlier, until Wenk leads him away, out of the frame.

After *Dr. Mabuse der Spieler*, Lang and Hoffmann worked together on another two-part film, *Die Nibelungen: Siegfried* (February 1924) and *Die Nibelungen: Kriemhilds Rache* (April 1924), an adaptation of Richard Wagner's four-opera cycle *Der Ring des Nibelungen* (1848–1874); Hoffmann was assisted on this project by cinematographer Günther Rittau, camera operator Walter Ruttmann (uncredited), and special-effects camera operator Eugen Schüfftan (uncredited). The first section, "Canto 1: How Siegfried Slayed the Dragon," opens with mid shots of a blacksmith's assistant pumping a bellows and of Siegfried (Paul Richter, who played Edgar Hull in *Dr. Mabuse*) hammering the blade of the sword he will use to slay the dragon, and close-ups of Mime the blacksmith (Georg John, Pasch from *Dr. Mabuse*) admiring the clanging sound, and mid shots of him inspecting the blade and confirming its sharpness by letting a feather fall on it.

The next shot sequence looks ahead to Siegfried's destination, the castle at Worms, on the Rhine. The opening shot, of a royal procession of members of the House of Burgundy through the castle, is perfect in design, making maximal use of the action field of the stationary camera, which dominates in the film, in part to evoke through fixed images the ancient, precinematic look of the medieval *Nibelunglied.* The wide shot consists of a row of knights standing guard, armed with their swords and shields, four of them in half-silhouette in the extreme foreground, two of them visible in the center, and half of the other knights visible in either side, and filling the entire vertical and horizontal axes of the frame; in the background is a brightly lit corridor. Hoffmann films the knights, who do not move, for five seconds, at which point the royal procession enters the frame from the right and, one by one, members of the House of Burgundy slowly cross the field of action, right to left, across the frame and behind the guard of honor. The shot, a single take, has a duration of 1:06 and perfectly balances stillness and action, in which respect it recalls the static shots of Wenk's office and Mabuse's counterfeit prison in *Dr. Mabuse*. The long take from a stationary camera is a defining characteristic of Hoffmann's cinematography. The processional shot also establishes a destination for Siegfried as a heroic quester in the Romantic mode, to journey to Worms to win the hand of Kriemhild, of the House of Burgundy, and of course to prove his valor by overcoming any obstacles he meets on the way, initially by slaying the dragon, a stop-motion cinematography larger-than-life model Hoffmann films with a sympathetic camera. By bathing in the blood of the dragon, Siegfried acquires invincibility. Later, he encounters Alberich the Nibelung (Georg John, in a double role), who, in exchange for his life, gives Siegfried the wonder cap, which empowers him to be invisible or to assume any material form. Hoffmann depicts the ethereal realm of the Nibelungen mainly through craggy set designs and backdrops enveloped in light and shade and with fog-machine atmospheres, and the liberal use of double exposures of empirical and fantastic live action, which special-effects cinematographer Eugen Schüfftan achieved by combining live-action mirror shots, a process termed "das Schüfftansche Spiegelungsverfahren" ("the Schüfftanesque mirage technique").[3]

Notwithstanding special effects, *Die Nibelungen: Siegfried* comprises mainly stationary-camera wide shots of processional action, such as Siegfried riding through the landscape, and of formal interactions of the royal family and attendants in the vast rooms of Worms castle; mid shots, for presence, of characters engaged in conversations and gestural exchanges according to the conventions of silent-film dramaturgy; and iris shots and cross-cuts as transitional devices. Lang and Hoffmann also use intercut shots of soothsayers, in a sense to foreshadow a coming scene, such as Gunther's court poet Volker (Bernhardt Goetzke) and Brunhild's *runemagd* ("rune maid") (Frida Richard), who predict Siegfried's arrival, and effect the transition to the scene of his arrival. Yet some of these conventional shots are remarkable in their compositional design and action, the protracted movement within the frame, like the overhead shots of Siegfried as he approaches the throne of King Gunther (Theodor Loos) to ask for the hand of Kriemhild, and to accept the condition he act on Gunther's behalf to win the favor of Brunhild, Queen of Iceland.

In contrast, in the sequence in which King Gunther courts Queen Brunhild (Hanna Ralph) on her condition, that he defeat her in three tests of strength—stone, spring, spear—Hoffmann uses double exposures to show how Siegfried, invisible because he is wearing his wonder cap, wins the tests as Gunther's superimposed double. These shots evoke fantasy more than artistry. In contrast, Hoffmann's normal-angle three-shot sequence of Gunther and Brunhild's arrival at Worms, with no special effects, is spectacular simply in its construction. The first shot is of a human bridge composed of shields laid flat and supported on each side by twenty-six uniformed and helmeted soldiers standing waist-high in the water: this anticipatory setup, by showing spectators where the bridge leads, to the shore, makes possible the next shot. It is a reverse-angle shot that extends to the other end of the soldiers' bridge, where it joins the ship: in the top half of the frame the shot shows the ship and a staircase down to the bridge, which stretches diagonally from the middle of the frame through the camera left corner. The vertical line of the ship's mast, the horizontal lines of the cross-beam and the side of the ship, the diagonal lines of the staircase and the walkway, and the erratically angled diagonals of the ship's long oars in repose combine to form a pictorial shot, a formally balanced image with powerful aesthetic values, composed of points, lines, and planes. It is a shot appropriate for a king and queen to enter. That Hoffmann holds the shot for fifty-three seconds, the time it takes Brunhild and Gunther to walk along the deck, down the stairs, and across the bridge through the camera left corner, a very long time cinematically, 0.62 percent of the entire duration of *Die Nibelungen: Siegfried*, means spectators can gaze on a meticulously composed image and ponder its cinematography and visual discourse. The third shot, reversing the angle again, shows Gertrude and Gunther crossing the rest of the bridge to the shore: the diagonal of the bridge intersects with two diagonal lines of soldiers on shore. This triptych of visual compositions is characteristic of the Lang-Hoffmann collaboration.

They follow up this sequence with an unconventional three-shot, a mid shot of three people: Brunhild, Gunther, and Siegfried. By winning the contest of strength, Gunther has gone only halfway toward winning Brunhild's hand: he must also break her will. Therefore, he enlists Siegfried again to act on his behalf by donning the wonder cap and this time assuming his form. Under the appearance of Gunther, Siegfried physically overpowers Brunhild in her chamber and makes her cower. Then he reports back to Gunther. Hoffmann shows them, the two Gunthers, in a split-screen, two-image, effect. Next Siegfried-Gunther removes his wonder cap and, in a match dissolve double exposure, the image changes over from Gunther back to Siegfried. The special effects complicate the conventional three-shot, because they involve four characters: Brunhild, Gunther, Siegfried, and Siegfried-Gunther. Within the heroic fantasy mode of the *Nibelungenlied* and Wagner's opera, Hoffmann's special photographic effects in *Die Nibelungen* are basic, but at contemporaneous screenings they were essential to audiences' suspension of disbelief. If the premise of Siegfried's wonder cap is plausible, so too is the match dissolve that depicts its power. Aesthetically, the form-over-content aspects of fantasy special effects, in which, wearing the wonder cap, Siegfried erases his form or takes the king's form in a form dissolve, and of shots and shot sequences remarkable primarily for their framing, their formal balance of composition, and of the stationary camera that effects them, are closely aligned throughout *Die Nibelungen*.

In part 2, *Die Nibelungen: Kriemhilds Rache [Kriemhild's Revenge]*, Lang opens with a stark establishing shot of Kriemhild standing, in the background, facing the camera, at the head of Siegfried's tomb in a crypt, with four female mourners, her attendants, on each side, all of them motionless. Hoffmann's shot establishes the premise for Kriemhild's revenge, Siegfried's murder by Hagen Tronje (Hans Adalbert Schlettow) at the end of part 1. But the shot also has to do with the formal aesthetic principles of the *mise-en-scène*. With Kriemhild, and the shadow she casts on the wall behind her, as the apex, the mourners, who stand in two diagonal lines that extend into the foreground corners of the field of view, form a pyramid, the lines of which the stone steps leading up to the tomb and the arches of the crypt accentuate. Kriemhild and the mourners wear long headdresses imprinted with ternary designs, the mourners' headdresses prominent because Hoffmann shoots them over-the-shoulder, so their faces are hidden. The back wall, decorated with two horizontal bands in a chevron pattern, replicates the ternary design, which is apparent in the architecture of Worms castle, the costumes of many at the Burgundian court, and the set dressings of several key scenes in both parts of *Die Nibelungen*, in the form of triangles, pyramids, and chevrons, and in diagonal lines and zigzag patterns. *Mise-en-scène* ternary design is a signature feature of Lang and Hoffmann's collaborative visual syntax here.

The film is noteworthy also as a catalog of shots for presence of Kriemhild the revenger demanding justice for the murder of Siegfried, initially of King Gunther on the occasion of a marriage proposal she has received from King Etzel (Etzel) of the Huns. Only when, out of loyalty to him, but also because of his own cowardice, Gunther refuses to surrender Hagen Tronje to Kriemhild does she agree to receive

Etzel's emissary. She marries Etzel and they have a child together, Ortlieb, but she has forged only a marriage of convenience to consolidate the power she needs to avenge her true love, Siegfried. For example, she takes advantage of his favor by asking Etzel to invite her Burgundian family to celebrate the summer solstice with them, as a pretext for trapping Gunther and Hagen Tronje. Hoffmann's presence shots of Kriemhild reacting to the refusal of her demand of Gunther and a succession of Burgundians that Hagen Tronje be surrendered to her to mete out justice are modeled on the opening establishing shot of her standing like a statue at Siegfried's tomb, in which she is silhouetted against a backdrop that accentuates her sorrow and her resolve. In each of these shots, whether wide, mid, or close-up, she appears standing alone, confronting the camera, her truculence discernible only in her passionate eyes. Thomas Elsaesser observes, "in *The Nibelungen*, none of the relations that the characters have with one another are ever directly dialogical. This is also true of other couples in Weimar cinema, who rarely if ever simply interact with each other, face to face, as it were."[4] This shot sequence culminates when Kriemhild finally decides to take what she has been denied, by ordering the Huns to annihilate Hagen Tronje and his forces, who are waging a losing battle against them, and in which he has murdered her and Etzel's baby. After a scene in which Margrave Rüdiger, having returned from his failed negotiations with Kriemhild and with Etzel (Rudolf Klein-Rogge) to plead for peace, returns to report to the surviving Burgundians that he has brought back not peace but a death sentence, Hoffmann cuts to an extreme low-angle shot of Kriemhild standing on top of a turret of the castle. The turret and battlements occupy the lower half of the field of view, their contour traversing the frame from the left foreground to the right background corners, with a monochrome sky filling the other half, backlighting Kriemhild's severely foreshortened figure overwhelmed by an environment that isolates her in the ignominy of death yet gives her an all-seeing perspective. Lotte H. Eisner states, "In *Die Nibelungen* also, the isolated human body is treated as a decorative element, absolutely static, deprived of individual life, and frozen in its symmetry."[5] Kriemhild will concede, "I died when Siegfried died" (intertitle). Hoffmann emphasizes her ambivalent position of dominance and vulnerability by holding the shot for six seconds. He follows up by intercutting two mid and one close-up reaction shots of her in the same position atop the turret, now gazing in horror at the carnage below, and multiple final wide and mid shots of her standing by, arms crossed, as she watches the destruction by fire of the castle hall in which the enemy is sheltered. Gunther and Hagen Tronje are the only survivors of the battle and the conflagration. The Huns promptly behead Gunther after he refuses to reveal where Tronje has hidden the Nibelungen treasure, and when Tronje too refuses to answer Kriemhild executes him by bludgeoning him with Siegfried's sword. Her revenge accomplished, Kriemhild now has only to die herself, according to tragic and operatic conventions. Avenging Tronje's death, Hildebrandt stabs Kriemhild from behind and she dies in a passion. Acknowledging Kriemhild loved only one man, Etzel now decrees that her body be transported to Worms Cathedral, where she will be installed in a crypt with Siegfried.

In two major two-part films, *Dr. Mabuse der Spieler* and *Die Nibelungen*, 1922–1924, Carl Hoffmann and Fritz Lang established a collaborative partnership based on (1) camera movement through action cutting, cross-cutting, and parallel cutting, rather than a fluid camera employing pans, tilts, and other traveling shots; (2) special effects, form dissolves, and masking, more than the dramaturgy of character interaction; and (3) formal balance shots more than content shots about narrative events. Compared to Karl Freund and F. W. Murnau in *Der letzte Mann* (1924), a technically groundbreaking film remarkable for its experiments and technical innovations in camera mobility, Hoffmann and Lang seem to have been interested in exploiting the stationary camera, essentially an objective camera, to demonstrate its optical properties, its imagination, in a sense, its capacity to form lasting images of formally balanced scenes and character tableaux, and to sustain these images in shots of the longest possible duration. This distinction between the fluid camera of Freund and Murnau and the static camera of Hoffmann and Lang is not just taxonomic: it is contextualized in early film history and the transitions to synchronized sound and dialogue technology and to the subjective, dramatic mobile camera. When Freund strapped a camera to his chest to capture fluid shots in *Der letzte Mann* he anticipated the contemporaneous adoption of the handheld camera in the last years of the silent era and the introduction of camera stabilizer technology in the mid-1970s. Whereas Freund incorporated the film camera, making it part of his body and linking its movements to his natural pantomime, Steadicam technology separates the camera and the operator's body, allowing them to move independently of each other. In the history of film optics, Freund's innovation was revolutionary, not only because it liberated the camera from its tripod but also because it made it an end effector, an extension of its operator. In comparison, Hoffmann and Lang's stationary camera in *Dr. Mabuse* and *Die Nibelungen* seems conventional and, like iris shots, obsolescent. Who is more responsible for reliance on a static camera in these films, Hoffmann or Lang, the cinematographer or the director, and are stationary camera shots merely a signature of their collaborative partnership on these projects? If Freund could adopt a new fluid camera technique working with Murnau, would Hoffmann find the same improvisational freedom working with him on *Faust: Eine deutsche Volkssage* (1926)? For example, Eisner notes, in reference to *Der letzte Mann*, "For Murnau the camera moving on a dolly was no longer enough: he tied it to his cameraman's chest and made him follow Jannings step by step, bending, learning, and twisting in order to shoot from the most complicated of angles."[6] In contradistinction, Elsaesser, drawing on Siegfried Kracauer, observes, "According to one of his chief cameramen, Karl Freund, Murnau rarely looked through the view-finder himself."[7] For Murnau to tell Freund to position and operate the camera in this way yet trust him to get the right shots on his own is not necessarily a contradiction. It is likely a sign that they were truly collaborating cinematographically, designing *Der letzte Mann* together.

Based on the tragedy *Faust* (1808–1832) by Johann von Goethe, *Faust: Eine deutsche Volkssage [Faust: A German Folk Tale]* stars Gösta Ekman as Faust and Emil Jannings as Mephisto. The film opens with an allegorical montage of double exposure, superimposition, traveling matte, jump and parallel cuts, match dissolves, and other mechanical effects that establish the premise: devils have been released from hell, including Mephisto, who, making a wager with an archangel (Werner Flutterer), elects to win the soul of Faust, whom he sees as a vulnerable moral hypocrite.

The prologue montage begins with two intertitles: "Behold!" and "The gates of hell are opened and the horrors of the masses hunt over the earth." These are followed by chiaroscuro shots of the heavens: fast-moving clouds of steam against a dark background, into which Hoffmann makes a lap dissolve to the image of three devils, depicted as skeletons on horseback through the clouds, and then he cross-cuts back and forth to shots of the sun, to establish that the riders are approaching the earth, and back to them riding, only now a mid close-up shot. The first intriguing shot in the montage is a wide shot of Mephisto (Emil Jannings), depicted as a rebel angel, his horned head, with luminous eyes, at the top of the frame, his wings filling the rest of the space, disclosed in a diagonal shaft of striated light that cuts across the dim field of view, followed by intercut two-shots of the archangel in white light in the top of the frame, with Mephisto in an over-the-shoulder shot and profile silhouettes in the foreground, in conversation about Mephisto's desire to dominate the world. The archangel shows him two visions of Faust lecturing to his students and conducting experiments to discover the Philosopher's Stone. The montage ends with a frontal tilt-up close-up of Mephisto making his wager to "wrest Faust's soul from God" and, in Hoffmann's sudden backward tracking shot, appearing to drop out of frame.

The first scene opens with an establishing framing shot of Faust's village, which in the *mise-en-scène* is a miniature model of buildings with smoke (steam) emanating from several chimneys and a painted backdrop sky shrouding the sun (lightbulb). From here follow several shots of performers at a fair, jugglers, wrestlers, acrobats, shadow puppeteers, all with attentive audiences. Then Murnau and Hoffmann return to the establishing shot, but now Mephisto, a huge winged form appearing in the background, looms ominously over the town. The *mise-en-cadre* is simple: Hoffmann films a backlit Jannings, in costume as Mephisto, who stands behind the village model, but in contrast to the prologue montage, which is mythological and fantastic, the manifestation of Mephisto in a mundane setting, even if it is a replica, is shocking, specifically when he spreads his wings, blocking out the sun and darkening the entire village. Hoffmann's foreshadowing, his cross-cut to the fair to show the shadow-puppet screen going dark, is chilling, particularly because it leads to the spread of the plague through the village, which Murnau and Hoffmann represent as a windblown smoky vapor, or steam distributed by generator fans, and shot through a dark lens filter. The plague is occasion not only for special-effects shots but also for Hoffmann to demonstrate his *Neue Sachlichkeit* cinematography. The initial shot sequence of this kind in the film concerns a single event: a young woman asks Faust to come to help her mother, who is dying. The first shot is an extreme close-up of the mother, lying supine, horizontally in the immediate field view, with only her face in profile visible in the darkened room; her daughter, her face in three-quarter profile, leans over her, with her right arm placed around her mother's head. As the daughter pulls back, raising her body, her face now in three-quarter profile from behind, her head and torso illuminated, Faust enters the room through a door in the background, moving from shadow gradually into the illumination. He stands by the bed, examining the mother's condition: now he is in three-quarter profile, and the daughter (upright) and the mother (supine) are in full profile. He pushes the daughter away, indicating he wants to be alone with the patient. When he leans over the body to inspect the face closely, Hoffmann cuts to a tilt-up shot of the woman's face. The next shot shows him pulling back and removing a vial from a pocket in his garment. Again Hoffmann cuts to the close-up, as Faust raises her head to pour some medicine from the vial into her mouth: now in a tilt-up three-quarter profile in which her neck, chin, and mouth are prominent, the woman's face is luminous. Hoffmann cuts back to a mid shot that shows the woman rise, grab the collar of Faust's cloak, and then fall back lifeless, now onto her side into shadow, facing the camera. Again Faust leans over the woman, but this time to confirm she is dead. He casts the vial away, shattering it on the floor, which Hoffmann shows in an intercut close-up, and then cuts back to Faust standing over the body and turning away to fetch back the daughter. A shot reveals him filling the doorway; when he moves slightly to one side, he reveals the daughter, with another child, in the next room, framed by the door opening. She squeezes past him, then raises her hands in horror upon seeing her mother is dead. The next shot, a chiaroscuro close-up, shows her, the light illuminating first her forehead and then her entire profile, embracing her mother's body, with only the face visible, framed in deep shadow. Then the sequence fades to black. With a duration of just two minutes, and comprising a variety of close-ups and mid shots, this sequence establishes (1) the film's central themes on the fragility of human life and the fallibility and moral ambivalence of Faust, and (2) principal aspects of the cinematography, such as Hoffmann's use of a sympathetic camera for evoking emotion and his use of a *Neue Sachlichkeit* camera for realism. Robert Herlth, who along with Walter Röhrig was an art director on *Faust*, recalls Murnau's attitude to lighting:

> And when Carl Hoffmann lit the first set for *Faust*, Murnau said, "Now how are we to get the effect in the design? This is too light. Everything must be made much more shadowy."
>
> And so all four of us [Murnau, Hoffmann, Herlth, Röhrig] set about trying to cut out the light, with screens 23 cm. by 50 m. high. We used them to define the space and create shadows on the wall and in the air. For Murnau the lighting became part of the actual directing of the film. He would never have shot a scene without first "seeing" the lighting and adapting it to his intentions. Hoffmann has made masterly use, ever since, of what emerged from a single one of Murnau's experiments.[8]

Further, Eisner observes, "Carl Hoffmann's camera gives the terrestrial part of the film extraordinary modelling and has the power of impregnating everything, down to the cloth of a garment, with diabolism."[9] Yet in this sequence, and elsewhere,

Hoffmann's camera is "terrestrial" because it is humanist, revealing cloth not just as a "diabolic" garment but as an affective extension of the body, as when, in her final passion, before she expires, the woman clutches at Faust's collar. His reactions to the woman's death, and specifically to his failure to supply her with medicine to save her life, are to tell people on his doorstep, imploring his help, "Belief will not help you, nor shall knowledge" (intertitle), and, when he is in his laboratory, to cast his research tomes into the fire. For Faust to lose faith in the intellect and knowledge in this way is his humanist response to the absurdity of existence and the human condition of mutability and frailty. His seduction by Mephisto in the mythological mode is a metaphor of his condition.

When, relying on an occult text he rescued from the fire, Faust calls on Mephisto to resolve the human predicament, Murnau and Hoffmann represent his materialization through a number of fire-and-smoke chiaroscuro special effects, and expressly through a double-exposure superimposition of Mephisto in the human form of a learned man that, despite Faust's efforts to evade him after the invocation, shows up wherever he goes, and finally in his own laboratory. Superimposition dissolves are the stock in trade of Mephisto, who, to sway Faust, unrolls a blank scroll on which a printed message to renounce god appears, and, to persuade him to try signing his allegiance to him for one day, produces a giant hourglass for this purpose and promptly turns it over. More appealing cinematically than the spectacle of dissolves, however, is the cross-cut from an extreme close-up of Faust peering into the hourglass, his face filling half the left side of the frame, with the timepiece filling the other, to a matching shot of Mephisto looking at Faust from the other side of the device, his face on the right side of the frame, the hourglass on the left.

Hoffmann complements this later with a two-shot in which Mephisto dissuades Faust, already disillusioned with his allegiance with the devil, from attempting suicide by drinking poison. An extreme close-up in which Faust's countenance fills the frame with Mephisto, with the lower half of his face visible in the camera right corner, whispering in his ear, is followed by a cut to a standard close-up of them in the same positions, and finally to a mid shot, in which they change positions. The shot composition, camera angle, and shot sequences are technically innovative, and they are enhanced by the arch facial displays of such emotive actors as Gösta Ekman and Emil Jannings. The multiple-exposure special effects that follow to display the fire-based magic Mephisto works to give Faust back his youth are not as favorably impressive as the amazing two-shots, and the startling profile shot of thirty-five-year-old Ekman without makeup, when Mephisto reveals him. *Faust* is a montage of these two types of shot, the special effects and *Neue Sachlichkeit* humanist framing shot. For example, Hoffmann follows the two-shots of Faust and Mephisto with two clever special-effects shots: in one shot, a traveling matte, Mephisto draws a small mirror from his pocket to reveal on its surface the image of the old Faust, stating, "We've caught the old man" (intertitle); in the other, a form dissolve, a new image of Faust, as a slick, silk-clad vampire, emerges from his old form, that of a disheveled peasant, and, in a split screen, which is another matte shot, gesturing to his alter ego to disappear, which Hoffmann effects with a cross dissolve. "In Dr. Murnau's *Faust* he gave us an unconventional Mephistopheles. In the prologue his appearance was gross and obscenely evil, but when he becomes the gallant companion of Faust he is a creature of comedy."[10] After awakening the young Faust, Mephisto shows him a vision (a double-exposure superimposition) of the Duchess of Parma (Hanna Ralph, Brunhild from Lang's *Die Nibelungen*), who will be his means of tempting him to renegotiate his one-day wager. When Faust expresses his desire to be taken to the duchess, Mephisto envelops him and takes him through the window to fly over the village. Hoffmann achieves this special effect with a traveling matte combining the image of the bodies of Faust and Mephisto (miniature models shot from behind) with a moving overhead shot, with the camera mounted on rails above, of the miniature model of the village and with an image of the actors standing side by side on Mephisto's flying cloak, against a traveling matte background of cloud formations, forests, mountains, rivers, and Parma, where, Mephisto discloses to Faust as a temptation, the Duchess of Parma is getting married today. Robert Herlth, art director on *Faust*, further recalls,

> There was still no crane at that time, so when we had to film the flight on Mephisto's cloak, our solution used Hoffmann's idea of building a narrow plaster ramp on which a carriage with large rubber-tired wheels and the camera mounted on it could be rolled. The plaster ramp went up and down like a roller coaster. That was supposed to convey the up-and-down movement of the flight. The landscape consisted of models, for aerial shots would have been limited and, being real, would not have conveyed a medieval, romantic atmosphere.[11]

The package of special effects is innovative cinematographically, since it uses three types of traveling-shot technology, as well as miniature models. More important, it experiments in camera mobility in the crane-like shot overhead of the village and landscape models, in the zoom illusion as Mephisto and Faust approach the campanile of the duchess's villa, and in the elevator shot that descends to show the activities of the wedding guests on two levels of the campanile and on the ground floor the duchess and duke embracing, and some of their guests celebrating.

> The movement of the mobile camera is less easy to follow than in *The Last Laugh*. In the two-year interval Murnau had learnt to gauge the depth of his tracking shots and the range of his pans, and to subordinate his enthusiasm to the rhythm of the film as a whole.[12]

Posing as guests, Faust, now dressed like a nabob, presents the couple with lavish gifts, Mephisto works magic to immobilize everyone and then awakens the duchess, who immediately falls in love with Faust and runs away with him. Murnau contextualizes these scenes at the villa with intercut shots of the sand in the twenty-four hourglass running out, to emphasize his seduction of Faust.

When the duke comes to and realizes the duchess is gone, he draws his sword and impales Mephisto, who drops to the floor, apparently dead. But through a form dissolve, Hoffmann shows him appearing to rise from the corpse, alive again, extract the sword, and run the duke through. When he first withdraws the sword, the image of Mephisto's corpse vanishes; similarly, when he stabs the duke, the scene fades to black, leaving only him in the light, and then he too fades out. Only when young Faust returns to his room with the duchess and starts making love with her does Mephisto confront him with the hourglass, which has run out. When he threatens to return him to as he was, Hoffmann represents the choice he faces in a double-exposure image of old Faust, an in-progress form dissolve, which aborts when young Faust promises to serve Mephisto forever. This interplay between special effects and live action is typical of the cinematography in *Faust*. For example, after winning Faust's soul, Mephisto vanishes in an image dissolve; he materializes in another dissolve above the bed in which Faust and the duchess are making love, drawing his cape over them for propriety's sake, to initiate the cross-cut to the next scene, which shows Faust alone in a misty setting, sitting on a rock, contemplating his fate, when Mephisto appears in a flash by leaping up from behind a rock, in a live-action move that for Hoffmann also parodies his typical special-effects dissolves, a parody that is further evident when the rock formation from which Mephisto appeared also serves as a frame for a traveling matte background scene, Mephisto's evocation of Faust's childhood home.

> Along with Lang's *Die Nibelungen* (1922–4) and *Metropolis* (1926–7), *Faust* was not only in subject matter a "national" production, it also became the outstanding technical achievements of the Weimar cinema, with such a dazzling display of special effects that it remained unsurpassed until Stanley Kubrick's *2001—A Space Odyssey*, almost fifty years later.[13]

Yet in film history and particularly in reference to cinematography, *Faust* is arguably less remarkable for its special effects than for its compilation of special-effects and live-action shots, of fantasy and humanism, because it has much to do with the history of spectatorship, and with how *Faust*'s spectators learn to perceive its different levels of cinematographic mimesis. These include even some comic moments that seem out of place in such an earnest existential drama, such as when, standing outside the church during an Easter mass, Mephisto, like a child, sticks his fingers in his ears to block out the sound of a hymn, when he grimaces as if inflicted with a grievous wound when he catches a glimpse of the celebrant holding up the consecrated host in a monstrance, when he laughs heartily after Faust orders him, "Do as I command" (intertitle), in defiance of his counsel that he pursue one of the "more obliging" girls of the village, rather than Gretchen (Camilla Horn), whom he has caught sight of on her way to mass and become enamored with, and when, as he plants a talismanic necklace in Gretchen's home to make her feel the power of the devil, he scowls at a Madonna and Child carving as if he is enfeebled by the power of an image. When Gretchen finds the necklace with a heart pendant, imagining it to be a gift from her new admirer, Faust, she conceals it from her mother and goes to visit her Aunt Marthe Schwerdtlein (Yvette Guilbert), who practices folk medicine, as her first scene confirms, in which she sells a love potion to a young man. The irony is clear: Gretchen brings a talisman that can subvert her free will to preserve her honor to seek advice about it from an aunt who sees an elixir that is likely just a placebo to encourage a young man to be more willful in finding a lover. Yet this conflation of opposing theatrical properties, an efficacious object and a mild emulsion, is a correlative of the film's cinematographic structure, comprising special effects and live action, and its visual ironies of fantasy and humanism, magic and superstition, and tragedy and comedy. Similarly, after Gretchen leaves, Mephisto pays Marthe a visit, to give her the gift of a necklace, which he tells her he is bringing from her cousin in Lombardy. When in trying it on she is unable to find the clasp, Mephisto offers his help, and in the process of fastening the necklace from behind he puts his hands onto her shoulders and then fondles her breasts, a bold expression of desire that she makes no show of being unwelcome to her. The scene, which is in the comic mode, implies that this diabolic necklace, unlike her niece's, has no coercive power: Marthe has control of her free will. Analogically, Gretchen's necklace is a special-effect property in the fantasy mode, whereas Marthe's necklace is a live-action stage property in the humanist mode. Later, however, when Marthe offers Mephisto a vessel of her love potion, he refuses, and offers to concoct a drink of his own using her ingredients. When he blows into it, fire issues from the vessel, which suggests a satanic brew. But Marthe's reaction upon downing it is only to strong and foul libation, and her subsequent amorous play, which Mephisto fends off, seems an expression of her natural desire, not an involuntary resolve. It turns out Mephisto has administered the drink to her as an anti-inhibitor, to discourage Marthe from halting the budding courtship of Gretchen and Faust, who, Mephisto assures her, is "a prince of noblest blood."

The most graphic example of the confluence of special effects and live action occurs in Faust's seduction of Gretchen the evening of the day they meet. After assuring Faust that Gretchen's brother, Valentin (William Dieterle), will interfere with them, Mephisto actually goes to the pub to cast aspersions on her honor and then inform him her lover is currently with her in her bedroom. Arriving at the house before Valentin, Mephisto conjures up an enormous wind to circulate throughout the house, alarming her mother and prompting Gretchen to go to her assistance. The wind, which Mephisto generates simply by blowing, is a mechanical effect generated with large fans. When Valentin arrives to find Faust in the bedroom, he engages him in a sword fight that spills out into the street. Despite at first appearing to be simply an observer, scrutinizing the terrible mischief he has caused, Mephisto draws his sword and stabs Valentin in the back, killing him. He simply intervenes physically, not in any supernatural manner, not through any special effect, such as a match dissolve, in which their forms could merge to show Mephisto taking over Faust's body to administer the fatal blow, much as in Fritz Lang's *Die Nibelungen: Siegfried* Karl Freund exploits a match dissolve to show Siegfried taking over Gunther's body in his test of strength with Brunhild. Instead, Murnau and Hoffmann represent the physical, not the metaphysical, act of murder, without any special-effects intervention. This is noteworthy, given that the murderer, Mephisto, is the tester of all the special effects in this film. For instance, at the beginning of the film he fatally impales the Duke of Parma in conjunction with a form dissolve that shows him reappearing and his corpse, lying on the floor, vanishing. When, after killing Valentin, Mephisto leaves the scene of the crime and runs around the village crying "Murder," thus falsely implicating Faust as the murderer, Murnau and Hoffmann exploit dramatic irony in part to emphasize they did not use a match dissolve and thus raise the issue of whether Mephisto committing murder while occupying the body of Faust would implicate him. Rather, Mephisto implicates Faust through the unmediatized human acts of projection and lying, which he perpetrates as a means of controlling him absolutely, which is evident when he helps him evade capture and spirits him away from the village on a flying beast, a mechanical effect.

Hoffmann's sympathetic camera is most evident in the aftermath of their departure, when Gretchen is publicly shamed as a "whore," manacled in the stocks and displayed in the public square, and the following winter when she gives birth and she and her baby are homeless, her baby freezes to death, and she is charged with murdering it: all along Hoffmann pans to follow her walking traumatized in a daze, when everyone, including her mother, has ostracized her and rejected her. As Gretchen in these climactic scenes, Camilla Horn delivers a great tragic performance, which is especially remarkable (1) because of the wide arc of her performance trajectory, from an *ingénue* to *pécheresse* to *tragédien*, and (2) because the *mise-en-scène* of plastic snow and wind machines and the premise of a woman who simply wanders aimlessly with her baby in her arms, and never tries to find temporary shelter from the elements, is not entirely convincing, and Horn has to maintain her performance for the camera and to inspire pity and terror in the audience. Hoffmann captures her performance through pan shots that often make her the sole focus of the field of view but also through close-ups that show her profound emotion. "Jannings wiederholte den Mephisto, den er 1922 am Lessing-Theater verkörpert hatte, und nachdem zuerst Leni Riefenstahl für das Gretchen im Gespräch gewesen war, ging die Rolle schliesslich an Camilla Horn"[14] ("Jannings reprised the Mephisto he had played at the Lessing Theater in 1922, and after Leni Riefenstahl had first been talked about for Gretchen, the role eventually went to Camilla Horn" [St. Pierre's translation]). Horn was an unknown, working as an extra on the Ufa studio lot, when Murnau noticed her and cast her as Gretchen, a role that launched her film career. His casting decision had to do not just with Horn's appearance, her looking the part, but also with her photogenic potential for Carl Hoffmann and his humanist camera, given that the character of Gretchen is not associated with special effects: her reaction to the talisman necklace Faust gives her is just that of young woman flattered to have an admirer.

When in desperation she cries out for Faust to save her, she is credible as a woman in love, despite the fact her lover murdered her brother and abandoned her and her unborn child. Sensing her plea, Faust demands Mephisto take him to her: "You are still my servant. Bring me to her. Otherwise the pact is broken" (intertitle). Whereas his earlier defiance, "Do as I command," provoked Mephisto to laughter, this challenge is in the tragic mode, an ultimate proposition worthy of the damned. Mephisto returns him to the outskirts of the village, where Gretchen is to be burned at the stake. When Faust curses his youth, Mephisto seizes the opportunity to extract the mirror on which he has preserved the image of him as an old man, and he smashes it, just as he reaches the execution site in the hope of saving Gretchen. Realizing he has been transformed back, he at first asks her for forgiveness, and then he elects to join her at the stake and die with her. When she recognizes Faust, seeing the young man in the old, he becomes young again. Even though Hoffmann generates this transformation through a form dissolve, his humanist camera suggests it happens through Gretchen's perception of him, because she discerns Faust's youthful facial features in his much older self, which has to do with spectatorship also, since spectators have had to exercise this discernment throughout, and ultimately because the word *love*, which Mephisto does not know, is efficacious in dissolving an eternal pact with the devil. The conclusion of *Faust*, in which Faust and Gretchen, immolated together on the stake, are purged of their sins and ascend to heaven as angels, is principally a matter of closure, of bringing the film to a precipitate and tidy end within a moral paradigm of spiritual redemption in which God necessarily trumps Satan. In its visual syntax, however, *Faust* is about another kind of conflict, a textual conflict between the word *love*, which Faust invokes, and Hoffmann represents as an intercut animated image, against Mephisto in the end, and the contract in which he signs over his soul to Satan for all time. To invoke closure, the film argues that *love* can break the pact, based on the earlier evidence, in Faust's arguments "Do as I command" and "You are still my servant," that the contract can be annulled, should Mephisto fail to do his bidding regarding Gretchen. Therefore, the conclusion of *Faust* is premised on the specious argument that (1) if Mephisto can annul the contract by failing to do what Faust commands of him, then (2) Faust can annul the contract by issuing a command to Mephisto to love, or at least to acknowledge love, something that by his diabolical nature he cannot do, which the film has illustrated in his evading Marthe's expressions of love and his dedication to ruining Faust and Gretchen's love. So how does Faust's text *love* annul the text of Mephisto's contract?

> The text constitutes a parasitic message designed to connote the image, to "quicken" it with one or more second-order signifieds. In other words, and this is an important historical reversal, the image no longer *illustrates* the words; it is now the words which, structurally, are parasitic on the image.[15]

In *Faust* both texts, the word *love* and the diabolic contract, are also images, in the obvious context of film, but also because each appears on the screen, as an image, in an intercut shot. Clearly, the text of the contract is a "parasitic message," for the obvious reason that the sender, Mephisto, is a parasite who feeds on human organisms, that is parasitic on its screen image. The text *love* also could be considered parasitic on its screen image, but its message, "love one another," is fundamentally different from Mephisto's message, which is predicated on hatred. In this respect, in the conclusion Faust's image does illustrate the word *love*, and in reference to spectatorship it functions to remind that the film is a romance as well as a tragedy and a comedy.

Faust is the most conspicuously collaborative of Carl Hoffmann's feature films. His partnership with Murnau was ambitiously speculative, addressing a new language of filmmaking, with a battery of special effects, camera angles and movements, and a diversified shot repertoire. Helmut Schanze has gone so far as to call *Faust* a *Gesamtkunstwerk*, a multimedia work of art, a performance: "Murnau's *Faust*, seen as kitsch by some art critics, could be described as a generic *Gesamtkunstwerk. Mise en scène*, shooting and montage form an assemblage of pieces of art, a diversity within a technical unity."[16] On the contrary, *Faust* is *gesamt* or "whole" precisely because it is the idiosyncratic collaboration of two great artists: Murnau deferred from looking through Hoffmann's viewfinder, and Hoffmann did not contest Murnau's shooting script or shot breakdown, as his array of shots confirms, from phantasmagoric bilocational form dissolves to sympathetic moving shots, running shots, and close-up shots for presence, whether to focus on Mephisto's panoply of diabolic and mischievous facial displays (Jannings's mugging for the camera) or to close in tight on Gretchen's face to evoke her abject suffering (Horn's POV poses). The German language has two words for collaboration, *gemeinschaftsproduktion*, which denotes the teamwork of coproduction, principally in media arts, including film, literally "community production," and *zusammenarbeit*, which denotes cooperation, literally "working together." While they have no established taxonomy in film criticism, the collaborative relationships of German directors and cinematographers in the Weimar period could be categorized as *coproductions*, in which directors and cinematographers team up to make films with their imprints, and *community productions*, in which directors and cinematographers work together to make films with the entire crew, as a collective endeavor that bears the stamp of ensemble production. According to these categories, therefore, *Faust* is a *gemeinschaftsproduktion*, or coproduction, because Murnau and Hoffmann had equal responsibilities in the production and the final cut has an original and distinctive cinematography with its own technical armature and visual syntax in which traces of the film's means of production are apparent. Fritz Lang's *Die Spinnen: Der Goldene See* (1919) and E. A. Dupont's *Varieté* (1925), on which Hoffmann worked as assistant cinematographer to Karl Freund, was for him more a *zusammenarbeit*, or community production.

> To a great extent the knowledge base of the cinematographer overlaps with the knowledge base of the director. The cinematographer must have a solid familiarity with the terms and concepts of directing, and the more a director knows about cinematography the more he or she will be able to utilize these tools and especially be better equipped to fully utilize the knowledge and talent of a good DP. Any successful director will tell you that one of the real secrets of directing is being able to recognize and maximize what every member of the team can contribute.[17]

A common knowledge base implies an equal working relationship between directors and cinematographers, a *gemeinschaftsproduktion*, but sometimes this data base and labor model extends to the entire crew, in which case the production can be termed a *zusammenarbeit*. All film projects, of course, are based on teamwork, and most are a combination of coproduction and community production. Whatever the model, however, the "solid familiarity" of the director and the cinematographer is central, and the more knowledge they share, the better the picture.

As a *gemeinschaftsproduktion*, a film in which the director and cinematographer have equal responsibilities, *Faust* also demands equal recognition for them in the production. But film history has not given the same kind of recognition to the cinematographer as to the director in projects on which they collaborated. For example, Helmut Schanze refers to *Faust* as "a milestone in Murnau's cinematographic work"[18] and states of Murnau, "He controlled every detail to perfection. Carl Hoffmann's camera work was renowned for its devoted professionalism."[19] These remarks can be interpreted as implying a hierarchical relationship, based on two types of work, one type, cinematography, producing a filmic achievement, and the other, the operation of a machine, producing a commitment to the job. Barthes defines the filmic nonhierarchically: "The filmic is that in a film which cannot be described, the representation that cannot be represented. The filmic begins only where language and metalanguage ends."[20] Films comprise shots, scenes on film, which are representations that have characteristics subject to scrutiny and analysis, and which lend themselves to description. It does not follow, however, that films themselves can be described, because they consist of the filmic, not just shots, which Barthes calls a "third meaning," a structural meaning beyond "obvious" and "obtuse" meanings, which are describable. The filmic has two principal elements in the aesthetics of collaborative filmmaking in the Weimar period. First, the filmic is the artistry, the engineering, and the labor of selecting and executing shots in a film camera, representations that are in contradistinction to images, what is represented on the film stock. Second, the filmic is the collaborative endeavor of the director and the cinematographer, which, because it is nonhierarchical, not artistic labor that can be divided and attributed to one and the other, or to the other more than the one, in which respect it is nonmimetic shared labor. Barthes proposes a beginning to the filmic, "only where language and metalanguage ends." Within a collaborative filmic model, the terms *director* and *cinematographer* are language, and terms such as *cameraman* and *camera operator* are metalanguage. To begin the filmic and the collaborative, classist industrial terms such as *director, cinematographer, cameraman, camera operator*, and other words that perpetuate the division of labor in film production, must end. All these can be replaced with *filmemacher*, or filmmaker, because, whether the project is a coproduction or a community production, it is a collective endeavor based on teamwork: every member of the film team, even spectators, is a filmmaker. This collaborative model is endemic to the Weimar film industry, as Janet Bergstrom has noted:

> Murnau's own media image as a film artist, not just a director, clearly fits into the larger picture of his industry and its desire to build and maintain an audience. The German film industry took pride in presenting itself as superior to other national cinemas artistically, and had developed a commercial appeal for its films based on a "high art" self-identification.[21]

In this regard, the *filmemacher* is an artist in the company of a participatory spectatorship and both the *zusammenarbeit* and the *gemeinschaftsproduktion* models extend to the entire film crew, including the analytical audience, which is part of the filmmaking community and production. *Faust*, along with other German fantasy and Expressionist films that rely heavily on special effects, appeals directly to spectators to react to its trick photography, in awe of the film magic and with a sophisticated deductive intellectual fascination with experimental technology, much as they were terrified by Mephisto yet more intellectually intrigued by Jannings's portrayal of him. Acknowledging the technical innovation of German film in the 1920s, Silberman notes

> a reputation for the intense collaboration of directors and actors, set and costume designers and camera crews, a reputation supported by the increasing international marketability of their skills. This may seem all the more astonishing since the diverse German studios did not hold a set of production values or practices in common prior to the Third Reich. I propose, rather, that the cinema's coherence is to be found on a more abstract plane, as a response to the change in the aesthetic consciousness of modernism and as the search for adequate means to transform this consciousness into images. Contrary to the traditional view of classical German cinema, then, I see it not simply as the sum of two polar styles—Expressionism in the first part of the 1920s and realism in the second—but rather as an ongoing search for a visual language that began in the 1910s.[22]

Notwithstanding that collaboration in German film followed the *gemeinschaftsproduktion* and the *zusammenarbeit* models, and cinematographers distinguished themselves as filmmakers within their camera crews, directors and cinematographers like Murnau and Hoffmann were exploring the imagery of modernism within the *Neue Sachlichkeit* movements in the visual arts. In *Faust* this imagery is evident in the realism and humanism of Hoffmann's camera, and in the coalescence of objective shots and standard camera movement with spectacular special effects.

But, as Roland Barthes suggests, Hoffmann's filmic expertise is fundamentally in "the representation that cannot be represented" on screen, his ideas, perceptions, dexterity, ingenuity.

> In this production he used the Agfa Ortholtinu film, a Debrie Parvo and a Cameraeclair combined with arc lamps and mercury vapor units. The film included toned takes that rendered many life-like scenes. Filtered light was intensively used in the most varied conditions and intense smoke was used to produce the required atmosphere. In many cases igniting nitrate film or mixing hydrochloric acid with ammonia obtained the smoke near the stage entrance. Varied resources were adopted for shooting, such as the camera on rails moving over a large miniature to show an aerial view of cities, woods, landscapes and villages in Faust's travel. Large amounts of salt were used for the snowstorm. Hoffmann controlled the lighting of the scene very carefully and had built extremely high gobos [framing devices that block light from the camera lens or part of the set] to control the size of long shadows.[23]

This combination of life-like shots and atmospheric special effects was the signature both of Hoffmann's cinematic style in *Faust* and the imprint of the cinematic knowledge he shared with Murnau in their *gemeinschaftsproduktion*. Although his rapid cuts and long takes in Lang's *Dr. Mabuse* and his form dissolves and pictorial *mise-en-scène* in Lang's *Die Nibelungen* also are cinematographically distinctive, they are indicative more of the *zusammenarbeit* filmmaking model.

NOTES

1. Norbert Grob, "'Bringing the Ghostly to Life': Fritz Lang and His Early Dr. Mabuse Films," trans. Julian Raymer, in *Expressionist Film: New Perspectives*, ed. Dietrich Scheunemann, 95 (Rochester, NY: Camden House, 2003).

2. Thomas Elsaesser, *Weimar Cinema and After: German's Historical Imaginary* (London and New York: Routledge, 2000), 156.

3. Rudolf Arnheim, *Film als Kunst: Mit einem Vorwort zur Neuausgabe* (Munich: Hanser Verlag, 1974), 234.

4. Elsaesser, *Weimar Cinema and After*, 88.

5. Lotte H. Eisner, *The Haunted Screen: Expressionism in the German Cinema and the Influence of Max Reinhardt*, trans. Roger Grieves, rev. ed. (1952; Berkeley and Los Angeles: University of California Press, 1969), 163, 166.

6. Ibid., 191.

7. Elsaesser, *Weimar Cinema and After*, 245.

8. Qtd. in Lotte H. Eisner, *Murnau*, rev. ed. (1964; Berkeley: University of California Press, 1973), 62.

9. Eisner, *The Haunted Screen*, 285.

10. Liam Ó. Laoghaire, "Jannings: The Portrait of an Actor," *Irish Monthly* 78.926 (August 1950): 389.

11. Qtd. in Klaus Kreimeier, *The Ufa Story: A History of Germany's Greatest Film Company, 1918–1945*, trans. Robert and Rita Kimber (Berkeley: University of California Press, 1999), 107–8.

12. Eisner, *The Haunted Screen*, 291.

13. Elsaesser, *Weimar Cinema and After*, 242.

14. Frank Noack, *Emil Jannings: Der erste deutsche Weltstar* (Munich: Collection Rolf Heyne, 2012), 164.

15. Roland Barthes, *Image—Music—Text*, trans. Stephen Heath (New York: Hill & Wang, 1977), 25.

16. Helmut Schanze, "On Murnau's *Faust*: A Generic Gesamtkuntswerk?" in *Expressionist Film: New Perspectives*, ed. Dietrich Scheunemann (Rochester, NY: Camden House, 2003), 230.

17. Blain Brown, *Cinematography Theory and Practice: Image Making for Cinematographers, Directors, and Videographers* (Amsterdam: Focal, 2002), ix.

18. Schanze, "On Murnau's *Faust*," 223.

19. Ibid., 229.

20. Barthes, *Image—Music—Text*, 64.

21. Janet Bergstrom, "Sexuality at a Loss: The Films of F. W. Murnau," *Poetics Today* 6.1/2 (1985): 192.

22. Marc Silberman, "What Is German in the German Cinema?" *Film History* 8.3 (1996): 303–4.

23. H. Mario Raimondo-Souto, *Motion Picture Photography: A History, 1891–1960* (Jefferson, NC: McFarland, 2007), 135.

5

Fritz Arno Wagner, with F. W. Murnau, Fritz Lang, and Arthur Robison

When he came to work with G. W. Pabst on three films 1927–1931, Fritz Arno Wagner (1894–1958) had transcended the foundational categories of *camera operator* and *cinematographer* and achieved the more collaborative position of *director of photography*. He had shot only five films, notably with proven director Paul Wegener on *Der Galeerensträftling* (1919), when he worked with Murnau on *Schloss Vogelöd* (1921), the film on which Wagner developed his signature light and shade Expressionistic cinematography. He enhanced this technique in Murnau's *Nosferatu, eine Symphonie des Grauens* (1922), the first masterwork of German Expressionist film, a designation attributable as much to Wagner's arresting visual imagery and haunting special effects as to Murnau's virtuoso direction and Max Schreck's iconic performance as the title character. His achievement is particularly apparent in a comparison to the restrained visual grammar in Wagner's first half of *Der brennende Acker*, Karl Freund having shot the second half, a Murnau film released just two weeks after *Nosferatu*. Wagner's distinctive Expressionist cinematography is prominent in Arthur Robison's *Schatten: Eine nächtliche Halluzination* (1923), apparent in his representation of shadow puppetry as a correlative of psychological horror, but is less pronounced in Robison's *Pietro der Korsar* (1925). Wagner perfected his use of light and shade as signifiers of character, temperament, and thematic mood in the three major films he made with Fritz Lang. In *Der müde Tod* (1921) he evokes an ambiance of horror, by maximally lightening and darkening the set and characters to establish an ambient visual mood appropriate to a macabre allegory about confronting Death. The distinctive visual grammar of *Spione* (1928) pertains to the shifting realities of espionage and the suspense of impermanence, and in *M* (1931), arguably Lang's most humanist film, Wagner evokes a vacillating mood of horror and intrigue and concentrates it in the movements and facial displays of the protagonist, played by Peter Lorre. Wagner's most productive collaboration was with G. W. Pabst in three complex psychological dramas: *Der Liebe der Jeanne Ney* (1927), a story of love and war, *Tagebuch einer Verlorenen* (1929), a morality play featuring Louise Brooks in her second film with Pabst, and *Die 3 Groshen-Oper* (1931), based on Bertolt Brecht's musical *Die Driegroschenoper* (1928), an evocation of Weimar decadence. In his collaborations with Pabst, more than with any of his other director partners, including Murnau, Lang, and Robison, Wagner executed daring shots to record some of the most representative images of the Weimar *zeitgeist.*

Fritz Arno Wagner was born on December 5, 1889, in Schmiedefeld am Rennsteig, Thüringen, Germany. After studying commerce at the University of Leipzig in 1909, he attended the École des Beaux Arts, in Paris, and in 1910 took a clerical position at the Pathé Frères film company, where he developed an interest in cinematography and was appointed manager of its offices in Vienna and, subsequently, Berlin. In 1913, Pathé assigned him to New York, where he served as manager of *Pathé Weekly* and as a reporter and newsreel camera operator, and covered the Mexican civil war. He returned to Germany in 1914 for military service in the cavalry, but was discharged after ten weeks of training when he severely injured his arm. In 1919, electing to pursue a career as a feature camera operator, he came to the notice of Ernst Lubitsch, who appointed him assistant to cinematographer Theodor Sparkuhl and stills photographer on *Madame Dubarry* (1919) and *Sumurun* (1920), with the Projektions-AG Union (PAGU), which was instrumental in promoting domestic film production during World War One, when the German government banned the screening of non-German films. Having established himself with Lubitsch as a cinematographer of note, Wagner worked with several leading directors on major projects through the Weimar period, specializing in *kammerspielfilm*, Expressionism, Gothic representation, chiaroscuro, *Stimmung* (atmospheric lighting), the mobile camera, image framing, heterodox camera angles, Naturalism, and the transition to synchronized sound and dialogue technology, and he made some enduring contributions to the history of cinematography.

After the rich experience of shooting two Lubitsch films, Wagner dedicated himself to building up his portfolio, as assistant cinematographer to Sparkuhl again, on Georg Jacoby's *Vendetta* (1919), and to Frederik Fuglsang on Rochus Gliese and Paul Wegener's *Der Galeerensträfling* (1919); and as principal cinematographer on Victor Janson's *Das Skelett das Hern Markutius* (1920) and Paul L. Stein's *Martyrium* (1920) and *Die geschlossene Kette* (1920). His next appointment was a big break, as cocinematographer, with Russian cinematographer Lásló Schäffer on F. W. Murnau's *Schloss Vogelöd [The Haunted Castle]* (1921). That this was Schäffer's first film meant Murnau drew more on Wagner's experience.

The film opens with a standard establishing shot of the setting, a wide shot of Castle Vogelöd, represented in a miniature building and the surrounding landscape. Wagner uses this shot to open each but the last of the film's five acts, and elsewhere to signal daytime and nighttime, as a proxy of the interior setting. Because *Schloss Vogelöd* is a *kammerspielfilm*, literally a "chamber play film," a theatrical mode that is noted for spare and bleak interior settings, as well as for using intertitles sparingly, the formative establishing shot is actually of the interior of the castle, a drawing room where guests are waiting out a storm before going out on a hunt. Wagner first shoots Lord von Vogelschrey (Arnold Korff) as, holding a box of cigars, he crosses the room, toward the camera, coming close to a presentative moment by acknowledging it, and then the guests shot-by-shot: one man standing over another sitting reading a newspaper, a man writing at a desk, another man with a newspaper, and four men at a card table, whom Volgelschrey approaches to offer cigars. Thus Wagner establishes *schloss*, *kammer*, and *spieler*.

He cuts to a shot of a double door, through which a servant enters to announce the arrival of Count Johann Oetsch (Lothar Mehnert), an uninvited guest, thus initiating the plot: Count Oetsch is suspected of having murdered his brother four years ago, to become the sole heir. He is the first husband of one of the houseguests, Baroness Safferstätt (Olga Tschechowa, who would go on to play Parysia in E. A. Dupont's *Moulin Rouge* [1928]), expected to arrive that evening; though clearly unwelcome at the gathering, Oetsch insists on staying to prove his innocence, as the plot reveals. In his office Vogelschrey implores Oetsch to leave, to save Baroness Safferstätt embarrassment, while the district court judge (Hermann Vallantin), the anxious man (Julius Falkenstein), and the others in the drawing room gossip about his guilt: Wagner cuts back and forth between the two scenes to enhance the mystery of his presence, which Oetsch does not explain to Vogelschrey. Wagner concludes the scene with an iris-out, a device typical in this film, and the most conspicuous evidence of a moving camera. For example, an iris-in, iris-out, followed by a cut from the film's usual sepia tinting to black and white film, later marks the transition to Baroness Safferstätt's recollection to Father Faramund, in the form of a flashback to her happy life with her first husband (Paul Hartmann). Otherwise, *Schloss Vogelöd*, specifically because it is a *kammerspielfilm*, consists mainly of passing shots, in which the camera is stationary and people move through the visual field. Typically, Wagner sets up his camera (1) in the foreground of a vestibule, landing, or similar open space in the castle, which people walk into and out of, such as to and from staircases and in and out of doors; and (2) in the foreground of large, high-traffic passageways, such as rooms or the castle gate, in which people, horses, and carriages enter from the background, approach the midground in the direction of the camera, and then move laterally out of frame. Because vestibules, landings, passageways, and gateways are architectural sites about mobility, Wagner found he could restrict his camera movement in them.

Take, for example, a scene in which Lady Vogelschrey (Lulu Kyser-Korff) tries to comfort Baroness Safferstätt, whose anxiety over Count Oetsch's presence has been complicated by the arrival of the Reverend Father Faramund, a Franciscan friar and a relative of her late husband, who also presumes the count's guilt. After a servant announces Faramund will now receive her, the baroness stands up, pulls away from Lady Vogelschrey's embrace, and turns to walk to the door. Here Wagner cuts to an over-the-shoulder mid shot of the baroness as she enters the field of view in the camera right corner of the frame and walks tentatively toward the door, partly visible in the left corner, but stops in the middle of the field and slowly turns to look back to Vogelschrey, and the camera. Here Wagner cuts again, to a mid shot of Safferstätt running to Vogelschrey, who is seen from behind. He cuts to a mid close-up of them embracing, and then to another over-the-shoulder shot of Safferstätt as she enters the camera right corner of the frame and walks across the foreground to the door and exits into the next room. This five-shot sequence, which is neither complicated nor self-reflexive, functions principally to heighten Safferstätt's pathos and apprehension and the film's bleak atmosphere and languorous pace. The irony of Wagner's cinematography in *Schloss Vogelöd* is that his brief shots and scenes and quick cuts, devices usually associated with rapid-action films like Lang's *Dr. Mabuse*, slow up the pace here. Thus, in this sequence, Safferstätt starts to leave in one shot, but she comes back in the next shot, and then in the following shot does leave the room: thus, the camera moves through its cuts.

The supernatural mode enters the film with the disappearance of Father Faramund, who has been listening to Baroness Safferstätt's confession about her first marriage, and the investigation of his room, which reveals his bed has not been slept in and he has not been staying there. For instance, the nervous man later has a nightmare, comprising live action and a model miniature, in which he imagines a hooded figure with a large attenuated taloned hand, which anticipates *Nosferatu*, that opens his window, reaches over to his bed, pulls him out, and pulls him through the window. Given the character's type, this dream sequence is more comical than horrific. Murnau confirms the comic mode in the next scene, also a dream sequence, that of a naughty kitchen boy who is reprimanded in a previous scene for dipping his fingers in the batter and who now imagines he is the chef and Father Faramund is spooning him batter as the chef who reprimanded him looks on. Thus, both the nervous man and the kitchen boy are haunted by the mysterious disappearance of Faramund, and Murnau and Wagner confirm the castle is haunted, and haunting has to do with travestying the supernatural more than with Expressionism. In the next scene, however, at dinner, Count Oetsch shocks all the diners when he accuses Baron Safferstätt of having committed a murder, and then explains it was merely the subject of his dream last night. The count's indiscretion, which empties the room, is not comic, but part of a strategy that till now he has exercised superciliously to solve the mystery of his brother's murder.

When Father Faramund returns to the castle with no explanation for his absence, as mysteriously as he disappeared from it, he first approaches Baroness Safferstätt, who offers to make a confession to him, on her presumption of priestly confidentiality, which Wagner represents with an iris-out mask and a cut to a flashback scene in which she, feeling alienated because her husband has become a religious extremist, states, in the presence of Baron Safferstätt, who is enamored with her, that she would like to see "something utterly evil . . . a murder" (intertitle). Interpreting her literally, she tells Father Faramund, the baron murdered her husband to oblige her, and remove his rival, and he confessed to her two days later. Here Wagner cuts again to the flashback to represent the devastating moment immediately after the baron's confession. His shot is the most compositionally and aesthetically arresting of the entire film, a fade-in foreshortened wide shot of a vast, high-ceilinged corridor, with two open doorways in the background and narrow floor-to-ceiling alcoved windows along the walls. Dominated by the cavernous space, she leans against one wall, shattered, the baron against the other, overwhelmed, his hand against the windowsill, inconsequential figures who are motionless and almost imperceptible in the architecture. Wagner sustains the shot, which resembles a still, for eighteen seconds before closing it with an iris-out. After Baroness Safferstätt finishes her confession and swears him to secrecy, Father Faramund offers his equivocal agreement, "I understand you," the only words he speaks in the film, consistent with his name, in that the German word *mund* denotes "mouth." Then Wagner shoots him crossing the corridor to confront Baron Safferstätt in his room, initially by removing his disguise of eyeglasses, fake beard, and wig, to reveal what spectators, no doubt, have know all along, that he is really Count Oetsch, and then by urging him to act like a man, which he later interprets as not confessing but committing suicide, which he does off-camera. The story ends with a passing shot, that has dominated Wagner's camera operation in *Schloss Vogelöd*: a servant opens the gates to let in the real Father Faramund (Victor Blütner), whose arrival Oetsch has forestalled in his scheme to expose Baron Safferstätt as the murderer. In the final shot, Faramund negotiates the passageway, the symbol of disclosure and movement in the film, from corridors and landings to the view field itself, and exits the frame.

On their next project together, Murnau's *Nosferatu, eine Symphonie des Grauens [Nosferatu: A Symphony of Horror]* (1922), Wagner was principal cinematographer, assisted by Günther Krampf (uncredited). The film is an unauthorized adaptation of Bram Stoker's novel *Dracula* (1897). The epigraph, from "Account of the Great Death in Wisborg, Anno Domini 1838," introduces the name of Nosferatu, "like the deathbird calling your name at midnight," and the horror genre, and conveys a warning, "Beware you never say it—for then the pictures of life will fade to shadows," which hints at Murnau and Wagner's transition from realism to Expressionism in this film. *Nosferatu* begins with a high-angle live-action establishing shot of Wisborg, with the cathedral steeple visible in the foreground, the public square in the midground, and the rest of the town in the background. "Murnau shot *Nosferatu* on location in the summer of 1921, with Fritz Arno Wagner as cameraman. Location shooting was a novel idea at the time, and in the case of *Nosferatu*, most likely a response to a limited budget. Thus, the heightened artificial settings so typical of expressionist films are absent, the director and photographer resorting instead to carefully plotted visual compositions, with the camera immobile. Night scenes were shot in broad daylight, then tinted deep blue for release."[1]

The following shots, a sequence set in the home and garden of Hutter (Gustav von Wangenheim) and Ellen (Greta Schröder), establish the young married couple's happy, loving relationship, but also the possibility it will be disrupted, the foreshadowing evident in Ellen's curious reaction to the bouquet of flowers Hutter has picked from the garden and presented to her: "Why did you kill them, such beautiful flowers?" (intertitle). Murnau and Wagner sound this note of foreboding again in the subsequent shot of Hutter, who is rushing down the street on his way to work, in the direction of the camera, when he is intercepted by an older acquaintance in the immediate field view, who greets him with the witticism, "Not so fast, my young friend! No one can outrun their fate" (intertitle). These blatant warning signs, which are part of the establishment package of the horror plot, are consistent with the associations of Hutter's name, in that the German word *hut* denotes "hat" and the idiom *auf der Hut sein* "to be on one's guard."

The next scene establishes the character of Knock (Alexander Granach), the unscrupulous estate agent, and Hutter's employer, who, as a consequence of his sale of a house in Wisborg to Count Orlok of Transylvania (Nosferatu), puts Hutter and Ellen in his direct sphere of influence. When Hutter sets out to Transylvania to secure the sale, on Knock's recommendation, of the abandoned building across from his and Ellen's house, spectators see one of Wagner's typical shot sequences in this film: a wide shot of a scene with a simple cut to a mid shot of the same scene. In this case, Wagner films a wide shot of the house and of Hutter and Ellen emerging for his departure, and then cuts to a mid shot of them saying good-bye with an embrace and a kiss. This is an example of fundamental camera movement, in which the position of the camera is changed from shot to shot and the image seems to move. Wagner uses it again strikingly at the castle, the first time Hutter witnesses Count Orlok going into his coffin at dawn: a wide shot of Orlok standing at the coffin, followed by a mid shot, the transition suggesting Hutter seeing something startling and then having to take a closer look. But *Nosferatu* features actual motion of the camera within the shot, typically through pans and tilts. For instance, as Hutter makes his journey on horseback into the Carpathian Mountains, Wagner intercuts a sweeping traveling shot of the landscape, a subjective view that implies what he sees and also how he feels about it, but in the extent of the perceptual arc suggests also that he would turn his head and, given he is on horseback, twist his torso, to take in the view. An elementary shot is packed with information. Reaction shots also are an important device in Wagner's repertoire, evident initially when Hutter, who has stopped at an inn, shouts after his server to bring his dinner quickly because he is eager to get to Count Orlok's castle. Everyone in the inn reacts with horror to his remark: Wagner shows their reactions one by one in a sequence of mid and close-up shots. When the innkeeper warns him not to travel farther tonight because the werewolves are about, Hutter laughs him off, yet elects to stay the night. Intercut shots show a "werewolf" prowling in the vicinity of the inn and frightening the horses, and Hutter, unsuspecting, seeing this through the window in his room. He takes a book from the bedside table, *Of Vampyres, Terrible Phantomes, and the Seven Deadly Sins*, and glances at the first page, about Nosferatu, "who liveth and feedeth on human blood." First thing in the morning he looks through the window on a sunny bucolic landscape; he looks again at the book and dismisses it with a laugh. Dramatic irony is a prominent trope in the film.

This first shot of Count Orlok (Max Schreck), marking the film's transition from Realist to Expressionist visual aesthetics, is of a deeply shaded arched passageway from which he slowly emerges, tall, slender, his hands folded chest-high, head bowed, black clad, in a word, *sinister*. He awaits Hutter, who arrives near midnight; then together they walk into the shadowed arch, an undefined enclosed space that Wagner emphasizes by concluding the scene with an iris-out. As Jean Mitry observes, in reference to title cards in Expressionist films, which, he argues, serve more an evocative than an expositional purpose, the words "'As soon as he crossed the bridge, the spirits came to meet him' suggest the crossing of a border, a journey into another world, with no other explanation of the story."[2] In reference to visual syntax, symbolism, and iconography, however, Hutter crosses this threshold when he moves from light into shadow. This is first evident when, distracted at dinner, Hutter accidentally cuts his thumb and Orlok at first comes over to him to express concern but then grabs his hand, pulls it to his lips, and sucks the blood. Here Orlok crosses into the shadowy space of vampirism, but also homosocial desire. Significantly, the following morning, awaking in a chair beside the hearth, where they were talking after dinner last night, to find Orlok absent, Hutter checks his appearance in a hand mirror, in which he first notices mysterious incisions on his neck, in an image, in a shadow. (After breakfast, in a letter to his wife, he shrugs off the incisions as mosquito bites.) Later, when Hutter's photo of Ellen falls out of his pack, Orlok immediately becomes enamored with her image, observing drolly, "Your wife has a lovely neck" (intertitle), and only then agrees to buy the house. As Hutter reads in his book on Nosferatu, which he took from the inn, "Beware that his shadow does not engulf you like a daemonic nightmare." But he does not associate his image of Nosferatu with the shadows he casts; in the film itself, of course, all the shadows are images.

Sensing Hutter has discovered his secret, Orlok confronts him in his bedroom. The door to the room, like many doors in the castle, is self-activating. Orlok first appears framed in the arched doorway, intensely backlit and threatening. Wagner cross-cuts to a shot of Ellen's bedroom: Ellen sits up in with a start, gets out of bed, and starts to sleepwalk out the room and along a balustrade outside. Harding (Georg H. Schnell) and his sister, Ruth (Ruth Landshoff), who are staying with Ellen in Hutter's absence, alerted by her activity, intervene to save her, and then call a doctor.

The interplay between the simultaneous scenes, which have no immediate logical connection other than Ellen and Hutter's romantic love, serves Wagner in heightening suspense and mystery. Orlok's backlit figure, shot from behind, casts an ominous elongated shadow. It is first as a shadow that Orlok attacks Hutter, who cowers from him in his bed, eyes closed, shutting out the unthinkable, whether the vampiric or the homoerotic. Koebner explains, "In his craving for blood Nosferatu makes no difference between men and women. If one wants to understand his blood lust as a puritan code for sexual appetite, one has to concede to him a reckless bisexuality, hetero- and homo-eroticism."[3] When Ellen, in another cross-cut, calls out Hutter's name, Wagner cuts back to Orlok's shadow hovering over Hutter, which now withers, at the sound of her voice, because, since seeing her image, Orlok has been obsessed with her as his next sacrifice. That he has heard Ellen is apparent in Wagner's shot of him after his shadow fades: he appears in profile, at first raising his head after hovering over Hutter, and then turning 180 degrees clockwise so that he is facing and looking through the arched doorway, when Wagner cross-cuts to Ellen sitting up in bed and looking vacantly into space, thereby making her look like the object of Orlok's vision. A supernatural connection has a logical explanation in Wagner's cross-cut. That cutting can be magical Wagner shows when Hutter decides to investigate Orlok, who has just left through his doorway, his height and posture matching the shape of the arch. Elsaesser notes how the film "sets off the more dramatically the appearance of the vampire himself, always framed in angled doorways and coffin-shaped apertures."[4] Now, Wagner films Hutter walking up to the same arch, and then cuts to him on the other side, creating the visual effect of him slipping over the threshold imperceptibly, as Orlok might. This shot sequence, like the wide shot, mid shot combination, is a peculiarity of Wagner's cinematography. By likening their passages through the same threshold, Wagner links them through movement. Their common trait explains how Hutter can now go to the crypt to expose Orlok in his coffin. Murnau and Wagner explore the character parallel further as Orlok, concealed in a coffin, makes his passage by ship to Wisborg and Hutter, after a period of hospitalization, returns on horseback. Onboard, the entire crew, excepting the captain and ship's mate, succumb to the plague of Orlok's infection. When the ship's mate, armed with an ax, goes below in a desperate attempt to discover the source of the malady by breaking into the cargo of coffins, he confronts Orlok in one of the most iconic shots in film history, in which his rigid body rises in a perfect vectorization arc to a standing position. Wagner achieved this reverse-motion shot, in which Orlok moves opposite to how he was filmed, by operating the camera upside down and, during the printing process, turning the footage upside down again, so that when the edited film is projected, the footage that shows Orlok rising from the coffin looks as if it is running forward.

After he witnesses this event, the ship's mate commits suicide by leaping overboard, and Orlok takes control of the "death ship" by murdering the captain (offscreen), the last remaining crewman. Wagner films the mysterious progress of Orlok's ship mostly in wide shots, but one shot stands out because its point of view is from the deck of the ship itself. It is a live-action acute tilt-up shot of the main mast, executed from the base. Although the camera is stationary, the rise and fall of the ship on the waves implies camera movement as the background shifts between a monochromatic gray sky and a polychromatic sky with the horizon line and the sea. The shot recalls Karl Freund's pulley-shot up the ship's mast to the observation deck in Fritz Lang's *Die Spinnen: Der Goldene See* (1919), except that there the camera movement is actual.

Murnau and Wagner focus on a variety of objects of perception in *Nosferatu*: thus, shots of the ship's mate witnessing Orlok's amazing resurrection, of the ship rising and falling on the waves, the derelict building across the street, which Orlok now inhabits, and Ellen, moments after Hutter's return, who points to it and says, "That is what I look at—every night" (intertitle). These shots have much to do with spectatorship, with how spectators view characters, objects, events, images, shadows, light, and other phenomena, how they see what the camera sees in film.

In the end, Ellen elects to sacrifice herself to save the community infected with Orlok's vampiric contagion, by allowing Orlok to bite her in order to distract him past the cock's crow and thus kill him. Here Wagner's unrestrained Expressionist camera of the horror genre is most evident in his two shots of Orlok as he approaches Ellen's bedroom, both of them in silhouette, showing his hideously distended shadow cast on the staircase wall and towering over her door. Wagner follows these up with two climactic shots: one shot is of Ellen flinching in bed as Orlok's shadow spreads over her body, and the other is a wide profile shot of Ellen, unconscious in bed, as Orlok, seen overhead because he is leaning forward, kneels on the other side, feeding on her neck, only part of his face and right hand visible in the dark room. These chiaroscuro shots, like the reverse-motion shot of Orlok rising from the coffin, are iconic in film history. After Ellen succeeds in distracting him till dawn, Orlok self-immolates. Cinematographically, his death consists of a simple dissolve, followed by a puff of smoke. *Nosferatu* is remarkable for using match and form dissolves sparingly and for creating horror through dramatic pantomime, such as when Orlok comes to Ellen: one shot shows the doors to his home and the next him standing in the open doorway, whereas elsewhere in the film he walks through material barriers.

Wagner collaborated with Fritz Lang on *Der müde Tod* [*Destiny*; literally "The Weary Death"] (1921) in between working on *Schloss Vogelöd* (1921) and *Nosferatu* (1922) with Murnau, and along with cinematographers Erich Nitzschmann and Herrmann Saalfrank, each directing one of the film's three episodes, set in the Renaissance Venice, Persia, and China. The film begins with a wide shot of a cemetery and a mid shot of a treed area in which, through a lap dissolve, a black-clad human figure, a stranger, materializes from a puff of dust or smoke. The first establishing shot is of the interior of a horse-drawn coach, in which a young engaged couple (Lil Dagover and Walter Janssen) and an old woman are passengers. When the woman is let off the coach, the stranger gets on. When the young couple gets off in town, so does he and follows them into a pub, sitting at their table. In an earlier scene a group of men have discussed an urban legend of a stranger who came into town and persuaded the town council to sell him the property adjacent to the cemetery, around which he constructed an impenetrable high wall, with no points of entry or egress. The dark-clad stranger at the couple's table, the owner of the walled property, is Death (Bernhard Goetzke), who, during the woman's brief absence in the kitchen, mysteriously disappears with her fiancé. The woman searches the entire town for them, but to no avail. Defeated, she leans against the compound wall, where she is shocked to see a crowd approaching her, the spirits of the dead, including her fiancé, double-exposed images that pass by her and through the wall into the realm of Death. In her trauma she loses consciousness. Later, an old apothecary finds her body lying outside the wall, revives her, and takes her home with him. There she finds a bottle of poison, pours herself a glass of it, and, just as she raises it to her lips, finds herself inexplicably, but actually through a match dissolve, standing in the realm of Death. In a chamber of candles, each of which represents a human life, Death explains to her that he is weary of being blamed simply for doing God's work, and eventually he offers her a chance to persuade him to spare her fiancé: showing her three flickering candles, representing people who are in danger of losing their lives, he tells her if she can save just one of them, he will do her bidding. All these events establish the main characters and frame the three main narratives of the film.

In the Persian narrative, Zobeide (Dagover), the caliph's daughter, tries to save the life of an infidel, Franke (Janssen), who is also her lover, while El Mot the gardener (Goetzke) observes her actions. When she discovers her lover's dead body buried in the garden up to the neck, El Mot, standing by, transforms to his appearance as Death through a match dissolve. Then Wagner, Nietzschmann, and Saalfrank cut to a shot of the three candles, in which one of them goes out.

In the second narrative, set in Renaissance Venice during Carnival, Dagover plays Mona Fiametta, who is courted by Giovanfrancesco (Janssen) but is betrothed to Girolamo (Rudolf Klein-Rogge), who vows to kill his rival. In the end, Giovanfrancesco is killed in a duel, although not by his opponent, Girolamo, but by his servant, the Moor (Louis Brody), who stabs him in the back. In a match dissolve based on posture, the Moor (Brody) transforms into Death (Goetzke). And again a cut to a shot of the three candles now reveals a second candle going out.

The third narrative, set in China, begins with a letter the magician A Hi (Paul Biensfeldt) receives, a cordial scroll from the emperor, inviting him to perform at his birthday celebration tomorrow, noting in a postscript, however, that should he fail to delight, he will behead him. When he calls his daughter, Tiao Tsien (Dagover), to tell her the news, she is indoors exchanging kisses with Liang (Janssen). Instead of showing her and Liang the scroll by handling it, he invites it to rise from the ground like a snake and then fly away like a bird, which Wagner et al. represent in stop-motion animation photography, and then he flies the three of them on his magic carpet to the celebration, which they shoot against the background of several traveling mattes. At the celebration, A Hi performs his magic tricks to the amazement of the emperor and his guests, which are executed in the film with animation, miniaturization, form and match dissolves, and traveling mattes, yet the emperor states he would prefer to keep Tiao Tsien as his birthday gift. When she tries to run away, the emperor sentences A Hi to death by beheading in the morning. Death stands by as a witness to all these events in the person of the emperor's archer (Goetzke). Although the archer mistakenly kills Liang, when he magically is in the form of a tiger, to make amends he yields to Tiao Tsien the power to "turn the fate" (intertitle) by returning to the living, where, within the period of one hour, she must find someone, preferably already near the end of their life, willing to exchange their life for that of her lover. He sends her back to the apothecary shop, to the moment she raises the glass of poison to her lips, when the scene continues: now the apothecary intervenes, knocking the glass out of her hand and saving her, but he then rejects her plea to give her his life.

Subsequently, she makes the same plea to a beggar and to a group of very old and feeble hospital patients, but they all refuse indignantly. But later when she notices the hospital is on fire, she helps in the rescue operation and is responsible for saving many lives, including, at great personal risk, the last person left in the almost consumed building, a baby. Witnessing her valor, Death takes her to the body of her fiancé and reanimates it, which Wagner et al. represent in a form dissolve and in double exposure, but he activates the corpse only in spiritual form. The film ends as Death and the young couple, spiritual beings, walk off together. When they reach the top of a hill, Death disappears in a form dissolve, leaving the couple behind in an ambiguous form, either spirits together in death or living beings. An expert in special effects, Wagner gave *Der müde Tod* his distinctive cinematographic imprint.

Between his major collaborative partnerships with Murnau and Lang, Wagner filmed *Schatten: Eine nächtliche Halluzination [Warning Shadows: A Nocturnal Hallucination]* (1923), the third film directed by Arthur Robison, a German American who graduated in medicine at the University of Munich and made his film directorial debut in 1916. *Schatten* is an intense study in Expressionism and, in the style of Murnau's *Schloss Vogelöd* (1921), a *kammerspielfilm*, the principal conventions of which are close, oppressive interior spaces, signifying settings, and the absence of intertitles. Wagner, for example, refers to "boring sub-titles which interrupt, if they do not wholly destroy, the pictorial continuity. In 1922 Arthur Robison, [art director and costume designer] Albin Grau and I created *Warning Shadows*, a film without sub-titles, in order to avoid this dilemma."[5] While mainstream Expressionism and a conventional *kammerspielfilm*, *Schatten* is a pure silent film with no intertitles, in which Robison designed a distinctive visual syntax.

A historical drama, the film begins theatrically, with the curtain drawn to reveal a film screen on which appears a combination live-action, shadow-puppet show, executed through match dissolves, performed by the Shadowplayer (Alexander Granach), which introduces the main characters one by one: the Man (Fritz Kortner), the Woman (Ruth Weyher), the Youth (Gustav von Wangenheim), three Gentlemen (Eugen Rex, Max Gülstorff, and Ferdinand von Alten), and the Servants (Fritz Rasp and Carl Platen), the Maid (LilliHerder), and the Traveling Entertainer or Shadowplayer, who emerges from the prompter's box below the center-front stage.

The Romantic plot is allegorical: the Man and Woman are married, but she receives the Youth, her lover, along with the three Gentlemen, her suitors. The Shadowplayer sits outside, observing guests arriving at the door and watching the people inside silhouetted in the windows. Within the house, the husband is the tortured cuckold, observing his wife's flirtations and infidelities in his imagination, in shadows cast on the walls, and in her physical activities. Although uninvited, the Shadowplayer managed to gain entry to the house, where eventually he performs a shadow play for the benefit of all, projecting the consequences of their interactions. Cinematographically, the shadow stencil puppet show depends on lighting: the entire set is intensely lit centrifugally, so characters pantomime themselves in the shadows they cast on walls and form silhouettes, visible to outside observers, when they are framed by glass windows. Wagner films the shadow play in a wide shot, with the woman and her four suitors, backs to the camera, sitting at the dining table, and her husband, in three-quarter profile, standing on the side. Using a match dissolve, he films the Shadowplayer, his show over, moving them hypnotically to the other side of the table, thereby informing them that they too are shadows to be manipulated.

Here Wagner demonstrates the principle of shadow play with a special effect. Next he exploits more ambitious perspectival aesthetics. As the people are awaking from their hypnotic stupor, the Woman and Young Man slip away to her bedroom to make love. When he notices they have left the table, the Man goes to confront them. Stopping outside the bedroom door, he appears to see, confirming his suspicion, the Young Man, stepping backward into the doorway as he bids his lover adieu, through the paned-glass windows of the double doors to her room. As the Young Man steps back into the corridor, however, it becomes clear that the image of the double doors was a reflection in a mirror mounted on the wall outside her door. Clearly, the Man deliberately exploited the mirror to observe his wife and her lover and remain undetected himself, which becomes clear when the Young Man is shocked to find him standing there. For spectators, however, the mirror shot is an equally shocking *trompe l'oeil* not just about an event, when a husband discovers his wife cheating on him, but also about the filming of the event and the elision of appearance and reality, shadow and substance, desire and consummation in the film. The man exacts his revenge by arming the three Gentlemen with rapiers and forcing them to impale his wife while the Young Man watches. Wagner films the instant the blades penetrate her body in silhouette in an intercut shot: because of the imagery in the shadow play earlier, the motion of the rapiers looks like *legerdemain*, but the return shot confirms that the Woman is dead. Afterward, the Man goes to stand outside his wife's bedroom, where Wagner films him in the same mirror shot: he knocks several times on the door, as if he thinks she is inside, then, as he turns away he moves into the mid shot, still in the mirror, then he acknowledges his own mirror image, pointing an accusatory finger at himself, and finally he enters the field of view between the mirror and the camera. This shot sequence, like the earlier mirror shot, is about *seems* and *is*. Walking back along the corridor, he notices his image in another wall mirror: it seems to confront him and, in a futile attempt to distinguish between *seems* and *is*, he smashes the mirror. When he returns to his wife, her four suitors confront him and kill him, throwing his body out the window. On the pavement below, his body vanishes in a dissolve. In the next shot, Wagner tracks back to reveal the Shadowplayer's screen and the Man, the Woman, the Young Man, and the three Gentlemen all watching the end of the narrative of betrayal and retribution, the film itself, but as an imaginative correlative of the shadow play and of its allegory. In the end, the shadow play differentiates between *seems* and *is* and the Man and the Woman are reunited.

After shooting *Der brennende Acker* (1922) with Murnau, *Schatten: Eine nächtliche Halluzination* (1923) with Arthur Robison, and *Die Liebe der Jeanne Ney* (1927) with G. W. Pabst, and working as cinematographer on many other feature films through the 1920s, Wagner again collaborated with Lang on *Spione* (1928), like his

Frau im Mond (1929), a late-era silent film, and *M* (1931), the director's first film with synchronized sound and dialogue. Wagner said:

> I believe in the Talking Film because speech does not necessarily prevent a film from becoming a work of art, once the question of material has been settled in principle. Speech will then enhance the film, provided that the dynamic quality of the film today, namely Rhythm, whether applied to Sound or Scene, is fulfilled and the visual and audible components create a harmonious whole.[6]

Wagner generated the rhythm of *M* through the intonation of high- and low-angle shots and the musical motifs of Hans Beckert's whistling the melody of Grieg's instrumental music to Henrik Ibsen's *Peer Gynt* and in the criminal network's signaling system comprising various whistles.

Spione [Spies] is an espionage thriller in the style of Lang's *Dr. Mabuse der Spieler* (1922) and that marks his transition to *Das Testament des Dr. Mabuse* (1933). Also, as in the two Mabuse films, Rudolf Klein-Rogge is cast in the starring role, in *Spione* as the protagonist Haghi. The establishing shots of *Spione* recall those of *Dr. Mabuse der Spieler*, particularly because they both focus on the theft of a secret document: fast-paced with short scenes and multiple cross-cuts, a *bricolage* of visual fragments establishing less the setting than a chain of events. The first shot is an extreme close-up of a pair of rubber-gloved hands, left hand on top of, the other turning the dial of a combination lock to open a safe key box, and then, with the right hand, inserting a key to provide full access. The second, also an extreme close-up, focuses on these hands placing an envelope into a larger envelope and sealing it with the fingertips, possibly raising the question how they became damp enough to moisten the adhesive on the seal. The envelope has no addressee, but it is embossed with a sender's address: "Ambassade de la République Française, Shanghai." The third is a cross-cut, an extreme low-angle close-up of a motorcyclist in motion, the camera positioned lower than the front wheel, probably in a trench, and it reveals the spinning front wheel, the engine, gas tank, handlebars, light, and face of the rider, who is wearing a helmet and goggles and appears to be smiling, or perhaps just taking in oxygen. The cross-cut, if it signifies action continuous from the previous two shots, suggests the rider is fleeing from the scene of the safe job. The point of view is one no spectator would have seen before in film, and only those run over by motorcycles would have experienced in life. The fourth shot, another extreme low angle, is an animation of two telegraph towers sending out a message, represented by expanding concentric circles of electrical energy emanating out from transmitters at the top. The fifth shot is of the text of the message, about the theft of documents from the French Embassy, Shanghai. The sixth shot is analeptic, interrupting the temporal continuity of the previous shots by showing how the document was stolen: a live-action exterior, with the camera mounted on the hood, it shows an ambassador riding in the back of an open, chauffeur-driven limousine, when another car, also open, and with three occupants, pulls alongside, and from which a sniper rises to shoot the ambassador in the back of the head, and then, in an intercut close-up of a hand, someone reaches over to grab his briefcase from the seat. In the seventh shot, a reporter phones in his story of an assassination attempt on the minister; in the eighth a newspaper headline screams the minister has died and documents have been stolen. Then follows a montage of shots of editors and journalists on the phone tracking down the story. Next, a series of shots shows the ambassador's chauffeur running into a government building and into the office of a military official, but just as he reports "I saw the man" (intertitle), two shots are fired through the window, killing him. In shock, the official asks himself, "Almighty God—what power is at play here?" (intertitle). The establishing shots completed, Lang and Wagner now cut to a close-up of the person who has engineered this sequence of events: Haghi.

The story begins with an explanation of the government secret service and the counterintelligence to Haghi's intelligence, specifically in the character of No. 326 (Willy Fritsch), an undercover agent who, posing as a vagabond, receives a summons to report to the police, as a pretext to meeting secretly with his superior, Burton Jason (Craighall Sherry). At the police station he is taken to Jason's office, where he notices one of his assistants fiddling with his lapel pin and, though he is in handcuffs, he wrestles him to the floor and removes the pin, which he reveals is a miniature camera. The assistant is exposed as a double agent working for Haghi, whose identity is unknown to the authorities, as is the general incompetence of the secret service.

Next Wagner exposes Haghi and something of his highly mediatized operation, the Haghi Bank, first in an eye-level mid shot of him sitting, in a wheelchair, at his desk, and then in a high-angle shot mid close-up of him rolling a cigarette and then barking orders into an intercom telephone: "Copy photos 4 and 6 . . . Distribute to all members of the surveillance squad" (intertitle). Even though No. 326 confiscated the double agent's camera, Haghi has managed to procure photos of him by other means, such is the reach of his network. Subsequent shots reveal his headquarters as an industrial-model penal operation. While Haghi is conducting business, a broken man dressed in a prison uniform is brought to him, Hans Morrier (Louis Ralph), whom his men have abducted from a state-imposed execution. Although Morrier is deeply grateful to him for intervening to save his life, falling to his knees and kissing his hand, Haghi shows no emotion, assuring him he did it only because he is useful to him, and threatening to impose his own death sentence should he let him down. The scene is designed to demonstrate Haghi's coercive power, which is apparent in on over-the-shoulder tilt-up shot of Morrier, on his knees, looking up at Haghi. He extends his power also through state-of-the-art media of the day, for example a wall-mounted electronic monitor that issues current data about the geographic locations and even the destinations of people he is monitoring, like Colonel Jellusic (Fritz Rasp).

Wagner first shoots Jellusic for presence: tall, elegantly dressed, and with a manicured handlebar mustache. Then he films him at a *post restante* window. Initially Wagner shows him through the frosted glass as he removes a fountain pen from his pocket and writes his box number on a piece of paper, and then from the clerk's side of the open window as he makes his transaction. Immediately after he leaves with his mail, a police agent who has been watching him all along approaches the window, flashes his credentials to the clerk, and demands to see the box number of the man who was just there. Wagner intercuts three close-ups of the ticket, first when Jellusic presents it to the clerk, next when the clerk pierces it on a nail, and finally when the agent demands to see it. In the latter close-up, however, the number vanishes before the clerk can retrieve it, because Jellusic wrote it in disappearing ink, and because Wagner shot it using a match dissolve, a device that evokes the atmosphere of intrigue around espionage, including the issue of increased government public surveillance in Germany in the late 1920s. Elsaesser notes:

> *Spione*, watched today, is striking for its sharp look at conspiracies: criminal ones at the ostensible plot level, but perceiving how much Haghi the master spy is made to resemble Lenin, and his headquarters a prison designed by Piranesi, one wonders what this parallel wanted to point up.[7]

That Haghi resembles Lenin, on which Philipp Stiasny concurs when he refers to him as "a banker, who looks like Lenin" and observes, "Lang has drained the political subtext from the anti-Bolshevist iconography he employs,"[8] is an oversimplification. First, while in portraying Haghi Rudolf Klein-Rogge wears a mustache and goatee that resembles Lenin's, he is not bald, as Lenin was during his leadership. Second, Lenin had died in 1924, and was succeeded by Stalin, who was still in power in 1928. Of greater concern to Lang was the political situation in the Weimar Republic, where Hitler had been active for a decade. Third, Haghi's principal spy is a Russian revolutionary, and the romantic lead of the film, opposite No. 326; Klein-Rogge's role is secondary, not that of a round enough character to share a likeness with Lenin. Rather, the only likeness he bears is to Dr. Mabuse. Thus, disappearing ink denotes not international espionage, but rather local issues of free speech and censorship. In addition, audiences would have found this shot thrilling, for the concept of disappearing ink, the *coup l'oeil* of the trick photography of the match dissolve, and the appeal of Fritz Rasp's performance. After he leaves the post office Jellusic gets into the back of a chauffeur-driven car with Sonja Baranilkowa (Gerda Maurus), who is spying on him, and also charged with investigating No. 326, for Haghi. Wagner films them in a live-action stationary shot through the rear window as the car pulls away, which contemporaneous audiences would likely have found as fascinating as the disappearing ink dissolve shot, but this shot not for its special effect but specifically for its actuality, because they had observed people departing in cars in everyday life. A subsequent scene at the Haghi Bank, in which Lady Leslane (Hertha von Walther) declines Haghi's request that she spy on her husband to procure information about a pending Japanese treaty, reveals his supreme power of control over people, evident in his threat, which he backs up with incriminating photographs, to divulge details of her private opium use should she not deliver the data soon. When she tries to bribe him in exchange for his silence, he brusquely refuses, assuring her, "I'm richer than Ford" (intertitle). He coerces Baranilkowa into continuing to investigate No. 326, who, she tells him, reminds her of her brother, a revolutionary executed in Russia, when actually she is falling in love with him.

No. 326 and Sonja go out on a date to Daniella, a fashionable nightclub, the general activities of which Wagner films initially in an extreme high-angle overhead shot, of a boxing match in the center and, after its conclusion by a knockout, the movement of spectators from their dining tables onto the dance floor around the boxing ring. Then Wagner moves to a mid shot of the dancers, focusing on No. 326 and Sonja dancing, weaving in and out of the other dancers, until someone slips her a note to see "J. H." immediately, at which point he cuts to a long shot of Haghi at a table. Feigning illness so No. 326 will take her back to their table, she casts a disapproving glance at Haghi as they pass his table, furtively rips off her necklace and throws it to the floor, and then, once seated, announces she has lost her necklace and asks No. 326 to return to the dance floor to look for it, when a stranger arrives to deliver Haghi's instructions to her and she makes her escape, catching the first cab out, in which she reads she is to pay Jellusic his asking price for some mobilization plans, on condition he flee the country tonight. Subsequently, Haghi takes Sonja Baranilkowa prisoner, keeping her under house arrest in his compound, because of her allegiance to No. 326, and he has Colonel Jellusic exposed as a traitor, with the result that, facing military prosecution and as a point of honor, he commits suicide. Haghi has neutralized another major opponent, Dr. Masimoto (Lupu Pick), by planting one of his operatives, Kitty (Lien Dyers), to seduce him and steal a secret agreement he has brokered for the Japanese government, and which could prevent the outbreak of war in Asia. He too commits suicide. Now Sonja Baranilkowa's fate is wholly contingent on Haghi's final battle with No. 326. She agrees to courier the agreement out of the country for Haghi, in exchange for No. 326's life.

Wagner shoots Sonja settling into her private compartment on the train before departure. She glances up and notices through the window No. 326 in the compartment directly opposite hers, in a train on the adjacent track. At first she tries to hide, in case he should notice her, and until he pulls down the blind. The shot itself, which looks through two perfectly aligned windows, is fascinating, because it resembles a mirror shot, in the sense that a mirror conventionally adds an element to the larger image, No. 326 to Sonja's room, as it were. In this respect, the special effect is of a mirror image, as if the window of Sonja's compartment is a mirror, which at first suggests that he is in her room. This *coup l'oeil* effect evokes what Sonja perceives, the man she wants to be with, and it confirms the film's romantic theme that Sonja and No. 326 belong together. The mirror effect is fleeting; it is soon recognizable for what it is, a shot through two panes of glass. The scene ends as his train pulls out of the station, with a shot of Sonja looking through her window, as No. 326 might have seen her, and as she notices the number on his carriage: 33133. Wagner's double window shot of the train pulling away recalls his shot of Jellusic and Baranilkowa through the rear window of a departing car earlier in the film, except that here her opportunity is not to betray a man but to save one and redeem herself.

This is the number of the last carriage on his train, which Haghi has sabotaged by arranging it to be separated from the rest of the train and stranded in a tunnel to collide with a train traveling in the opposite direction. Wagner captures some riveting shots from the doomed train, from a camera mounted to the sides of cars and under a carriage, as well as external shots; all of these are mostly to heighten the suspense of the impending crash. When she learns about the accident to car 33133, she recalls seeing this number on a slip of paper in Haghi's hands. Sonja boards a Red Cross train, to help in the rescue and in hopes of finding No. 326 alive. She does. In the climax, Haghi is holed up in his secret room in the bank, surrounded by police. But now he is holding Sonja and No. 326's chauffeur hostage as a means of negotiating his escape. Eventually they manage to free themselves, and all Haghi's men are apprehended as they emerge from their escape tunnels, sewers, ventilation shafts, and other passages. Haghi, however, manages to escape, because, it turns out, he is not bound to a wheelchair, which was a property of his persona. Now he disguises himself as the clown Nemo in an attempt to hide out in the circus, where eventually Sonja, No. 326, and the police manage to track him down, in the middle of his performance. Recognizing he is surrounded and this time cannot escape, he, like Jellusic and Masimoto, chooses to die honorably, precisely because he has not lived so. The chilling mid shot that shows him putting his pistol to his temple and firing it, which is the final image of *Spione*, recalls, in its audacity and its shock effect, Edwin S. Porter's shot of the gunman who defiantly fires his revolver at the audience in the last image of *The Great Train Robbery* (1903).

As *filmemacherin* Lang and Wagner were collaborative auteurs, with a shared vision of film. But Wagner was also an adaptive cinematographer, who seemed equally adept at producing special-effects shots, fast-paced cross-cuts, experimental optics shots, and formal balance shots.

> From the start, the common practice with an auteurist critical perspective would be to investigate, for instance, the films of Fritz Lang as a consistent personal vision that expresses itself according to identifiable cinematic figures or forms, seen across his films—in this case, perhaps shared themes about the dark impulses of society and a consistent stylistics of blocking groups of characters within the mise-en-scène of these films.[9]

In a collaborative auteurist relationship between a director and cinematographer with a shared vision, however, these cinematic tropes are evident more in their projects, in the aesthetic appearance of the films they make together than over one or the other's career trajectory. Thus, *Dr. Mabuse der Spieler*, *Spione*, and *Das Testament des Dr. Mabuse* (1933) have the distinctive look of Lang-Wagner collaborations, in part also because they are fast-paced films in the thriller genre and they have common scenic elements, shot repertoires, and actors, notably Klein-Rogge. In *M* (1931), however, a film "about the dark impulses of society," the protagonist, Hans Beckert (Peter Lorre), is unlike Mabuse and Haghi, whose compulsions are about criminal infrastructures and macro-domination. Rather, Beckert is a pedophile and murderer

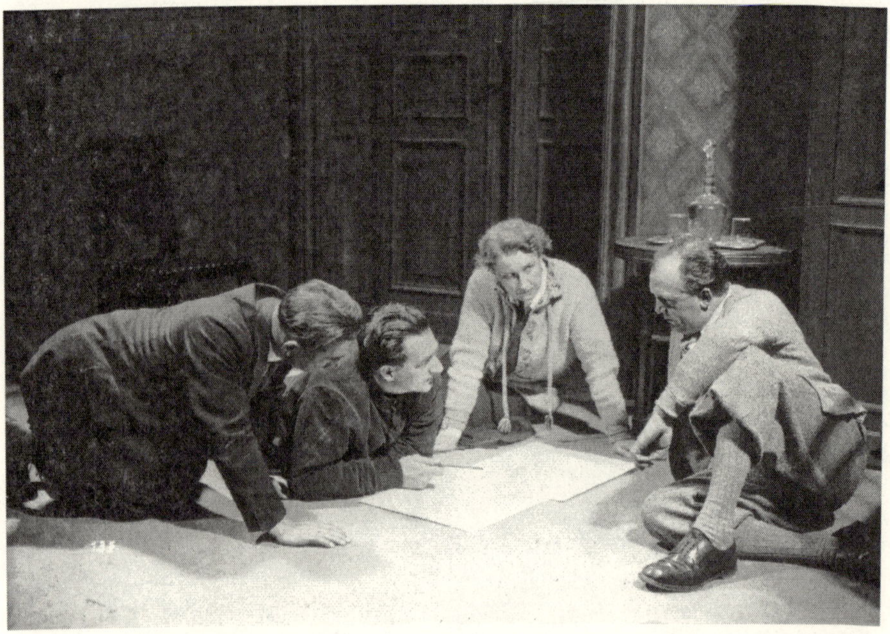

Figure 5.1. ***Left to right:*** **Art director, Fritz Lang, Thea von Harbou, and Fritz Arno Wagner on the set of *M* (1931). Copyright: Horst von Harbou–Deutsche Kinemathek.**

whose instincts lead him to control the individual, one child at time, and also his own individuality, as an abject subject, a sociopath and predator, and, within the plot, as the prey, the murderer everyone is trying to catch. "The film is based on authentic events, namely the search and capture of Peter Kürten, a serial murderer in Düsseldorf who randomly assaulted and murdered 30 children and adults between February and May 1930."[10] This is the film's historicity. Its verisimilitude is its cinematography.

M begins with a high-angle shot of young girls, gathered in a circle, playing a game in which a girl at the center rhythmically counts off the others by repeating a chant that, each time it ends, with the word *up*, eliminates one of the players: "Just you wait, it won't be long / The man in black will soon be here / With his cleaver's blade so true / He'll make mincemeat out of you!" This voyeuristic shot, along with the subject matter of the chant, establishes the film's predatory mood. Next Wagner pans left and tilts up to a second-floor balcony to show a woman hanging out her washing, who leans over the railing to order the children, "I told you to stop singing that awful song." Clearly, she is complaining because she finds the song content disturbing, not simply that the children are noisy. In the subsequent scene, Wagner shows the woman struggling to carry a basket of dried clothes upstairs to another resident, Frau Beckmann (Ellen Widmann): the washerwoman recounts her experience with the children, explaining that her objection has only to do with the fact that a murderer is on the loose. Frau Beckmann, however, rationalizes the chant, arguing that as long as she can hear the children's voices, she knows they are safe.

After Frau Beckmann, who is doing washing and cooking on the stove, hears the school bells ring at noon, dismissing the children for lunch, Wagner cuts to a series of shots focusing on her daughter, Elsie (Inge Landgut), walking home from school through town: when she steps off the curb to cross the busy street, a passing car honks at her and she steps back, but a policeman comes directly to her assistance and guides her across. Wagner follows her laterally in a dolly shot as she bounces a rubber ball along the sidewalk and then up against a street-lamp pole, which is off-camera until he pans slightly right and then tilts up to show that she happens to be throwing it against a printed poster that, when he zooms in, can be seen to bear a message about a 10,000-mark reward for the apprehension of a murderer and about the recent disappearance of two children, a brother and sister, suspected to be victims of a crime similar to one perpetrated last fall. The silhouette of the head and upper body of a man in profile now enters the frame, his shadow cast over the text of the wanted poster, and it leans forward and down as the man, still only an outline, speaks to the child, admiring her ball before asking her name, which, off-camera, she tells him, "Elsie Beckmann." Wagner now cross-cuts back to Frau Beckmann, preparing lunch, anxious that, at 12:20, Elsie is not back yet, hopeful when she hears children climbing the stairs, disappointed when she finds her daughter is not among them. Then he cross-cuts back to a high-angle shot of Elsie at a street vendor's with the man, shot from behind, who is buying her a balloon. He casts his shadow on her, of which the balloon, with a human form, is an extension.

> The early cinematic shadow—when foregrounded by isolation from its human source and by juxtaposition to other characters or objects within the frame—frequently enabled a simultaneity of multiple narrative, a diegetic complexity, otherwise achieved later through the use of sound, as in Fritz Lang's *M*. . . . In the decade separating *Nosferatu* and *Warning Shadows* from *M*, there is discernible first the adoption and then the rejection of the shadow as metaphor within the conventions of the cinematic code.[11]

There is nothing distinctive about the man, particularly in shadow and from this restricted point of view. His dress is commonplace: dark overcoat, dark fedora. Yet he is whistling, a melody from "In the Hall of the Mountain King" from Grieg's incidental music, Suite No. 1, Opus 46, to Ibsen's *Peer Gynt*, the dominant motif of the film and the clue that eventually leads to the child-murderer's arrest. The beggars who eventually apprehend him do so in part because of their communication system based on whistling. Whistling functions as a signal that Lang, in his first film with synchronized sound and dialogue, is exploiting sound to its fullest extent. Elsie and the man now walk, hand in hand, out of the frame camera right. Wagner then cross-cuts back to Frau Beckmann, who is setting the table for Elsie's lunch. She answers the doorbell, only to find it is the postman, who assures her he has not seen Elsie. She goes out onto the landing to look down the stairwell and shout Elsie's name, where, to capture what she sees, Wagner points the camera straight down into an abstract maze of seven flights of empty stairs. Coming back into her apartment, she sees the time is now 1:15. She opens the window to the courtyard where the children were chanting earlier and calls after her daughter twice, and then three more times, her voice rising in desperate passion, as with each of these additional cries Wagner cuts to the places the mother is looking for her daughter: an overhead shot of the stairwell, a wide shot of the attic, where clothes are drying on lines, and finally a high-angle shot of Elsie's empty place setting and vacant seat at the table. When he cuts to a high-angle wide shot of her ball rolling out onto the grass from a wooded area and a mid close-up of her balloon, caught for a moment in overhead electrical wires and blowing out of frame, and fades to black, Elsie's fate, Frau Beckmann's apprehension, and the unidentified man's motive all become clear, especially because of the continuity of circle symbols: the ring of children, their round of song, the ball, and the balloon.

> Wir hören nur den ständigen Ruf nach Elsie und sehen dabei das leere Treppenhaus . . . Elsies unberührten Platz am Küchentisch, ein Stück Rasen, über de Elsies Ball rollt, ihren Luftballon, der sich in den Telefondrähten verfangen hat.[12]

> We hear only the repeated call of "Elsie," and see the empty stairwell . . . Elsie's untouched place at the kitchen table, Elsie's ball rolling over the grass, her balloon caught in phone wires. (St. Pierre's translation)

Completing the aural motif of the Grieg melody and the symbolic motif of circles is Wagner's visual motif of high-angle, counterbalanced with some low-angle and overhead shots.

> The high angle is, of course, impersonal by its very nature. As with subjective and objective camera views on the lateral plane, we can see camera angles that diverge from eye level as increasingly objective, more third person in terms of our literary analogy. This applies especially to higher angles.[13]

The second section of *M*, after the fade to black, begins a high-angle shot of newsboys and an overhead shot of corner news vendors doing brisk business selling the extra edition with details of Elsie Beckmann's murder. Wagner follows these with a high-angle over-the-shoulder shot of the murderer, identifiable because he is whistling Grieg, writing a cryptic letter to the press about his crime, in which he complains the police have ignored him and affirms this will not be his last murder. Wagner proceeds next to an over-the-shoulder traveling shot of members of the public who are reading the reward poster on the wall of a kiosk: the shot initially focuses on the poster, with four hats visible at the bottom of the frame; then he pulls the camera back through the crowd, with no apparent break in it, to reveal a much larger group of people. This shot, along with the opening shots of people buying newspapers, signifies that everyone is talking about the murder of Elsie Beckmann, but in its composition and formal balance and as a demonstration of Wagner's fluid objective camera, it marks an amazing technical and artistic achievement also.

Next, Wagner films a high-angle mid shot of a group of five affluent middle-aged men sitting at a round table at a pub, while one of them reads a newspaper story about how vulnerable children are to predatory abductions, the poor response from the police, and the lack of clues, to which he intercuts close-up reaction shots, including commentary on the crisis, until, from a high angle, one of the men hints another might be the murderer and the gathering breaks up in chaos. He explores the perspectival motif further in a street scene in which a little girl asks a small older gentleman for the time, after which he advises her to go straight home. A tall, burly man who witnesses the conversation confronts the man, demanding what business he has inquiring into where the girl lives. Wagner now films their initial exchange in opposing shots, a high angle, the burly man's perspective of the gentleman, and a low angle, the gentleman's perspective of the burly man. Soon a crowd gathers and they apprehend the gentleman and call for the police, who have just arrested a pickpocket on the bus. The pickpocket complains that the police should catch the murderer instead of concentrating on petty crime, a crowd gathers, presuming the man in custody is the murderer, and chaos ensues. Lang designs the scene to show that fear is universal; Wagner shoots the scene affectively, but also uses it to develop the film's perspectival motif. All high-angle and tilt-down shots are correlatives of the perspective the *kindermörder* has on a child.

Spectators see the face of the murderer for the first time when Wagner suddenly cuts away from a forensic conference, at which, from his handwriting analysis of the note to the press, a graphologist is building up a profile of the killer, to a mirror shot, in which Peter Lorre's character, Hans Beckert, looks in the mirror, while the graphologist's address describing him continues as a voiceover, and the murderer inspects his features and changes his expression, at the mention of madness even posing as insane, as if he hears the address. His narcissism implies he is curious about what people are saying about him, and his reaction to the voiceover manifests this. Lang exploits the same device when the criminal secretary discusses the case with the police chief over the phone, and Wagner displays the latter's account of various investigational activities in a series of intercut scenic shots in which police seem to enact the voiceover content.

One of these events is a police raid of the Crocodile Club, a pub patronized by criminals. As the police approach the location in force, the film carries no voiceover or soundtrack of any kind, not even ambient noise. A police whistle, a signal to begin the operation, interrupts this silence. One shot shows the people in the bar alerted by the whistle to the impending raid: they flee up the winding staircase tunnel to the ground floor, but just as they near the top the police start to descend it, so all the patrons are forced to go back. Wagner films this bidirectional movement of people with a high-angle shot from the top of the staircase. Initially, he takes a passing shot in which the camera is stationary and the pub patrons move upstairs toward the camera and then, when they realize they cannot escape, back downstairs. Next, as three police side by side, then another three, enter the camera's field of action and start to herd everyone back downstairs, Wagner takes a moving shot, in which the camera follows them in paralletic movement, in an over-the-shoulder shot of the police and everyone they are pushing back down the stairs and into the pub. Here the police interrogate everyone, demanding to see their papers, and uncover much evidence of criminal activity, such as false passports, stolen goods, and tools of the trade, although primarily they are looking for the child murderer. This scene is crucial in the film, because in the end it is the criminal underground that catches the killer. Criminals are motivated to do this because they want to put a stop to their profile-based harassment by the police, and because, knowing criminal behavior, they feel they are better qualified than the police to conduct the search. The Crocodile Club raid provokes their vigilante action, but within the context of perspectival shots and camera angles, the high-angle passing shot and the paralletic movement shot set them on their way. The towering overhead shot of the stairwell and seven flights of stairs in the apartment building at the start of the film signals Elsie Beckmann is not coming home, whereas this high-angle and fluid shot of the staircase at the pub signals her murderer will be found. Lang and Wagner seem to signify everything of importance in this film through distinctive shots, angles, and camera movements. Thus, although they first show the murderer in a silhouette, and subsequently from behind, in an over-the-shoulder shot, they elect to reveal his face in a mirror shot, which is a passing shot, and in the paralletic movement of his face-making.

Wagner exploits cross-cuts liberally to display the simultaneous actions, the two narratives, of the crime syndicates and criminal networks, including beggars, led by Schränker (Gustaf Gründgens), and the police, led by Inspector Karl Lohmann (Otto Wernicke). When Schränker decrees they will put the entire city under surveillance and monitor the movements of every child, Wagner cuts to a three-shot of men's silhouettes on the wall, signifying the secrecy of their operation and invoking how Beckert first makes acquaintance with children, as a shadow. He favors the beggars' community with inventive fluid camera movements, such as when with a portable camera he wanders unfettered from table to table and throughout the café where they congregate, panning, tilting, and zooming to show the dignity of these men who are able to survive by salvaging food, cigarettes, and cigars, saleable junk because of their attention to detail. The best example of this kind of preferential camera work is a shot sequence Wagner executes to reveal the beggars queuing up to register as volunteers for Schränker's surveillance work. He reveals the men gradually, beginning with a shot of the menu board at the café, then remotely, in a tilt-up shot from the menu board to a second-story paned-glass window through which the queue of men is visible, and finally intimately, in a justified dolly shot with a lap dissolve in which the camera seems to pass through one of the panes of glass into the room and then moves across the registration desk to focus on Schränker leaning against a wall. Wagner uses this shot sequence primarily to emphasize the men's high moral principles, but he constructed the through-the-glass effect also to acknowledge his indebtedness to cinematographer Karl Freund, who executed a similar shot in the scene where the porter is demoted in *Der letzte Mann* (1924).

Wagner shows the beggars at work in the field, initially in a high-angle shot of a hurdy-gurdy player performing to a few children gathered in a loose circle, as in the opening scene of the film, and in a high-angle close-up of the shoes and upturned hat of a "visually impaired" beggar wearing a "BLIND" sign, and of the shoes of two passing pedestrians, a man with a girl, who throws a coin in the hat, followed by a mid shot of the beggar thanking her and then lifting his glasses to scrutinize the couple, whom the next shot, a dolly shot, follows along the sidewalk to the door of the school, where the man, who is now verifiable as the father, drops the girl off.

Wagner builds upon the perspectival motif of mirror and window shots in a sequence of intercut shots that display Inspector Groeber (Theodor Loos) conducting a search of his apartment while awaiting Beckert to return, and of Beckert shopping in town. After making a purchase at a fruit stand, he is distracted by a J. A. Henckels knife and cutlery shop window. Wagner shoots him from within the store through the glass, his head framed in a diamond-shaped reflection of some of the knives in the window display, and then this diamond reflection from outside, in which Beckert sees framed the reflection of a young girl. Then Wagner returns to the first shot, which now shows how Beckert reacts to the object of his perception, the reflection of a child within the reflection of knives. This shot connotes the violent threat Beckert poses to this girl, and to other children, but in its panoply of images it suggests also his complex sociopathy.

> In *M* Wagner turned all his expressive force with light and image composition to enforce the drama of the theme, even though it was a realistic film. These effects were notable in the scene when the shadow of the sadist falls on the innocent child, like fate marking its victim, or the reflection of many pocket knives reflected on a shop window around the killer's face. Wagner's brilliant cinematography was also present in the light treatment in night city scenes, the lighting and compositions of staircases, and the indoor scenes where the underworld gets together to judge the surprised psychopath.[14]

Wagner moves back and forth between the interior and exterior shots, of Beckert and the girl within the diamond frame, until the girl walks out of the frame and his temptation seems to be removed. But Wagner continues to focus on this girl as she looks into other shop windows, as the soundtrack of Beckert whistling the Grieg melody confirms, ominously, he is following her, until she meets her mother, who enters the frame. As they walk past, Beckert is hiding in a doorway. Later this melody registers with a visually impaired balloon vendor (Georg John), who recalls having sold a balloon to the man with Elsie Beckmann, just before she was murdered. That in the bundle he is holding is a balloon identical to the one he sold Beckert that day confirms he is the same vendor and his memory is reliable, and also points to Lang and Wagner's attention to detail. The balloon seller tells another tramp, who spots Beckert with another girl and tracks them to a fruit shop. Again, Wagner uses a high-angle shot, evoking the perspective of the tramp looking at them from street level down through the front window of the basement store. When Beckert and the girl emerge onto the street, the tramp, from his hiding place, observing him pull out a switchblade to peel an orange the girl has offered him, seizes the opportunity to expose the killer: with a piece of chalk he writes the letter M on the palm of his hand then deliberately jostles Beckert and slaps his back, imprinting his overcoat with M, signifying he is a *Mörder*, on the pretext he is offended because Beckert is littering by dropping orange peelings on the ground. Although a mark made in this fashion would reproduce in reverse, it reads M forward and backward, in which respect Beckert's M is like a mirror image and like a reflection in a window. When the beggars corner Beckert in the street and block his exit, Wagner shoots the scene in a high-angle shot that stresses his isolation, especially now that panic has forced him to flee the girl. Taking advantage of a diversion, he manages to escape into an office building, where he hides in a wood-slatted storage locker, and Wagner shoots him cowering in a low-angle shot, trapped in a cage, and later an overhead mid close-up shot of him struggling to smash the lock. Meanwhile the criminals, knowing he is hiding inside, take over the building after hours and apprehend him.

They take him to an abandoned warehouse. With his jacket pulled over his head, they push him up one flight of stairs, then down another, in low-angle followed by high-angle shots, into an ad hoc courtroom, where in a high-angle panoramic shot Wagner scans a large crowd of criminals and beggars, enough to pack the field of view, who will now pass sentence on Beckert. In his own defense, he pleads his compulsion to kill, arguing, "I have to roam the streets endlessly, always sensing that someone's following me. It's me! I'm shadowing myself!" Here Lang and Wagner (in a medium close-up of Beckert for presence, neither the high-angle nor the low-angle shot with which he typically distances and separates him) draw to a close the motif of shadows, mirror images, and over-the-shoulder, overhead, and acute angle shots that has distinguished him as the elusive Other and has dominated *M*. When in the denouement the police arrive to disrupt the mock trial and arrest Beckert to try him under the law, he does not make another appearance in the film, not even in the concluding scene, a wide shot of the courtroom where he is to be tried because, having exhausted his visual motif, his shot repertoire, he has been isolated. He no longer has access to a filmic signifying system to prowl streets and cast his shadow over girls since, as he states in admitting his guilt at the mock trial, he shadows himself.

NOTES

1. David J. Skal, *Hollywood Gothic: The Tangled Web of Dracula from Novel to Stage to Screen* (New York: Norton, 1990), 84.

2. Jean Mitry, *Semiotics and the Analysis of Film*, trans. Christopher King (Bloomington and Indianapolis: Indiana University Press, 2000), 152.

3. Thomas Koebner, "Murnau—a Conservative Filmmaker? On Film History as Intellectual History," in *Expressionist Film: New Perspectives*, ed. Dietrich Scheunemann, 113 (Rochester, NY: Camden House, 2003).

4. Thomas Elsaesser, *Weimar Cinema and After: Germany's Historical Imaginary* (London and New York: Routledge, 2000), 228.

5. Fritz Arno Wagner, "I Believe in the Sound Film," trans. A. L. H. Moore and S. P. Larcombe, *Film Art* 8.111 (1936): 11.

6. Wagner, "I Believe in the Sound Film," 8.

7. Ibid., 148–49.

8. Philipp Stiasny, "Humanity Unleashed: Anti-Bolshevism as Popular Culture in Early Weimar Cinema," in *The Many Faces of Weimar Cinema: Rediscovering Germany's Filmic Legacy*, ed. Christian Rogowski, 63 (Rochester, NY: Camden House, 2010).

9. Timothy Corrigan, "Teaching Film Auteurs," in *Teaching Film*, ed. Lucy Fischer and Patrice Petro, 20–21 (New York: Modern Language Association of America, 2012).

10. Anton Kaes, "The Cold Gaze: Notes on Mobilization and Modernity," *New German Critique* 59 (Spring–Summer 1993): 108.

11. James C. Franklin, "Metamorphosis of a Metaphor: The Shadow in Early German Cinema," *German Quarterly* 53 (March 1980): 179.

12. Rudolf Freund, "M: Mörder unter uns," in *Deutsche Spielfilme von den Anfängen bis 1933: Ein Film Führer*, ed. Günther Dahlke and Günter Karl, 257 (Berlin: Henschelverlag Kunst und Gesellschaft, 1988).

13. Blain Brown, *Cinematography Theory and Practice: Image Making for Cinematographers, Directors, and Videographers* (Amsterdam: Focal, 2002), 57.

14. H. Mario Raimondo-Souto, *Motion Picture Photography: A History, 1891–1960* (Jefferson, NC: McFarland, 2007), 234–35.

6

Fritz Arno Wagner, G. W. Pabst, and the Weimar *Zeitgeist*

In the eight films he shot, 1921–1933, with F. W. Murnau, Fritz Lang, and Arthur Robison, notably Murnau's *Nosferatu, eine Symphonie des Grauens* (1922) and Lang's *M* (1931), collaborative works of exceptional cinematic artistry, Fritz Arno Wagner proved himself a versatile and eclectic cinematographer, capable of adapting to the directors' demands for special effects achieved both through photographic techniques and generated before the camera; passing shots in which the camera is stationary and subjects and objects move or in which the camera moves and subjects and objects are stationary; acute angle and heterodox shots; and a facility in the visual syntaxes of Expressionism and Realism. In the six films he made, 1927–1931, with director G. W. Pabst, Wagner established a fuller collaborative filmmaking partnership, in part because he demanded less photographic tricks and severities than a percipient eye, less the silhouettes and mirror shots of Expressionism than the images and montages of social realism.

On *Die Liebe der Jeanne Ney [The Love of Jeanne Ney]* (1927), Wagner was assisted by cinematographer Robert Lach, who had previous experience with Pabst, shooting his first three films with him: *Die freudlose Gasse* (1925), *Geheimnisse einer Seele* (1926), and *Man spielt nicht mit der Liebe* (1926). *Die Liebe der Jeanne Ney* concerns post–World War One unrest and the Russian civil war (1917–1923) that broke out after the Russian Revolution, precisely as the dispute spilled over into Crimea. The film opens with a close-up profile shot of a pair of men's shoes, propped against the wall. It engages with its curiosity but also provokes speculation beyond the borders of the frame, such as about the sitting position of the person wearing the shoes. Still in close-up, Wagner pans down the pant legs, across a newspaper, and along a cluttered desktop, when a hand enters the field of view to feel for a partly smoked cigarette butt and then returns to feel for a match. Here Wagner pans right to reveal in high-angle close-up a reclining man, Khalibiev (Fritz Rasp), now struggling to get the smoke alight through a cigarette holder. With this character established, Wagner cuts to the scene of a boisterous pub packed with drunken soldiers, paramilitary types, and civilians. He captures the raw emotion of the space in a montage of close-ups and mid shots, pans and tilts, all for presence, as he swings the camera in and out of the dense crowd in all directions through the tight space, seemingly recording indiscriminately whatever the lens crosses, but as if it is whatever crosses the lens. As in medical semiotics "the symptom is felt, the sign observed by some other person," so throughout *Jeanne Ney* the symptoms are the feelings evident in the performances, the signs how Wagner imprints them on film, whether those of the lead actors or those of supporting or bit players. A server carries a tray into a second-floor room, where, spectators learn, Khalibiev is, to deliver him some wine, which he drinks from the bottle, and Wagner films him doing it in an unflattering high-angle shot that focuses on the base of the upturned bottle, with his face obscured at the other end.

The next principal scene introduces Jeanne Ney (Édith Jéhanne), whose father, Alfred Ney, a political observer, informs her they will return to Paris because the situation in Crimea has grown too volatile. Wagner shows she is pleased with the decision when, in an over-the-shoulder close-up, she blows on a pane of glass to form condensation and with her finger writes the word *Paris* on it, and he establishes the protagonist as capable of surprising responses. After she complains she has no happy memories of her six years in Crimea, Wagner cuts to an antecedent action montage of her experiences, most of them pleasant enough, shared with Andreas Labov (Uno Henning). Next, Khalibiev pays a visit to Alfred Ney. When he enters the home, typically in a shot in which he is partly out of frame, he first notices Jeanne, still standing by the window on which she wrote *Paris*, and is clearly fascinated by her. He bows to her, she acknowledges him, then leaves, walking circuitously behind her father's desk and along the background wall to the door, his gaze tracking her across the room, which Wagner represents in two pan shots of her walking and crossing the threshold, alternating with two close-ups of him watching her and another close-up of him casting a lingering glance, before finally turning his attention to her father. The perceptual tracking shot, in which the fluid camera emulates a character's point of view, is typical of the cinematography in *Die Liebe der Jeanne Ney*. Wagner uses it again when Alfred's servant goes to a café to find Andreas: he shoots the servant initially through a paned glass window, as he verifies that Andreas is present, then as he enters the bar, greets several people, and looks around, which he represents in a pan shot that mimics his act of seeking through observation and physical movement, while establishing a cross-section of the patrons talking and playing chess, and the pan stops and tilts down slightly when he locates Andreas. Wagner continues his pan shot as, rather than walking directly there, the servant wanders from table to table commenting on chess matches under way, and then sits next to Andreas, on the pretext of observing his game. He casually tells Andreas about the transaction Khalibiev has just completed with Alfred Ney, selling him military information, a register of Bolshevik freedom fighters.

The next scene shows Andreas and a comrade confronting Alfred at gunpoint, demanding he surrender the list. When Alfred offers resistance, firing a pistol, which grazes Andreas's scalp, the comrade fatally shoots him. Alerted by the bang, Jeanne comes to investigate, which Wagner records in a fast-paced shot sequence: a mid shot of Jeanne in the doorway followed by an intercut shot, suggesting what she sees, Alfred's body fallen over the desk; a passing shot of Jeanne running to the body and, now filmed from behind, embracing it, standing up and throwing up her hands, and then suddenly turning around in close-up to face the perpetrators. Wagner cuts directly from her to a mid shot of Andreas that tracks in to a close-up to signify her recognition of him, her lover, and now, she realizes, a murderer. Now Wagner dissolves to one of the shots of the flashback montage earlier, in which Jeanne and Andreas seem a happy romantic couple, and then he cuts back to the present, where she stares at him accusingly. When he advises her to leave, because the Bolsheviks are about to mount an assault on the town, Wagner cuts to a shot sequence of the attack already under way, which he makes continuous through fluid camera action cutting through tracking and passing shots of the Red Army marching through the streets. This footage documents the 1920 victory of the Red over the White Army for control of Crimea.

When Jeanne returns to Paris, she contacts her uncle, Raymond (Adolph E. Licho), who tells her he has no place for her at his detective agency. But when his visually impaired daughter, Gabrielle (Brigitte Helm), begs her to stay with her because she is lonely, Raymond, seeing the advantage of a companion for his daughter, promptly dismisses his secretary and hires Jeanne in her place. Subsequently, Khalibiev tracks her down at the agency, where, on the recommendation of the late Alfred Ney, as he claims, he sounds Raymond on the business opportunities there, which for him, Wagner's point-of-view shots of him imply, are really occasions to steal assets from the company, which he attempts to secure by developing a romantic relationship with Gabrielle. His emotional insincerity, which is already apparent in his obsequious facial expressions, gestures, and postures, Wagner makes blatantly obvious in two extreme close-ups: one is of Gabrielle's eyes, after he has given her a bouquet of flowers, her vacant look emphasizing she cannot see how Khalibiev displays himself, that he does not want to kiss her; the other, in a later scene at a bar, Khalibiev, flirting with a woman bartender, Margot (Hertha von Walther), leans over the counter to give her a raunchy kiss. (In a later scene with her, he tells her in an intertitle, "After I marry the blind idiot I'll get rid of her and we can skip with the money.") Andreas also follows Jeanne to Paris, where he arranges to meet her on a bridge, but when the car bringing her arrives on an adjacent road on the bridge, he waves wildly to get the driver's attention and runs alongside the car. Wagner films him in a running shot and the car in a wide pan shot: the shots merge when the roads converge, Andreas and Jeanne finally meet, when he films them in a mid shot for presence and also tracking back as they walk toward the camera.

Das Auto, das sie zum Rendezvous bringt, lässt Fritz Arno Wagner beziehungsreich an Brückengeländern und Vorgarten-Gittern entlangfahren, die die Liebenden nicht zueinanderkommen lassen.[1]

The car that brings you to the rendezvous, Fritz Arno Wagner running along bridge railings and garden gratings, which do not allow the lovers to come together. (St. Pierre's translation)

Waiting for them back in the car, Gabrielle happens to tell his driver, Poitras (Hans Jaray), she is engaged to Khalibiev, at which point Wagner cuts ahead to the engagement celebration dinner that evening, which includes Raymond and Jeanne as well as Gabrielle and Khalibiev, who hardly seem in love. When Raymond leaves the table after dinner, Gabrielle moves over to be close to Khalibiev, who is seated on a love seat, and touches his hand, which his reaction shows disgusts him. With her hand still on his, Khalibiev slides over on the sofa toward Jeanne, who is seated on his other side, and, with his free hand he touches her hair and face seductively and then leans over to kiss her, which Wagner shows in a low-angle over-the-shoulder shot of him, whose seat is lower than hers, from behind and of her facing the camera, with her face and particularly her eyes visible, showing she is horrified by what he is doing. Then he cuts to a reaction close-up of Gabrielle showing her usual vacant stare, yet appearing shocked by what she is "witnessing." To quell any suspicion his fiancée might have, Khalibiev now covers her hand with his and squeezes it, and then slides back over to her side of the sofa, leaning into her and laying his head on her shoulder, but with a smug expression, looking as if he is satisfied with himself for carrying off this deceit and demonstrating his feelings for Jeanne, and he has done nothing to violate the engagement. Then, emboldened, he leans over to Jeanne again, touching her shoulder amorously; when she pushes him away and flees the table, he wrests his hand away from Gabrielle's to pursue her, into the next room, where Raymond has fallen asleep in his chair. Khalibiev corners Jeanne in a doorway, but his designs on her are interrupted when Raymond awakes, disturbed by the noise, to see them together. Khalibiev goes over to Raymond to defuse his indiscretion, which he brazenly blames on Jeanne: "Even in the Crimea she was always running after me" (intertitle). Wagner displays their mutual understanding about "women," in a pair of cross-cut shots: a high-angle tight close-up of Raymond, seated, from Khalibiev's perspective, and a low-angle shot of Khalibiev, standing. They laugh off the impropriety. Gabrielle is left alone in the dining room, abandoned by everyone. Her father looks in on her but only to turn off the light.

Wagner exploits a similar two-shot in a subsequent scene, in which Margot, the girlfriend from the pub, visits Gabrielle and bluntly discloses Khalibiev's plan to rob and murder her, kneeling at her feet to kiss her hand: a high-angle close-up of Margot looking up, and a mid high-angle close-up of Gabrielle looking down, followed by another high angle, and a low angle in which, Margot, telling her that Khalibiev plans to strangle her after the wedding, reaches up into the frame, into Gabrielle's shot, to put her hands around her neck to implore her. Subsequently, close-up shots of hands figure in a scene in which Raymond rehearses a fraudulent transaction scheduled for tomorrow, in which a client will pay him a reward of fifty thousand marks for the recovery of a stolen diamond, and he will split the reward with the diamond thief. Wagner films his pantomime, which comprises returning the diamond, accepting the reward, counting out the bank notes, and depositing the money in the safe, mainly in mid shots, close-ups, and extreme close-ups, as of his rapid hand movements and of his lips counting aloud, all for the presence of Raymond's unfettered greed. In pantomime, he levels the side of the stack of notes on the desk, then lays the stack flat and, with the fingers of his left hand, lifts the notes so that with the fingers of his right hand he can separate and count them. He images a future event. But it happens now, when the doorbell rings; he goes to the door, believing it is the client with the reward, but when he opens the door, he meets his murderer. Wagner films the murderer metonymically, focusing only on his hands reaching around the throat and strangling Raymond. Spectators know immediately the murderer is Khalibiev, because they have seen his chokehold before, when Margot uses pantomime and touch to persuade Gabrielle he intends to strangle her. As the killer enters the office to retrieve the diamond, it is appropriate that she, her sleep having been disrupted by the noise of the murder by asphyxiation, comes first to witness the crime. Khalibiev manages to distract her and escape, after which she stumbles upon her father's corpse.

When Andreas, en route to Toulon, is arrested on the train for the murder of Alfred Ney, spectators know he is innocent, but Jeanne can confirm his alibi, that they spent the night of the murder, the eve of his departure, together in a hotel. Leaving the hotel in the morning, Jeanne catches a glimpse of Khalibiev on the stairs, despite his attempt to shield his face from her with his hand. He has spent the night there with a prostitute. Therefore, because she cannot give her alibi directly to the police, who could charge her as an accomplice to the murderer, she believes she can rely on Khalibiev to testify that Andreas was at the hotel with her the night of the murder. When he returns to his hotel room he is shocked to find her there waiting for him; fearing she will expose him, he immediately locks her in the room and flees. Observing him through the window, she overhears him give his destination, the Gare de Lyon train station, to a taxi driver. After alerting the hotel manager to unlock the door, she follows him by taxi to the station. Wagner first shows Khalibiev, along with other passengers, in a low-angle shot through the open door of his compartment. Almost all the interior shots are close-ups for presence, showing him, a murderer, in the company of ordinary travelers. For example, when a man withdraws his pocket watch, Wagner intercuts an insert close-up of the watch face, and then a three-shot mid close-up of the man showing his wife the time, with Khalibiev looking on, emphasizing that his concern with a punctual departure is different from theirs. He reveals Jeanne on the platform searching for Khalibiev in a high-angle close-up passing shot, with the tracking camera keeping pace with her as she walks alongside the train looking up into each compartment. Close-ups and tracking shots are striking throughout this film, as acute-angle and tracking shots are in Lang's *M* (1931).

Close-ups, including two-shots and over-the-shoulder shots, give *Die Liebe der Jeanne Ney* a kind of perspectival intimacy that in the late twentieth century would be associated with television. This closeness is apparent when Jeanne enters Khalibiev's compartment just as the train pulls out. She immediately grips his arm with both hands and leans into his body, mainly to prevent his escape, but in a manner that makes the other passengers, an older couple, think they are lovers and her late arrival has something to do with their romance, but she is simply making her appeal to him and, at this point, hopeful he will respond reasonably. When the other passengers acknowledge them, offering them some of their bread and sausage, Jeanne resolves to take advantage of the attraction he has always had for her as a platform in her persuasive negotiations with him, by feigning affection for him and even encouraging him to reciprocate. In this regard, Wagner's intimate close-ups are razor-edged, given the mortal danger she is in. When the other couple suddenly gets off at the first stop, Jeanne tries to leave with them, pushing Khalibiev to the door, which he shuts and bars, leaving them alone. Now that there are no witnesses, he begins to respond to her show of affection in the only way he can, through coercion and violence, as when he promises to return with her to Paris on the condition she show him now she loves him. Wagner films their deliberations in a sequence of alternating over-the-shoulder two-shots, or dirty singles, over the shoulder of one to a close-up, tight close-up, or mid close-up of the other. She closes her eyes, as if to permit him to kiss her, but clearly this would not be enough for him, and he rejects her overture, saying, "That's not enough. You must show that you really love me" (intertitle). Seeing a folded newspaper in his pocket, which Wagner reveals in an intercut close-up of the paper and another of her shocked reaction, she realizes he has known about Andreas's arrest all along. He goes to the other side of the compartment, to sit by the door. She follows to sit with him, grabbing his lapels, turning his body toward hers, and imploring him. He responds by kneeling at her feet and initiating rough play. She jumps to her feet and pulls the emergency handle, forcing the train to stop. Clearly her gesture of approaching him at the door was only a pretext to get close to the alarm. When she screams for help, he tries to silence her by stuffing her mouth with his handkerchief, forgetting that he has used it to wrap the stolen diamond. When she struggles against him, the handkerchief falls to the floor, exposing the diamond in her hand, proof he is the murderer. When the conductor and some passengers arrive to investigate what emergency stopped the train, she exposes him as a murderer. He tries to flee in the countryside, but they manage to apprehend him. The film concludes as Jeanne gazes into the diamond as the proof that will exonerate Andreas, but also as a prism in which she now envisions him as a free man again, walking toward her, which Wagner represents in a double exposure. Jeanne looks up as if she can see him in the compartment and holds the diamond to her heart.

After completing *Die Büchse der Pandora* (January 30, 1929), with cinematographer Günther Krampf, and starring American actor Louise Brooks in her German film debut, Pabst collaborated with Wagner on five consecutive films over two years: *Tagebuch einer Verlorenen* (September 1929) and *Westfront 1918: Vier von der Infante-*

rie (May 1930), *Skandal um Eva* (June 1930), *Die 3 Groschen-Oper* (February 1931), and *Kamaradschaft* (November 1931).

In *Tagebuch einer Verlorenen [Diary of a Lost Girl]* Pabst relied on Wagner's expertise in close-up shots to detail the sexual development of Thymian Henning (Louise Brooks), the shy daughter of a pharmacist, Friedrich Karl Henning (Josef Rovensky), from repressed *ingénue* to uninhibited *fille de joie*, as discernible in her facial displays. Instrumental in her transition is Meinert, the pharmacy manager, played by Fritz Rasp in his signature miscreant role, recalling his Khalibiev in *Die Liebe der Jeanne Ney*. The film's opening shot is a tight close-up of the hands of someone untying the string securing a packet. Wagner tilts up to reveal a woman, Thymian's Aunt Frida (Vera Pawlowa), who looks up from her task to reveal her face from under a broad-brimmed hat, taking notice of something out of frame. Wagner cuts to a wide shot of what she has seen, through the translucent curtains of French doors, which reveals two human forms, and whence an establishing scene unfolds: a housekeeper, Elisabeth (Sybille Schmitz), is leaving her position with the family. She comes through the doors but then returns to the room, where she opens her suitcase and removes a knitted baby sweater that she holds up to Thymian's father in a desperate appeal for support, which Wagner films in a high-angle shot of her on her knees, followed by a low-angle shot of the father, who shrugs his shoulders. When Aunt Frida comes to investigate, her observation, "So you had your way with this housekeeper too" (intertitle), confirms the story the preceding shot sequence has told and also establishes the double moral standard governing sexuality and gender behavior in the film, which the entrance of Thymian emphasizes: dressed in white, with a band of white flowers in her hair, for the occasion of her Confirmation, she begs Elisabeth not to go. Yet Wagner focuses more on Elisabeth, whom he follows in a pan shot as she descends the curved staircase to the door and exits through the pharmacy, where, in mid shots, he shows Meinert watching her, and bending down to offer to help her, by placing his hands on her shoulders, when her suitcase breaks open.

When Thymian runs after her, to give her the packet Aunt Frida opened, Meinert stops her in the doorway by blocking her way with his arm and his hand over hers on the handle, and draws her back in by pulling her hand to shut the door. His conduct is more threatening than when he touches Elisabeth. It represents men's control over women's bodies, like the father's over Elisabeth's pregnant body, and it recalls how Khalibiev shuts the door to trap Jeanne on the train in the climax to *Die Liebe der Jeanne Ney*. When Thymian asks Meinert why Elisabeth had to leave, the disparity between a naive woman and a worldly man is clear in Wagner's alternating dirty singles, shots of a type associated with courtship, as an anticipatory setup to a kiss, for example, rather than exchanging information. Wagner confirms his foreshadowing of a sexual relationship between Thymian and Meinert in two intercut shots, a mid shot of Mr. Henning, behind the pharmacy counter, observing their conversation knowingly, and, from the father's point of view, a mid close-up reaction shot of Meinert winking at him, implying their male complicity. After promising to tell her why Elisabeth had to leave, Meinert secretly writes in her diary, the Confirmation gift Aunt Frida unwrapped, requesting she meet him in the pharmacy late tonight. That he would make the first entry in her diary foreshadows how he intends to take her virginity. At the reception, he watches her lasciviously as she adjusts her skeleton-key pendant and slips it down the neck of her dress, and her father greets the new housekeeper, Meta Koch (Franziska Kinz), on her arrival and introduces her to the guests, who react wryly, familiar with his reputation as a sexual predator. Thymian discovers the truth about the relationship of her father and Elisabeth after the reception, when some men bring a dead body on a stretcher to the pharmacy: Elisabeth has committed suicide by drowning herself. When Thymian runs upstairs to inform her father, Wagner films her in a perspectivally inventive passing shot through the railings of the staircase and of the mezzanine to his room, where, finding him sitting in a love seat, with his arm around Meta, she appears to grasp why Elisabeth may have taken her own life, and then she faints. Thymian's suspicion about the relationship of her father and Meta is warranted, as it turns out, because after bidding him good night, Mr. Henning casts Meta a glance as if to confirm an arrangement they made when he embraced her, and now she follows him into his bedroom.

Despite the events of the day—the death of Elisabeth, her disturbing insight into her father, and her blackout—Thymian keeps her late-night tryst with Meinert in the pharmacy. They come together emotionally when she complains she is all alone, and he assures her she can count on him, but they form a bond in Wagner's close-up two shots of them, one shot in which they both are facing forward, to the camera, she in front of him, and the other in which he is behind and she is in profile, having turned to hear his explanation about her father's relationship with Elisabeth. Then in a mid shot they embrace, she faints, he kisses her, carries her to his bed, and, as the *mise-en-scène* and fade to black imply, rapes her when she is still unconscious.[2] The following scene is nine months later: Thymian has given birth, Meinert is identified as the father, the baby is taken from her and put into the custody of a midwife, and she is sent to a penitentiary-like reformatory for wayward girls, operated by a strict and sadistic married couple.

> In Pabsts *Tagebuch einer Verlorenen* wird das Erziehungsheim-Milieu forgendermassen eingefürt: man sieht zunächst das harte . . . böse Gesicht der Erzieherin; dann, dass sie rhythmisch auf einen Gong schlägt; dann fährt der Apparat weiter zurück, und es zeigt sich, dass sie an der Kopfseite eines langen Tisches steht, an dem Die Zöglinge zu Mittag essen, und zwar indem sie mit militärisher Exaktheit den Löffel nach dem Takt der Gongschläge zum Munde führen.[3]

> In Pabst's *Diary of a Lost Girl*, the reform school milieu is introduced as follows: first you see the hard . . . angry face of the governess, who then beats rhythmically on a gong; then the camera pulls back, and it turns out that she is at the head of a long table, at which the girls are eating lunch, namely by raising their spoons to their mouths with military precision to the rhythm of the gong. (St. Pierre's translation)

Her institutional experience hardens her and she eventually escapes with her only friend Erika, also an inmate, and with the help of Count Nicolas Osdorff (André Roanne), a family friend. In addition, Mr. Henning and Meta marry; they forgive Meinert yet disown Thymian.

When she tries to see her child and the midwife summarily informs her it is dead, she looks up Erika (Edith Meinhard), who she discovers lives and works in a brothel, as Thymian soon comes to do. Whereas Wagner shoots most of the scenes at the reformatory in wide shots, to emphasize the sterile environment of an industrial complex, he shoots the scenes at the brothel in shots for presence: in moving shots that circulate through quite a vibrant and diverse community, especially in comparison to her dysfunctional family, which includes Count Osdorff, and in close-ups and two-shots, including two-shots of the feet of dancers, that individualize the madam, the prostitutes, and the customers and distinguish them as a community, a free society.

> Unique in German art of the late 1910s and early 1920s, the many depictions in bedrooms of mutilated prostitutes with legs splayed and bellies or vaginas cut open . . . suggest that the transgression of traditional gender codes (in this case by women whose sexuality seemed more like that of men in that it was not strictly reproductive and performed outside the bounds of traditional marriage) was more threatening in Germany than elsewhere. Though clear-cut gender boundaries were being similarly eroded in all industrialized countries by working women (including prostitutes), new dress codes and visible homosexual subcultures, nowhere else was there the literary and visual obsession with the masculine woman and her feminized male counterpart than there was in Germany.[4]

One of the reasons G. W. Pabst cast Louise Brooks, in both *Die Büchse der Pandora* and *Tagebuch einer Verlorenen*, was for her look, that of *une garçonne*, of which her bob hairstyle was the signature, which he felt would emblemize the *zeitgeist* in Germany as it entered the 1930s, which in painting is best represented by Otto Dix in his painting *Portrait of the Journalist Sylvia von Harden* (1926), "a prime (and popular) example of a Weimar type. Dix's Harden embodies the so-called 'garçonne,' or masculinized woman, whose appearance challenged existing notions of sexual difference, as do Aenne Biermann's [photograph] *Woman with a Monocle* [1928] or a photograph of Bauhaus students Elsa Franke and Gerhard Kadow."[5] Dancing with her first client, Thymian appears to pass out again, as she fainted upon seeing her father with Meta and in response to Meinert's amorous advance, but lying on the bed, she comes out of her swoon to kiss the man passionately. The shot fades to black, leaving their lovemaking to the imagination. In the morning Thymian awakes, somewhat disoriented and incredulous, to find the madam and one of her women standing by her bed. Wagner films the three of them in two shots, notably as the madam presents Thymian with an envelope of bank notes, her earnings from last night, and tells her, "He also leaves his regards" (intertitle), and then a particularly clever sequence, consisting of a three-shot, with the madam and the other women sitting on the bed, then a two-shot close-up of the madam and Thymian as she turns away, shocked by the implications of being paid for sex, and then a tight close-up for intimate presence, a choker shot showing Thymian's face in profile, framed by her arm, from the top of the head to her mouth.

Once Thymian adjusts to her new life, Wagner shoots her freely moving about the community, often in an upscale party atmosphere, in passing shots in which the camera is stationary and the characters circulate around the frame and in which the camera is fluid, moving with their flow. The first crisis for her in her new life arises when Mr. Henning, Meta, and Meinert go out on the town, and Meinert, having decided to show them "the seamy side of the big city," takes them to dinner at the brothel, where they see Thymian under unimaginable circumstances: the women have set up a charity lottery to benefit the brothel, which is insolvent, with Thymian as the prize, in which capacity she now, standing on a stage, exhibits herself to everyone. Wagner films their moment of recognition in two combination perspective-reaction, take-double take, mid shots. He follows these up with parallel cutting shots of Thymian surrounded by men ingratiating themselves to her and of her alone, struggling to cross the crowded floor to reach her father, and three-shots of him, Meta, and Meinert as if deliberating from a position of moral superiority how to extricate themselves from this embarrassing situation, and then of Meta and Meinert as they usher Mr. Henning out of the room. Mr. Vitalis (Kurt Gerron), a prostitution reformer who is now a regular client at the brothel, shows his empathy for Thymian in her degradation, and sheds a tear, which Wagner reveals in a close-up for presence and, although he assures her, "Yes, Thymian, you're a lost girl now . . . just as we're all lost" (intertitle), the wider shot reveals, on the contrary, she does have a loving family—the empathetic extended family of her brothel sisters and community—for the first time in her life.

The subsequent scenes advance the plot three years, as Thymian, who is still active as a prostitute, reads a bereavement card from Meta, notifying her of the death of her father and the need for her, as the legal heir to Henning's estate, to attend the reading of his will. When she mounts the curved staircase of her former home to the room assigned for the reading, Wagner films her with a passing shot that recalls the earlier one of her rushing to inform her father of Elisabeth's death, except that now he shoots her mounting the stairs, not directly through the uprights of the banister, which evoked her fragmentation, but in a wider slightly down shot that enhances her self-assurance, now that she is Countess Thymian Osdorff, having married Nicolas to give herself a new identity, and her elegance, as she is accessorized in a stylish fur-trimmed cape. At the conclusion of the reading, the lawyer kisses her hand, but when Meinert offers to shake hands with her she refuses and walks out, which prompts him to call her a "filthy slut" (intertitle). The lawyer reacts to his slur by slapping Meinert across the face, which Wagner represents in an over-the-shoulder shot, looking over the lawyer to a close-up of Meinert's wide-eyed reaction to the insult. Still within this shot, the lawyer bows to Meinert, from which Wagner cuts to a mid shot of his reaction, at first just standing there, mortified, and after the lawyer has left the room and when, having collected himself and remembered his manners, he bows back.

When she returns to the brothel to announce she gave away her inheritance to Meta and her two children, who are her half-siblings, Count Osdorff, who has been planning to spend her inheritance on renovations to the brothel, commits suicide by leaping out a second-floor window. After the burial, she meets her late husband's uncle, the Elder Count Osdorff (Arnold Korff), who, regretting he repudiated his nephew in life, now resolves to make amends for this to her. She accepts his offer to come to Swinemünde, at the seaside, where she joins the leisured class and makes some important personal connections, like with the Society for Saving Young Girls, where she confronts the old warden of the reformatory and takes Erika into her custody. Old Count Osdorff approves of her actions, observing at the end of the film, in an intertitle, "With a little more love, no one on this earth would ever be lost!" Ironically, Thymian does not find romantic love with anyone. Count Osdorff wins her in the lottery; she marries him as a means to a new identity. Her love for Erika stems from this opportunism, but it is also empathetic, based on their shared experiences in the reformatory, the brothel, and in cinema: as Wagner films Thymian on the staircase twice, he films her and Erika meeting a second time at the reformatory.

In *Westfront 1918: Vier von der Infanterie [Westfront 1918: Four from the Infantry]* (May 1930) Pabst and Wagner developed their collaborative partnership by venturing, with the aid of Charles Métain (assistant cinematographer), K. Brodmerkel (sound photography), and W. L. Bagier Jr. (sound montage) into their first film with synchronized sound and dialogue. *Westfront 1918* begins with an orientation mid wide shot of the facade of a small house in an occupied French village, and of a soldier, carrying a bucket of water, who enters the frame camera left and walks across the field of action to the front door, followed by a reverse-angle mid shot of him standing in the open doorway. The ensuing sequence of mid shots and close-ups shows him with six other soldiers, who flirt with the student soldier's French fiancée, Jacqueline (Jackie Monnier), and cavort with one another as she makes them coffee. The only reference to war, other than the soldiers' uniforms, is an allusion to "nothing but trouble from the Prussians," in reference to Prussian strategizing of German forces. This extended interior scene of frivolity ends suddenly in a blackout accompanied by the sounds of an aerial bomb attack, followed by scenes showing the men taking cover in the cellar, and some love scenes between the student, Otto (Hans Joachim-Möbis), and Jacqueline. Next Wagner films a sequence of exterior scenes, showing soldiers inspecting a nearby bomb site, soldiers and civilians rushing through the streets of the village, and soldiers mobilizing for action, followed by a sequence of battle scenes, notably a high-angle passing shot of soldiers advancing along a trench, a low-angle stationary shot of Karl (Gustav Dissel) and another soldier desperately struggling to hold up a collapsing dug-out room ceiling, and action cut mid shots and close-ups of soldiers panicking over a friendly-fire barrage with collateral damage and sending out a messenger dog to inform the artillery that their bombs are landing short. These and most of the war scenes are most remarkable for Wagner's close-ups for presence and his fluid camera, such as when it pans along a line of men to read their life-and-death facial displays. When the messenger-dog strategy seems to have failed, the Lieutenant (Claus Clausen) asks for a volunteer to carry the message to regimental battle headquarters, and the student steps forward. On the battlefield, he comes across the dead messenger dog, and then proceeds through no-man's-land. When he reaches his destination, he delivers the message and then collapses with exhaustion. Pabst and Wagner's social realism, which gives all the battlefield scenes a documentary style, is here particularly apparent as Wagner films the student in a lingering mid shot as he drinks a glass of water, as if, his mission accomplished, the war has been suspended for him for now. Subsequently, in a dinner scene at headquarters, a server sets an officer's place at table and then removes food from each of the two serving dishes and puts it on a plate that, just before the officer arrives, he hides behind his back: in a passing shot Wagner follows the server as he walks backward out of the officers' mess, having secured a good dinner. This shot blends into the next scene, as the server passes two officers who are addressing the artillery problem over the telephone, and Wagner stays with them. Although his passing shot of the server seems to function merely to transition out of a scene, Wagner picks it up in an exterior passing shot, showing him still backing up until he reaches the student, who is recovering: the server has brought him dinner. Thus the transition is not to the officers, but through them to a beautiful act of kindness. Wagner uses a two-shot to show the student eating ravenously, but after he has had enough food he thanks the servant and exits the frame, when the servant picks up the plate and eats the rest of the meal. This sequence of social-realist shots outside the theater of war evokes the men's bio-signature. Pabst shows another aspect of humanity when Wagner films the student on his return to the front and he passes several soldiers who are constructing wooden crosses as markers for the dead, a reminder that even when war seems suspended for water, food, and acts of humanity, it continues. He asks the carpenters for directions to Bezincourt, his destination, then walks out of the action field. But Wagner keeps his camera focused on the carpenters, as one of them crank starts the engine of a gas-powered rotary saw for cutting lumber for more crosses. Thus he shows that even the act of turning a crank, maybe like turning the crank of a film camera, is a significant human gesture.

At Bezincourt, he visits the house where Jacqueline and a group of billeted soldiers are sleeping, and taps on the window until he awakens her. Wagner films him looking through the window, from her perspective, in a low-angle shot, and her sitting on the edge of the bed to put her shoes on, from his perspective, in a high-angle shot. Their reunion in the doorway, combining a hug and a passionate kiss, resumes the narrative that structures the film and is the antithesis of war. A complementary scene shows Karl on leave at home, where he discovers his wife (Hanna Hoessrich) in bed with the butcher, with whom she is sleeping in exchange for meat for herself and his mother. Although he forgives his wife, Karl willingly returns to the war front. While Karl, the Bavarian (Fritz Kampers), and two other soldiers are out on a special mission to engage the enemy, the French forces, directly, as they mount an attack by crossing the barbed-wire barrier, they happen upon the dead body of Otto, the student, who never made it back after delivering the message. They improvise a quick burial by scraping dirt over his body. In all these scenes Pabst and Wagner show that infidelity and death are significant aspects of humanity, not just love and goodwill. Thus, Jacqueline and Otto's love affair crosses enemy lines, but her collaboration with the enemy and his senseless death have equal actuality. In the major battle that ends the film, Wagner uses a wide passing shot in which the camera is stationary and soldiers move and stop moving and the film as a whole shows the brutality and senselessness of war. The antiwar message is evident mainly in the fate of the protagonists, the four friends of the title. The student and the Bavarian die in battle. The lieutenant goes insane on the battlefield and is hospitalized. Karl also is hospitalized and dies of his wounds. In the final scenes, Wagner focuses on individual hospital patients and their intense physical and psychological suffering.

Less than a month after the release of *Westfront 1918: Vier von der Infanterie*, Pabst and Wagner completed *Skandal um Eva [Scandals About Eva]* (June 1930), their fourth collaboration, second sound film, and first comedy. The film opens with a wide shot of a vacant school hallway in a vanishing-point perspective that leads to a closed door, while a bell rings. A man enters the frame from the background, an intersecting hallway; then a girl enters from a side staircase; the man waves at the child and turns down the stairs out of frame; then the girl down the hall toward the camera and out of frame. The opening shot of the vacant hallway is restored. This establishing shot, which is about a setting and characters (teacher and student) and activities found there, is also about spectatorship, the perception of film and the act of reading the field of vision as a data. In other words, when first one character, then another enters a *mise-en-scène* that spectators can identify as a school hallway, they immediately make a connection between them, that he is a teacher, she a student. Thus spectators exploit the establishing shot to process visual information. (They will later learn that the school is the Margarethem Lyceum.) Now, three more teachers enter the frame, and Wagner follows one of them, panning left and then cutting to a mid shot to show her entering a room and then to a wide shot of a class of girls standing to greet their teacher, a traditional older woman. In a mid shot he shows her take her desk at the front of the classroom, and then he tracks back to take in the students as the teacher orders them to sit down, stand up, sit down, stand up, and finally sit down. Her arbitrary commands are her means of establishing order at the start of the day, but they also suggest that education is about conformity, an idea that becomes further evident when she requests that one of the students read the poem "Belsazar" by Heinrich Heine. When every hand but one goes up, she asks the reluctant child, who has a stammer. Then the principal enters the classroom to conduct an observation. Again the teacher makes her request, but when the girl who started the reading stands up, she calls upon another girl, whose fluent reading suggests she is the best student in the class. Thus, the teacher changes her teaching method to conform to the standard of one higher in authority. The principal then absents himself from the observation to investigate a persistent noise coming from the classroom above. There he finds another teacher, Dr. Eva Rüttgers (Henny Porten), whom he addresses as Fräulein Doktor, who is celebrating with her class of older girls the news of her engagement to be married. The principal takes her aside and scolds her, gently under the happy circumstances, but she charms him by plucking a flower from a bouquet she is holding and putting it in his *boutonnière,* and she ironically asks him to extend her thanks to "Fräulein Belsazar" downstairs. This second classroom scene establishes that this teacher is younger than her downstairs counterpart, and more liberal, innovative, lighthearted, and subversive. Spectators draw these inferences from the *mise-en-scène,* from the actors' performances, primarily, but also from the director and cinematographer's shot selection and camera angles and movement, deductions about scene content the establishing shots of the vacant hallway and the transitional shots into the first classroom have taught them how to make.

Next, Pabst and Wagner take Eva Rüttgers to the workplace of her fiancé, Dr. Kurt Hiller (Oskar Sima), the minister of education in the government, where she has come to say good-bye before she leaves for a two-day field trip with her students. While looking through the congratulatory messages they have received on their engagement, she mistakenly opens a personal letter to him, describing (intercut shot) a four-year-old boy he has, named Gustav, whom he has never seen. Instead of handing over the letter to Kurt, such as with an explanation or apology, she pockets it. When she returns from the field trip, she and Kurt get together and end up discussing the life they will have together. Thinking she is giving him a chance to confide his secret to her, she mentions that she would like their first child to be a boy and to name him Gustav, but his reaction is ambiguous, and dramatically ironic. Spectators are aware of an ambiguity in the letter of which Eva seems unaware: the letter might state that Kurt has a son he knows about but has never seen, or it might inform him for the first time that he has a son. Wagner films this scene with a stationary camera in a mid side-by-side two-shot in which Eva and Kurt move in and out of profile, facing each other and turning away as the conversation goes, fraught with double meanings. Part of the comedy comes not from the shot itself, but from how the actors use it, and from the fact that Wagner tends to film Eva in passing and other moving shots, and in the two-shot she seems trapped with Kurt, specifically in the scandal of what she believes is his past life. Wagner exploits the same mid side-by-side two-shot when Eva discusses the undisclosed child issue with her friend Käthe Haack (Käte Brandt), to whom, after showing her the letter, she confesses, "the funny thing is now I love the criminal twice as much." Käthe does not suggest Kurt may not know he has a child or propose Eva show him the letter.

But a subsequent scene implies that Eva realizes Kurt is unaware he has a child. She pays a visit to the authors of the letter, the boy's custodians, the Schlotterbecks (Claus Clausen and Frigga Braut), in Saxony, in the hope they will release the child into her custody so she can "surprise" Kurt. When Eva asks where Gustav's mother is, Herr Schlotterbeck, who claims to be her brother, tells a dubious story that she is now in a relationship with the local baker. Eva is allowed to see Gustav, who is sleeping: she sits on the bed and, in a close-up, Wagner shows her hand stroking his, suggesting she is already bonding with the child. In an intercut scene, however, of a conversation between him and his undersecretary, who is clearly in his confidence, Kurt mentions his son, as part of his past he might discuss with his wife one day. Wagner then returns to the Schlotterbecks' house, the following morning, where Eva is playing with Gustav and their bond is clear: she calls him by the diminutive form of his name, Gustl, and when she asks, "Tell me again, who am I?" he answers, "*mein mutti*" (my mommy). Her phrase *tell me again*, however, suggests she may have coached him to answer this way, particularly because she departs that morning to take the boy to his father. As they bid the Schlotterbecks goodbye, Gustav excitedly announces, "Now we're going to my daddy." When they return and join Kurt at a symphonic performance in the park, he and everyone present believes the child is hers, particularly because Gustav calls Eva "*mutti*." Kurt is indignant that she has kept this "scandal" a secret. He says, "A decent person explains about such things before the engagement," to which she replies ironically, "You're perfectly right; a decent person explains about such things before the engagement." Wagner films this exchange in a close-up two-shot: she is sitting with the boy in the open backseat of a taxi and Kurt is standing beside the car. In the close-up, they appear to be standing next to each other in the same space. But when the taxi pulls away, she leaves the field of action. Wagner splits a two-shot in half as a visual representation of the split between the two of them. At the park some people openly expressed their disapprobation of Eva as a single mother, but others supported her, questioning what difference it makes. In a subsequent scene, however, the leader of the Cleansing Party delivers a long speech before the city council demanding Eva Rüttgers be dismissed from her teaching position and claims he represents the view of many. In their depictions of public, personal, and bureaucratic responses in the park, between Kurt and Eva, and at city council, Pabst and Wagner are commenting on challenges to the German *zeitgeist* in 1930, when there was a growing backlash to liberal attitudes toward sexuality and public behavior, fascist parties were on the rise, and personal freedoms were under attack. In contrast, Eva is unconcerned about public opinion and enjoys playing the role of Gustav's mother: her scenes with him imply she believes she is his mother.

When Kurt arrives at her place to have a talk with her, Wagner shoots them in another kind of stationary camera two-shot, not side-by-side in a close-up, but sitting across a table from each other, a symbolic barrier in between, in a mid shot, with intercut close-ups of each of them, reaction shots of Kurt, but longer shots for presence of Eva, as she reminisces about her past relationships, which she is inventing on the spot to make him imagine he has a rival and be jealous. Wagner complements this scene with two-shots of Eva and visits from two teachers from the school: Professor Hagen (Paul Henckels), who, after encouraging her to quit her job, confesses to his fear the Cleansing Party will investigate, which includes, many years ago, receiving a small fine for "peeping" through a knothole at the women's bath house; Frau Vulpius (Adele Sandrock), the old teacher from the room below, who confesses to an indiscretion she now fears will come under the scrutiny of the Cleansing Party, that Professor Hagen once kissed her; and Direktor Rorbach (Ludwig Stössel), the school principal, who confesses to having received a fine for the same crime of voyeurism as Professor Hagen. The comedy here is charming, and rich in dramatic irony, particularly when Käthe has to move Professor Hagen into the pantry, to free the dining room so the Direktor will not find him there, and will feel comfortable making his confession; when Eva excuses herself for a moment from the Direktor to put Gustav to bed, and then asks "Uncle" Kurt to tell him a story and watch over him until he falls asleep; and when Hagen, Vulpius, and the Direktor, their confessions made, finally meet, and in a three-shot of them standing and facing the camera, the Direktor concedes that, each of them having failed in their bid to counsel Eva to submit her resignation, they should have worked together; and a massive street protest mounted by the schoolchildren, who rally in support outside Eva's house. After witnessing the students' show of goodwill, which includes a readiness to appeal to the minister of education himself, Hagen, Vulpius, and the Direktor find that, even by pooling their wills, they cannot issue Eva their proposition, so they postpone it until tomorrow. The children's show of solidarity with Rüttgers is Pabst and Wagner's expression of hope in the next generation, in contradistinction, for example, to the *Hitlerjugend* who emerged in the 1930s, which Frau Vulpius, the film's most venerable character, confirms when she says, in admiration of the children's protest, "In my youth, nobody would have dared such a thing."

When Kurt tells Eva he is leaving, she delays him by asking him if he would like to make his confession first, meaning tell her about his child. He pretends not to understand, but his response is interrupted by the doorbell, which Eva goes to answer. While he is waiting, Kurt starts to listen and look through the crack between the double opaque glass doors to the vestibule, which is his crime of voyeurism, where he overhears the voice of the new visitor, speaking German in a Saxon dialect and claiming to be a messenger from Frau Schlotterbeck, who could not come herself, and to have brought Kurt his son, to which Eva replies in disbelief that he has a child. When Kurt, his curiosity piqued, opens the doors, he is shocked to see, in profile, two veiled figures dressed in black, entirely concealed, an adult and a child. In two reverse-angle mid shots for the audience, Wagner reveals Eva to be one of the figures, performing both voices; the other figure is Gustav. In the second, she removes her disguise, opens and closes the door to simulate the Saxon visitor departing, and then leaves the boy to stand alone in the vestibule, for his father to find him. As Kurt disrobes the boy to reveal Gustav, and as his own son, Eva looks on through a crack in the door, which she widens to reveal herself as a spectator, a witness, and an agent of what is happening, and showing that in a liberal society voyeurism is not a crime. In Wagner's closing mid three-shot, Eva, holding Gustav in her arms, hands him over to Kurt, so she might attend to her guests. Their tender kiss before she leaves the room confirms the three-shot is of a family, the engagement is secure, and the marriage will be true. He cuts to a wide shot of this scene, from which Eva exits to

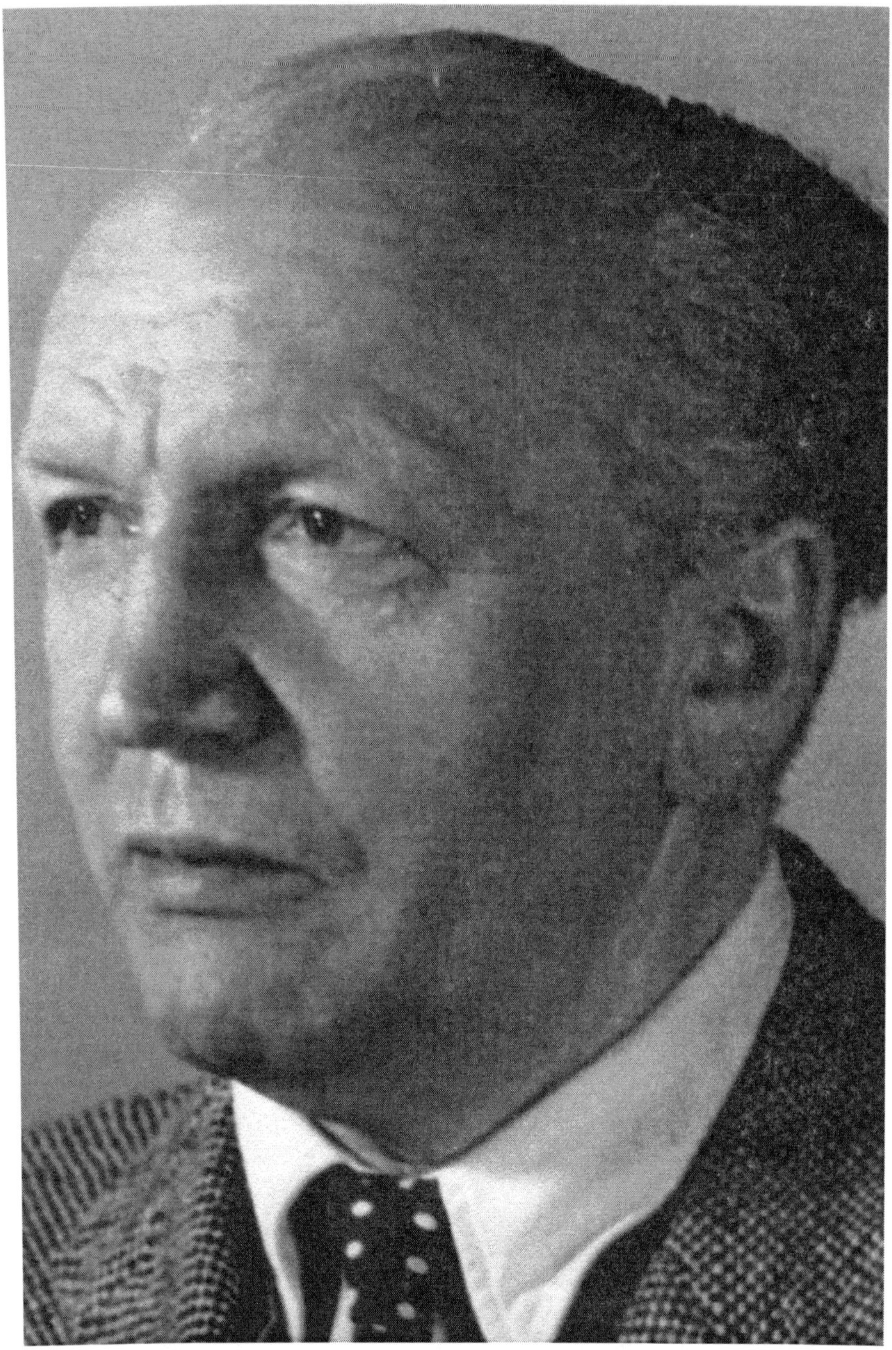

Figure 6.1. Fritz Arno Wagner. Source: Deutsche Kinemathek.

attend to her guests, and in which Kurt carries Gustav to bed, walking toward the camera and out of the frame.

In *Die 3 Groschen-Oper [The 3 Penny Opera]* (1931), which was released eight months after *Skandal um Eva*, Pabst and Wagner exchanged comedy for social satire but continued to address issues of gender and sexual freedom as the tenets of the Weimar Republic were eroding. For example, although the plot centers on the marriage of Mackie Messer to Polly Peachum, it focuses also on his visits to a brothel and his ongoing relationship with his previous lover, Jenny, and his former crime of having sex with minors, two sisters, who, he claims, told him they were thirty. The film is based on Bertolt Brecht and Kurt Weill's musical play *Die Dreigrosschenoper* (February 1928) and John Gay's ballad opera *The Beggar's Opera* (1728). Pabst concurrently directed a francophone version of the film with a French cast, *L'opéra de quat'sous* (June 1931).

The film opens with a wide shot as Mackie Messer[6] (Rudolf Forster) and Jenny (Lotte Lenya) come through a doorway and pause to let two women pedestrians pass, whom Wagner follows in a pan and zoom shot that opens up onto a street; when the women exit the frame by turning into another street, he quickly pans back to Mackie and his companion, now in a mid shot, because they have stepped forward from the doorway onto the pavement. In a single take with a fluid camera he draws attention to the protagonist, but also to his own cinematography. When Mackie breaks free from Jenny's embrace to investigate, Wagner follows him in profile and from behind in a passing shot down the street and around the corner, the path of the women, and then picks him up in a reverse-angle mid shot, looking ahead, and follows this up with a moving mid shot of what he sees, a busy street of strollers and shoppers, and of what he is thinking, as the shot moves around a corner and Mackie follows, to reveal, in a mid shot, a street performer singing Kurt Weill's *Mack the Knife*, about Macheath, Mackie in this film. Wagner pans through the street scene, showing the singer, the hurdy-gurdy player, the audience, passersby, and finally Mackie emerging from the crowd and walking camera-ward out of frame. His next shot is of the two women he and Jenny let pass, who stop to look at a mannequin in a wedding dress in the window of a bridal shop. When Mackie follows and stands beside one of the women, Polly Peachum (Carola Neher), his image appears, a reflection in the glass, as if he is inside the window, standing beside the bride. Then he cuts to a close-up of the woman, who is no longer looking at the mannequin but is now gazing back at him gazing at her in his reflection. When she turns to see who is there, Wagner pans right and tilts up to a close-up of Mackie in profile staring at her, and then cuts to a reverse-angle shot of all three standing at the window: when Mackie leans into the woman, she pulls away from him, and when she and her friend walk away, he pursues them until they agree to accompany him to a dance hall for drinks. Before following them through the doors, he glances back to see Jenny disconsolately looking for him, and instructs the doorman that he is not to be disturbed, and so to bar her from entering. Inside, he finds a dance partner for Polly's friend, and then, through the paned-glass windows of a room divider, Wagner films him saying something that pleases her, which subsequent events reveal to have been a marriage proposal. Rudolf Forster portrays Mackie as a dictatorial character, in the spirit of Brecht's Macheath. But his Mackie resembles other hypnotically imperious figures in contemporaneous German film, such as Rudolf Klein-Rogge's Mabuse in *Dr. Mabuse der Spieler* and Haghi in *Spione*. Over this shot sequence, from the doorway to the shop window and into the dance hall, the camera has scarcely stopped moving, pausing only for close-ups and shots for presence. Thus, Wagner announces his will be a fluid camera in this film.

He confirms the impending marriage, to take place this evening, with a close-up of a mannequin, from which he tracks back to a mid shot that reveals it is undressed, and then he pans left and tilts down to the door of the bridal shop, from which one of Mackie's gang members, in his company of thieves, emerges carrying the wedding dress Polly admired in the window earlier. Whether he stole the dress is unclear, but his gangsters steal all the other furnishings needed to adapt a derelict warehouse on the waterfront for a sumptuous wedding ceremony and banquet, although Mackie calls the arrangement "junk," and the only guests in attendance are some ragtag gangsters, a reluctant minister who performs the ceremony at gunpoint, and the chief of police.

Wagner's fluid camera is not like Karl Freund's in *Der letzte Mann* (1924), a device for displaying an array of innovative cinematographic techniques. Rather, Wagner exploits a fluid camera along with traditional shots and angles. For example, when in providing entertainment at the reception Polly sings a (Kurt Weill) song, he films her mainly in a low-angle wide shot from a stationary camera, letting her performance stand alone and making full use of sound technology. When the chief of London police (Reinhold Schüzel), Mackie's old friend Tiger Brown from "India, the Sudan, in a hundred battles," arrives at the reception late, Wagner films him in an extreme low-angle point-of-view shot at the top of a high stepladder, which when he has to climb it to leave, he describes as "this awful ladder," and Mackie in an extreme high-angle point-of-view shot at the foot of the ladder, exploiting these acute perspectives to emphasize the irony of a meeting of old friends who now find themselves on opposite sides of the law. This legal-criminal divide is triangulated when Tiger is introduced to Polly as the former Miss Peachum, and he deduces, for the benefit of film viewers, she is the daughter of London's beggar king. The pyramidal plot becomes clear later when Peachum (Fritz Rasp) attempts to blackmail Tiger by threatening to ruin him by disrupting the upcoming coronation of the queen with an embarrassing mass showing of the underclass, a flash mob, unless he arrests Mackie Messer.

Pabst initiates the transition to the Peachum section of the plot through a narrator (Ernst Busch), the street singer from earlier, who appears throughout the film as a linking device. Wagner introduces Peachum, "the poorest man in London" and a kind of capitalist human-rights activist for poor people, in a three-quarter profile close-up that, when he tracks back to a mid shot to reveal he is interviewing prospective beggars for his business, remains a close-up because his lower body is concealed behind the desk at which he is sitting. It is a subtle shot transition that suggests the ethical subtlety of his business, which involves the beggars in his network feigning disability and suffering to solicit monetary donations from the public, which they then hand over to him in exchange for his protection, and for sustenance, shelter, and other benefits. Wagner also favors high-angle–low-angle moving transitional shots in the multileveled warehouse setting, in conversations between Mackie (high) and his gangsters (low): as well as being visually impressive, these function in drawing attention to power hierarchies generally and to the class distinctions that inform the conflicts among the criminal, beggar, and police factions.

For example, when Mackie decides to go into hiding during the police investigation Peachum initiated, he places Polly in charge of his organization, which raises the issue of gender among the gangsters, who at first object, "What? A woman?" but later concede, "At a time like this, a woman is the right man." Later, drawing on the knowledge she has gained from her father, she buys a bank, reasoning a legitimate business will be more profitable than safe-cracking. As well as trusting his wife to handle the mob's current plan to stage a big bank robbery, he also promises to scale down his criminal operations in Soho, in deference to patriarchal entitlement, and move his operations in the city of London. Wagner then films him and Polly in a low-angle shot, from behind, climbing one flight of stairs, and in a reverse high-angle shot, facing them, climbing another flight, and then in two high-angle close-ups, one frontal, the other from an oblique angle, as they pause halfway up to discuss his departure, she begs him not to go the "ladies" of Turnbridge, to which he replies equivocally that he loves only her and then mounts the remaining stairs out of frame, leaving her alone in her sadness at the leave-taking, in a perspectivally fascinating acute high-angle shot, which is remarkable also because it lasts for twenty-nine seconds. Then, in a reverse low-angle pan shot, Polly turns to announce to the gangsters that she is in charge now, and she walks slowly down the stairs to confer with them about the bank job, which she promises to execute "in first-class style," as if her intention as leader is to subvert class hierarchy along with the gender hierarchy in the process. In a scene at the brothel, where Mackie goes directly after parting from Polly, Jenny, whom Mrs. Peachum (Valeska Gert) has persuaded to betray him, signals the police that he is present there. Wagner films her looking through an open window down to the police in the street in a low-angle wide shot, the police looking up at her in a high-angle wide shot, her issuing a hand signal in a return low-angle shot, and a reverse-angle interior mid shot of her, from behind, as she closes the window. Here she breaks out into a Kurt Weill song, and partway through, Wagner pans right to reveal that Mackie is watching her, standing tall in profile. As she continues the song, Mackie approaches her, walking toward the camera into a choker close-up in which only half of his face appears in a corner of the frame; when he sits down, his head pulls back into a regular high-angle close-up. Finishing her song, she notices Mackie watching, but after he reminisces with her about old times together she equivocally informs him he has been betrayed yet aids his escape; out on the street he evades capture when he stops to chat with a prostitute and ends up accompanying her home. When Mrs. Peachum reports to her husband that Mackie has escaped, Wagner films them with a similar acute-angle shot combination, he on a mezzanine, looking over a railing, she on the ground floor below, except here he uses mid shots, which are appropriate to a disclosure of information, as opposed to a hand-signaled betrayal, which demands distance. This information prompts Peachum to follow through on his threat to Tiger Brown by disrupting the coronation, which the beggars eventually do by carry placards with messages such as "This is military despotism," which is a sign also of changing times in Germany, the shift of the *zeitgeist* toward fascism. Once he has initiated the beggars' protest against the coronation, Peachum is unable to stop. Once Tiger Brown has issued the order for police to use violent force in attacking the beggars, he finds he cannot rescind it. Consequently, the beggars and police clash, and the coronation parade is disrupted. Pabst, along with Brecht, is alluding to the present day, when fascist political movements may be taking the Weimar Republic to a point of no return.

In the end Mackie, Tiger Brown, and Peachum, criminals, police, and beggars, join forces at the bank: Mackie because he realizes it is easier to steal from the public at large through a legal institution than by cracking small safes one at a time; Tiger Brown because he will be fired because of his mishandling of policing the coronation, and there is no safer place to land than with an old friend; and Peachum because he failed to control a mob protest and protect the most vulnerable members of a class-structured society, and his safest landing is with his daughter. In addition, both Brown and Peachum believe they will be able to apply their expertise to the bank. The hope for the Weimar Republic is in collaboration and working against the forces of division.

In their final collaboration, *Kameradschaft [Comradeship]* (November 1931), Pabst and Wagner drew upon some of the current themes of two recent films: from *Westfront 1918: Vier von der Infanterie*, in which the German soldier Otto and the French woman Yvette, who billets German soldiers, transcend their political and cultural differences to fall in love, they developed the theme of French-German cooperation in the face of disaster; and from *Die 3 Groschen-Oper* they developed the theme of collective action against the forces that divide society along gender, class, and political lines. *Kameradschaft*, which is set in the present and concerns a group of Germans who intervene to help rescue French laborers trapped in a coal mine disaster, is based on a historical event, a mine explosion that occurred on March 10, 1906, in Courrières, near the French-German border, and in which more than 1,200 miners died after inhaling toxic pit gases, and some German miners from Westphalia came to join with French teams in their rescue efforts.

The film begins with a shot of two boys playing marbles, with the goal of rolling them into a hole in the ground. Wagner then cuts to a scene at the border control, in which a German customs official informs two German young men that France is not admitting any unemployed people into the country, yet with a shrug lets them through anyway, since they have border passes. But at the French customs they, along with many other German job seekers, are refused entry.

Wagner cuts back to the boys, who now are in a disagreement over a game: one boy draws a line in the dirt with his shoe and dares the other to cross this "border" to retrieve the marble in dispute. Wagner films the job seekers returning, dejected, to the German side and complaining about French protectionism, and he intercuts sweeping pan and track shots of a massive industrial site, the French coal mine, the Thibaut Mine where the men had hoped to find work, initially external shots, as if from the German side of the border, and then internal shots of the work site, of rail lines, cable and pulley systems, smokestacks, and, further inside, workers operating heavy machinery and workers getting on a massive elevator, and finally workers in the mine shaft drilling coal and shoveling it onto rail carts. After a worker complains of a strong odor, two managers enter the shaft to investigate, ruling out a gas emission and attributing the smell to fires burning for several weeks, and prohibiting the use of dynamite blasting until a new brick retaining wall can be constructed on Sunday. Here Wagner intercuts a shot of three bricklayers building the wall. He also takes a long panning track shot along the mine shaft showing heavy planks of wood smoldering, and then exploits a 360-degree panoramic shot of the entire underground space. All these are establishing shots providing essential visual data about the workplace and the working conditions and also foreshadowing the mine disaster. But the factory and mine scenes in particular, in that they provide a facsimile of raw documentary footage of a heavy industry, exploit the representational conventions of the *Neue Sachlichkeit* aesthetics of verism and realism, which focused on industrial sites and machinery as cultural artifacts and, when painted, photographed, or filmed, as works of art. That Wagner recorded this documentary footage directly after filming Mackie Messer and Peachum's industrial warehouse headquarters as theatrical settings points to his versatility as a cinematographer and his collaboration with Pabst as very eclectic and adaptable. This contrast between documentary and theatrical industrial footage is clear in *Kameradschaft* in the next part, which is set in a French dance hall and shows three Germans buying tickets, getting their hands stamped, about which one of them observes, "like meat," and sitting down for a beer. Prominent on the dance floor are two young lovers, Émile (Georges Charlia) and Françoise (Andrée Ducret), he a miner, she a Parisienne on the last day of her vacation to visit her mother. When they sit down, in preparation to leave, the Germans approach her, and one of them asks her to dance. When she politely refuses, because she is tired and must depart in the morning, the German takes offense, believing she is prejudiced against Germans, and boasts he can dance as well as any Frenchman. The men return to their table, and the couple leave the dance hall. Outside, Émile and Françoise overhear engineers discussing the mine fire and the progress of firewall construction, which agitates her and prompts her to say she thinks she could not have a relationship with a man down the mines.

The film follows these characters next as Françoise prepares to catch a train: she talks to her mother, says good-bye to her brother, Jean (Daniel Mendaille), and to Émile, who has come to pick up Jean for work. On their way to the mine, they meet up with many other mine workers streaming out of the town. Next Pabst and

Wagner insert more footage of activities in the mine shaft, particularly the work of an engineer inspecting the new firewall, and of massive flames suddenly breaking through the wall and erupting through the shafts. Wagner films three fleeing workers in a close-up backtracking shot, and the dozens of other workers in wide shots as they run toward the camera. Then he intercuts shots of Françoise on the platform, saying good-bye to her mother, boarding the train, then, through the window noticing smoke billowing up from the mine and everyone at the station running across the tracks and down the platforms to the mine, and finally opening the door and attempting to jump off the moving train, until she is pulled back in by other passengers. Subsequently, Wagner films numerous scenes in the town as people learn of the disaster and rush through the streets to the mine, including many intercut shots, notably of an old retired miner (Alex Bernard), the grandfather of Georges (Pierre-Louis), a boy miner, one of the first to notice the smell of smoke in the mine yesterday, of a shopkeeper, an uncredited actor, standing outside his hat shop, looking into the distance to see what is wrong, and of a group of Germans at the border crossing, observing that something is amiss at the mine. Subsequently, he shoots miners' family members pushing up against the iron gates of the mine, wanting to get in, with police trying to hold them back from the other side. When they have to open the gate to admit an ambulance, they quickly shut it again against the mass of bodies. Wagner follows the ambulance into the mine superstructure, and as the car makes a turn, his shot picks up the figure of the old miner, who has found his way into the compound by hiding on the running board. Even though the rescue workers tell him he ought not to be there, he is in the way, he ignores them and steals a lantern, determined to conduct his own search for his grandson.

Wagner now cuts to several scenes revealing the German reaction, where mine workers, led by Wittkopp (Ernst Busch), one of the job seekers turned back from the French border at the start of the film, form a volunteer team to help in the French rescue effort, which their employer supports by providing the volunteers with their own mine's rescue equipment. As the volunteers depart, standing on the deck of a panel truck, Wittkopp's wife, Anna (Elisabeth Wendt), with their young child in hand, walks alongside the truck, angry her husband is going on the mission. The trucking shot of the woman with the child in tow, a mid high-angle shot, is intriguing, because spectators do not know until Wagner cuts to a reverse-angle shot of Wittkopp, in which he addresses the woman as "Anna," precisely what her connection is with the volunteers, specifically who is looking at her from the high angle. Wagner cuts back to Anna, this time in a close-up, as she gazes up at her husband then bends to pick up the child and, in a reverse-angle shot, lifts it up to Wittkopp to hold for a moment. As the vehicle pulls away, Wagner films the mother and child in the receding perspective of a backtracking trucking shot. These characters matter as visual content in the film, not just because they round out the figure of Wittkopp. Thus, Pabst and Wagner endeavor to personalize the main characters in *Kameradschaft*, who, given the documentary focus on events, tend to be rather flat, by detailing them with names, families, stories, and emotions, but they also valorize some of the secondary characters, such as Anna, by assigning them camera time and with vital shots whenever possible. Here they counterpoint Anna with Françoise, whom in the next scene Wagner films in a wide shot as she runs along a dirt road and toward the camera, which is positioned at an intersection. As Françoise nears the corner, Wagner pans right in an arc, until a right-turning truck enters the frame and completes the camera's arc, and then pulls over to the roadside, to wait for the woman. Thus, Anna, a minor character, is part of a protracted trucking shot, and Françoise, a major character, is part of a perfectly executed pan shot, and a kind of trucking shot. Similarly, the three German characters who appear in the dance-hall scenes at the beginning of the film figure quite prominently in the rescue operation scenes, because they have a backstory. Thus Pabst and Wagner attempt to personalize the rescue operation: the old miner finds his grandson, Émile rescues Françoise's brother Jean, and so on. The interaction between documentary footage and Wagner's innovative shot execution is typical in *Kameradschaft*, but it is also characteristic of his and Pabst's collaborative partnership over six films, 1927–1931, in which they developed a distinctive visual syntax comprising social realism, *Neue Sachlichkeit*, and objective mobile cameras for documentary and subjective fluid cameras for character development and visuals.

Wagner shoots the rescue operation both underground and aboveground. Thus, underground the old miner, Émile, and the three Germans represent the larger rescue team, and aboveground teams of rescue workers, including the German volunteers, are seen entering massive industrial elevators and making the descent eight hundred meters to the bottom, and also gatherings of family members, including Françoise and her mother, outside the gates awaiting news, ranging from high-angle pan shots over heads of the crowds to close-ups for presence, notably track-in close-ups of faces visible through the bars of the gate, which is a symbolic barrier separating peoples and cultures, like the international border, the firewall, and mine shaft. For example, when Émile, with Jean, first encounters a gas-masked German in the tunnels, he has a traumatic reaction, a flashback to his World War One experience, which Wagner represents in an insert close-engagement battle scene, which he begins and ends with clever match dissolves, notably in which Émile engages in hand-to-hand combat with a German soldier on the battlefield, which dissolves into his matching life-and-death struggle with Wittkopp in the mine. Thus, Pabst and Wagner represent the postwar lingering cultural conflict between Germans and French and how the German rescue effort is also a humanitarian gesture toward intercultural reconciliation. One scene in which the German rescuers devise a battering ram to break through a brick firewall to open a passage to the surface and to safety is symbolic of this rapprochement. Another scene contributes to this theme, but in the mode of social realism rather than symbolism: the three German rescuers, from the dance hall, along with the old miner and his grandson, all of them trapped in the engine room, happen to make telephone contact with French rescuers at the surface but find they also have to break through a barrier, not of a firewall but of the language difference, and one of them, after trying to communicate in German, manages to extemporize enough French to identify their number and location, five men in the engine room, tunnel eight. Pabst and Wagner depict their rescue primarily through sound: first, using wrenches and other heavy tools, the Germans tap on pipes and walls to signal their location to the rescuers, who are tapping signals on the other side; then when they realize they have been found and will likely be saved, the Germans and the French miner and his grandson express their joy spontaneously, each group in their own language, with no barriers to communication and with no cultural differences. On the surface, waiting for the truck to arrive to take him back to Germany, Kasper (Alexander Granach) boasts about how he was able to communicate in French over the phone with the rescue director, as at the beginning of the film he boasts he can dance as well as any Frenchman. Similarly, Émile delivers a speech in which he acknowledges Kasper, his rescuer, as his comrade.

NOTES

1. Christiane Mückenberger, "Die Liebe der Jeanne Ney," in *Deutsche Spielfilme von den Anfängen bis 1933: Ein Film Führer*, ed. Günther Dahlke and Günter Karl, 160 (Berlin: Henschelverlag Kunst und Gesellschaft, 1988).
2. Although the film does not show Thymian giving sexual consent to Meinert, she never refers to their intercourse subsequently, whether as nonconsensual, as sexual assault, or otherwise.
3. Rudolf Arnheim, *Film als Kunst: Mit einem Vorwort zur Neuausgabe* (Munich: Hanser Verlag, 1974), 103.
4. Maria Makela, "New Women, New Men, New Objectivity," in *New Objectivity: Modern German Art in the Weimar Republic 1919–1933*, ed. Stephanie Barron and Sabine Eckmann, 54 (New York: Prestel, Los Angeles: Los Angeles County Museum of Art, 2015).
5. Lynette Roth, "New Identities: Type and Portraiture," in *New Objectivity: Modern German Art in the Weimar Republic 1919–1933*, ed. Stephanie Barron and Sabine Eckmann, 260, 262 (New York: Prestel, Los Angeles: Los Angeles County Museum of Art, 2015).
6. The German *Mackie Messer* roughly translates as "Mack the Knife."

7

Günther Rittau, Günther Krampf, Optical Language, and Autonomous Collaborative Agency

In addition to serving as assistant cinematographer, under Carl Hoffmann, on Fritz Lang's *Die Nibelungen: Siegfried* (1924) and *Die Nibelungen: Kriemhilds Rache* (1924), Günther Rittau (1893–1971) has the distinction of having been principal cinematographer on two revolutionary films, each in its own way an icon of film history, Lang's dystopian fantasy *Metropolis* (1927) and Josef von Sternberg's immorality play *Der blaue Engel* (1930). Yet, hardly a director of photography in the manner of Fritz Arno Wagner, Rittau, who starting in 1919 had trained as a documentary filmmaker, learned camera operation mainly on his own initiative because of his interest in special-effects shots. The technical expertise he acquired enabled him to make a transition, in 1921, from documentary filmmaking to feature-film cinematography. That he landed *Siegfried*, which was only his fourth feature as cinematographer, and *Metropolis*, just his eighth, in what was essentially a self-regulated career indicates the singularity of his cinematic vision, which major directors found very attractive, notably German film pioneer Joe May, who had been instrumental in starting Lang's career and enlisted Rittau as cocinematographer, with Konstantin Irmen-Tschet, on his film *Heimkehr* (1928), and as principal cinematographer on *Asphalt* (1929), a breakthrough film of the Weimar period. Despite his appointments with leading directors like Lang, May, and Sternberg, Rittau more typically worked with several minor German directors of light comedy, romance, action, and dramatic pictures, notably Hans Schwarz, with whom he shot nine films, 1929–1931. Although he would appear, therefore, to have had his main ongoing professional relationships with directors like Schwarz, in fact he had complex and productive collaborative relationships with Lang, May, and Sternberg, and specifically with their film projects, in which respect his collaborations with them were occasional or project-specific. Like Karl Freund, Rittau was the kind of cinematographer that collaborated with several directors, as distinguished from working recurrently with one director, in the manner

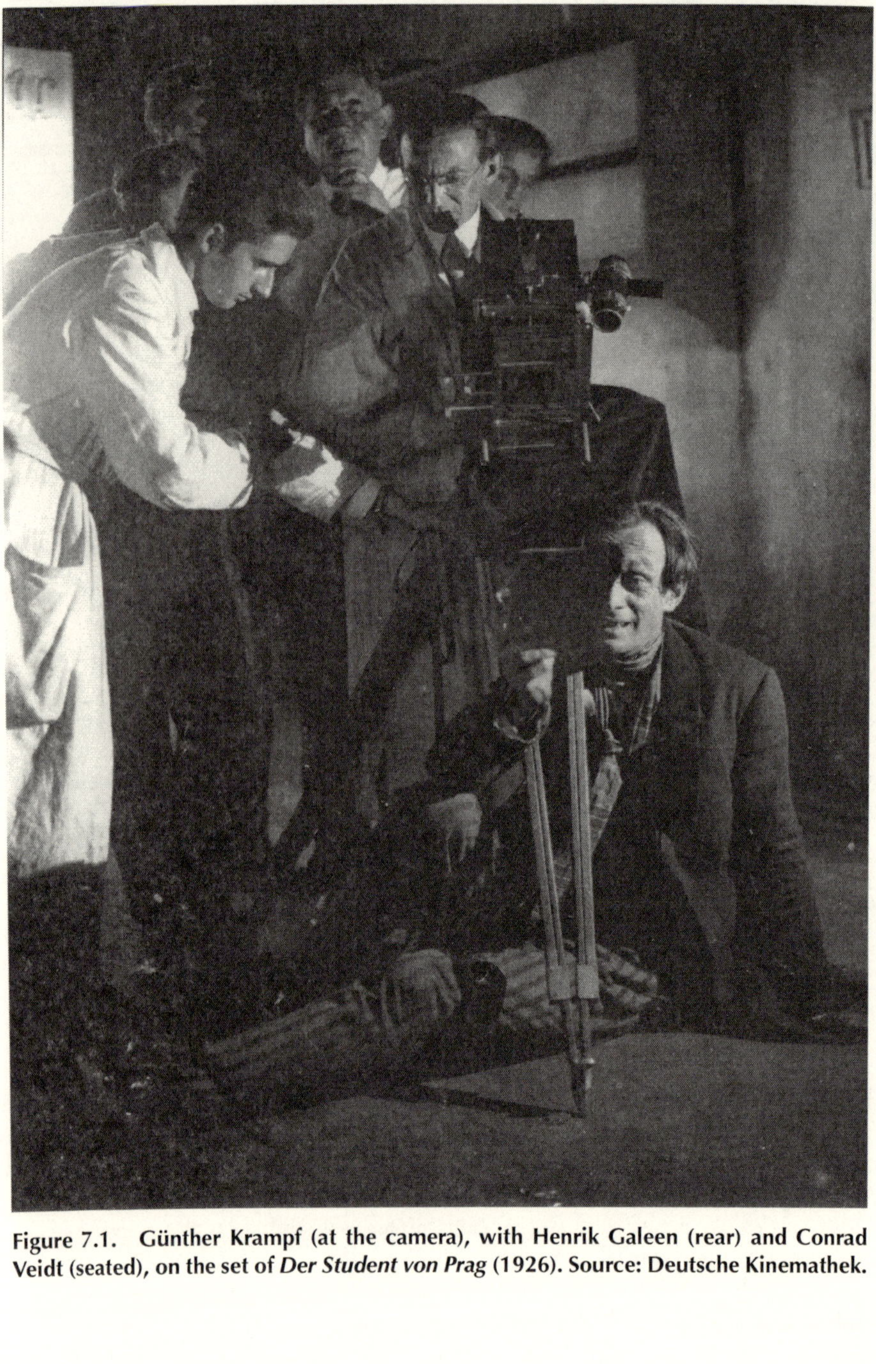

Figure 7.1. Günther Krampf (at the camera), with Henrik Galeen (rear) and Conrad Veidt (seated), on the set of *Der Student von Prag* (1926). Source: Deutsche Kinemathek.

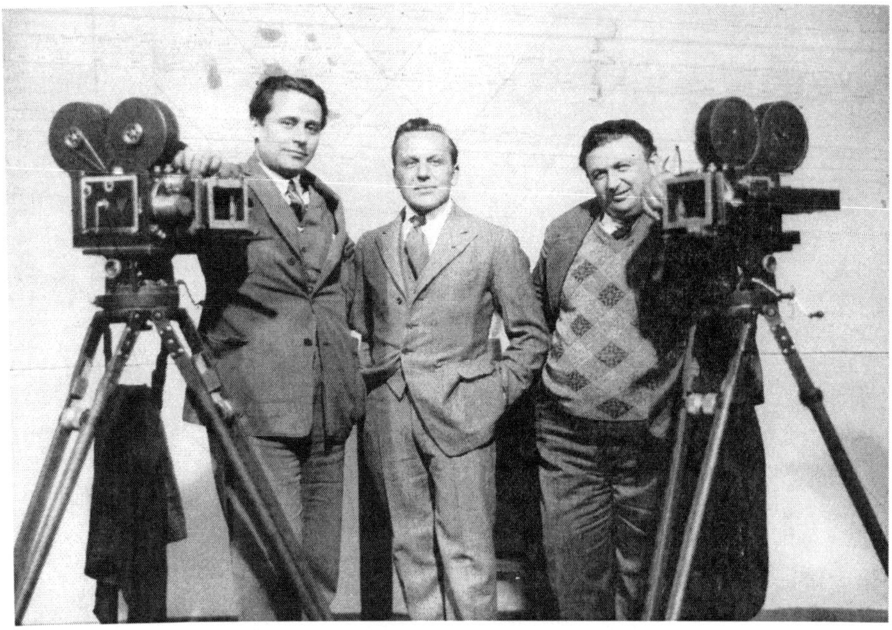

Figure 7.2. ***Left to right:*** **Günther Rittau, Charles Rosher, and Karl Freund. Source: Deutsche Kinemathek.**

of Theodor Sparkuhl with Ernst Lubitsch or Fritz Arno Wagner with Murnau, Lang, and Pabst. Yet because of his expertise as a camera operator and what they came to recognize as his special skills in project management, Lang, May, and Sternberg sometimes targeted Günther Rittau for their most demanding projects, knowing he spoke the same optical language as they, the highly specialized discourse of lenses, lighting, and other camera and optical dynamics. They trusted Rittau, more than other cinematographers, to satisfy the special optical requirements and representation demands of their most aesthetically ambitious projects.

Günther Krampf (1899–1950), equally adept at shooting in Naturalistic and Expressionist styles, was one of the most versatile cinematographers of the Weimar Period. He had served a brief apprenticeship, notably as assistant cinematographer, with Werner Brandes, on Joe May's *Die Legende von der heiligen Simplicia* (1920) and principal cinematographer on Hanna Hemming's *Am roten Kliff* (1921), when at age twenty-two he became assistant cinematographer to Fritz Arno Wagner on F. W. Murnau's *Nosferatu, eine Symphonie des Grauens* (1922). Here he learned the Expressionist visual grammar and camera techniques from Wagner, but, more important to his career, he also was able to observe the collaborative filmmaking model of Murnau and Wagner in action. He perfected his Expressionist style working as assistant cinematographer to Hans Androschin and under Robert Wiene's direction in *Orlacs*

Hände (1924) and *Pension Groonen* (1925). His preferred cinematographic style was Naturalism, however, which he pursued to acquire his personal stamp as principal cinematographer, assisted by Erich Nitzschmann, in Henrik Galeen's *Der Student von Prag* (1926), and a series of films he shot, 1926–1928, with directors such as Fritz Wendhausen, Johannes Guter, Fritz Freisler, Kurt Bernhardt, Josef Berger, Uwe Jens Krafft, and Alexander Lang, a record that attracted the interest of G. W. Pabst, who hired him for *Die Büchse der Pandora* (1929), believing he and Krampf shared an artistic vision about the revelation of character through unconventional and experimental camera angles and shot selections. Their collaboration produced a classic of silent film, established Louise Brooks as a lead actress in Germany, and marked the transition from Expressionism to Naturalism as the aesthetic marker in Weimar visual culture. Although he made only this one film with Pabst, it set the trajectory of his art, much as *Nosferatu* had established the foundation earlier, and it prepared him professionally for his transition to shooting films in Britain, where he relocated in 1931 to spend the rest of career. Working with both Murnau and Pabst, Krampf showed his mastery of two vastly different visual grammars and aesthetic configurations. Yet each director elected to go with other cinematographers on their next films, Murnau with Fritz Arno Wagner and Karl Freund on *Der brennende Acker* (1922), Pabst with Wagner and Sepp Allgeier on *Tagebuch einer Verlorenen* (1929). For Krampf, more than other Weimar cinematographers, collaboration meant working passionately with a director when an occasion arose for them to make one perfect film, rather than over a series of films. His specialist code as a cinematographer, thus, pertained to his autonomous agency in collaborative paradigms.

Günther Rittau was born on August 6, 1893, in Köningshutte, Germany (now Chorzów, Poland). He attended the Technical University, Berlin, where he specialized in photochemistry, a field in which he went to work, after serving as a sergeant in the Pioneers in the First World War. In 1918 producer Erich Pommer hired him as a technical manager to develop scientific films in the culture department at Decla-Bioscop and, in 1922, when it purchased Decla, at Universum Film AG (Ufa). From there he worked as an assistant cinematographer to Friedrich Paulmann on Eugen Illés's *Der Eisenbahnkönig: Mensch und Mammon* (1921) and *Der Eisenbahnkönig: Lauernder Tod* (1921), to Carl Hoffmann on Fritz Wendhausen's *Der Steinerne Reiter* (1923), Fritz Lang's *Die Nibelungen: Siegfried* (1924), and *Die Nibelungen: Kriemhilds Rache* (1924), and to Karl Freund on Lang's *Metropolis* (1927). Notably, on Lang's films Rittau drew on his technical expertise to execute double-exposure special effects, to film traveling matte and Schüfftan process mirror footage, and to film miniature models integrated into standard sets.

Günther Krampf was born on February 8, c. 1899, in Vienna, Austria-Hungary. He attended the Technical College, Vienna, and apprenticed as a camera operator there, and in Berlin and Florence. He was assistant cinematographer to Werner Brandes on Joe May's *Der Legende von der heilingen Simplicia* (1920), principal cinematographer on Erik Lund's *Die Geschichte von Barak Johnson* (1921) and three episodes of the serial *Die Geschichte des grauen Hauses* (1921), and Hannah Henning's *Am roten Kliff* (1921), assistant cinematographer to Fritz Arno Wagner on F. W. Murnau's *Nosferatu* (1921), and principal cinematographer, assisted by Erich Nitzschmann, on Henrik Galeen's *Der Student von Prag* (1926). He was an expert lighting camera operator in Expressionist and fantasy films, but his reputation as a cinematographer, notably in Pabst's *Die Büchse der Pandora* (1929), was for naturalistic and realist aesthetics.

When they came together to collaborate on *Asphalt* (March 1929), Joe May had already directed sixty-three films from 1917, whereas Günther Rittau was in effect still apprenticing, having been principal cinematographer on only one film, Aleksandr Razumnyj's *Fürst oder Clown* (January 1928), and an assistant on eleven other films, notably the film he made previous to *Asphalt*, May's *Heimkehr* (August 29, 1928), on which he worked with cinematographer Konstantin Irmen-Tschet. It was May who, on the basis of his work on *Heimkehr*, promoted Rittau from effectively a camera operator to a cinematographer and a director of photography.

Asphalt's front credits run over a montage of scenes showing a team of road builders pounding down a freshly laid surface of asphalt. The *noir* imagery and even the raw look of the footage immediately distinguish the film as a modern realist police thriller, in contradistinction, for example, to stylized *policiers* like Lang's *Dr. Mabuse der Spieler* (1922) and *Spione* (1928). The montage cuts into the opening scene of a Berlin street, in which Rittau tracks the camera in the opposite direction of cars, trolleys, and pedestrians, films vehicles moving toward the camera, executes a high-angle close-up of pedestrians' shoes and a montage of intersecting streams of traffic, thus initiating the film's urban pace, and concludes the sequence with a mid shot of a bird in a cage, from which he pans and tilts across the room until his shot rests on a man, retired Sergeant Major Holk (Albert Steinrück), slouching in a chair at the breakfast table and smoking a cigar, and then over to Frau Holk (Else Heller), sitting with good posture and mouthing the words as she reads the newspaper. Then he films their son, Sergeant Albert Holk (Gustav Frölich), in the hallway, putting on the cap to his police uniform, and then entering the dining room. Rittau now cuts back to the shot of the caged bird, which dissolves into another urban montage of circulating traffic, that comes to focus on a gloved hand, from which he tracks back to reveal Sergeant Holk, on duty directing traffic. The entire shot sequence, from the opening montage of workers through the two montages of traffic flow, and finally to Sergeant Holk, is orientational, establishing the urban and domestic settings and visual fields, but in its inventive and diverse syntax it seems to announce also, Rittau has arrived as a cinematographer.

Lotte H. Eisner interprets this sequence as evidence of May's overreaching for the avant-garde:

> In the end, all that Joe May's pretentions (sic) to avant-garde artistry and his skilful imitation lead to is an image which is highly symbolic of his own insignificance. A bird sits in its cage, and four superimposed trams bear down on it from the four corners of the screen. Here May seems to have been outclassed by techniques whose potency exceeded his own small talent.[1]

But as Eisner acknowledges, *Asphalt* "is a cogent example of the use that Ufa commercial films made of the results of artistic research."[2] Although it is clearly not avant-garde in the abstract nonrepresentational style of noncommercial German absolute films, such as Hans Richter's *Rhythmus 21* (1921) and *Vormittagsspuk* (1928) and Viking Eggeling's *Symphonie Diagonale* (1924), *Asphalt* is avant-garde in three respects: it is experimental, exploring new modes of representation and perspectival experience; it addresses the spatial and temporal properties of film images; and its subjective camera provides fluid impressions of the physical environment. In these respects, *Asphalt* is typical of the visual experiments German filmmakers were conducting at the time. For example, Rittau's impressionistic shots of bustling street scenes, in direct contrast to the Expressionist evocations of films earlier in the decade, are remarkably similar to Werner Brandes's establishing shots in E. A. Dupont's *Piccadilly* (1929), in which he "bleeds the blue lights into a blue darkness to create the amorphous ambiance of Piccadilly Circus, and a semiotically complex field of vision . . . in footage that resembles a film negative, through which omnibuses, automobiles, and pedestrians progress without disrupting it."[3] Thus, May the director was not "outclassed" by Rittau the cinematographer's techniques: he was simply doing what other German filmmakers were doing then, collaborating with his cinematographer to push the technical boundaries of camera management, image making, storytelling, and spectatorship.

The first event, the impetus of the plot, is a minor collision that knocks a convertible onto Sergeant Holk's traffic island. Holk first observes the driver, the shot suggesting his personal interest in her, then examines her driver's license, and finally sends her on her way, but not before propping up a large teddy bear in the back seat, as if he were correcting his father's poor posture. Afterward, Rittau turns back to his evocative shots of traffic streams and other street activities. Not all his shots are subjective in this manner, however. For example, in a pan shot he follows a line of people crossing the street, then people walking in a perpendicular line along the sidewalk, and ends the horizontal movement by focusing on the pole of a street lamp. Next he moves the camera vertically, not in a tilt shot, by moving the camera's head, but in a kind of early crane shot, to the two lights on top, which, in a match dissolve, are illuminated, indicating the temporal transition from afternoon to evening, or simply "later." That May and Rittau exploited such an experimental shot[4] merely to signify the passage of time proclaims that *Asphalt* is a modern film with an innovative visual syntax, and a self-reflexive film, concerned with its own status as film. Its modernity is evident also in its street scenes as signifying spaces. For instance, in a high-angle shot he films a large group of people gathered outside the Bemberg Strümpfe window display, in which a model demonstrates putting on a stocking. Rittau first shoots the model over the shoulder, with the affluent onlookers in the background, and then he pulls the camera close to shoot through the glass and pan among the various facial displays of the men and women watching her, voyeuristically, and then, in the film's second event, on the faces of a team of pickpockets as they mark a woman, jostle her, slip a hand into her purse, and make their escape. This event is important for two reasons: it establishes the undercurrent of crime in the city, an important element of the plot, and it sets up a later shot, in which, after tracking pedestrians along a busy sidewalk, he films a jeweler with a customer through the I. Bergen jewelry store window, and then cuts to a mid shot inside, where the customer, who is scrutinizing diamonds, is now identifiable as the driver from the traffic accident earlier, Else Kramer (Betty Amann). In a sequence of close-ups of the jeweler and customer and mid shots of other employees clearly fascinating by her beauty and elegance, Rittau shows how she manages to distract him from his work, so that, when one diamond falls to the floor, he does not notice, and she picks it up surreptitiously with the tip of her parasol, equipped with a hollow designed for this kind of shoplifting. Thus, the window shot of the pickpockets sets up this scene, introduced with a window shot, of another act of theft. Immediately after she leaves the shop, however, another jeweler notices one of the diamonds is missing. When they confront her down the street and she declines their polite request to return to the shop, a crowd forms around them, which Albert Holk, who has just finished his shift directing traffic, comes to investigate. He orders her to return to the shop, where, behind closed doors, she is strip-searched and, in her absence, he looks through her purse, fur muff, and other accessories, and eventually her parasol, from which he extracts the stolen diamond. Although the jeweler who was enamored with her pleads with Sergeant Holk to let her go, he insists on pursuing the matter according to the letter of the law. At the end of their cab ride to the police station, however, she pleads imminent destitution and, in tears, begs for mercy. Finally, she persuades him to permit her at least to return to her flat to collect her identification papers, where Rittau exploits tilt and pan combination shots to evoke his point of view as Holk performs a cursory search of her apartment and a close-up of the parasol, which he is still holding, from which he tilts down to his boots, tapping and shuffling his feet in impatience. In the scene in which Else achieves her goal in returning to the apartment, by seducing Holk, this close-up of his boots is fetishized in another close-up: dressed only in a negligee, she leaps onto his body to prevent him from leaving and, as she wraps her legs around him to hold on and engages him in a passionate kiss, Rittau cuts to another object close-up of his boots, specifically her bare foot as she rubs it erotically up and down the leg of a boot.

Subsequent scenes, as well as showing her romantic relationship to a gangster who poses as Consul-General Langen (Hans Adalbert Schlettow), currently in Paris, but is on his way to Berlin, reveal that sometime during their sexual encounter Else managed to steal Holk's police identity card. Her sending it back to him by messenger along with a gift of a box of cigars is the reason for their second encounter, when he pays her a visit to return the gift. Although he arrives angry, because he blames her for his having neglected his professional duty for the first time, he leaves happy, because Else is sincerely attracted to him and he responds to her accordingly. After their lovemaking, they fall asleep. Rittau signifies the passage of time as earlier in the film, by cutting to a wide shot down a city street in a vanishing-point perspective at the precise moment the street lights come on, first one side, and a moment later the other. As a temporal signal, the shot is superfluous, but in its formal balance, that of a painting, it is beautiful in itself, and it is self-reflexive, as a complementary allusion to the earlier shot of street lights coming on. This evocation of beauty and change proves to be ironic in the scenes that follow, in which Else and Holk discuss the possibility of an ongoing relationship; she confides to him that she is a professional thief, not someone in need; her gangster partner, just back from Paris, bursts in on them; and he and Holk have a violent brawl in which Holk strikes him fatally with an andiron. After fleeing the scene, he informs his parents, in a sequestering close-up, "I have killed someone." His father dresses in his old police uniform to arrest his son and take him in to the police station. Rittau's shot of them negotiating the apartment building's elaborate staircase is visually arresting: they walk, the father leading with authority, the son behind, hanging his head in shame, from the front door down one flight of stairs toward the camera, then across the field of vision, right to left, down another flight, then away from the camera down the next flight, then across the vision field left to right, and so on, the figures diminishing in size as they recede in the field. After Else, accompanied by Frau Holk, arrives at Holk's interrogation at the police station, to testify Holk killed the man in self-defense and in support to offer her confession, from her theft at the jewelry store and including their relationship. As a consequence of her evidence, Holk is released, and Else is taken into custody. Breaking away from his parents to run to embrace her before she is taken away, he promises to wait for her. The film ends with an over-the-shoulder wide shot through a barred door window, as Holk watches Else go, which corresponds to the two earlier window shots, at Bemberg Strümpfe and I. Bergen, both crime scenes. Here, the shot has to do not with crime but with two people's reparations for their crimes, because as a shot/reverse-shot lens the window between them implies they both are behind bars.

Günther Rittau's second major collaboration was with Austrian-born American director Josef von Sternberg on *Der blaue Engel* [The Blue Angel] (1930), Ufa's first film with synchronized sound and dialogue.[5] Sternberg hired Rittau as principal cinematographer on the project because of his exceptional visualization of the relationship of an ingenuous man and a sophisticated woman in *Asphalt.* Under the direction of Sternberg, a more ambitious and resolute filmmaker than Joe May, and with the assistance of cinematographer Hans Schneeberger, Rittau filmed the emotionally and psychologically complex relationship of Professor Immanuel Rath (Emil Jannings) and Rosa Frölich, known as Lola Lola (Marlene Dietrich), a *chanteuse* at The Blue Angel nightclub, with a less ostentatiously self-reflexive shot repertoire than in *Asphalt. Der blaue Engel* opens not with the flourish of a montage but with three simple and efficient establishing shots: a wide shot of a street scene in which merchants are preparing for the start of their business day; a mid wide shot of one shopkeeper, who pauses after pitching a bucket of wash water onto her front window, inside of which is mounted a large advertising poster of Lola Lola, to mimic her provocative pose, standing with legs apart and hands on the hips, and thus evoke the vamp as an object of desire to women as well as men; and a close-up of the door sign of "Prof. Dr. Rath," which dissolves into a low-angle wide shot up the stairs leading to his flat, where his housekeeper (Ilse Fürstenberg) is seen sending her daughter off to school, which dissolves into an interior shot of her puttering around as she prepares Professor Rath's breakfast.

Entering the scene through his bedroom door, Professor Rath immediately distinguishes himself as decorous and fastidious in his dress and comportment, and quite distracted in temperament. He interrupts his coffee, for example, to whistle a signal to his caged songbird. Investigating when the bird fails to respond, he discovers the bird is dead. When he appeals to his servant about what to do about it, she simply takes the corpse from his hand and disposes of it in the woodstove. Whereas in *Asphalt*, May uses the trope of the caged bird to symbolize Sergeant Holk's confinement in his parents' home and the order of the law, Sternberg uses it to evoke the disparity between her pragmatic and his fanciful response to unforeseen events and encounters. Rittau now shifts his shot sequence from the domestic to the institutional environment of the preparatory school, a classroom where the adolescent boys awaiting Rath's arrival are engaged in two activities: most of them are looking at provocative photographs of Lola Lola and one student is defacing the cover of Rath's notebook, altering his name to *unrath* ("filth"). Later his secret fascination with these Lola Lola cards inspires Rath to satisfy his curiosity by attending and then obsessing over her show and engaging her in a submissive-dominant romantic relationship. On his second visit to her dressing room, when he catches three of his students in her cellar and expels them from the club, they yell at him through the window, "*unrath*." Similarly, in Pabst's *Tagebuch einer Verlorenen* (1929) Fritz Arno Wagner films Meinert in the pharmacy, looking at "filthy" pictures moments before he seduces Thymian. In each case, women's images prompt the imagination to form a heteronormative behavioral model that the male spectator, in his capacity as a voyeur, attempts to act out, beyond imagination, dominantly or submissively. Professor Rath is first exposed to an image of Lola Lola during a class composition exercise when he confiscates it from a boy gazing at it instead of his paper, scolds him, and files it in his notebook. But this scene is as notable for its exploitation of sound as for its focus on an image, when he opens and closes a window in conjunction with his confiscation of the boy's picture.

> Towards the end of the scene, Professor Rath has set his students a writing task and turns to open a window. As he does so, we hear the sound of the school choir singing in an adjacent building. This continues over the several shots that follow: the teacher watches his students, cleans his glasses, discovers a student looking at a picture of Lola (the nightclub singer), and finally shuts the window again, but in a different set-up from the one in which it was opened, the sound of the choir is then cut off and the dialogue continues. Plainly, the off-screen choir was instructed to begin singing at the point when the window was opened then, after a period of time, which was predetermined to allow all the action to be included, the window would be closed again and the singing stopped.[6]

The main function of the window in the scene is twofold: first, it is an opportunity for Sternberg and Rittau to demonstrate their facility with new recording technology in synchronizing sound, dialogue, and images; second, it highlights one of the film's most salient themes, all stemming from Professor Rath's failure to hear the birdsong in his first scene, that of distraction and Lola Lola as the object of distraction that diverts the student's attention from his writing assignment here and diverts Rath's attention from his duties and responsibilities, from his life, as a teacher. But the opening and closing of the window serve the additional function of invoking symmetry: in opening and closing doors and windows, in Professor Rath's impersonations of a rooster crowing at his wedding celebration and in his final performance on the stage of The Blue Angel, in double mirror images, in the spotlight Lola Lola shines on Rath in the audience in his first appearance at the nightclub and the flashlight that the school janitor shines on his dead body at the end of the film, and also in camera-shot pairings, most remarkably in this climactic scene.

After school Professor Rath catches his best student with Lola Lola pictures. He orders him to accompany him to his home, where, in the process of reprimanding him, he learns about the popular fascination with the performer. He impounds the photographs and, when the boy has gone, scrutinizes them. The images of Lola Lola are less erotic than Rath's act of gazing at them. In one famous shot, Rittau films Rath in a close-up, holding up three of the photographs as if inspecting his hand in a game of cards, and blowing on the cards, once, then again and again, and looking around in fear the housekeeper might enter anytime and expose him, and the camera cuts to a reverse-angle close-up of the photos themselves, one of which has been modified to make Lola Lola appear to wear an *appliqué* grass skirt that blows up to disclose her stocking tops and garter. From this animate image, Rittau introduces a form dissolve from the photographic image to Lola Lola herself, on stage, whom he films in a wide shot singing a drinking song with a women's chorus, as an establishing performance for Rath's arrival, out of curiosity or for research or surveillance purposes, the latter possibility of which is confirmed in intercut shots of his students, backstage with Lola Lola and in the audience, who flee when they spot their teacher there, and of him when he recognizes one student and pursues him backstage, and particularly on this chase when he stumbles into her dressing room and, wryly, she asks him if he is the police.

> Sternberg had made only one sound film before *Der Blaue Engel* . . . but his work in the American studios had taught him how to use sound more effectively than the German film-makers of his day. An example to note is the play on doors, from which snatches of laughter or singing escape as soon as they are opened.[7]

Earlier, he mistakenly opens the door to the women's dressing room, immediately closing it when he realizes his impropriety, and out of which a man in a clown's costume appears to investigate the intrusion. The subsequent three-shot of Roth backed by two mirror images of him foreshadows how his image as a professor will change, as if Lola Lola is blowing on his *appliqué* of respectability, when he becomes her *homme passionné* and eventually replaces the clown in her act. Rittau exploits the shot again on his second visit to her dressing room when Lola Lola mischievously blows into the face powder he is holding for her, blowing onto his *appliqué*, as it were, and he goes to look into the double mirror to clean himself off. Their relationship develops in her dressing room through his voyeurism as she changes costumes in his presence and her accommodation of him as a pedantic curiosity but also, in a sense, a courageous man, a repressed man who is not put off by her unrepressed Weimar Republic New Woman personality. "In principle, [Gustav Friedrich] Hartlaub identified New Objectivity positively with Weimar democracy and a new conception of the individual, embodied (for example) by the emancipated New Woman."[8] Maria Makela also notes, "One of Berlin's most famous nightclubs, the Eldorado catered specifically to transsexuals and transvestites and featured performances by Marlene Dietrich, Claire Waldoff, and the Weintraub Syncopators."[9] In contrast to his first class, which Rittau shot from the back of the room, his class the morning after his encounter with New Woman Lola Lola is initially a reverse-angle over-the-shoulder shot of him sitting at his desk at the front of the room: the shot evokes not so much his perspective of his students as their perspective of him, informed by their knowledge of his nightclub antics, evident in their quizzical facial displays, which close-ups of several students confirm. The reverse-angle shot also suggests Roth has surrendered his point of view as a figure of privilege and authority.

Rittau evokes this shift in his point of view positively in filming Lola Lola's performance of "Ich Bin von Kopf bis Fuss auf Liebe Eingestellt" ("Falling in Love Again"), which Rath watches from a side gallery. She dedicates the performance to him and sings it to him directly, which Rittau films not in alternating high-angle and low-angle shots but in alternating close-ups of her looking right and up at him, and him looking directly down at her, which suggest both their connection through the shot sequence and their disconnection through the shots making it up. In the morning, their connection is confirmed in her bedroom at the club, where he has spent the night, when he awakes to birdsong and Lola Lola says, "Morgen, Immanuel," addressing him by name, he hears the school bell and has to run, yet she insists on kissing him before he leaves.

The principal, responding to a ruckus in his classroom, where the students have posted lewd caricatures of him on the blackboard, fires Professor Rath because of the scandal he has brought to the school. Rittau shoots him alone and despondent at the front of the empty classroom, the caricatures behind him, the camera positioned three rows from the front, then he tracks back slowly past three more rows, to expand his absurd environment, and lastly he fades to black. That he turns to Lola Lola, proposes marriage to her, and she accepts seems compensation enough for the disgrace of losing his job, but his role as her attendant in the variety theater, he comes to realize slowly, is demeaning. Initially, his task is to distribute her photo postcards to the audience after her shows, to help her put on her stockings, and to ensure her curling iron is hot. After a passage of four years, 1925–1929, Rath has taken the place of the clown in Lola Lola's act. Rittau films him in a mirror shot for indirect presence, disconsolately applying his greasepaint, bulbous nose, frizzy wig, and high collar. That her bill-matter now gives him credit—"Persönliches Auftreten von

Professor Immanuel Rath" ("With a Personal Appearance by Professor Immanuel Rath")—seems only to taint his academic name through self-caricature.

Professor Rath reaches a crisis when he becomes jealous of Lola Lola because of a younger performer's open expressions of affection for her, when he grows disaffected with his role as a clown, in which he is the support in a double act with Magician Kiepert (Kurt Gerron), and when, catatonic, he appears to be suffering from depression, melancholy, or a similar condition. In his performance with the magician, he is both the subject of his sleights of hand and the object of his derision. Rittau films their act, like all the variety acts, with a stationary camera from the point of view of the audience, but as Rath is exploited as the laughingstock and grows aware of Lola Lola and her admirer together backstage, his shot only segregates him and evokes pathos. He suffers an emotional breakdown on stage, attacks Lola Lola and her admirer, and frightens the other cast members, and in the end he has to be restrained with a straitjacket to pacify him. Released from his restraints, he dresses in his old cape and hat and sneaks out of the theater in the middle of the night, as Lola Lola is onstage singing "Ich Bin von Kopf bis Fuss auf Liebe Eingestellt," this time, pathetically, not to him. He walks through the city to his old school. Rittau films the climax in an Expressionist mode, as Professor Rath approaches the front of the building preceded by his distended shadow, the distorted image corresponding to his double mirror images earlier, emphasizing how far he has fallen from academic excellence and respectability. When the janitor lets him in, he goes directly to his old classroom, his path through the dark setting lighted only by the flashlight beam of the janitor, who is following him, and who arrives to find him dead at his desk, his hands gripping it in rigor mortis. In a slow track-back shot identical to the one with which he filmed Professor Rath in the empty classroom after he was dismissed from his job, Rittau now shows him alone in death, and he reveals that his tragedy was not his misplaced affection for Lola Lola or the failure of his imagination, but rather his fall from academic grace. He appears to have died of natural causes, possibly of old age, exhaustion, and a broken heart, but cinematographically Professor Rath dies in a slow track back and fade to black. The association between the two track-back shots in the classroom functions in three principal ways: first, the shot pairing confirms the idea that Rath dies because, when he lost his teaching position in his pursuit of an unattainable woman, he lost his purpose in life; second, in a self-reflexive manner, the back-track shot shows how Rath has backtracked on the teaching profession and backtracked to his old desk as a kind of bier; and third, it contributes to the film's overall formal balance in that it functions structurally by invoking the tidy closure of symmetry.

While the two empty-classroom tracking shots are structurally symmetrical, they are distinct in their execution. In the first instance, when Professor Rath stands at his desk, where Rittau films him in a wide shot in three-quarter profile, as he starts to track back, from the third row of desks, Rath slowly sits down, his hands in repose on the desktop, and then when the shot reaches the sixth and last row of desks it fades to black. In the second instance, Rittau starts the back-track shot from the first row of desks and slowly draws it back to the last row, when the shot fades to black. In both shots, Rittau uses an objective camera to depersonalize his subject, but in each the parameters of spectatorship, how spectators perceive the subject, are different. In this respect, both of Rittau's shots appear to expand the frame when they track back. In the first instance, the shot of Rath after he is dismissed, spectatorship is experiential as well as perceptual: spectators, aware the camera is moving backward and the frame appears to be expanding, becoming less limiting, know that Rath is not "delimited," his meaning determined by the frame. In the second instance, the shot of Rath's corpse, however, his body is a formal element in the expanding frame, ephemeral like his mirror images earlier and the shadows that precede his arrival at the school, which the interplay of the darkened room and the beam of light on his face now emphasize: spectators, aware the camera is withdrawing because the protagonist is dead and the film is ending, perceive Professor Rath with feeling, but primarily as the image of a body lying on the image of a desk, receding in the vision field and soon to vanish in a fade-out.

After assisting Fritz Arno Wagner on F. W. Murnau's *Nosferatu, eine Symphonie des Grauens* (1922), his work uncredited, Günther Krampf was cocinematographer on four films: with Erich Waschneck on Ludwig Berger's *Ein Glas Wasser* (February 1923); with Sepp Allgeier on Arnold Fanck and Holger-Madsen's *Pomperley's Kampf mit dem Schneeschuch* (March 1923); and with Otto Baecker on Johannes Guter's *Die Prinzessin Suwarin* (April 1923) and *Der verlorene Schuh* (December 1923). He was cinematographer, with the assistance of Hans Androschin, on Robert Wiene's *Orlacs Hände [The Hands of Orlac]* (September 1924), a film that launched his transition to principal cinematographer in the late 1920s. The horror film begins with a mid shot of Yvonne Orlac (Alexandra Sorina) lying in bed, reading a letter from her husband, expressing the love he will show her when he returns tomorrow, followed by an intercut shot of a newspaper article with the headline "Letztes Konzert von Paul Orlac" ("Paul Orlac's Final Concert"), and cross-cuts to Orlac (Conrad Veidt), performing in concert on the piano and to a close-up of his hands at the keyboard. Krampf completes the establishing sequence with parallel and action cuts to scenes of Yvonne preparing for her husband's arrival, his train passing through the countryside, a switchman mistakenly changing the tracks, two trains traveling in opposite directions on the same track, railway officials receiving dire news over the telegraph, and Yvonne arriving by chauffeured car at the train station, reacting in the film's first expression of horror when she encounters panicked travelers crying, "UN ACCIDENT" and "à MONTGERON," dialogue that, typical of mid-1920s film, appears as intertitles superimposed over live action, and then running outside to tell her chauffeur to drive her directly to Montgeron.

Krampf films several nighttime location road scenes representing their drive to Montgeron, in trucking shots taken from vehicles following or alongside their car. The crash site itself comprises a theatrical set of wreckage depicting train cars piled up, with many passengers and rescuers passing through the field of view simulating the rescue. After Yvonne arrives at the site with her chauffeur, she is quickly able to locate Paul in his numbered car, and confirm he is alive, much as in Lang's *Spione* (1928), Sonja manages to locate No. 326 alive in the train wreckage. Such astonishing independent rescues are typical of German thriller, adventure, and horror films. As in *Spione*, No. 326 is able to walk away without injury from a terrible crash, so in *Orlacs Hände* Yvonne manages to complete her rescue of Paul by instructing rescuers to place the stretcher bearing his body in the backseat of her convertible and then by driving him home, as if she has met his train, picked him up, and brought him home, but in a highly unconventional way. This sense of unreality is clearly in the horror mode, which the following divergent cut to an unrelated scene, to the unexpected, seems to confirm. A servant wakes Doctor Serral (Hans Homma), a medical researcher with his own private hospital, at 5:30 a.m. to remind him a prisoner named Vasseur is to be executed in half an hour, and then his body will be brought to the clinic. Then, as the professor is getting dressed, the servant informs him about the train wreck and that Paul Orlac was a casualty. Krampf cuts to a study, where the doctor meets Yvonne, who faints into his arms, then to an external overhead shot of other servants carrying Orlac's stretcher from the limousine into the clinic, then back to the study, where, hearing the professor's prognosis for her husband, she begs him to save his hands, which are his life, and finally to an internal overhead shot, presumably from the doctor's perspective through the window, of the hearse from which attendants are removing Vasseur's covered corpse on a stretcher, and finally a return shot of the study, where Yvonne again makes her desperate plea and the professor promises her he will try, although he does not tell her about the hand transplant, or that the donor hands have come from the body of the executed murderer, Vasseur. Dr. Serral performs the transplant surgery because he is enamored with Yvonne, as her subsequent letter, in which she tries to break off the relationship, confirms, and he believes it will be a means of permanently removing his rival for her affection, Paul Orlac. Subsequent scenes provide the rationale for this bizarre cross-cut sequence: although Orlac survives his injuries, which included a fractured skull, from which he recovers, they leave him with severely disfigured hands, an inability to pursue his career as a concert pianist, and a deep depression. When Paul has recovered enough to have his head bandages removed, Yvonne is able to be with him alone. Krampf films their love scene with a formal balance, showing him supine and her on her knees beside the bed and leaning over to kiss him, to reestablish their relationship, but also to disrupt it as Paul, with his hand grafts still heavily bandaged, has his first vision of Vasseur, appearing to him, head and shoulders, first in a small insert traveling matte on the back wall of the room, and then in an intercut full-screen close-up of him, a vision about which he comments to Yvonne, in an intertitle, "There . . . that head . . . isn't he looking at my hands?" Later in his recovery, when Paul asks what secret lies beneath his bandaged hands, the doctor promises to reveal it to him now, but only by removing the dressings, without disclosing anything about the transplant or the donor. Krampf films Paul reacting to this disclosure, sitting up in bed, in an iris mid shot in profile, in his first attempt to use his hands by tentatively pantomiming the playing of a piano keyboard on his raised knees.

In his performance of this scene Conrad Veidt is remarkable, looking at his hands as if they are recognizable as his own, yet also alien to him as a human organism. In the next scene Krampf shoots him in profile again, asleep in his hospital bed and having a nightmare, which he represents in the standard consciousness and supernatural technique of a double-exposure sequence, occupying most of the field of view, comprising a gathering of mist, the giant disembodied head of Vasseur, and his arm and clenched fist cutting a diagonal across the screen and thrusting at Paul's head. When Paul awakes in terror, spectators know the images he has dreamed, but they may be equally aware they have seen special effects derivative of silent film. Dismissing the nightmare, he tries to return to sleep but finds a note lying on his bedcover: "Your hands couldn't be saved . . . Dr. Serral gave you different hands . . . the hands of the executed robber and murderer Vasseur" (intercut shot). Paul now looks at his hands with horror, as if he would like to sever himself from them. Alarmed, he gets out bed and faints, dropping to the floor. In a scene the following morning he confers with Dr. Serral, asking him directly, in a paraphrase of the note, if he has "the hands of the robber and murderer Vasseur." Now Krampf films them in a mid shot, front-lit against a black backdrop, side by side in three-quarter profile, while Serral slowly rotates his body into a full profile, indicating he prefers not to answer, and Orlac lowers his body, as if he is bending his knees, until only his head is visible in the frame, indicating that Serral's silence has confirmed his worst fear, where the scene ends in a hard-edge wipe to black.

Despite several location shots, *Orlacs Hände* is primarily a *kammerspielfilm*, in the style of Murnau's *Der letzte Mann* (1924), notable for its spare interior sets, psychological mimesis, and demonstrative facial displays, such as Yvonne's wide-eyed astonishment and Paul's pendent arms and rigid hands. These qualities are most dramatically evident in the scene in which Paul, having returned home from the hospital, goes to the music room to try to play the piano again. Filming him in a mid shot and in profile and three-quarter profile, Krampf shows him embrace the grand piano using the complete span of his arms, before sitting on the stool, opening the lid, and, in a tight close-up, playing. Standing in the background, Yvonne cringes at the sounds Paul is producing. Krampf cuts to a close-up of him, devastated by the implications of his failure, and of his hands as he pulls them away from the keyboard, and then back to a profile mid shot of him, leaning back on the stool, his arms limp at his side, his hands rigid, as Yvonne crosses on stiff legs from the background to the midground of the piano, to embrace him from behind. His sequence of close-up two-shots of Yvonne and Paul front-lit against a black backdrop, at this moment of profound dismay and terror, is impressive visual content, particularly when Paul reaches to take his wife's face in his hands, but has to stop himself, afraid of what he might do.

His doubts about his capability through Vasseur's hands prompts him to purchase the back issue of the newspaper with an account of his murder of an old moneylender by stabbing him through the heart; Paul learns Vasseur was convicted on fingerprint evidence taken from the knife handle, with its distinctive X-symbol engraving. In

Krampf's *kammerspielfilm* shots of Paul, he is alone in a nondescript basement bar except for the server, who leans against a wall. In the black surroundings the only details to stand out are the server's crisp white apron and Orlac's deathly white face. These shots are among the most stylish of the film, particularly one unusual close-up shot of Paul after he drops the newspaper, devastated by the article: Krampf films the tight close-up as a three-quarter profile shot that appears high angle, because the subject is tilting his head down. When he starts to raise his head slightly, Krampf cuts to a wide shot that reveals his entire torso hunched over the table, with the server still visible in the background: here he reverses the ground focus from sharp in the foreground (Paul) and soft in the background (server) to soft in the foreground and sharp in the background, and then soft in the background as well. Here he dissolves into a soft extreme overhead close-up of a hand wielding a knife in a stabbing action.

Returning from this shot to the bar, Krampf reveals it to have been Paul's imagination, a portent. Back at home, Paul is horrified to find Vasseur's knife, with the X handle, stuck in the front door. Krampf cuts to a mid shot of the door; Paul enters the frame in a diagonal line to the center midground, leaning forward, more than walking, to the door, reaching to extract the knife, and then holding it openly against his chest, rather than hiding it with the newspaper inside his overcoat. Later he conceals the knife under the lid of the grand piano, unaware a maid was watching him. Krampf then takes several fine horror shots of him, frontal close-ups in which Paul holds up his hands like so much tissue and bone he would like to reject, murder weapons impossible to conceal. Later, alone in the bedroom, he crosses the space in a diagonal line midground left to foreground right, with his arms extended in front of him as if murderous hands are drawing him. His diagonal trajectory in this scene, combined with his trajectory when he reaches to remove the knife from the door, from foreground right to midground left, traces an X across the visual field. Krampf shows him entering the music room hands first, then, instead of filming the rest of his body crossing the threshold, cuts to show him in the room. He walks, arms extended, to the piano, where he lifts the lid, removes the knife, and, holding it up like a devotional object, focusing on it hypnotically, he walks back to the doorway, where he is enveloped in the darkness. A subsequent scene reveals him holding the knife over his head and making repeated downward stabbing gestures, as Yvonne listens from the other side of the door. When she enters the room, he conceals the knife behind his back and warns her not to come near him and to go immediately. Alone he withdraws the knife and, in a raw mid shot with a black backdrop, he makes as if to stab his left hand, but stops himself, slowly lowers the knife until it is outside the frame, when Krampf cuts to a wide shot that shows his body collapse, as if losing his murderous impulse, and drop to the floor in self-reproach and exhaustion. In the following scene, the figure of Vasseur, with no special-effects modification, shows up to confront the Orlacs' maid, whom he has been coercing to do his bidding to manipulate Paul: when she timidly refuses to cooperate with him further, he utters a cryptic threat to go to Paul's father unless she "seduce his hands" (intertitle). When she goes to Paul, she approaches him on her knees and kisses his hand, to which he responds by placing it and then the other hand tenderly on her head: although at first receptive to his show of affection, she begs him to stop, noting that his are the hands of a murderer. Her response implies that her seduction of his hands is not sensual but incriminatory.

> Paul, unable to caress or even approach his wife, is quite happily able to do so to the maid. The latter, by virtue of her social position, is of course figured as socially inferior to Paul—a fact emphasized by the spatial positioning, as she kneels and crawls towards him. With the maid, then, Paul feels secure in his superiority, and is thus able to react towards her "as a man."[10]

In alarm, Paul flees the house and runs to the private hospital, where he begs Dr. Serral to amputate his hands, to which he replies only with the aphorism that the head governs the hands. Meanwhile, Yvonne pays a secret visit to Paul's father (Fritz Stassny) to seek his monetary help, because, with no concert-performance income, their creditors are threatening to seize their house. Orlac bluntly refuses, explaining that he hates his son and would welcome their destitution: the truculence he shows here provides a mitigating circumstance, along with the volition of a murderer's hands, when in the horrific climax of *Orlacs Hände* Mr. Orlac is bludgeoned to death. When Yvonne returns home empty-handed, the maid, carrying out Vasseur's demands, advises her that Paul himself should now visit his father, precisely to give him an opportunity to surmise he may murder him. Later, he wanders through his father's house, only to discover his dead body, with the X-signed knife through his heart. When he brings the police to the crime scene, the inspector, kneeling over the corpse, immediately identifies the murder weapon as Vasseur's, and when he goes on to identify his fingerprints on the knife handle and table top and his handwriting in an incriminating letter, used to lure Mr. Orlac's servant away from the house, Paul begins to think he must be the murderer, despite the fact he cannot remember committing murder. Slipping away from the investigation scene, he encounters Vasseur in the street, and after a moment follows him into a bar. There Krampf films them in the camera left midground of a wide shot, small figures sitting on opposite sides of a table, brightly lit from an overhead fixture. Then he cuts to a mid shot of them in profile and a frontal close-up of Vasseur as, reminding Paul he is his father's heir, he demands he bring one million francs by tomorrow, payment for his hands. Then Vasseur shows his metal prosthetic hands and forearms, which he has concealed beneath his cloak in all his previous scenes, and, uncovering a deep neck scar, he attributes his survival of his execution by the guillotine to one of Dr. Serral's assistants, who reattached his severed head. He threatens to incriminate Paul as the murderer, should he fail to deliver the money on time. Krampf's close-up two-shot of them emphasizes their profound power differential: Vasseur stands menacingly, camera right, half in the frame, shot from behind, in one-quarter profile; Paul cowers in abject fear, leaning back severely from his sitting position, his body a diagonal line that extends from the center of the frame toward the background left corner. Because Vasseur is looking down at Paul, in a diagonal line that crisscrosses the line of Paul's body, the shot forms an X design and it resembles a high-angle over-the-shoulder shot, though it is actually eye level. Later, after conferring with Yvonne, and for the first time in the film, he takes her advice to tell the prosecutor the whole story; they embrace and kiss, also for the first time, in Krampf's two-shot. When, now in an undercover operation, Paul meets Vasseur at the arranged time and place, the police swoop in to make an arrest, and in the process expose Vasseur as the alias of Nera (Fritz Kortner), Dr. Serral's onetime assistant and "one of the most talented crooks in the world" (intertitle). The inspector exposes his prosthetic hands and neck scar as fake, and Yvonne arrives with the maid, who confesses Nera, a friend of Vasseur, made plaster casts of his hands, which he used to make rubber gloves bearing his fingerprints to stage Paul's crime. She reveals that Nera killed Mr. Orlac, and he also murdered the moneylender and framed Vasseur, who was an innocent victim. This testimony frees Paul Orlac of the murderous impulse he imagines he has.

> And, regardless of the "innocence" or the "new" hands he has been given, Paul's identity, after all, has been irrevocably changed: his body is still a hybrid one, his hands—symbols of his livelihood and of his will—are still those of another man. In other words, we might still read the final shot as an expression of some level of continued aggression towards Yvonne.[11]

In the end, however, knowing his donor hands are from an innocent man, framed and falsely accused, a man whose circumstances are very much like his own, and therefore freed from an evil imperative, Paul can at least continue with his recovery. But the film's final shot is not "an expression of some level of continued aggression towards Yvonne." Krampf's close-up two-shot of their embrace, enclosed in an iris mask, he in profile, she in three-quarter profile, he holding her head and touching her hair, she resting her head on his chest, and finally their heads nestled together with his hands exposed to the camera, confirms the romantic desire for her that he expresses in the letter than opens the film, in which he writes, "I will embrace you . . . my hands will glide over your hair . . . and I will feel your body beneath my hands" (intercut shot). This final embrace, because it recalls how he embraces his piano when he first returns home from the hospital, may even suggest that he will recover some degree of an executant bond with the piano, even if that means only playing as badly as Vasseur played or as well as he might have learned to play. Outside the horror genre, a transplant recipient of this type, having overcome rejection, as Paul surely does, could, through recovery and therapy, come to accept the donor hands as his own. That he is able to manipulate his hands to "glide" them over Yvonne's hair and feel her body, in the manner, his letter suggests, that he would before the accident, seems to indicate he may now have the manual dexterity to learn to play the piano again and perform professionally.

Throughout *Orlacs Hände*, exploiting an exclusively stationary camera, Günther Krampf takes advantage of the maximally spare *kammerspielfilm* settings of the Orlac mansion, in which each of the massive, darkly lit rooms is typically furnished with a single piece of furniture, such as a bed, a piano, or a settee positioned in the background, and no adornments other than doors and door frames on the halftone stone walls. Within each vast space, Krampf alternates between wide shots of characters on their marks in the background and midground, where they are discernible in the "whiteness" of their exposed skin, mainly faces and hands, and mid shots of gestural displays and close-ups of facial displays for presence, usually tortured, grotesque, affective ones. Although his camera is immobile, Krampf creates the illusion of camera movement through passing shots as he films the characters, who in their silent-film dramaturgy have to move about within the vast interior spaces for wide shots, and for close-ups they must adopt frightful facial displays like bulging eyes. The implied camera movement of the passing shot is prominent in the film's many images of Orlac's hands, which Conrad Veidt holds out in front of his body as they seem to lead him through space, which he holds up before his eyes in disbelief, with which he embraces the knife, the piano, the maid's head, and finally Yvonne's head, and which he conceals behind his back, when he refuses to take Dr. Serral's extended hand in his terrified reaction at the murder site when the police verify Vasseur's fingerprints. Krampf's cinematography in *Orlacs Hände* is stark and spare, in the *kammerspielfilm* and the horror modes, in which Robert Wiene was adept. Their collaboration was inventive but not avant-garde.

After completing *Orlacs Hände*, Günther Krampf worked as cocinematographer, with Hans Androschin, on Robert Wiene's *Pension Groonen* (1925). He went on to shoot fourteen more films, 1925–1928, and to distinguish himself as a principal cinematographer when he came to collaborate with G. W. Pabst on *Die Büchse der Pandora [Pandora's Box]* (1929), although in the front credits he is identified as Kameramann ("cameraman"). The film opens with a delightful shot sequence that serves to establish the character of Lulu (Louise Brooks) and how she interacts very openly with other people. Krampf shows her coming out of her flat to pay her gas bill but first to pour the meter reader a glass of liqueur; then, hearing a knock at the outer door, the meter man opens it to find someone who appears to be a beggar demanding an alms. When he prepares to give the man some change, Lulu addresses him by name, as Schigolch (Carl Goetz), and immediately fetches him off the doorstep and takes him into her apartment, where, delighted to be together, they dance in circles and again embrace as she sits on his lap: Krampf evokes their moment of affection and intimacy in a series of warm mid and close-up two-shots. She also indulges him, to take money from her purse and drink liqueur straight from the bottle, because he is in need but also because he is her first dance instructor. Today he has come to offer her, through his associate Rodrigo Quast (Krafft-Raschig), who, as he points out, is waiting on the sidewalk, an opportunity in variety theater to perform again as a dancer. Krampf shows Lulu and Schigolch looking down at Quast from the balcony, in a high-angle mid shot that, by appearing to shorten the physical distance of a conventional wide shot, suggests that they are looking at him intently. When Lulu notices her romantic partner, Dr. Ludwig Schön (Fritz Kortner), a newspaper editor, approaching (off camera), she asks Schigolch to crouch down and hide on the balcony while she receives him. Although they greet as lovers, he does not kiss her and seems inexplicably remote, until he informs her he is getting married, to which, as a free woman, she embraces him and replies, "You won't kiss me just because you're getting married?" (intertitle). He explains he and she are the object of public gossip because of their scandalous relationship, which he informs her now they must break off. When her barking dog, which also happens to be on the balcony, exposes Schigolch hiding there, Lulu simply introduces him to Dr. Schön as her first patron, implying he is her current patron, which gives him an excuse to leave, and which prompts Schigolch to signal down to Quast it is convenient for him to come up now.

Subsequent scenes establish: (1) Dr. Schön is engaged to another much younger woman, Charlotte Marie Adelaide von Zarnikov (Daisy D'Ora), whose father disapproves of her choice because of the scandal around him; (2) Dr. Schön's son, Alwa (Franz Lederer), is a composer for the musical theater, who, along with his artistic director, Countess Anna Geschwitz (Alice Roberts), a free-spirited modern woman, is a friend of Lulu; (3) in Dr. Schön's opinion, Lulu is of a lower social and moral class than Charlotte and Countess Anna, so less fit for marriage; and (4) Dr. Schön recommends that Alwa cast Lulu as a dancer in his variety show, which he does. All these characters appear in the wings at the premiere of Alwa's show, where Krampf films the backstage bustle with a fluid camera and multiple cuts between brief shots, all amplified with the movement of the actors, managers, stagehands, and guests, particularly as it is fragmented by stagehands moving scenery and large properties through the crowd as the acts change on stage. This shot sequence is joyous and celebratory, as is particularly evident when a pulley-operated platform bearing three artificial trees drops down, stagehands immediately remove the trees, and then the stage manager (Sig Arno) unwittingly steps onto the platform just before it is drawn back up into the scaffolding: Krampf films his comic ascent in an eye-level elevator shot, likely with the camera fixed to the platform of a rope and pulley system identical to the one in the shot. Elsewhere, when Lulu is in a costume change, Krampf shows Charlotte staring at her, in her elegant gown with an open back and bare on the shoulders: the shots of the two women show Lulu's beauty, Charlotte's envy, and the disparity in social class between a fiancée and a mistress. When Lulu turns around and sees Charlotte together with Dr. Schön, she becomes instantly jealous and refuses to go onstage, and threatens to join a trapeze act. When the show's producer appeals to Dr. Schön to reason with Lulu, she informs him she will not perform for Charlotte. When he takes her into a property closet to persuade her to return, she throws a tantrum, and then attacks him physically, a tussle that turns into a tumble onto a mattress and a romantic embrace. As they are kissing, Alwa and Charlotte open the closet door. Her smirk and glance at Charlotte signifying her victory, Lulu now runs into the wings, just in time to make her entrance into her act. Dr. Schön confirms her victory when, Charlotte having walked out on him, devastated, he informs Alwa that now he will have to marry Lulu, adding he believes this will be his undoing.

At the wedding reception scene, Pabst and Krampf exploit an envious-glance shot similar to that of Charlotte backstage. Now the shot reveals Anna looking hostilely at Alwa and Lulu, as if the latter is a rival and a threat. But the scene develops when Lulu goes to talk to Anna and then they go together onto the dance floor, where they are the only same-sex partners. Krampf follows this dance with a fluid camera and shot cuts for presence and intercut shots to show onlookers. Anna and Lulu dance a slow two-step, cheek to cheek. When Dr. Schön cuts in on the pretext of introducing her to some of the guests, he is also cutting off a show of affection he finds threatening. Krampf's two shots of Anna alone on the dance floor, clearly enamored with Lulu, acknowledges the Weimar period's liberal attitudes to nonheteronormative sexuality. The painter "Jeanne Mammen regularly chronicled gays, lesbians, transsexuals, and heterosexuals touching, caressing, embracing or otherwise intimately and deeply engaged with one another. Indeed the breakdown of traditional gender boundaries that typified the Weimar era was not just chronicled by many, it was celebrated."[12] Krampf confirms his reference to a romantic relationship between Anna and Lulu in a later shot: after Lulu signals to Dr. Schön that she is ready for them to leave the reception to enjoy their wedding night, Anna seizes the moment to walk over to give Lulu a final hug. She lets go of her hold on her body as if freeing her, giving permission, to pursue her heteronormative relationship, which implies they may have had a sexual relationship in the past.

> Pabst places Lulu's sexual attraction to others invariably in the context of ambiguous gender attributes, though the film never comments on any of them, except by carefully differentiating the encounters. Throughout the relationship with Dr. Shön, for instance, she is the androgynous Pierrot sporting a sylph-like body. With Alwa Schön an incestuous and homosexual element is always present. At her wedding to Dr. Schön, Lulu reserves her most sensuous dance for the lesbian Countess Geschwitz, and on the gambling boat, she allows herself to be seduced by a young sailor, in order to exchange clothes with him.[13]

Pabst and Krampf explore this theme antithetically in a subsequent scene, in which Ludwig Schön enters the bedroom to discover Lulu there in the company of Schigolch and Rodrigo Quast, both guests at the reception, and very drunk. They went there to scatter roses over the marriage bed, but afterward Schigolch showers his affection on Lulu, while Quast helps himself to a bedside bottle of wine. When Ludwig arrives, he sees Schigolch with his arms around Lulu, sitting on the edge of the bed. He first attacks Quast, knocking the glass out of his hand, who responds by trying to hit him with the wine bottle, but Lulu intervenes. Then he pulls out a pistol concealed in a bookcase to shoot Schigolch, whom he considers his wife's paramour, but again Lulu intervenes, shouting that Schigolch is her father. Both men manage to escape to the reception, where Ludwig pursues them, his pistol raised to fire, but some of the older guests manage to calm him down. His violent intrusion puts an end to the party and all the guests leave, excepting Alwa, who is going away for a long time and, expressing his love to Lulu, begs her to come with him. When his father comes across them, still brandishing the pistol, he sees Lulu seated and Alwa kneeling at her feet, with his head on her lap. Rather than murdering them, he simply taps Alwa on the shoulder, stands him up, seizes him by the lapels, and then reminds him he could miss his train. Krampf's close-ups of Ludwig, his downcast face the surface of his inner condition, indicate marrying Lulu was a terrible mistake, whose unrepressed sexuality has already been his undoing. He watches Lulu as she starts to undress, narcissistically, at a mirror, and approaches her from behind until his menacing image appears with hers. When she withdraws in fear, he confronts her with the pistol, forcing it into her hand, turning the barrel to her face, and demanding she kill herself, to save him from having to murder her. In an over-the-shoulder close-up, in which Krampf films him from behind, towering over her, they wrestle for control of the weapon, which discharges, striking him. When he walks out of the frame, Krampf cuts to a shot of him as he sits down on the bed, and then back to Lulu to reveal she is holding the pistol, with the barrel still smoking. Managing to stand up, he stumbles over to Lulu to force himself on her as her husband, but he is overcome by his injury and collapses. Alwa enters, presumably alerted by the sound of gunfire, and his father dies while he is trying to embrace him.

The next section of *Die Büchse der Pandora* is set at the summation of Lulu's murder trial. In his closing remarks to the male jury, her defense counsel argues Lulu did not murder Ludwig, who, rather, "was the victim of tragic circumstances" (intertitle), including, he emphasizes, her abject upbringing, and he reminds them of the deceased's son's testimony in support of this argument. In a close-up tracking shot he surveys the reactions of her closest supporters sitting together in the front row, in the facial displays of Alwa (dejected, head downcast), Schigolch (smiling, turning to Quast), Quast (laughing at what Schigolch has said, and turning to tell Anna), and Anna (solemn, turning away to ignore Quast). The state prosecutor begins his summation by recounting the Greek myth of Pandora, a flatterer, whom the gods gave a box with all the world's evils, which she opened and set free. After dismissing the defense counsel's argument as specious, he demands the death penalty. Krampf's additional close-up shots, such as of journalists and photographers, and of Lulu, in mourning clothes, looking variously ebullient and grave and raising and lowering her veil accordingly, effectively evoke the courtroom milieu of exhilaration with the verdict imminent. When the court reconvenes after the jury deliberations, the presiding judge sentences Lulu to five years in prison on the lesser charge of manslaughter. Cutting to a scene in the corridor outside, in which one man intentionally sets off the fire alarm and panic ensues in the courtroom, Krampf films the streams of people trying to get away to safety mostly in close shots, mid shots to evoke everyone moving at once, and close-ups to show a group of men, those responsible for the diversion, and clearly her supporters, who circle around Lulu to shield her and facilitate her flight. The final shot of the sequence is a wide shot of Alwa, leaning against a back wall, the last person in the courtroom, apparently unconcerned about any danger. In the next scene, at the Schön mansion, where she is hiding out, Alwa finds her and is indignant she has now involved him. But, no match for her charms, he soon finds himself her accomplice, agreeing to help her flee Germany. With typical insouciance she informs him Countess Geschwitz has agreed to lend her her passport. In the next scenes, on the train, a disreputable character, Marquis Casti Piani (Michael von Newlinsky), who recognizes Lulu from her photograph in the newspaper, blackmails Alwa for five thousand marks. Krampf films these scenes mostly in mid shots and close-ups, in which the long, narrow corridor, with cabin doors receding on both sides, forms a modified vanishing-point perspective background to Alwa and Casti Piani's rivalry for Lulu's attention, which soon includes Schigolch and Rodrigo Quast. Casti Piani advises Alwa not to take Lulu to Paris, where she will be too conspicuous, but to come to his place, which will offer them discretion, which turns out to be a casino ship at dockside, where, the scene reveals, when Anna comes to visit her, she has lived for three months.

The shot, in which a crewman leads Anna down two flights of stairs, with wooden treads but no risers, to the gambling room, is among the most visually arresting of the film: positioning the camera at floor level on the landing, Krampf first uses a wide shot to film the crewman and Anna, followed by two other crewmen carrying her luggage, as one by one they descend the first flight of stairs, in the direction of the camera and the midground of the visual field, and then as the lead crewman turns around on the landing and descends the next flight, the vectorization of which is in the opposite direction, away from the camera. But as Anna takes her first step onto the second flight, Krampf lowers the camera below floor level now to shoot her descent through the spaces between the wooden treads. This is a more aesthetically complex shot of a constricted space, combining a *mise-en-shot* with an elevator shot, than the typical shot of the train corridor.

The film reaches a crescendo at the casino, where Alwa is a compulsive gambler heavily in debt, where Casti Panti, on the threat of turning her into the German police for the reward, negotiates to sell Lulu into sex slavery to an Egyptian man, and where Quast, using the same threat, is trying to extort money from her. When Anna gives Lulu a large sum of money to free her from sex slavery, she gives it to Alwa instead, in the hope he will win big at the gambling tables, seemingly aware of the implications should he lose. To help ensure his win, Schigolch slips him a trick deck of cards. When Lulu asks Anna to throw herself at Rodrigo Quast to dissuade him from turning her in, she is at first disgusted, but agrees because she is in love with Lulu. Krampf makes their unrequited bond clear in his close-up two-shot of them, standing very close together: both face the camera, Anna directly, her eyes downcast, Lulu in three-quarter profile, looking at her, and they are holding hands. Then Anna turns around to face Lulu, so both subjects are in three-quarter profile; Lulu's hand is on Anna's shoulder and then she moves it to caress her cheek and chin with her fingers, as if they are about to kiss. Here Anna, holding Lulu's hand, turns away from her, back to the camera, her face now visible, her expression one of resolve. Krampf cuts to a mid shot of Rodrigo at the bar, vulgar and drunk. Such is Anna's courtly love for unattainable Lulu that she is willing to debase herself with Rodrigo. Later, when he sexually assaults her in his cabin, she kills him. After winning a fortune at cards, Alwa loses everything when he is exposed cheating; consequently, Lulu has no choice but to go with the Egyptian slave trader, to avoid being turned in to the police. Nevertheless, Schigolch, Alwa, and Lulu (disguised as a sailor, after having exchanged sex for his uniform) escape from the casino in a rowboat. Eventually, they relocate to London, where the final section of the film shows them living in a dank tenement in abject poverty and Lulu working as a prostitute to make ends meet. It is while walking the streets that she meets Jack (Gustav Diessl), also known as Jack the Ripper. When they climb the wooden staircase to her flat, Krampf shoots them in the manner in which he shot Anna on the stairs of the casino ship, in the spaces between the risers. He shoots the tenement stairs, however, from the side, not straight on, and in a low-angle shot, and with lighting that casts the shadows of the risers on the wall, and the spaces between them as light. When spectators first see Jack, he is a stranger walking out of the mist to a Salvation Army–style Christmas charity: initially he is in silhouette, but his features become clear. When they see him again, he is reading a poster warning the public about a man who lures women into dark places, where he murders them. For the first time this character is associated with Jack the Ripper. Krampf shoots him in three-quarter profile, with little of his face visible under his broad-brimmed hat and with his overcoat collar up, but his image is clear at first: then Krampf tracks back slightly as Jack turns his head into a full profile and away from the light source, and appears in silhouette. These two appearances, one in which Jack progresses from silhouette to clear image and the other from clear image to silhouette, anticipate the climactic shot on the tenement stairs, where the interplay of light and shadow on the wall signifies Jack the Ripper as spectators have come to recognize the stranger. These staircase shots mark the end of her passage through the spaces of gender, sexuality, class, and social structure in the film. While making love with her, Jack stabs Lulu to death, which Krampf signifies as his silhouette envelopes her face.

Clearly, his shot repertoire in *Die Büchse der Pandora* is more diverse and ambitious than in *Orlacs Hände*. The greater sophistication of his cinematography is attributable partly to the advances in camera technology in the five years between the films, but mainly to his working relationship with Pabst, who trusted Krampf to perfect "the true meaning" of the film's Naturalistic look, through close-ups and mid shots of the main characters, for the ubiquitous presence of Lulu's smile or facial displays during life-and-death crises, and of crowd scenes, at the reception, in the courtroom, and on the gambling ship. But Pabst also gave him license to experiment with shots, angles, camera movement, and action-field configurations. Krampf wrote:

> In the good days of the German film, 1919–25, the primary consideration of first-class men like Lang, Pommer and Pabst was always this. The cameraman in Germany was the king of the studio. He worked closely with the director on the preparation for a film and his job was to convey the true meaning of the story through the camera and the camera only. It was the director's job to co-ordinate the work of the artists and technicians and to direct the acting. The rest was in the hands of the cameraman.[14]

Die Büchse der Pandora marks the apex of camera-driven film aesthetics in Germany. The project was a *gemeinschaftsproduktion*, in which the director and cinematographer had equal responsibilities, and in which Günther Krampf came into his own as an *auteur* and *filmemacher*.

NOTES

1. Lotte H. Eisner, *The Haunted Screen: Expressionism in the German Cinema and the Influence of Max Reinhardt*, trans. Roger Grieves, rev. ed. (1952; Berkeley and Los Angeles: University of California Press, 1969), 267–68.

2. Ibid., 266.

3. Paul Matthew St. Pierre, *E. A. Dupont and His Contribution to British Film:* Varieté, Moulin Rouge, Piccadilly, Atlantic, Two Worlds, Cape Forlorn (Madison, NJ: Fairleigh Dickinson University Press, 2010), 84.

4. Given that the invention of the crane shot is usually attributed to the film *Broadway* (May 1929), directed by Pál Fejös, with cinematography by Hal Moher, which was not screened in Germany until 1930, it is likely May and Rittau's execution of a crane shot is a significant example of the phenomenon of multiple discovery.

5. Sternberg made two versions of *Der blaue Engel* simultaneously, one in German and the other in English and German, marketed for international distribution. I have relied on the German version.

6. Don Fairservice, *Film Editing: History, Theory and Practice; Looking at the Invisible* (Manchester: Manchester University Press, 2001), 237.

7. Eisner, *The Haunted Screen*, 314.

8. Olaf Peters, "New Objectivity and 'Totalitarianism': The Reception of Weimar's Modernity in the Third Reich and the German Democratic Republic," in *New Objectivity: Modern German Art in the Weimar Republic 1919–1933*, ed. Stephanie Barron and Sabine Eckmann, 78 (New York: Prestel, Los Angeles: Los Angeles County Museum of Art, 2015).

9. Maria Makela, "New Women, New Men, New Objectivity," *New Objectivity: Modern German Art in the Weimar Republic 1919–1933*, ed. Stephanie Barron and Sabine Eckmann, 59 (New York: Prestel, Los Angeles: Los Angeles County Museum of Art, 2015).

10. Anjeana Hans, "'These Hands Are Not My Hands': War Trauma and Masculinity in Crisis in Robert Wiene's *Orlacs Hände* (1924)," in *The Many Faces of Weimar Cinema: Rediscovering Germany's Filmic Legacy*, ed. Christian Rogowski, 111–12 (Rochester, NY: Camden House, 2010).

11. Ibid., 112.

12. Maria Makela, "New Women, New Men, New Objectivity," 61.

13. Thomas Elsaesser, *Weimar Cinema and After: Germany's Historical Imaginary* (London and New York: Routledge, 2000), 266.

14. Günther Krampf, "The Curse of Dialogue," *World Film and Television Progress* (April 1936–March 1937): 4.

8

Guido Seeber's Promotion from Special-Effects Technician to Cinematographic Artist

A pioneer of silent-film cinematography in Germany, Guido Seeber (1879–1940) invented several fundamental techniques of camera operation, having to do with the special effects of light and shade that could be best produced in tracking shots, and he was a precursor of the Weimar visual language of Fritz Arno Wagner, Karl Freund, Carl Hoffmann, and other cinematographers. Seeber began his career shooting nearly fifty actuality, documentary, and other short films 1898–1913, working with directors Emil Albes, Julius Pinschewer, Stellan Rye, and Urban Gad on multiple films. His most prolific relationship during this apprenticeship, however, the working relationship most resembling an artistic collaboration, was with Gad, for whom he shot twenty-seven films 1911–1915. The first major film on which he worked with technical distinction as the principal cinematographer was Stellan Rye and Paul Wegener's codirected *Der Student von Prag* (1913), a film whose visual grammar is most characterized by Seeber's remarkable special effects, an achievement that helped to establish a particular critical perspective on a variety of cinematography that is elided with light-and-shadow trick photography as a distinguishing feature of German Expressionist film. With codirector Henrik Galeen in *Der Golem* (1915), and with codirector Paul Boese and principal cinematographer Karl Freund in *Der Golem: Wie er in die Welt kam* (1920), Wegener again relied on Seeber's expertise in special-effects photography for a distinctive look to combine legend and the horror genre. His innovative cinematography on *Der Golem: Wie er in die Welt kam* earned him positions as principal cinematographer on Fritz Lang's *Das wandernde Bild* (1920) and as assistant cinematographer, with Reimar Kuntze and Josif Rona, on Wegener's *Lebende Buddhas* (1925). The collaborative relationship that distinguished his career, however, was with G. W. Pabst, with whom he worked on four films, as principal cinematographer on *Grafin Donelli* (1924), as lead, with Robert Lach and Kurt Oertel, on *Die freudlose Gasse* (1925), *Geheimnisse einer Seele* (1926), and *Man spielt niche mit der Liebe* (1926). Concentrating on making Naturalistic dramatic films, Pabst relied on Seeber less for special-effects light-and-shade trick photography, as had Wegener and Lang, than for exploiting a sympathetic lens and supplying probing camera angles and establishing tracking shots appropriate for leading players such as Greta Garbo, Asta Nielsen, Ruth Weyher, Lili Damita, and Werner Krauss. His collaborative partnership with G. W. Pabst in the Naturalist mode revealed Guido Seeber as both a camera technician and a visual artist of the first order.

Friedrich Konrad Guido Seeber was born on June 22, 1879, in Chemnitz, Sachsen, Germany. His father, Clemens Seeber (1851–1905), was a factory worker who became a photographer, opening his own institute in 1879, Kunst Anstalt für Photographie; Germany's first photojournalist; and a film pioneer, devising a rotating camera and film reels in the late 1890s. In 1896, he purchased a projector and films from Oskar Messter, a developer of silent actuality films, including balloon-sourced aerial films of Berlin, and in 1897 he launched film screenings of "Seeber's lebenden Riesen-Photographien." With Messter, Seeber invented and patented a mobile film camera-projector called the Seeberograph in 1903, and in 1905 accessorized it with the Seeberophon, a gramophone that allowed sound to accompany film images, and started making and screening his own sound films. Guido Seeber grew up working in his father's photography studio. In 1895–95, he apprenticed to photographer Carl Pietzner in Karlsbad and Vienna and, inspired by the actuality films of Louis and Auguste Lumière, he purchased his first film camera in 1896, which launched his self-directed apprenticeship in filmmaking. He directed and shot thirteen documentary short films, 1898–1904, beginning with *König Albert von Sachsen wird in Chemnitz empfangen*. In 1908 he assumed the position of technical director and camera operator at Deutsche Bioscop Gesellschaft, in Berlin (to 1911) and Neubabelsberg (1911–1914), where he shot fifty short documentary, performance, and dramatic short films, 1909–1914, starting with *Zepplin III in Berlin am 29.8.1909* (1909), and culminating in his first feature film, Stellan Rye's *Der Student von Prag* (1913), in which he distinguished himself for his double-image effect of actor Paul Wegener and his *doppelgänger*. In 1914 he enlisted in the German Navy, and in 1915 became head of the Film and Photography Department of the Seeflugzeug Versuchsanstalt ("Seaplane Experimental Institute"). He rejoined Deutsche Bioscop in November 1918 as a technical director and joint managing director. When Ufa bought out Deutsche Bioscop in 1921, Seeber became a freelance cinematographer. His chance to work with Fritz Lang on *Das wandernde Bild [The Wandering Image]* (1920), though he was still an emerging director, who had made his directorial debut one year, and five films, earlier, and his reputation for special effects, original shot composition, and new techniques were key factors in his hiring.

Appropriately, *Das wandernde Bild* begins with traveling shots, not of a moving camera, but of train travelers heading to a village in the Alps. The opening shot is of Wil Brand (Rudolf Klein-Rogge) and another man standing together on the train platform; the second shot shows Brand leaning out a train window and talking to the same man on the platform. In both shots the man offers Brand his condolences

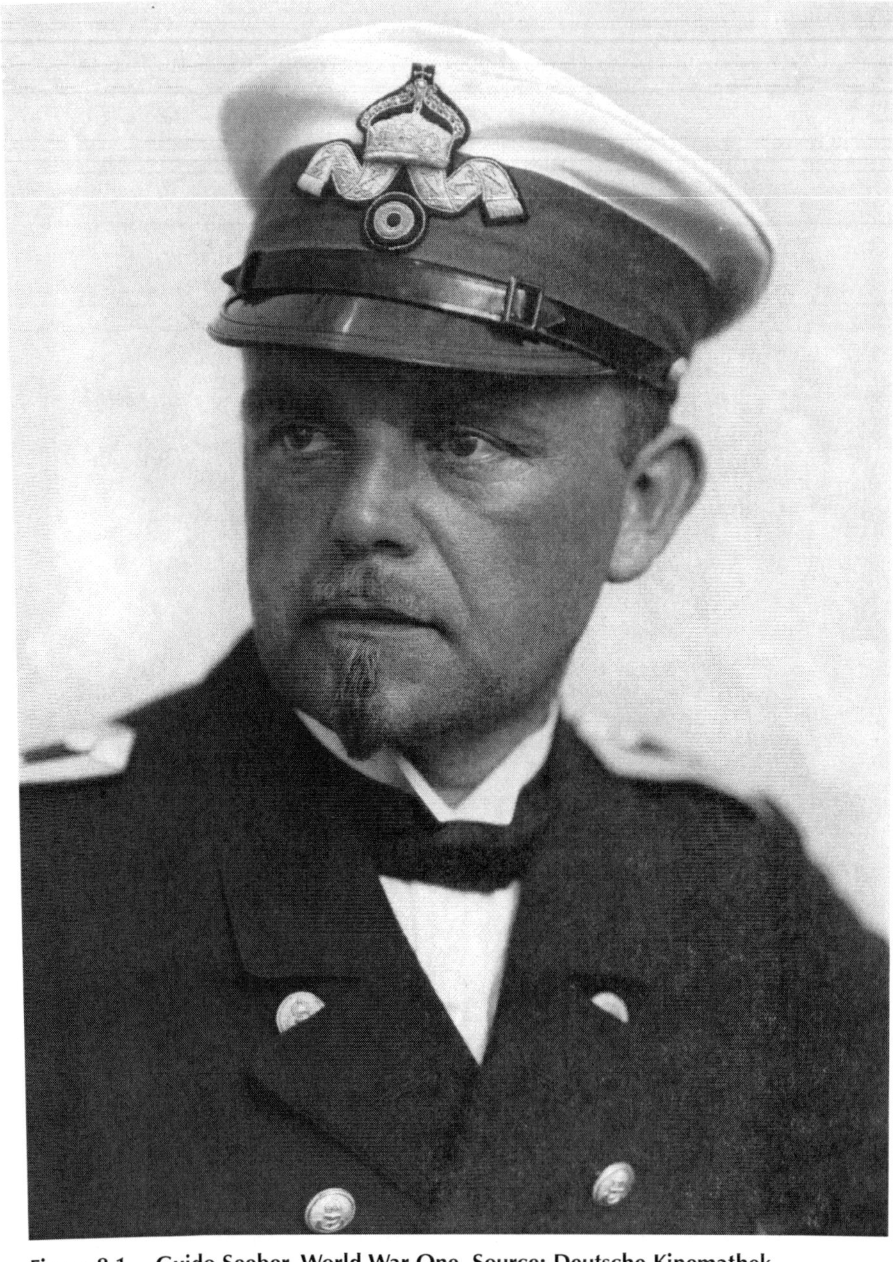

Figure 8.1. Guido Seeber, World War One. Source: Deutsche Kinemathek.

on the death of his cousin. The third shot is of the train interior, in which a woman, Irmgard Vanderheit (Mia May), walks over to stand at an observation window at the end of the car. By shooting her first from a distance, through the corresponding observation window of the adjoining car, and then cutting to a close-up of her in three-quarter profile directly through her window, Seeber introduces Irmgard and the theme of surveillance prominent in the film. This shot, like all the outward-looking shots on the train, is remarkable because it is on location, so the moving backdrop is live, as opposed to a traveling matte.

When the train pulls in to a station, an official on the platform delivers a telegram to her, but not without Wil Brand taking notice. She reads the telegram from her observation post, only now in a profile shot with no window framing her: "Irmgard Vanderheit if you think you can escape you are wrong. John." Brand also watches as she tears up the message and scatters the pieces out the window, and breaks down emotionally, covering her face with her hands; then Brand writes in his notepad, which in the next shot, from the next platform on the route, he throws down to a conductor with instructions to send the urgent message as a telegram; addressed to H. Marcus, Munich, it reads: "Suspend temporarily the issue with Irmgard Vanderheit" (intercut shot of the conductor reading the message on the platform). Next, Lang shows Irmgard at her destination, in front of the station, ordering a cab under her name before marriage, "Lady Karen Svenden." Upon arriving at her hotel, she learns her reservation has not been kept. Here, Brand, showing up in the next cab, intervenes to offer Irmgard his own reservation, which she declines. The cab driver informs her of rooms available on the other side of the lake. Seeber complements the live-action shot of a boatman rowing Irmgard to the other side, with a live-action shot of John Vanderheit (Hans Marr) as he arrives in his motorcar at the hotel and inquires about the widow of Georg Vanderheit, Irmgard's deceased spouse, as Brand looks on, taking particular interest when John asks of the cab driver, "Sir, can't you see that my wife has a mental disorder" (intertitle). Brand immediately hires a boat to the other side of the lake, moments ahead of John, where he forewarns Irmgard about the man making inquiries about her and offers her his protection should she need it. Instead, she seeks the assistance of a maid at her pension, who stores her overcoat and provides her with a veil and walking staff. As she walks out of the village for her hike into the mountains, she thanks Brand for his offer of assistance.

Lang and Seeber represent her journey intermittently, in shots of her encounters with a hermit, a mysterious hooded figure who does not make eye contact, at his hut and with a goat herder, who gives her directions to the landmark called "the stone from hell," and a warning to avoid the quarry, which is being excavated for road construction, and intercut shots of John, who is petulantly cross-examining the maid at the pension and accusing her of covering for his wife and even hiding her in the closet; when he finds her coat, exposing the maid in her lies, he attacks her physically, but a worker, alerted by her cries, bursts in to rescue her and chase him away. When the hermit sees Irmgard hiking high on the mountain, into the snow, he decides to go after her. There she encounters a Madonna and Child stone statue and seeks its intercession. Seeber films the statue in a close-up for presence, much as he would a biological mother holding her child, capable of response. At the mountaintop, John catches up to her and threatens to push her off the precipice, but the hermit arrives to distract him with a show of violence that allows her to escape. With daylight fading and the weather threatening, the hermit and Irmgard head to the nearest hut for shelter. Meanwhile, John steals explosives from the road-building crew and plans to blow up their hut. In an interior shot, Seeber films the hermit and Irmgard and a double exposure of a skeletal arm ringing a bell, a sound with which the villagers are familiar as an omen of death. Moments later a rock slide crashes into the hut, trapping them inside; it alerts the entire village. In his desperate effort to free them, the hermit pulls back the hood that has always concealed his face: Irmgard recognizes him as Georg, her "dead" husband, who also is portrayed by Hans Marr. When she passes out in shock, Georg, also traumatized, thinks about how he and Irmgard married: she was seeking a job as a maid so she could look after her aged mother; Georg asks her to marry him, to which she agrees on the condition she can keep it secret from her mother. He believes in the principle of free love, however, so they marry in common law. But when she gets pregnant, he accedes to her wish that they have a sacramental marriage in the church. But Georg feels he cannot go on living, having violated his philosophical principles, so he fakes his suicide by drowning and pursues the hermetic life in the mountains. Other analeptic shots show him on the train going into the Alps and making a vow at the Madonna and Child monument on the mountainside that he will not leave his retreat unless the statue walks, meaning, of course, he will never leave. Here the flashback ends and Seeber cuts from a high-angle shot of him at the monument to a low-angle shot of him in the hut, recalling his and her past. Now, Irmgard regains consciousness. Her conversation with Georg prompts another flashback, to the reading of his will, leaving his entire estate to her because they were legally married. His brother John's hostility to Irmgard arises from this will, his belief theirs was a common-law marriage in Georg's mind, and his disapproval of Irmgard's lower class. When he makes a sexual advance to her in the garden, she whips him with a switch. Another time, when he tries to assault her sexually in the house and she rebuffs him, he tells everyone that she is insane. For her safety she and her son go to live with her mother, but when John continues to harass her, she flees to the mountains in a drastic effort to find security. Here the second flashbacks ends. Seeber now pursues a shot sequence about the rescue effort of a group of mountaineers from the village, led by Wil Brand. They manage to remove enough rubble to free Irmgard and Georg through a hole in the roof of the hut; meanwhile, one of the mountaineers climbs the peak in pursuit of the bomber. Some complications arise, a fight ensues, and John falls to his death. As Georg helps Irmgard back down the mountain, they pass the Madonna and Child statue, where she begs him to return to the world with her, and he tells her of the vow he made.

They part here, and Brand accompanies her the rest of the way. In the village, he informs her that had she not married Georg legally, he would have inherited all. Subsequently, Seeber films Irmgard dressed as the Madonna praying over her son for the guidance to do what is right for Brand, particularly because he saved her life on the mountaintop. While helping a poor family, a new mother who is ill, Irmgard takes her baby away to give her some respite. While dressed as the Madonna, she carries the baby up the mountain for some fresh air. There Georg sees them walking across the snow, and he believes they are the statue walking. Relieved of his oath, he comes down the mountain and finds Irmgard in the pension at dinner with Brand, about to share her inheritance with him. But when Brand sees his cousin alive, he knows he has no prospects. The parable ends in a three-shot, comprising a crestfallen (seated) and then indignant (standing) Brand, and George and Irmgard finally together as husband and wife when she rises to embrace him and he takes her into his arms for the first time. Then, with closure, resolution, and reconciliation incomplete, Seeber leaves the rest to the parabolic imagination by fading to black.

In the antecedent action of its flashbacks, *Das wandernde Bild* is a closet drama about family structure and conflict: elder care, de facto and de jure marriage, social class, property, and inheritance. For instance, after finding her coat hidden in the closet, John is able to find Irmgard, the impediment, he believes, to preserving his family. In its current action, the film is a poetic allegory about idealism, truth, discovery, and justice: Georg, Irmgard, Brand, and John all withdraw from the world, as represented by the city, the family, and the village, to climb to the mountaintop. Georg studies the philosophy of free love; Irmgard seeks security and enlightenment; Brand is both protector and opportunist; John wishes only to exact vengeance against Irmgard by smashing the mountain, so he is sacrificed. In its cinematography, the film is self-reflexive, about "wandering images," not just the statue that appears to walk across the snow, but also a catalog of traveling shots, shots that depict travel: by train from the city to the village in the Alps (Irmgard, Brand), hansom cab from the train station to the hotel (Irmgard, Brand), automobile from the city to the village hotel (John), rowboat to and from the far side of the lake (Georg, Irmgard, Brand, John), and hiking and climbing (Georg, Irmgard, Brand, John). Although in *Das wandernde Bild* Seeber's camera is not fluid, it wanders in his well-constructed images of movement. As Graham Bader observes of *Neue Sachlichkeit* images in painting and photography, "In thus rendering their figures and cityscapes, these artists aligned themselves with a general shift in Weimar-era cultural criticism toward the privileging of surface in attempts to analyze the age."[1] The film is notable for its live-action repertoire: shots of objects and subjects moving through space, and of landscape changing, appearing to move, behind them, and also shots of immobile surfaces such as windows, walls, floors, furniture, and rock faces.

> Die Bilder allein, die von erlesener Schönheit, Schärfe und Tönung sind, müssen das Herz aufgehen lassen, wenn man nicht ganz verstockt is. Guido Seeber war der treffliche Aufnahmekünstler; ihm gebührt uneingeschränktes Lob. Wieviel Arbeit, wieviel Mühe mag oft notwendig gewesen sein, den Kurbelkasten "in Stellung" zu bringen.[2]

> The pictures alone, which are of exquisite beauty, clarity, and tonality, leave everything to the heart, unless it is completely hardened. Guido Seeber was the excellent recording

artist; he deserves unqualified praise. How much work, how much effort must have been needed to bring the crankcase "into position." (St. Pierre's translation)

The logistics of recording live-action, on-location footage are quite complex, of meticulously supporting, manipulating, and hand-cranking the camera at appropriate speeds and with appropriate image stabilization to capture both what moves and what appears to move by changing form and tonality behind what moves; for example, Irmgard, visible through two sets of windows standing on the observation platform on the train, and moving, and behind her, visible through one set of windows, the changing landscape through which the train is passing. These live-action, on-location passing shots, with subjects and natural background settings moving, at least perceptually, in opposite directions required more than a steady hand and eye: they demanded attention to camera lenses and focus. For example, in the window shots of Irmgard, Seeber would have used a long lens to compress the space or limit the depth-of-field between the subject and the landscape, making the moving background appear closer and thus softening the focus on the woman in the observation box to depict it as her psychological space.

Between Fritz Lang's *Das wandernde Bild* (1920) and G. W. Pabst's *Die freudlose Gasse* (1925), Guido Seeber shot sixteen films, mostly with directors of the second rank, excepting Pabst's *Gräfin Donelli* (1924), on which he was chief cinematographer. On *Die freudlose Gasse [The Joyless Street]*[3] Pabst appointed him to lead a team that included Robert Lach and Curt Oertel. The film opens with a title card: Wien 1921. The opening shot sequence establishes how the film will be shot, more than the setting, a narrow road that intersects with an alley at an arch. Seeber films four older characters as, one after another, camera-left, they enter into the field of vision and walk away from the camera and toward the arch in the background: a man who walks slowly with a cane; a woman who walks behind, yet appears to be with him; a woman in a shawl; a man with a disability, who hobbles along, with a wooden prosthetic leg and a cane. After the woman in the shawl turns to the side of the road, presumably to wait for the man with the disability, Seeber cuts to a mid pan shot of the first man and woman, now walking arm in arm, followed by the other man and woman, still in single file, as they pass under the arch into Melchiorgasse ("Melchior Alley"). He shoots them laterally in a close-up, where their progression across the vision field, close to the camera, seems much slower than their foreground-to-background movement in the previous shot. This slow-motion effect may be attributable both to the actors' protracting their movements for the shot and to Seeber's deliberately overcranking the camera, running it at a higher-than-normal pace so the film would project slower than normal.

Next, Seeber completes the establishing sequence by cutting to another shot of Melchiorgasse, showing young children playing, running back and forth, and various pedestrians, and introducing the butcher, Josef Geiringer (Werner Krauss), identified as the local tyrant, instructing a large group of women to queue up for rationed frozen Argentinean meat; the Lechner family, who live in a cellar, where Frau Lechner

(Sylvia Torf) is scrubbing clothes by hand, using a washtub and a washboard; and Herr Lechner (Max Kohlhase), the man with the disability, returns home angry because there is no margarine for his bread, and the court counselor Rumfort, the man with the cane, who lives on the first floor of the same building with his daughters Greta (Greta Garbo), who accompanied her father through the arch, and Mariandll, where they are at a dinner of cabbage soup, with the promise of meat tomorrow. Here Seeber cuts back to the Lechners' flat, to show the daughter, Maria (Asta Nielsen), the woman with the shawl, who has returned home without the margarine and must endure her father's wrath. Now Seeber cuts back to the Rumforts' flat, where, dinner over, Greta leaves to join the long queue for meat, even though she has to rise early tomorrow for work, and again to the Lechners', where he shows Maria in her bedroom, writing a letter to her boyfriend, Egon, begging him to let her come to live with him, when her mother looks in to remind her she is late to join the meat queue. All these scenes establish Melchiorgasse as an affective postwar space with resourceful working-class people, and show, in Pabst's Naturalistic representation of domestic and street settings, they are not Marx's *lumpenproletariat.* Still, Pabst does expose another person, like Geiringer, who exploits the resources of resourceful people, Frau Greifer (Valeska Gert), owner of a fashion salon, and the second most powerful person in Melchiorgasse, who is seen scolding her casual employee Else (Hertha von Walther), who wishes to buy a winter coat on credit when she already owes her for a dress, reminding her she made no sales in the past week, and then begrudgingly gives her the evening off so she can queue at the butcher shop. He also provides a perspective on the affluent part of Vienna, as represented by the Hotel Carlton, where in the restaurant a rich Chilean businessman, Don Alfonso Canez (Robert Garrison), conducts an investment meeting with the banker Max Rosenow (Karl Etlinger), who arrives accompanied by Frau Rosenow (Ilka Grüning) and their daughter, Regina (Agnes Esterhazy), and is later joined by his private secretary, Egon Stirner (Henry Stuart), Maria's boyfriend. Their business plan, based on the class and power differentials of the postwar Austrian economy, is to start a rumor of a workers' strike, driving down stock prices to open up an investment opportunity, and then to quell the rumor, driving the stock values back up, and then to sell the shares at a huge profit, "a million in gold" (intertitle). In 1922, Fritz Lang attributed an identical stock market scam to Dr. Mabuse in *Dr. Mabuse der Spieler*. In his allusion to Lang, Pabst implies postwar business speculators are simply unscrupulous "gamblers" like Mabuse, a megalomaniacal gangster, murderer, and villain. The deal struck, Egon and Regina venture onto the dance floor, where Seeber tracks them with a handheld camera as they two-step their way through the other dancers and into an adjacent room, where they can talk privately. She preemptively quells his courtship, reasoning that either he would have to be as rich as she, or she as poor as he, for her to believe his feelings for her. Her attitude is indicative both of the modern Austrian or German woman who is open about sexuality and takes the initiative, and of plutocracy as a suprasystem that exploits the postwar economy and reinforces class hierarchies. When he vows to try to accrue her level of wealth, she says she does not care whether he makes the money honestly or dishonestly. They return to the dance floor, where they are joined by Rosenow's lawyer, Dr. Leid (Alexander Murski), and his daughter, Lia (Tamara Geva), who takes the initiative to cut in and "steal" Regina's man. She leads their dance into the room where he was courting Regina and demands he do the same with her. After they kiss, she suggests they adjourn to a hotel she knows in Melchiorgasse and wear disguises, he in a fake beard, she in a veil. Learning of his plan, Regina even encourages Egon to exchange sex for money, assuring him, "You may obtain your money THIS way as well, if you wish" (intertitle). Later, Regina rejects her father and his wealth and becomes poor like Egon.

The scene shifts back to Melchiorgasse and shows Frau Greifer, who, behind the facade of her fashion salon, runs a nightclub, arriving in her automobile. Seeber films the scene in a sequence of three shots. In the first shot, the car turns into Melchiorgasse and, moving in the direction of the camera, starts to pass the queue of women, children, and men, who will stand in line all night, till the butcher shop reopens in the morning. The second shot is a reverse angle, as if illuminated by the headlights and guided by the trajectory of the car, a close-up trucking shot that moves along the line of faces, revealing the subjects' humanity and the affect of poverty and deprivation but also the rift between Frau Greifer in her automobile and people in the street. This trucking shot is one of the greatest in German film history because of (1) its synthesis of human and mechanical elements in its execution and composition; (2) its use of close-ups to reveal the individuality of the women, children, and men in line, including those spectators recognize in this way, like Maria, Greta, and Else; (3) its application of the reverse angle to evoke the aloof perspective of Frau Greifer, implying how she sees these human faces in the headlights as she passes them by, but continues on her way; and (4) its introduction of slow-motion—as in the earlier shot in which Counselor Rumfort, Greta Rumfort, Herr Lechner, and Maria Lechner walk through the archway—to film the faces as the arc of the car's trajectory is completed, which appear to move closer to the camera as the car swings past them: the close-ups become tighter and more extreme, and the subjects' gestures appear to slow down and lose focus in projection, because Seeber is deliberately overcranking the camera or, as he himself described this technique, getting "the crankcase 'into position.'" The concluding shot in the sequence reveals the rear end of the car as, moving away from the camera, it continues up Melchiorgasse.

By cross-cutting between simultaneous scenes that disclose the self-indulgence of patrons at the nightclub and the self-restraint of people waiting at the butcher shop, Seeber emphasizes the acute socioeconomic disparities of postwar Austria, and by implication Weimar Germany, particularly when Greta faints from fatigue and her parents have to come to replace her in line and, as an intertitle informs, "Six hours later the majority of those waiting knew there was no meat waiting for them": their suffering is attributable to deprivation and to their knowledge of it. Lingering after the police disperse the disappointed crowd, Maria and Else learn about another aspect of postwar capitalism as they observe two prostitutes who tap on the window of the butchery to signal to Geiringer their willingness to exchange sex for meat. Pabst exploited the same trope in *Die Büchse der Pandora* (1929), when Lulu trades sex for a sailor's uniform to ensure her escape from the gambling ship and the threat of imprisonment, and when Karl's wife trades sex for meat in *Westfront 1918: Vier von der Infanterie* (1930). When she sees her father drunk in the street and anticipates the beating awaiting her if she returns home without meat, Maria suggests she and Else do what the other women did. When they tap on the window, Geiringer lets them in. He takes Else into the meat cooler, has sex with her, and afterward cuts her a slice of beef. He cuts another slice and offers it to Maria but, unwilling to make the trade, she flees, after which he contemptuously throws the meat to his dog. Else takes her home with her, to the stable where she lives, rent free, at the inn, introduces her to her husband and their baby, and instructs him to divide the meat and give half to Maria, which he does, but in the end she refuses because she has decided she would rather not go home at all than go home with meat.

Again Seeber exploits cross-cuts to emphasize economic and social disparities: in one sequence, Counselor Rumfort accepts a redundancy buyout from the civil service, two years' salary in cash, most of which he later invests in the stock market, in a risky venture linked to falling coal prices and the Petrowitz shares that banker Max Rosenow is manipulating for Don Alfonso Canez; in another sequence, Maria goes to live with Egon Stirner, who welcomes her, but essentially as his dresser and housemaid, where she learns about his guiding principle that the accumulation of wealth, as opposed to living sustainably within one's means, ensures happiness.

In a subsequent scene at the office where she has a clerical job, Greta is summoned by the boss, Herr Trebitsch (Raskatoff), presumably to take dictation. But Trebitsch immediately starts to harass her sexually, suggesting she looks tired because she was out partying last night and then stroking her chin and patting her on both knees. When she shows her disapproval of his treatment of her by standing up to leave, he offers "a little advance to help you feel better" and slips some bank notes into a thigh-high front pocket of her dress, an act whose salaciousness Seeber emphasizes in an intercut close-up shot. The visual parallel he and Pabst draw between two capitalist exchanges, nonconsensual touching for money and coercive sex for meat, is clear. They expand this motif in a later scene, where Maria goes to see Frau Greifer at the shop to sound her on getting a one-hundred-dollar loan, which she plans to give to Egon, believing it is all the seed money he needs to accumulate wealth and happiness. While she is waiting for Greifer in an inner office that is also the secret entrance to the nightclub, however, she meets Dr. Don Alfonso Canez, who has been partying inside, and tells him about her investment plan. He immediately offers her the money and indicates he wants sex in return. They go to the Hotel Merkl next door. Afterward, she sends Alfonso away so she can satisfy her curiosity about some noises coming from the next room: through an adjoining transom window, she sees Egon and Lia, in their disguises, making love. Egon returns to the party at the Hotel Carlton, with Lia to show up discreetly ten minutes later, as if returning from the opera, but someone reports that she has been murdered at the Hotel Merkl. Frau Merkl (Edna Markstein) informs the police inspector that Lia Leid was in the room with a man who has a mustache and goatee, Egon's disguise, and that two people, Don Alfonso and Maria, were in the next room. When the inspector interrogates them, Alfonso, who has a mustache and goatee, claims diplomatic immunity as the Peruvian consul, whereas Maria appears nervous and edges her way to the door to evade detection, but, surprisingly, he intervenes on her behalf, lying to the inspector that she is his consular secretary.

When they leave together, he promises to look after her. For example, he takes her to a private fashion show, where he offers to buy her any outfits she likes, and to a jeweler, where he wants to buy her a pearl necklace. But she remains aloof and cold throughout. Her only desire, she tells him, is to return to Greifer's club tonight. Once there, she tells him she wants to go back to the Hotel Merkl, where she confesses that she wanted to return to the same room because, after he left last night, she witnessed a murder, and she identifies Egon as the killer. In contrast, Greta, caught modeling her new fur coat (purchased with her father's new money) at the office, is called into the office. There the boss, deducing from the rich coat that she has a boyfriend, and therefore must be sexually experienced, starts to assault her sexually, but she manages to fight him off and then she promptly quits, although she later finds out that her father has lost his entire investment in the stock market. With Greta gone, the boss simply summons the next pretty girl from the typing pool. Seeber films her as she follows him up the stairs to his office, in three shots: a mid close-up that shows her lower body and focuses on her shoes as she takes the stairs with a bouncy step; a mid shot that shows her body in full and the rest of the office; and a close-up that shows only her lower legs and again the bounce in her step. Seeber and Pabst have already indicated through several open relationships that sexual exploitation is cyclical in postwar Austria and Germany. Still, that they enhance this theme ironically here by focusing the camera on an uncredited minor actor and her peculiar walk, as if she is happy, with a spring in her step, because she has got a promotion, points to the subtlety of their storytelling; social and political satire; major, and also minor, character treatment; and, particularly, shot composition.

The fluidity of relationships and shot composition is apparent also as Greta struggles to put her family's financial situation in order: both she and her father are unemployed, and his investment failure has left him heavily in debt. She begins by renting out a room in the house, to a young, attractive American soldier, Lieutenant Davis (Einar Hanson), who is clearly attracted to her, and offers to pay her more than she is asking for rent. But within minutes of renting the room, one her father's creditors calls, and she gives him all the rent money. In the next scene she is at the salon for an arranged meeting with a moneyed friend of Frau Greifer, who turns out to be Josef Geiringer. First Greifer receives him in an adjoining room to get him ready. Seeber films him walking toward the camera, pans to follow him as he turns to face a mirror, and then cuts to a close-up mirror-image shot of him preening himself, by flattening and arranging his well-oiled hair and sprawling mustache. He returns to Greifer, who has a flower ready for his *boutonnière*. Seeber cuts to an extreme close-up of his lapel, in which are visible also the lower quarter of his face and her hand as she slips the stem into the buttonhole, more than halfway, and then releases it: the shot shows the stem drop the rest of the way, as if animated, more than by the force of gravity, and in slow motion, as in his shots of the people under the arch and in the butcher queue. When Greifer introduces him to Greta as "my niece Leocadia," he does not recognize her from the crowd outside his shop or the Melchiorgasse neighborhood. In the end, he finds he is attracted more to Frau Greifer, an androgyne, than to Greta, and he rejects her as a partner. Greifer has a *Bubikopf* and the trace of a mustache, and wears plain shifts with simple lines. Valeska Gert, the actor who portrays her, had popularized the style of the androgyne before Otto Dix painted his *Portrait of the Journalist Sylvia von Harden* (1926) and made it her emblem in her memorable character roles in films like *Tagebuch einer Verlorenen* (1929), *Die 3 Groschen-Oper* (1931), and, later in her career, as Pijma in Federico Fellini's *Juliet of the Spirits* (1965).

After Egon Stirner is arrested for the murder of Lia Leid and is set to face trial, Maria comes to police headquarters and confesses to the murder. Her confession takes the form of a flashback to the night she spent at the Hotel Merkl with Don Alfonso. Seeber initiates the analepsis with a close-up of Maria, dressed in silk, satin, and feathers, and then a match dissolve to Maria as she looked that night, plainly groomed and dressed. The scene plays out now as it does earlier in the film, showing Don Alfonso preparing to leave the room and Maria listening in to the adjoining room, where Egon and Lia are having their rendezvous in fetish disguise. Now when Maria looks through the window transom, Seeber films more of what she sees, chiefly Egon and Lia breaking off their lovemaking and him departing. He also films Maria in a low-angle shot through the other side of the window transom, her eye focused on a clear flower-petal pattern, and the rest of her head blurred slightly behind the frosted glass. This shot exposes her as a voyeur. The next shot shows how she commits murder, by quietly opening the adjoining doors to the other room, creeping up behind Lia, and strangling her. The close-up profile shot of Lia, freshening her makeup in a handheld mirror, while Maria's hands enter the frame camera left and her fingers are about to touch her neck, suddenly fade to black as Seeber cuts back to the close-up shot of Maria making her confession at police headquarters, specifically that she murdered Lia out of jealousy, because she loved Egon and was living with him. Pabst and Seeber designed the shot of Lia holding a mirror up to her nature to recall Maria doing the same to admire the jewelry she is trying on when Don Alfonso tries to make her over into his mistress, and Geiringer admiring his mirror image before his interview with Greta at Greifer's. Pabst and Seeber's exploitation of mirror images, specifically as images that move, points to the function of the *tableau vivant,* meaning "moving picture" in French, in the final act of the film. Thus shots incorporating mirrors and *tableaux vivants* correspond self-reflexively to the moving images of film. Within the frame of a mirror the images move with the onlooker, whereas within the *tableau vivant* frame the living models pose but do not move, like a static frame in cinema.

The climax of *Die freudlose Gasse* is not Maria's confession but an evening of *tableaux vivants* at Frau Greifer's club, at which Greta has reluctantly agreed to appear. The crisis is the confluence of individual and group forces for and against this event. When Greta notices Lieutenant Davis among the guests at the club, she refuses to change into her costume, but the costumer forces her. Meanwhile, when her father learns she is at the club, he goes there to stop her. Inside the club the patrons are restless for the start of the show. Seeber films a sequence of wide shots of the crowd waving their arms and calling for the performance to begin, and close-ups of people stamping their feet. He cross-cuts this sequence with a sequence of working-class people in the street rallying against the staging of *tableaux vivants* and threatening to storm the club to stop them. Notable in these sequences are the high-angle shots of poor people raising their arms, shaking their fists, and crying for justice; the strange, yet typical of the interpretive dancer Velska Gert, intercut close-up of Frau Greifer poking her head through the curtains and mugging facial displays and screaming ecstatically; and the intercut shot of the first *tableau vivant* comprising three naked woman who are standing arm-in-arm, posing to form a pyramidal living sculpture. When Herr Rumfort arrives, he runs into Lieutenant Davis and apologizes for having treated him badly as a houseguest. In the end the mob in the street launches a rock attack against the club, shattering windows and sending projectiles across their tables, and effectively disrupting the scheduled performance, including the possibility of Greta's participation onstage. Seeber cuts to a scene in the attic home of Else; her baby, whom she is no longer able to nurse; and her husband. Desperate for food, she runs to the butcher shop and demands meat of Geiringer, and when he cruelly refuses, she forces her way into his shop, murders him with his own meat cleaver, and flees down Melchiorgasse. The close-up of Geiringer's bloody face at the small cellar window that women used to tap at to signal their willingness to trade sex for meat provides a horrifying image, the most cathartic in the film, because it also references his earlier facial display at the window, signaling to two prostitutes to come inside. Later, the small crowd that has gathered around his shop witnesses Else's family's attic as it bursts into flames. Using red tinting evocatively, Seeber films interior shots of the family as the fire engulfs them and as they manage to save the baby by lowering it in a sling from the window to the crowd looking on below. In the final scene, the people claim the baby as belonging to everyone in Melchiorgasse.

In their collaborative production of *Die freudlose Gasse*, Pabst and Seeber concerned themselves with two principal factors: (1) the social realism of postwar inflation, speculative economies, class disparities, unemployment and workplace harassment, sexual exploitation and abuse, and hunger and other forms of deprivation; and (2) the use of the subjective and fluid camera both self-reflexively and as the applicator of a cinematic style independent of social realist themes. For example, Don Fairservice observes, "Pabst always denied that he was a realist, insisting that he chose realist themes with the intention of being a stylist, and that he saw realism only as a means to an end."[4] Thus, social realism is their means to the end of a social critique of the Weimar Republic, masked as Vienna and particularized as Melchiorgasse. But it is also their means to the end of the visual style or syntax of *Die freudlose Gasse* and of the style of their collaborative partnership as filmmakers, which is distinguished by meticulously handled close-ups for presence, remarkably of Frau Greifer peeking through the curtains and of her attaching Geiringer's *boutonnière*, and also by fluid shots, like the wide-arc, slow-motion tracking shots of the Lechners and Rumforts under the arch, and people queuing for rationed meat. Seeber's use of the *entfesselte kamera* ("unchained camera") is evident in his trucking shots of crowd scenes at the nightclub and the Hotel Carlton, in Melchiorgasse, and in Greifer's automobile's movement past the line of customers outside Geiringer's butcher shop and as it continues up the street. Seeber, along with the director Lupu Pick, specially devised a compact wheeled cart to facilitate extensive, albeit mostly linear, camera movement on the set of Pick's film *New Year's Eve* (1924), on which he worked as cocinematographer with Karl Hasselmann.

> This equipment was built by the cameraman Guido Seeber, and the director of that film, Lupu Pick, and it consisted of a central rolling platform with rubber tires; two sections made up of tubes emerged from the platform where two electrically operated cameras covered the scene simultaneously while the whole unit was being displaced.[5]

The invention of the *entfesselte kamera*, likely an instance of multiple discovery in camera technology, has also been attributed to F. W. Murnau and Karl Freund on *Der letzte Mann* (1924). The camera on a tripod was mounted on the platform between the two front large rubber tires, which ensured a smooth ride, behind which Seeber sat on a small bench. Two assistants at the back end, standing between the two smaller rear tires, pushed the cart in straight lines by gripping a railing and could turn it by lifting the back end and guiding it on the front tires only. Seeber also devised larger, spoke-wheeled platforms with armatures for mounting and extending the reach of the camera, in the manner of a boom shot, and he improvised a winter shot by mounting the camera and tripod on a very long sleigh, which was dragged by several assistants.

In *Geheimnisse einer Seele [Secrets of a Soul: A Psychoanalytic Film]* (1926), Pabst and Seeber exchanged social realism for psychological realism, yet their cinematic style remained constant, despite the addition of much special-effects photography. This unusual film actually begins with its front matter, two title frames following the opening credits, explaining the premises about human psychology: (1) unconscious desires and the psychological illnesses that can arise from them; and (2) the importance of psychoanalysis, particularly Freudian, in the treatment of these illnesses. In addition, the front matter declares the events of the film are taken from medical case history and are true to life. These premises and claims provide a model for viewing.

The film's opening shot is a close-up of a hand stropping a straight razor, followed by an extreme close-up a man's face in a small mirror: raising his chin, the man begins to apply shaving soap with a brush. Then Seeber cuts to a wide shot of the man, Martin Fellman (Werner Krauss), dressed in pajamas, in the bedroom, where

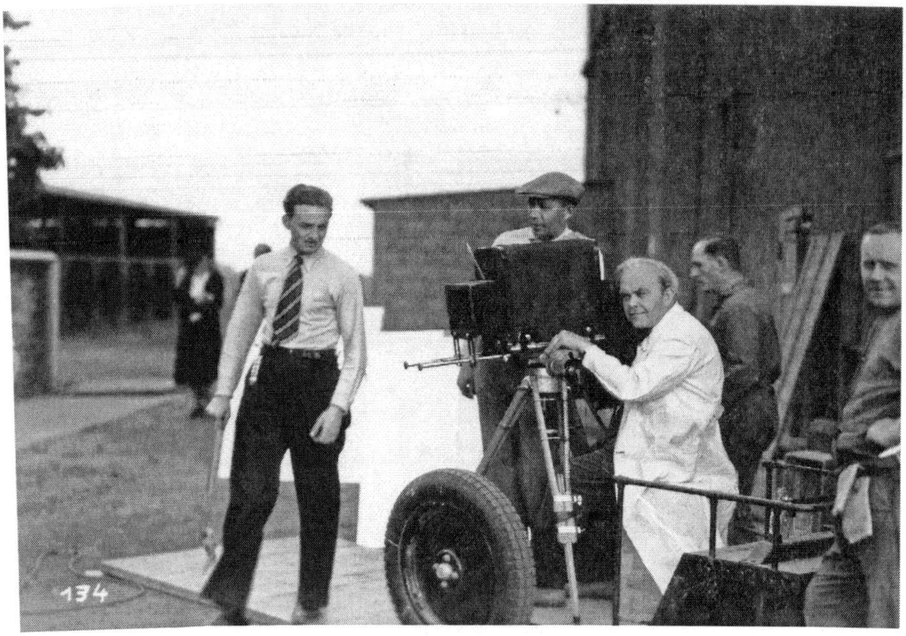

Figure 8.2. Guido Seeber on the *entfesselte kamera* platform he designed. Source: Deutsche Kinemathek.

he is standing at a window, preparing to shave. Then he cuts to a complementary sequence: a profile mid shot of Frau Fellman (Ruth Weyher), who is in another bedroom, seated at the dresser mirror, where she is brushing the back of her hair and, using a hand mirror, inspecting the hairline on her neck, followed by an extreme close-up of the hairline, and then by a reverse-angle profile mid shot of her brushing the back of her hair. Then she turns around, in the direction of the camera, and calls her husband in the next room, whom an intercut shot shows in the midst of shaving with a straight razor, and calls him again, whom another intercut shot reveals has completed his shave, yet now starts to lather his face again as he responds to his wife's call by going to the adjoining room. There, she shows him her hair problem, which he proceeds to correct by brushing her neck with soap and trimming her hairline. Here Seeber makes an abrupt cross-cut to an external scene in which a woman opens her shutters and screams "Help!" into the street. The juxtaposition of this shot with the previous implies she is reacting to the sight of Fellman shaving his wife's neck, believing he is cutting her throat. A close-up reveals that, as if startled by the scream, he has indeed cut her neck slightly. In fact the shots are independent of each other, images of disconnected events, yet with a contiguity.

When the Fellmans open the window, they see the woman yelling "Help!" and a crowd gathering outside her house, which Seeber films initially in close-up and mid shots of the body parts of people moving in the same direction, such as backs, legs, and feet, notably the boots of a police officer who is running to the emergency. Then he abruptly concludes with a fade to black. His next shot is of the Fellmans, now dressed and groomed for the day, as they come downstairs and then down a hallway, in both instances walking toward the camera, and press a buzzer to alert the maid, who an intercut reveals is outside investigating the emergency. Now Seeber cross-cuts back to show the arrival of an ambulance and the attendants as they carry a stretcher into the house, and then back to the Fellmans as the maid (Renate Brausewetter) runs upstairs and as she breezes past him, drops a bowler hat and a walking stick into his hands and disappears around the corner. Mr. Fellman kisses his wife good-bye and leaves through the front door. An exterior shot shows him lingering at his gate to observe the event across the street, especially the ambulance attendants carrying back the empty stretcher, and possibly to overhear someone gossiping, "Last night—with a razor!" Thus, the two earlier independent shots and disconnected events are shown to have a relation, in the idiom *with a razor*, in the correlation of cutting edges, and in the shot contiguity. Mr. Fellman walks to the road, where Seeber films him in a high-angle wide shot and picks him up in an eye-level wide shot as he walks past the ambulance and crowd on his way to work, to look over toward the event with mild curiosity and maintain his brisk pace throughout.

Seeber now cuts to an orientation shot of Fellman's workplace, a research laboratory, in which his assistant (Hertha von Walther) is working with her back to the camera at a table of beakers and test tubes. Fellman enters the office, and in a mid shot, with his back to the camera, removes his cane, hat, and jacket and changes into a white coat. He and his assistant do not acknowledge each other. While he is sitting at his desk opening his mail, a woman with her young daughter enters the office. He goes to them, crouches next to the child, and invites her to open a box of candies he offers her. In a reverse-angle intercut shot, taken from the other side of the lab table, Seeber offers the first glimpse of the assistant's face, the lower part obscured by an apparatus. Then he cuts from a mid close-up of the mother, admiring her daughter, as she turns her face from a profile, camera right, to a three-quarter profile, camera left, and smiles, not looking at the assistant, who acknowledges her in a frontal close-up, her face still obscured by the apparatus. Announcing, "Come—Papa's expecting us," the mother leaves with the child, walking away from the camera. Fellman, still crouching with the candy, smiles, then frowns; he goes to stand beside the assistant at the lab table, backs to the camera. The shot fades to black.

With the emergency event and the workplace established, Seeber now shoots the Fellmans, with the maid serving, at home at the table, after dinner, and then seated at the hearth, where in a tight over-the-shoulder close-up she shows him a newspaper article with the headline "Woman Gruesomely Murdered." Curiously, he seizes the newspaper from her and throws it into the fire. When a police inspector pays a visit to inquire about the homicide in the house nearby, he extends his hand, palm upward, but instead of taking it, Fellman simply lowers his head to look closely at it, as if unfamiliar with this convention of greeting. After Fellman responds to his inquiry by observing he heard only cries for help this morning, the inspector leaves peremptorily.

When Fellman returns to the hearth, he finds his wife waiting for him with a surprise, which she is shielding by standing in front of a small table. The surprise is an Indian small statue in ivory, a mother and child with acolytes, and what it represents, an imminent visit by her cousin Hans (Jack Trevor), who is introduced in two photographs of him, dressed in colonial white linen and a pith helmet and sporting a pipe, along with a letter (intertitle) that discloses he will be coming from Sumatra, Indonesia, then a Dutch colony, under the jurisdiction of the Dutch East Indies, and alludes to "presents." The next shots are of Fellman sitting next to the fire, showing him from two angles unsheathing a long Sumatran knife like a *parang*, the knife in a close-up, and Frau Fellman looking on in a close-up. After holding up the knife for closer inspection, Fellman suddenly throws it and the sheath onto the table, as if afraid of what he might do with it. Clearly, the knife, the newspaper article, and his own straight razor represent his unconscious desire to kill his wife, and suggest he did hear the outcry "Last night—with a razor!" in the morning, just as he heard the cry for help earlier. Thus, when he admits to the police inspector he heard this cry, he is disclosing his conscious knowledge; in contrast, he sublimates his unconscious desires yet does have some intimations of them, which his instinct is to reject or preclude precipitately. Subsequent scenes confirm the idea of the suppression of desire: of the maid reading the account of the murder in the newspaper she has salvaged from the fire, and, in contrast, of the Fellmans in their separate bedrooms, in which he sits brooding for a while before preparing to retire and she starts to get ready for bed, but then decides to lock her bedroom door from the inside. The next section of the film, titled "The Dream," explores a *bricolage* of his dreams on a stormy night in the form of a psychoanalytic depiction of their unconscious desires, a mixture of the real and surreal, starting with an exterior shot of the house on a dry moonlit night, followed by a close-up of Hans, perched in a tree in the garden.

Seeber amplifies this first manifestation of unreality or minimal mimesis—the man in the tree—by drawing liberally on his expertise with *der trickfilm* or special-effects shots. For example, when Fellman, dressed in pajamas, comes out onto the patio, he notices Hans in the tree and tries to run back into the house, but finds the door is locked. Meanwhile, Hans targets Fellman, raising arms into the position in which he would hold a rifle and then producing a pop gun instantaneously, which Seeber effects in a match dissolve. To avoid getting shot, Fellman starts to jump and wave his arms, as if trying to fly away. Seeber cuts to a traveling matte shot of him elevating from the ground, and then an overhead fast-motion track-back shot, to evoke his perspective during his ascent; of the patio below, for which he used a miniature model; and a traveling matte shot of him rising through the dark sky. A mid shot shows Hans aiming at Fellman and discharging his weapon, a cork on a string. Then he reverses the shots of Fellman's ascent: the traveling matte shot now shows his fall, and the overhead fast-motion shot now tracks forward. As Fellman falls to the patio, Seeber cuts to the mid shot of Hans, who salutes and then vanishes in a match dissolve. Then he cuts to a shot of Fellman in bed, stirring in his REM phase of sleep. Seeber explores this phase further with another shot repertoire. He shows Fellman, again in pajamas, walking through a pointed archway toward a statue that resembles Hans's gift. But by crossing the threshold he encounters an alternative reality, which Seeber represents in a montage comprising double exposure, dissolve, and traveling matte, and light-and-shadow shots of Fellman wandering through space, encountering barriers such as an iron railing, two trains, one superimposed over the other, and the image of Hans waving from a train compartment window; encountering the statue in giant form with a human face; witnessing an animated city rise from the ground and seeing, in a close-up, the pealing bells atop a tower dissolve into the swinging heads of his maid, his wife, and his assistant. He runs up the external spiral staircase of a set replica of the animated bell tower and looks down to see, in close-up, a multiple-exposure collage of men's faces laughing at him. Here Seeber cuts to a shot of Fellman restless in bed, and then a transitional shot of Frau Fellman in her bed, who wakes to the lightning flashes of the storm and the sound of her husband in the next room, which introduces the next dreaming phase, which concerns the murder yesterday in a neighboring house, which Fellman envisions in window silhouettes of a man and woman engaged in a deathly struggle, a shadow play in which he appears, dressed in a suit and bowler hat, outside on the balcony and shaking his fist and his walking stick in an attempt to intervene. Suddenly, in an animate shot the balcony railing rises to enclose the entire facade of the house, when Seeber cuts to a high-angle shot of Fellman hanging from the top rail, and then to a mid shot of Hans, tapping as if on glass. Here Seeber introduces a trial montage, consisting of as many as five exposures produced with masks one on top of another per frame and shot through lenses with small focal lengths, with Frau Fellman presiding, three top-hatted gentlemen and other figures as judge and jury, and giant drums, both stage properties and live-action silhouettes of drumming, representing justice, and Fellman, standing in his pajamas, as the accused. At one point, Frau Fellman, in an over-the-shoulder shot, lifts the back of her hair to expose the razor scar at her neckline. Clearly, the coincidence of Fellman's accidentally inflicting this wound and the fatal knife attack against a woman in the neighborhood is what has provoked his dream about his unconscious desires. In his next dream phase, he is with his assistant, trying to look outside a high barred window. He grabs an armful of books from a tabletop and throws them on the floor under the window, but, finding the pile is not high enough, he returns to the table, where, in a match dissolve, another stack of books has appeared. Still the pile is not high enough: another match dissolve, another stack of books. Finally, he gains the perspective he requires: through the bars, which in an exterior close-up resemble prison bars, he sees a romantic scene: his wife with Hans in a rowboat on a tranquil pond: in a reverse-motion shot, Frau Fellman draws a baby doll out of the water, a child she has had with Hans. They wave at Fellman as the boat passes under his window. In a close-up Seeber reveals him imprisoned, screaming with rage. He returns to the office, from which he now grabs the Sumatran *parang*, and when the image of his wife appears in a double exposure, he stabs at it repeatedly, until the image vanishes, when Seeber cuts to a close-up of Fellman waking, sitting bolt upright, and screaming in terror. When his wife comes running into his room and throws her arms around him warmly, Seeber films them in a wide shot that reveals their complete body interaction and marks the only time they have expressed any physical affection for each other.

> Eine besondere Wesenart des stummen Films was der Trick. Seine Existenz begann mit der des Films überhaupt und er ist nicht nur allgemein verbreitet und benutzt worden, sondern man hat ihn ausgebaut, wie selten ein anderes Verfahren. Der Filmtrick oder besser der Trickfilm, hatte sich zu einer Spezialität entwickelt; er war in seiner Anwendung und Ausführung praktisch ohne Grenzen.[6]

> A special feature of silent film was the trick. Its existence began with film itself, and it has not only been used extensively, but it has developed more than any other method. The film trick or, better, animated film, had evolved into a specialty; in its application and execution it had virtually no limits. (St. Pierre's translation)

Nevertheless, in *Geheimnisse einer Seele* Seeber had to test the limits of special effects, precisely because Pabst elided the borders of visual characterization beyond thought to the unconscious, which could be represented convincingly only through heterodox shot-and-image combinations. In *Orlacs Hände* (1924) Robert Wiene explored a similar theme of the murderous impulse and the trope of knives, and cinematographer Günther Krampf also used special effects extensively, within the high conventions of the horror genre and Expressionism in German film. Eisner notes,

> Certain shots representing the dreams of a repressive could never have been filmed had it not been for Expressionism. In this style Pabst discovered a means of giving a luminous and unreal relief to objects or people, of deforming architectural perspective, and or distorting the relative proportions of objects.[7]

In contradistinction to horror and Expressionism, Pabst was breaking new ground by taking representation into the discipline of psychoanalysis, for which there were no filmic traditions. Luis Buñuel and Salvador Dalí in *Un Chien andalou* (1929) would provide the next great example of a psychological film. Pabst required a radically new visual language, and a repertoire of special effects that in evoking dreams draws much more on Surrealism than on Expressionism. For example, a later scene, a visualization of his session in psychoanalysis, in which Fellman, dressed in black and shot from behind in near silhouette, walks toward the light source, a window, and closes the blinds, darkening the room, owes much to Surrealist painting and performance in its stark, dispassionate, and dreamlike avant-garde depiction of an encounter with light and space.

In the morning Fellman looks at himself in his shaving mirror as he did yesterday, but his routine breaks down when he tries to strop his straight razor and drops it, alarmed that his hand slipped. Leaving the razor lying on the floor, he goes to the barbershop for a professional shave rather than facing this first manifestation of the unconscious desires he explored in his dreams. Seeber shows the barber stropping his razor, applying the lather, and shaving Fellman, in close-ups, exposing him in his extreme anxiety as the barber strokes his neck and chin in particular. Later at work, he enters the room, changes into his white coat, and sits down at his desk to open the mail just as he did yesterday, but today he panics when he reaches for the letter opener. In contrast, when Seeber focuses the camera tightly on the letter opener, its form is that of a knife but its function is different, to slit rather than cut. He confirms the function of the tool when he tears open the envelope by hand. That he is not yet facing his unconscious desires is apparent when his assistant informs him his wife called to say her cousin has arrived for a visit and, although he smiles upon hearing the news, his shock makes him drop a test tube, which Seeber represents by cutting between close-ups of his hand releasing the tube and of it smashing on the checker-tile floor, which recalls the pattern of the patio tiles onto which he crashed in his dream.

In a film structured on two such mimetically diverse planes of reality—oneiric and empirical, unconscious and conscious—and focused on characters who learn to cross the threshold of identification and acceptance between them, Pabst and Seeber had to establish interpretive channels, thematic and cinematic, to link them to achieve unity. For example, thematically, they explore parallels between the razor murder and shaving with a straight razor and, cinematically, between the production of images through the faculty of imagination and the medium of the film itself, blatantly through the special effects of *trickfilm*. When the film shifts to the first nondream scene of the visitor, Seeber shows Frau Fellman and her cousin Hans looking at photographs of themselves as children, and thus he contrasts these fixed archival images of human relationships with the fluid images of Fellman's dream, in which his wife has a sexual relationship with her cousin, which has issued a child. But if "photographic seeing has to be constantly renewed with new shocks, whether of subject matter or technique, so as to produce the impression of violating ordinary vision,"[8] then the shocks of dream images, which are both subject matter and technique, and including the initial implied image Fellman forms of his wife's cousin when he first learns he has arrived for a visit, which startles him into dropping the test tube, then Pabst and Seeber's collaborative endeavor in *Geheimnisse einer Seele* would seem to be about *the shock of the adaptable image*, in reference to psychological experience and psychoanalytic interpretation or spectatorship, and about "violating ordinary vision" through an array of special effects and a fluid camera that is also an adaptable camera. Thus, only a cinematographer with an adaptable camera could create the complex effect of the trial scene of Fellman's dream by layering five frames of exposures, as distinguished from double exposures. When Fellman returns home from work and meets Hans at the hearth, they embrace and exchange greetings warmly, with no hint of anxiety, yet they also turn directly to looking at the photographs, a more stable form of human interaction, because fixed, not fluid, like the contents of the test tube spilled on the floor. Later at dinner, while Frau Fellman and Hans eat normally, Fellman has some psychological problems dealing with knives: when he notices three knives in his place setting, he immediately covers them with his napkin; when his wife hands him the knife to carve the meat, he subverts etiquette by deferring to her; and when he is faced with cutting the food on his plate, he breaks down and makes his excuses peremptorily: "You must excuse me—I cannot eat with you" and "I can't touch the knife!" (two intertitles). Subsequent scenes reveal he has sought refuge at a *ratskeller*, and Frau Fellman, who is on the porch, is looking for him on the property. Seeber shoots him finishing his drink, emptying his change onto the table to pay the server, and then walking out, forgetting to pick up his house key from the table. A close-up shot of the key indicates a man at a neighboring table has noticed this, and a subsequent shot of him shows he could intervene, but elects not to. A morally ambivalent figure, the man could be a criminal, intent on stealing the key, or simply indifferent and amoral. In the next shot, Seeber films Fellman, followed by another man, as he arrives at his front gate and discovers he does not have the key with him. The other man, who as he walks toward the camera is revealed as the man from the bar, now approaches Fellman and gives him the key, which Seeber films in the close-up of his hand holding the key, with only the end ring exposed. Fellman takes the key and thanks the man, who then asks a question: "Is there some reason you're reluctant to enter your own house?" (intertitle). His query is not inappropriate, because it confirms a suspicion spectators may have had about his forgetting the key, which was conspicuous on the table and not likely to be missed. Thus, spectators now realize that the close-up of the key, representing his noticing it on the table, actually signified the man's deduction about Fellman. Not indifferent, the man focused on a seemingly small incident and drew an astute inference about Fellman's unconscious motivation. When he sees Fellman is unwilling to respond, the man apologizes for asking the impertinent question, explaining "it's part of my job" (intertitle), which suggests he may be a psychoanalyst.

Inside, his wife comes downstairs to find Fellman sitting by the fire. All in close-up shots, she crouches next to him, and as they embrace, he runs his fingers through her hair and exposes the small scar on her neckline; then he glances over to the mantelpiece, where he notices the unsheathed *parang*, and he tries to suppress the intimations of his unconscious desires. Holding her head down with his left hand, he reaches with his right hand to the *parang*, which is barely evident in the foreground of the field of view, then in a close-up he places his open hand over the handle, in another close-up his facial display shows his crisis of conscious and unconscious will, and finally in a mid shot he breaks his hold on his wife and flees the scene, rushing toward the area immediately in front of the camera lens and, out of focus, in a fade to black blur, exits the field of inaction. The next scene reveals where he has fled to, the home of his mother (Ilka Grüning). Meanwhile, Frau Fellman, along with Hans, reports Fellman's disappearance to the police, where she inadvertently raises suspicion about him by establishing a timeline between his strange behavior and the neighbor's murder, although she implies only that he has been completely distraught. When the police inspector informs her the murderer was arrested today in Munich, any suspicions spectators may be entertaining that Fellman is the murderer are quelled.

Back at his mother's home, after Fellman has confessed his impulse to murder his wife and his mother asks him, "Do you know of no one who can help you?" Seeber cuts to a close-up of him, with his mother, in which he is manipulating his house key, a mnemonic of his encounter with the psychoanalyst. While the visual connotations of the key are obvious to the film's spectators, Seeber needs to show Fellman makes the connection, which he does in a tight point-of-view close-up in which he is holding the key up to his eyes, which dissolves into a double exposure with the close-up shot of the analyst's face from the earlier scene, as Fellman remembers it now. Returning to the *ratskeller*, Fellman makes some inquiries about the man, learns his name, Dr. Orth (Pavel Pavlov), and that he lives nearby, and then pays him a professional visit, where the consultation must be conducted mainly through intertitles, which distract from the flow of Fellman's confession, but also through facial displays, which fill in these gaps. The consultation does establish (1) that Fellman may have a serious mental illness and (2) that Dr. Orth believes he will be able to help him through psychoanalysis. Orth telephones Frau Fellman to inform her he is to take charge of Fellman's treatment, which requires he live away from home for three months. Seeber constructs her reaction shots creatively: a close-up of her facial display, expressing sadness and disappointment, and a close-up of her torso, in which her left hand is visible and her right hand replaces the telephone out of frame, and she sits down, bringing her face in three-quarter profile into the shot. In two shots and character movement, he records her whole reaction.

In their sessions together, Dr. Orth instructs Fellman to tell him what is in his mind's eye, which seems also a self-reflexive allusion to the "Dream" section of the film. Thus, when Fellman recounts his experience on the morning of the murder, Seeber illustrates it not in intertitles, the medium for representing their dialogue to this point, but in the visual syntax of the unconscious mind. The shot in which Fellman shaves the back of his wife's neck, for example, is quite different from the shot at the beginning of the film. Now, Seeber shoots them both from behind and against a matte background that almost eliminates the illusion of three dimensions, in a flat space with no spatial definition other than that of their bodies. Sitting on a stool, with her head bent forward, obscured from view, as he stands leaning over her, wielding the straight razor at her neck, she initially looks as if he has decapitated her. Suddenly, they both turn around, which an intercut shot of the neighbor crying "Help!" through her window, confirms as the noise they heard. A close-up of Fellman in three-quarter profile, in which he turns away from the camera, and the cut to a close-up of Frau Fellman's neck, which her husband is poised to shave with the razor, show how he ignored his neighbor's desperate petition and the entire emergency that morning and concentrated instead on satisfying his unconscious impulses, not by trimming his wife's hairline but by deliberately cutting her. The juxtaposition of the window shot and the neck shot shows the association Fellman makes between the two events in his unconscious mind. The next shot, also against a monochrome matte background of negative space, shows Fellman, as he was on his way to work, observing the murder site and the gossip of onlookers: "Last night—with a razor!"

Seeber intercuts these *tableaux* memories with close-up psychoanalysis shots of Fellman, lying down, with Dr. Orth, leaning over him, both of them facing the camera.

In their elision of the foreground, midground, and background of the vision field in these scenes of psychoanalysis, reconstructing the events of the morning of the murder, Pabst and Seeber depict Fellman's unconscious impulse for violence with the flatness of *Neue Sachlichkeit*:

> On a perceptual level these realist artworks, engaged in a precise form of mimetic representation, challenge stylistic commonalities: some are cold, sober, anti-emotional, and allegedly objective; some appear timeless (though sometimes in unexpected ways) and are often labeled Classicist; finally some are very literal and graphic in their depiction of violence, abnormalities, sexuality, and social inequalities and are frequently categorized as Verist. Yet in one way or another, they all make visible an alienated relation to the real, sometimes in the form of a dangerous and unpredictable outside world, one that is either devoid of humans or populated with ugly bodies and hyperbolic faces that appear as if filtered through a ghostly and uncanny present.[9]

Thus, the minimally mimetic scenes reconstructing Fellman's confessional testimony, cross-cut and counterpointed with the maximally mimetic scenes of Freudian psychoanalysis, "make visible an alienated relation to the real," the relation of the unconscious to the conscious mind.

When Dr. Orth speculates on the cause of his anxiety by inquiring if he recently quarreled with his wife, Martin's negative response is enacted in a wide-shot *tableau* of the Fellmans standing on a patch of earth, he bearing a shovel, she a shoot: he digs a hole in which to place it, which they do together, each with a hand on the stem, crouching together. Then Seeber cuts to a close-up of their hands together, holding the plant in place and filling the hole with soil. In subsequent analeptic scenes, the Fellmans enter their first apartment as a married couple, which is totally stark, with no furnishings except in the room designated as a nursery, but in a match dissolve the crib and accessories vanish and the nursery becomes an empty room, which represents their inability to conceive children together. Other scenes explore his erotic fantasies about his wife's sexual relationship with her cousin, in orgies and at parties, at which he is present as voyeur and cuckold, and finally in a stark *tableau* in which all three of them appear at a formal leave taking, when Hans, Martin's lifelong friend, departs to his new life in the tropics. Fellman attributes his illness to the day he learned Hans was returning to visit with them, and he envisions his sense of separation from his wife in a park scene where they are disparate bodies.

Fellman's breakthrough moment in analysis pertains to his dream, which Seeber reprises in some of the original special-effects footage, specifically of three converging trains, of Hans shooting him out of the sky with his popgun, of a montage of trains with Hans in one of the cabin windows, and of him caught behind railings. He also recalls being traumatized by the news Hans had arrived, when he dropped the test tube in the laboratory, standing before an Indian idol, a large replica of Hans's gift, and climbing the bell tower with the pealing bells and severed heads. His recollection of the visit of the mother and her daughter to his laboratory, however, is different from the original. It is set in the flat space with the matte background. He offers the girl a box of candy, as in the first iteration of the scene, but this time Seeber cuts to a close-up of the mother and his assistant standing side by side, who are looking at him amusing the girl, and then turn to each other and laugh at him, as if knowing he is childless has made him a ridiculous figure to them. Then Seeber focuses on the assistant in a close-up as she smirks at him. This shot marks a breakthrough in Fellman's therapy, because it provides unrestricted access to a character who is usually filmed in a wide shot from behind, or in profile and three-quarter profile mid shots in which her face is obscured by laboratory equipment, and with whom Fellman has little direct interaction. An intercut shot of Fellman, still on his haunches and holding the candy after the girl has gone, shows he has noticed the assistant sneering at him and he feels humiliated by her. At this point Dr. Orth confirms the diagnosis most spectators have made based on visual evidence: "In your nightmare, the small wound on your wife's neck flowed together with the crime in the nearby house—for this reason you saw yourself condemned as a murderer." He concludes, "So this psychological illness kept you from killing your wife." In a subsequent session with Dr. Orth, Fellman discloses his dream about his wife, Hans, and their doll baby in the rowboat, but his visualization of the memory of the dream is different from the visualization of the dream earlier in the film. In this representation, Fellman is at his office, with his assistant, and it is she who points out Frau Fellman with Hans in the rowboat, in a double-exposure image in the room.

In memory, he traces the dream scene in which Frau Fellman give the doll baby to Hans, to an experience in which as children the three of them were photographed, as in the picture she and Hans look at earlier, and his wife gave his and her doll to Hans, which greatly hurt Martin's feelings. As Dr. Orth interprets the recollection, "The pain you experienced when your wife gave 'your doll' to your cousin has remained awake in your childless marriage" (intertitle). Martin further recalls when he attacked the appearance of his wife with the *parang*, but in his visualization of the event now there is no double exposure of his wife, and he simply thrusts the weapon at the air, a gesture that he imitates now in the office, with a knife he has grabbed from his desk, which Dr. Orth interprets as a positive sign he is beginning to shed his phobia about knives and razor blades. Having made this breakthrough, he returns home. He first sees his wife looking through the window as he approaches the house. He seems to recognize her framed reality as markedly different from a dream, from the framed appearance of Hans in the window of a train cabin. Inside the house, he embraces his wife, and Hans, when he enters the room moments later, and he apologizes for the trouble he has caused them through his long absence, and the scene implies his terrible dreams as misrepresentations of him. The reconciliation scene is oversimplified, but Seeber's mid shot of Frau Fellman smiling as she looks on at her husband and cousin, friends again as they were in childhood, does invoke a form of visual closure on the film. Nevertheless, the film does not end here but continues in an epilogue, which functions as a maximally mimetic corollary of Fellman's dream and his re-creation of it through psychoanalysis.

The epilogue is set in a bucolic setting, a cottage in the Alps, where the first shot reveals Frau Fellman relaxing on the porch, and the second shows Martin fishing at the river: he catches a fish and throws in into a bucket of water, with several other fish; then he heads back to the cottage along a path on the riverbed; when he sees his wife standing on the porch, holding up a bundle, he drops his bucket and fishing rod and starts running to her. Seeber films him from behind as he scrambles up the steep grassy hill to the cottage, and in front as he nears the top, using a handheld camera that follows him very closely with a spontaneous and unsteady flow of images, camera movement that follows the terrain and imitates his movements and point of view. It is a remarkable live-action shot, the most energetic, inventive, and memorable of the film, and, compared to the special effects that form the majority of the shot repertoire, an avant-garde shot appropriate to what Martin Fellman finds at the top of the hill, his wife holding their new baby. It is a triumphant scene, highly sentimental, of course, but not inconsistent with marital experience.

G. W. Pabst and Guido Seeber made one more film together, *Man spielt nicht mit der Liebe* (1926), which has been lost. Their collaborative partnership rests on *Die freudlose Gasse*, remarkable for Seeber's sympathetic camera and social realist cinematography, and *Geheimnisse einer Seele*, notable for his *trickfilm* photography and psychological realist cinematography. Common to both films are *die Kamera-Realität*, an adaptable fluid camera suited to sociological and psychological representations, and to a variety of visual and technological experiments. Seeber worked productively with Pabst, designing slow-motion photography, five-exposure, short-focal-length special effects, wide-arc trucking and tracking shots, and live-action handheld shots. His expertise as a camera operator and technician with such a diverse shot portfolio made Seeber the ideal cinematographer to record Pabst's radical visions of human sexuality and psychology.

NOTES

1. Graham Bader, "Life in the Democracy and the Aftermath of War," in *New Objectivity: Modern German Art in the Weimar Republic 1919–1933*, ed. Stephanie Barron and Sabine Eckmann, 130 (New York: Prestel, Los Angeles: Los Angeles County Museum of Art, 2015).

2. "Das wandernde Bild," in *Das wandernde Bild: Der Filmpionier Guido Seeber*, ed. Norbert Jochum, 74 (Berlin: Elefanten, 1979).

3. *Die freudlose Gasse* was subject to severe censorship in Germany. Extant copies of the film distributed internationally also were extensively cut and adapted. Filmmuseum München's reconstruction (2012), which it describes as "an approximation," is still missing 600 meters (or about half an hour) of film from the original 3,738 meters.

4. Don Fairservice, *Film Editing: History, Theory and Practice; Looking at the Invisible* (Manchester: Manchester University Press, 2001), 173.

5. H. Mario Raimondo-Souto, *Motion Picture Photography: A History, 1891–1960* (Jefferson, NC: McFarland, 2007), 100.

6. Guido Seeber, "Trick und Ton," *Das wandernde Bild: Der Filmpionier Guido Seeber*, ed. Norbert Jochum, 125 (Berlin: Elefanten, 1979).

7. Eisner, *The Haunted Screen*, 31.

8. Susan Sontag, *On Photography* (New York: Farrar, Straus and Giroux, 1973), 99.

9. Sabine Eckmann, "A Lack of Empathy: On the Realisms of New Objectivity," in *New Objectivity: Modern German Art in the Weimar Republic 1919–1933*, ed. Stephanie Barron and Eckmann, 27 (New York: Prestel, Los Angeles: Los Angeles County Museum of Art, 2015).

9

Rudolph Maté, Carl Theodor Dreyer, and the Framing Principle of Cinematography

Rudolph Maté (1898–1964) served his apprenticeship in his native Austria as principal cinematographer on six films, 1920–1922. He entered the German film scene in 1923, as assistant cinematographer, with Axel Graatkjaer, on Peter Paul Felner's *Der Kaufman von Venedig*, based on Shakespeare's *The Merchant of Venice*, and, with Stephan Lorant, on Felner's *Dunkle Gassen*. He began to establish his distinctive style as a cinematographer working as assistant to Karl Freund on the Danish director Carl Theodor Dreyer's *Mikaël* (1924). William Everson reported about Maté, "With an unaffected modesty, he disclaimed credit for the 1924 Dreyer film *Mikaël* on which I assumed he had collaborated with Karl Freund. 'Freund really did all the work there, but had to leave for another assignment before the film was finished. I was called in to complete it, and it didn't amount to more than a few days' work.'"[1] Because he saw in Maté a potential collaborator compatible with his Naturalistic vision for film, as was apparent in his experience in the intervening years working as assistant cinematographer on Arthur Robison's *Pietro der Korsar* (1925), and as principal on Conrad Wiene's *Unter Ausschluss der öffentlichkeit* (1927) and Martin Berger's *Die Hochstaplerin* (1927), Dreyer appointed him principal cinematographer on his *La passion de Jeanne d'Arc* (1928), a film that bears the stark images of their common visual grammar and iconography. His experience with Dreyer and the earlier relationship he established working with Fritz Arno Wagner on *Pietro der Korsar* led to his opportunity, the year after Wagner had filmed her in G. W. Pabst's *Tagebuch einer Verlorenen*, to photograph Louise Brooks in Augusto Genina's *Prix de beauté* (1930). Maté worked with Dreyer again, along with assistant cinematographer Louis Née, on one of the director's most stylistically innovative films, *Vampyr* (1932), a *bricolage* of Naturalistic narrative and Expressionistic light-and-shadow images. Maté and Dreyer's working relationship on three films over eight years is one of the most versatile cinematographer-director collaborations in the Weimar period.

Mikaël is a film about artistic sensibility as well as homosexual love. It resembles a series of *tableaux*, with each setting and each frame composed as a painting. Although this painterly imprint is attributable more to principal cinematographer Karl Freund than to Maté, it was on this film that Maté learned Dreyer's aesthetic principle that the camera lens is a framing device and the operator's task is to find not just the right shot but also the moving painting, as distinguished from the moving image, because it records action and modifies frame content through camera movement, as in tracking shots, close-ups, wide shots, and cross-cutting. Although the emotions of *La passion de Jeanne d'Arc* are fundamentally spiritual, not erotic, although they are sometimes sexualized, and those of *Vampyr* are pagan as well as spiritual, Maté and Dreyer adapted the framing shots they designed in *Mikaël* for the more complex visual grammars of these films.

Rudolph Maté was born Rudolph Mathéh on January 21, 1898, in Krakau, Galicia, Austria-Hungary, now Kraków, Poland. His father was Hungarian. After attending the University of Budapest, where he studied art, graduating in 1919, Maté began working in the film industry as a laboratory assistant and then an assistant camera operator for the Hungarian director Alexander Korda at the Corvin Film Company, where he also shot three films for other directors. In 1919 Korda had been appointed to the Communist Directory for the Arts, responsible for nationalizing the film industry. But when the conservative Miklós Horthy came to power in Hungary in 1920 and the film nationalization program was scrapped, Korda, along with Maté, relocated to Vienna in 1921, to work for Sasha-Film. In 1924, Maté went to Berlin to take up an opportunity to work as a second-unit camera operator for producer Erich Pommer, who had produced some of the greatest of German films—such as Lang's *Harakiri* (1919), *Die Spinnen* (1919, 1920), *Vier um die Frau* (1921), *Der müde Tod* (1921), *Dr. Mabuse der Spieler* (1922), and *Die Nibelungen* (1924); Murnau's *Schloss Vogelöd* (1921) and *Die Finanzen des Grossherzogs* (1924); and Wiene's *Das Cabinet des Dr. Caligari* (1920)—and was instrumental in shaping filmmakers' careers. He gave Maté a formative opportunity when he appointed him as assistant to the great cinematographer Karl Freund on Carl Theodor Dreyer's *Mikaël* (1924). His contribution to this film's visual imprint influenced Dreyer to designate him principal cinematographer in 1927 on the Paris location shoot of his *La passion de Jeanne d'Arc* (1928).

> Dreyer found Maté eager to help evolve a photographic style that would subserve this intelligent dramaturgy, and together they hit upon "frog perspective"—i.e., the cameraman lies or squats on the ground and shoots up, and upon the utilization of white in decor, costume, and the lighting itself, to sharpen the impressions the audience receives. Finally, to these fundamentals of whiteness and "frog perspective," Dreyer and Maté added a third: very large full-face close-ups.[2]

In other words, Dreyer considered Maté a suitable candidate for a collaborative partnership on *La passion de Jeanne d'Arc*, a *gemeinschaftsproduktion* on which director and cinematographer have equal status as filmmakers and thus equal responsibility to design this new visual syntax.[3] Their film aesthetic concentrated on (1) close-ups of the expressive facial displays of actors wearing no makeup and shot with panchromatic film, high-resolution film sensitive to all the wavelengths of visible light and designed to record subtle gradations in skin tone and movement; (2) variations in high-contrast (hard) and low-contrast (soft) lighting for the purposes of sculpting the *mise-en-scène*, a massive concrete set in the style of medieval architecture, and humanizing the characters as fallible by disclosing the imperfections of the actors' skin; and (3) extreme low-angle "frog perspective" shots, and including shots in which the camera was placed into a hole to augment the angle and depict Joan's judges, interrogators, and clerics as inimically as possible. In shooting actors without makeup Dreyer and Maté were observing the portraiture conventions of *Neue Sachlichkeit* and its humanist depictions of ordinary people during a period of recession.

> In the worst years of the German depression Helmar Lerski made a whole compendium of distressing faces, published under the title *Köpfe des Alltags (Everyday Faces)* in 1931. The paid models for what Lerski called his "objective character studies"—with their rude revelations of over-enlarged pores, wrinkles, skin blemishes—were out-of-work servants procured from an employment exchange, beggars, street sweepers, vendors, and washerwomen.[4]

In its front matter following the opening credits, *La passion de Jeanne d'Arc [The Passion of Joan of Arc]* describes the discovery of a rare manuscript in the library of the Chambre des Députés, Paris, a transcript of the court testimony at the 1431 trial of Joan of Arc. The opening shot is of this document, a close-up of the handwritten manuscript and a man's hands turning its pages. Intertitles[5] intercut with shots of this manuscript further describe its contents, "the judges' questions and Joan's responses are recorded with great precision," and its claim that "a reading uncovers Joan as she was, not dressed in helmet and armour—but simple and human . . . a young woman who died for her country." In Maté's orientation shots Pabst establishes the parameters of both his Naturalistic style and their *gemeinschaftsproduktion*.

The film's opening dramatic shot is a slow, long-duration high-angle horizontal tracking shot across the length of the courtroom, front to back, and establishing that in this film the boundaries of the visual field will be transgressed. Maté concludes this panorama by cutting to the low-angle shot of the Bishop Pierre Cauchon (Eugène Silvain), which also tracks in to him reading the charges against Joan, and he pans to show a first glimpse of Joan (Maria Falconetti), a head shot, before cutting back to the bishop. He moves back and forth between the two shots to show her as she walks to the front of the courtroom, in three-quarter profile and frontal shots and in mid shots, close-ups, and tight close-ups, and then to a close-up of her manacled ankles as she takes a few tentative steps. After swearing her oath on the Bible, Joan takes her seat, a stool, in front of and below the judge as he interrogates her, asking her name and age. Her answers are thoughtful: her name is Jeanne, but she is called Jeannette; she calculates her age on her fingers and replies, "Nineteen years, it seems" (intertitle). Here Maté cuts to a close-up of the judge, and then swiftly tracks out to reveal another judge on the bench, and both of them laughing paternalistically at the naiveté of her response. He reverses the shot when he quickly tracks in to a close-up of a priest who asks her if she claims that God has sent her, to which she responds straightforwardly, "Yes." When she sees she has perplexed her interrogator, she adds, "To save France" and "It was for this that I was born" (intertitles), as if the truth will mitigate his confusion. Her interrogators first humor and then sexualize Joan, who in appearance and behavior is an androgynous figure, by asking her about her apparition of St. Michael, how he was, whether he had wings, if he was wearing a crown, what he was wearing, how she was able to know whether he behaved like a man or a woman, and, to follow up, if he was naked and "Pensez-vous que Dieu n'ait pas de quoi le vêtir?" ("Do you think God has nothing to clothe him?"). The reference to clothing prompts Bishop Cauchon to address her androgynous appearance as irreligious, by asking, "Pourquoi avez-vous pris cet habit d'homme?" ("Why do you wear men's clothes?" or, literally, "Why have you adopted a man's religious habit?"). Acknowledging her androgyny as a strategic form of dress, a "habit," she responds that only when the mission God has conferred on her is complete will she again adopt women's clothing.

> A corollary to the exaltation of androgyny, in Bakhtin's carnival, is the practice of transvestitism, or men dressing as women and women dressing as men. Transvestitism per se is not necessarily progressive or feminist. It can be seen, as Mary Russo points out, as an ambivalent "acting out of the dilemmas of femininity." On the one hand, transvestitism can be motivated by dreams of androgyny, parodying patriarchal dress, or operating what Kaja Silverman calls "male divestiture," the symbolic stripping away of masculine privilege. On the other, transvestitism can easily degenerate into misogynistic caricature. The point I would like to emphasize here, however, has to do with the relation between transvestitism and the historical evolution of codes of dress.[6]

That the clerical judiciary in their religious habits are men dressing not only patriarchally, in imitation of the pope or patriarch, but also in a form of women's attire, so cross-dressing, makes their intolerance of Joan's male dress, through which she parodies male and religious privilege, one of the key issues in her trial, as important to them symbolically as her religious apostasy.

Thus when they ask about her apparition of St. Michael what he was wearing and whether he was naked, they are acknowledging that her codified dress is her dream or apparition of androgyny. While the members of the judiciary confer about her answers, which in the end, after Joan admits to her hope that God will reward her for her work with the salvation of her soul, they rule to be blasphemous, although one priest stands up to defend her as a "saint," Maté follows them around the table, in both directions, with a low-angle tracking close-up shot that focuses on each man's facial display frontally and, as one man turns to confer with the next, in profile, and in three-quarter profiles that establish new diagonal perspectival and action lines.

This tracking shot, like most of the shots in *La passion de Jeanne d'Arc*, is directional, rather than symmetrical or centered. After their conference all the priests in their habits can think to ask Joan is if God has ordered her to wear men's clothing. Maté's fusion of a fluid camera with the minimal field size of his close-ups, along with Dreyer's shot breakdown calling for a full range of facial close-ups of Joan and her clerical accusers—medium (head to waist), close (head to chest), head and shoulders, choker (head and throat), tight (hairline to chin), extreme (eyes and/or mouth), clean single (one character), and dirty single (one character and part of another)—and low-angle (priests) and high-angle and eye-level close-ups (Joan) that signify differently in the film, is one sign of their constructive collaboration. Jean Mitry observes, "We have only to imagine Dreyer's *The Passion of Joan of Arc* shot in wide-shots rather than close-ups and mid-shots: nothing would have the same meaning."[7] For example, when Joan confesses she expects God will reward her with the salvation of her soul, one priest stands and approaches to attack her, which Maté shoots (1) in a directional low-angle two-shot with her in the bottom left corner and he in the upper right corner of the frame; (2) in extreme close-ups of his mouth berating her; (3) in these extreme close-ups intercut with dirty singles, close-ups of Joan, where the priest's mouth is visible, and in the last of which he deliberately spits on her cheek; and (4) in an entire sequence whose directionality is composed on the diagonal line of the field of vision. According to Luft:

> Maté regarded . . . Dreyer as a genius. "He has a very clear mind and absolute integrity," Maté told me. "He never compromises, and is intransigeant about the artistic imperative. He understands all phases of filmmaking and is a very precise craftsman, planning his picture long before shooting begins. He also reviews each night the work for the following day. He is apt in divining the fortes and lacks of his players and collaborators."[8]

Clearly, Dreyer and Maté shared a sense of what was vitally important aesthetically and visually in *La passion de Jeanne d'Arc*, which was partly the spirituality and historicity of the figure of Joan. Equally important to them aesthetically was the original visual syntax they made together.

This perspectivally intimate style is attributable also to contemporaneous developments in film camera technology, visual aesthetics, and the protocol of spectatorship in the Weimar Republic. For example, in *Die Liebe der Jeanne Ney* (1927), Pabst and Fritz Arno Wagner also fostered a cinematic style based on a preponderance of close-ups and tracking shots. Maté had assisted Wagner on *Pietro der Korsar* (1925), where the younger cinematographer may have picked up some camera tricks. On the set of *Mikaël* (September 1924), he had worked with Karl Freund, who was then padding his repertoire of close-up and tracking shots to use on F. W. Murnau's *Der letzte Mann* (December 1924) and may have influenced Maté's style. In addition, many other contemporaneous German filmmakers were experimenting with close-up shots:

> Some working-class Berliners in Robert Siodmark's film *Menschen am Sonntag* (1929) are having their pictures taken at the end of a Sunday outing. One by one they step before the itinerant photographer's black box—grin, look anxious, clown, stare. The

movie camera lingers in close-up to let us savor the mobility of each face; then we see the face frozen in the last of its expressions, embalmed in a still. The photographs shock, in the flow of the movie—transmuting, in an instant, present into past, life into death.[9]

More important than questions of attribution, of direct stylistic and aesthetic influence, however, are new art movements and modes of representation like *Neue Sachlichkeit* and the phenomenon of multiple discovery. For the first twenty-five years of film history, 1895–1920, the camera had been heavy, bulky, stationary, excepting tilt and pan shots, and remote from its subjects, from its own field of view, in a sense. But in the 1920s cinematographers started to experiment with smaller and more mobile cameras, with tracking, trucking, and other vehicle-assisted moving shots, beginning with Freund, when he strapped a camera to his chest in *Der letzte Mann*, and with directing the camera closer to the subject, action, and setting, thus controlling the field view.

In *La passion de Jeanne d'Arc* this control is most evident in passing shots, specifically, (1) close-ups that through camera movement become dirty singles: for example, the profile close-up of a soldier who raises and turns his head as Maté tilts and pans in the same direction to reveal the priest he is looking at; (2) extreme close-ups, from the eyes to the top of the head, in which the subject raises his head from the bottom of the frame, thus converting extreme into conventional close-ups; (3) shots of a monochrome background into which the subject raises his head from the bottom of the frame into the field of vision, thus converting the original blank shots into conventional close-ups; and (4) close-up shots of lances and the crowns of helmets visible at the bottom of the frame as soldiers walk in single file across the vision field but mostly out of frame. Maté later takes a shot similar to this one of the soldiers, when the judges vote with a show of hands on Joan's guilt and he tracks the camera across the group, showing only their heads and raised arms. These are the principal forms of character movement in passing close-up shots, but Dreyer and Maté seemingly explore every conceivable form of head movement in their shot breakdown. What most of the close-ups, both passing and tracking shots, have in common in their composition is some variation of the extreme close-up, in that the camera films part of the face, in frontal shots the top or bottom of the head or one-half of the face, and in profile shots the line of profile only, but not the head that gives it definition. These "incomplete" close-ups emphasize both the multifaceted aspect of the judiciary and, in relation to Joan, whose facial close-ups are always entire, their fragmentation. Her facial close-ups are usually frontal, but sometimes, as when she is listening and responding to a question, Joan moves within the shot from a profile to a frontal orientation. It might be said, *La passion de Jeanne d'Arc* is about character, but not about characterization. Nevertheless, it does focus on a form of visual characterization: spectators come to know the main characters by how Maté elects to shoot them and, in a sense, by how they display themselves, grotesque because magnified, in the natural pantomime of facial expressions, postures, and gestures, in front of the camera. He also exploits the antithesis of the close-up by subverting the form. For example, when Bishop Cauchon asks her if God has promised to deliver her from prison, and Joan replies "yes" but adds she does not know the day or hour, he is furious because of her allusion to the dogma that no one knows the day or hour of their death. Maté films him in a close-up, from which he tracks out swiftly and far back, diminishing the bishop to the eye, but also suggesting how he is casting his glance at Joan, in his vision but out of the vision field. When the trial adjourns, one of the priests observes, "If she is not willing to make a confession with softness, then one must try to extract it out of her by cunning." One scene shows priests forging a letter from King Charles VII, which they intend to use to incriminate Joan. In contrast, in her detention room, a soldier twists her wrist to allow him to steal her ring, but when a priest notices the theft, he confiscates it and returns it to her, and tells her of the pity he feels for her. Maté shoots their poignant exchange in two shots, a close-up of Joan, who is seated, looking up at him as she replaces the ring, and a mid close-up of the priest looking down at her from the doorway. Then, even while knowing they are being watched, which Maté confirms in a track-in close-up of the square spy hole in the door, in which the face of the guard is framed, as in a frame of film, the priest warns Joan of what is to come in the trial by asking if she is familiar with her king's signature. When he discerns in her face that she is not, he presents her with the forged letter, which suggests that the theft of her ring and his intervention in returning it were part of a ruse to earn her trust. A second shot of the guard framed by the spy hole, closer than the first, now reveals only his eye, which signifies not his surveillance but his confirmation of the priest's "cunning." Joan takes the letter from the priest, looks at it, and then confesses that she does not know how to read. This scene exposes the priest, the guard, and all the clerical judiciary as literalists: literate, educated, privileged men, but they are also interpreters who take the Bible, and who enforce its dogmas and teachings, literally.

Joan could not say she was familiar with the king's signature, not because she is unfamiliar with it, but because she could not read it. The priest reads her the letter: "I am preparing to march with a large army on Rouens. I am sending you this devoted priest. Have faith in him." Then, led by the guard, one after another a group of seven clerics enters the cell camera right, each passing against the background of the open barred door in a diagonal trajectory and leaving the field of vision in the foreground left corner. They ask her some of the trick questions posed in the courtroom: if Jesus is the son of God, does she consider herself a daughter of God; would she care to recite the Pater, or "Lord's Prayer"; does she believe God will deliver her from this prison; has God promised her that she will be in heaven and that she is certain to be saved. On the latter two questions, however, she glances over to confer with the priest, who each time nods his assent. She responds affirmatively to all questions. When the cleric who in court voiced his support for her rises up now to caution her that her assertion she is sure of her salvation is crucial, Bishop Cauchon very angrily shouts him down. They go on to twist her words, asking whether, given her assurance of salvation, she no longer needs the Church, and if she is in a state of grace. As she ponders the latter question, and as he represents his responses to all the questions, Maté cuts to a three-quarter profile close-up of her tilting her head up to her interrogator. This time, however, recognizing the gravity of the question about grace, she touches her mouth with her fingers, weighing her options. But in an improvisational moment, a housefly crawls down her forehead and onto her eyelid, when she brushes it away with her hand. Given the many facial imperfections the program of close-up shots reveals, this spontaneous and transitory flaw in a shot that easily could have been retaken makes it the greatest of them all.[10] Her answer is appropriately great, given that her counselor priest refuses to help her on this one; in effect she says, if she is in a state of grace, it is by the grace of God.

Maté films the clerics' individual reproachful reactions in a sweeping tracking mid shot across eight faces. Corresponding to this shot is the close-up of Joan in profile and looking up as Bishop Cauchon berates her after she asks if he would allow her to attend mass: from this position she slowly turns her head to show her other profile looking down, thus tracing a diagonal line across the vision field in conveying her desolation. Later, in the torture chamber, Pabst makes reference to this shot when a judge tells Joan, "Ne voyez-vous pas que c'est le diable qui vous a tourné la tête" ("Do you not see that it is the devil who turned your head?"). In addition, the judges inform her that her revelations come not from God but from the devil. As if in reaction to what he perceives as her show of humility in turning her head, the bishop, on the advice of a priest, offers to permit her at mass if she gives up her men's clothing. When she refuses, the bishop, with typical scholastic excess, concludes that she loves men's clothing more than attending the mass and, hence, she is not a daughter of God but the minion of Satan. He orders her to be taken to the torture. Even though he is drawing on the testimony of her trial, Pabst, by linking her torture to the transgression of cross-dressing, refers to gender fluidity in Weimar Germany, when boundary-crossing in gender, sexuality, and clothing was acceptable. After the clerics leave, the door guard and two other guards, knowing she is to be tortured, enter to mock her, such as by tickling her face with a piece of straw and squeezing her chin. Maté's close-ups of them sadistically laughing as they ridicule her are the most grotesque in the film.

Initially the judges torture her with insults and, when she refuses to sign a retraction, threaten her with excommunication, which to frighten her they tell her will leave her alone. But Joan is already alone in her mostly single close-ups, which seem to protect her from her accusers, or as she puts it, "alone with God." Next they show her the mechanisms of torture, such as spiked wheels, serrated blades, nozzles for dribbling boiling oil, which Maté films in close-ups and mid shots in the style of *Neue Sachlichkeit* paintings and photographs of industrial machines.

After fainting upon seeing the instruments of torture, she falls gravely ill and is taken to the infirmary, where almost all of Maté's shots are oblique angle, of Joan lying in bed, the monks opening a vein in her arm to allay the fever, and the priest celebrating a last-rite mass for her. As well as evoking her delirium, these oblique-angle shots, in which the camera is positioned between the vertical and horizontal, are typical of shot composition throughout the film, in which subjects, in posture, gesture, and expression, position themselves, pose, between the vertical and horizontal axes. The climax, comprising the extensive sequence of outdoor scenes that lead up to her execution by burning at the stake, is remarkable for both types of oblique shots, those in which the camera rotates twenty to forty-five degrees and those in which the subject turns twenty to forty-five degrees, in either direction. When Joan finally signs the document, retracting her military, social, and gender positions, the bishop rescinds her excommunication and declares that she is again in good standing with the Catholic Church, but he also sentences her to life in prison. Dreyer and Maté cross-cut close-ups of Joan having her hair shorn for her incarceration, with wide tracking shots of an adjacent sideshow, showing contortionists and sword swallowers who are practicing. This counterpointing of dysmorphic subjects seems to justify Joan's decision to recant again and reclaim her original position, the consequence of which is she is sentenced to be executed immediately *sur le bûcher*. Maté shoots the soldiers marching to prepare her pyre in a complex overhead shot that begins with a ninety-degree-plus shot that discloses them partly upside down walking into the ninety-degree overhead and out of it into a high-angle shot in which they walk under a raised iron gate. He exploits the inversion of this shot to show the people as they hurry to witness the execution: high-angle, overhead, and two ninety-degree-plus shots. He complements these overhead shots with panoramic low-angle tracking shots of the spectators gathered around her on the pyre. In the final scenes of the film, after Joan's death, Maté again uses mostly overhead and high-angle shots, including some ninety-degree-plus and extreme high-angle shots to film the skirmish between rioters who believe they have witnessed the martyrdom of a saint and soldiers ordered to quell the uprising with maximum force, including spears and cannons, inflicting fatalities. Maté's final shot sequences of her are of two principal kinds focused on two stages of her martyrdom: (1) low-angle close-ups of her head, positioned at various angles, passion shots for presence, in which, lashed to a pole, she is wholly recognizable and is wafted in smoke rising from a source out of frame, presumably the pyre in which she is standing; (2) low-angle mid shots of a model figure of the charred body, which at this point may be attributable to Joan only in the profile outline of the head and of course the circumstances with which spectators are familiar, in the midst of the flames, martyrdom shots for presence, and in which she appears, in the religious paradigm, as a holocaust, a burnt offering wholly consumed, and, in the cinematic paradigm, as an ironic special-effect silhouette, as if Dreyer introduces it to mark an end to Expressionism, and a credible Naturalistic depiction of a cadaver.

La passion de Jeanne d'Arc is a humanist biography, whose standard of narratological mimesis is historicity and whose standard of cinematographic mimesis is the frame of the field of view. Thus, in that the film comprises mainly single close-ups, of Joan, Bishop Cauchon, the principal judges, and several of the guards and soldiers, each shot is conspicuously framed; similarly, the subject of each shot is framed, in the manner of the portrait subject of a painting or photograph. But Maté's subjects move around liberally within the portrait frames and, in its mobility, his camera renders

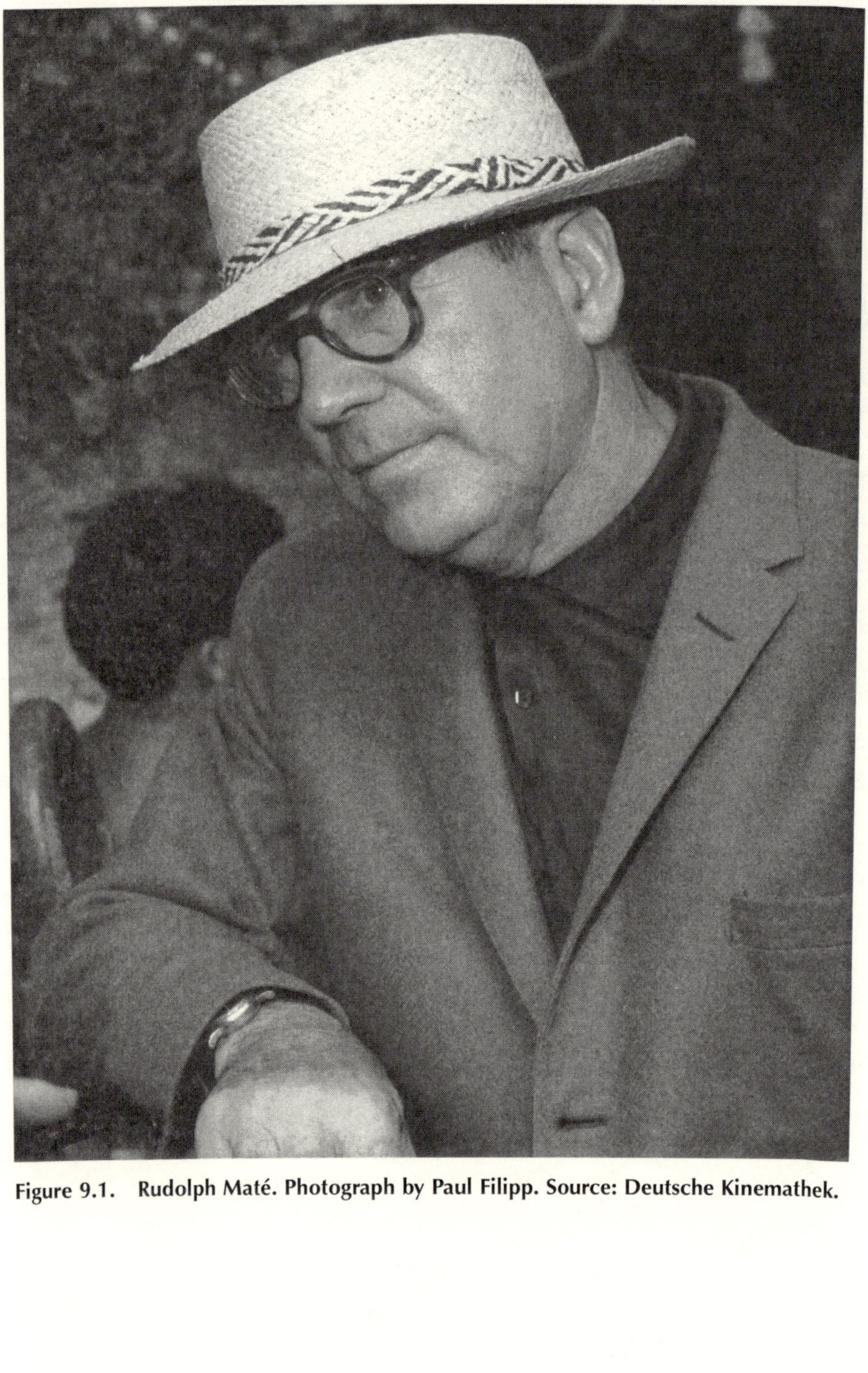

Figure 9.1. Rudolph Maté. Photograph by Paul Filipp. Source: Deutsche Kinemathek.

the frame borders elastic and arbitrary. Similarly, spectators drawn into close-ups are always aware of what is going on outside them, of whom Joan is looking at.

In *Vampyr* (1932), the collaborative partnership of Dreyer and Maté reached its apogee. Between *La passion de Jeanne Arc* and *Vampyr*, Dreyer had made no films, devoting himself to cowriting the 25,000-word screenplay of *Vampyr* with Christen Jul, and Maté had worked on eleven minor short and feature films, with the exception of *Prix de Beauté* (1930), directed by Augusto Genina and starring Louise Brooks. *Vampyr* is mainly a silent film, but it does feature several brief passages of dialogue in its German, French, and English versions.[11] A horror film, it begins with a front-matter narrative study of the protagonist, Allan Gray (Julian West, the stage name of French actor Nicolas de Gunzburg), a scholar researching the history of vampires and demonism, who becomes so consumed by his subject that he can no longer distinguish between the subjective appearance of the supernatural and the objective reality of the material and empirical. His peripatetic quest for supernatural phenomena now brings him to the town of Courtempierre, to a secluded inn by the river in late evening, where Maté takes his first shots.

He films Allan Gray, well dressed in suit and hat, and with a long-poled fishnet slung over one shoulder and a fish bag over the other, in a wide shot as he enters the frame, camera right, walks a few steps along the riverbank, and then turns and walks a few more steps toward the camera. A low-angle intercut shot of a metal sculpture sign, in the figure of an angel, from which Maté tilts down to show the word *HOTEL*, discloses his destination. He takes the first mid shot of Gray from inside the bar, through the window as he knocks the door to find no one there. The next shot, exterior, is of a lighted window of a room: Gray enters the frame to tap the glass. Immediately, the light goes out, when he hears a voice say, "Who's there?" Maté now cuts to a low-angle shot of the roof, where a young woman has raised a skylight and is shouting down directions to the entrance to the hotel. He appears back at the bar door, again in an interior shot. The next shot, a point of view, shows that he notices a man with a scythe over his shoulder, walking away from him and to the river. An interior shot now shows the innkeeper opening the bar door from the inside, and an intercut to a mid shot from behind the sower, his scythe now appearing massive, as he rings a bell three times to call the ferry to take him across the river. This may be the film's first horror image: Death calls upon Charon to ferry him across the River Styx.[12] Or it may simply be the image of a worker returning home after spending a day sowing fields. That spectators see this scene from Gray's perspective illustrates his confusion over appearance and reality. That they later see a pole-navigated flat barge ferry arrive at the dock, not from Gray's perspective but from the camera's point of view, indicates his confusion may be theirs too. From his hotel room, Gray looks out the window, when he sees, in a frontal mid shot, the reaper sitting in the boat, his scythe propped up against his shoulder: his face is visible for the first time, bearded, that of an older man, weary-looking, but definitely not appearing to be Death. Yet because spectators have adopted his perspective, they too wonder about appearance.

Closing the blind, Gray now walks around his room with a lighted candle: Maté follows him in a tracking shot, probably from a handheld camera, as becomes more evident in a subsequent shot sequence. Now he uses the candle to illuminate a framed engraving, on the grotesque theme of death. When he hears a loud voice coming from somewhere in the hotel, possibly sounding like somebody in distress, he goes out to investigate. Maté follows him down the hall with a handheld camera, shaking with a quivering motion, and as he ventures upstairs. On the next floor he encounters a grotesque little old man who has just opened his door: whether he is the source of the noise or is investigating it like Gray is unclear. But Gray's immediate reaction is to retreat downstairs into his room and lock the door behind him, in a track-in close-up, as if he has encountered the supernatural, which the following intertitle confirms, in reference to the interplay of light and shadow that night: "Allan Gray felt a sinister force descend upon him." Maté confirms the phenomenon of chiaroscuro in a cross-cut to a low-angle shot of the hotel-sign angel against a sky of dark clouds penetrated by moonlight. His foreboding is confirmed when, lying awake on his bed, he hears a loud knock at the door, sees the key turning in the lock, and then witnesses a man entering his room, the Lord of the Manor (Maurice Schutz), an older gentleman, well dressed in pajamas, a mohair housecoat, and a silk necktie. When Allan asks him to identify himself, he walks to the window and rolls up the blind, and then, pointing to the ceiling, indicating the room upstairs, says, "Quiet" and "She mustn't die. You understand?" Then he walks to the desk and places on it a bound envelope, taken from his pocket, on which he writes, "To be opened upon my death," and, nodding deferentially to Allan, leaves the room. Allan now gets up and, handling the envelope and sensing a soul is in danger, dresses and goes out to investigate the mystery by leaving the hotel. Dreyer and Maté intercut two more shots of the angel sign, which by now have become a motif to invoke the supernatural. On the riverbank Allan witnesses the shadow of a human form pass along the water on the other side, but with no human being casting it, and through a doorway in the wall around a derelict house, the shadow of a gravedigger at work, but in reverse-motion footage, catching shovelfuls of dirt and filling a grave. Entering the outbuilding, he sees the shadow of a man on the opposite wall, his silhouette like that of a veteran soldier with a prosthetic leg (Georges Boidin), who proceeds to climb a ladder. Maté achieves these disembodied shadows, that is, independently moving shadows with no visible human bodies and light sources producing them, through the use of double exposures. When an old man enters the room and walks toward him, Allan retreats.

Outside, he again sees the gravedigger's shadow, and then through an opening in the wall he sees a new phenomenon in which shadow and body are united: the veteran with the prosthetic leg, now in bodily form, is sitting at one end of a bench, where he is soon joined at the other end by his shadow; the human body, seeing his shadow, imitates its posture, which Maté engineers in a match dissolve, at which point the two start to move in unison, in response to a command from the old man. Later, Allan sees a more elaborate shadow play, that of two couples dancing and musicians performing, all cast on a wall, until the Old Woman from the Cemetery (Henriette Gérard) enters from the basement, in a high overhead shot, shakes her cane, and demands "Silence!" In the first circus shot of *Vampyr*, Maté films Allan coming into a room in the building, from which he pans right and moves clockwise into a 360-degree tracking shot across the four walls and shows their macabre content, and ends with Allan walking across the camera's field of view. When he enters the next room, Maté executes the same circular tracking shot, only counterclockwise, with him again crossing the view field. In an extreme low-angle shot, the antithesis of an overhead, from Allan's point of view, he shows a hand moving along the banister of a staircase landing one floor above. The figure of the village doctor (Jan Hieronimko) appears, walks down the stairs, past Allan, taking no notice of him, and walks into a corridor, investigating an unusual sound. He turns around and asks Allan if he heard the sound. Allan believes it was the voice of a child and the sound of dogs barking, but the doctor insists there are none in the house. After showing Allan out of the house, having not questioned what he was doing there, the doctor receives the Old Woman from the Cemetery, who presents him with a bottle of poison, which he seems to have been expecting. On the grounds of the derelict house, Allan witnesses more disembodied shadows passing over the grass. This time he follows them to an estate, where he encounters the old man who appeared in his room at the hotel, with his two daughters, Gisèle (Rena Mandel) and Léone (Sybille Schmitz), both of whom are bedridden, currently asleep, but also recovering from unusual wounds to their necks, and under the surveillance of a nursing sister (Jane Mora). Outside, looking in through a window, Allan witnesses in an upside-down silhouette the figure of a man drawing a rifle and firing. Maté cuts to a shot of the Lord of the Manor, collapsing as if the bullet has struck him in the back. Allan urgently attracts the attention of a servant, who lets him in; he rushes upstairs to the aid of the old man, but all he can do is spoon him tea to moisten his mouth and lips as he, now accompanied by Gisèle and the nurse, watches as the old man dies. Maté films the man's death scene mainly in an overhead close-up, into which Allan's hand appears with spoonfuls of tea. The shot is all about Maurice Schutz's acting, notably his impassive stare, his helplessness, and his resignation to die.

After helping to move the body to a dignified resting place, a servant invites Allan to stay at the mansion, to which he agrees. Later, he removes the bound envelope from his suit pocket, which earlier in his hotel room the man marked "To be opened upon my death." In it he finds a small leather-bound book titled *Die Seltsame Geschichte der Vampyre* (*The Strange History of Vampires*) (1770) by Paul Bonnat, whence Maté intercuts a shot of the first page, which reads:

> Accounts from many ages and lands tell of terrible demons called vampires. These are the bodies and souls of the dead whose terrible deeds in life deny them repose in the grave. Under the bright light of the full moon, they rise from their graves to suck the blood of children and young adults and thus prolong their shadowy existence. The Prince of Darkness is their ally and lends them supernatural power among the living and the dead.

As well as explaining all the shadow and silhouette phenomena to this point in *Vampyr* and enlightening Allan about the elision between supernatural and natural events, this excerpt makes a specific allusion to F. W. Murnau's *Nosferatu, eine Symphonie des Grauens* (1922) and to a similar scene, in which Hutter finds the book *Of Vampyres, Terrible Phantomes, and the Seven Deadly Sins* and reads the first page, about Nosferatu, "who liveth and feedeth on human blood." Clearly, Murnau made *Nosferatu* and another Expressionist film, *Schloss Vogelöd* (1921), earlier in his career, and before turning to the cinematically ingenious *Der letzte Mann* (1924) and to theatrical films like *Herr Tartüff* (1925) and *Faust: Eine deutsche Volkssage* (1926). For Dreyer, in contrast, *Vampyr* was a thematic and stylistic departure from films like *Mikaël* and *La passion de Jeanne d'Arc*, and it was for him, a Dane working in the German film industry, a paean of praise for the Expressionist tradition as exemplified by *Nosferatu* and for one of its greatest practitioners in Murnau. Still, *Vampyr*, while it has the vampire theme and light-and-shadow special effects in common with *Nosferatu*, lacks its visual shock value, notably in the grotesque performance of Max Schreck as Count Orlok. Appearing at the end rather than the beginning of the decade, and particularly as an early sound film, *Vampyr* seems an anachronism, yet is much more than a catalog of special-effects shots. Dreyer and Maté's shadow effects, for example, are not meant to be visually spectacular, with the exception of the match dissolve in which the disparate forms of an actor and a shadow start to move in unison. Allan notices the shadows, and they even inspire him to continue his search, but he is not frightened by them; he seems to perceive them as he perceives all phenomena, unquestioningly. Even the astonishing match dissolve me-and-my-shadow phenomenon does not shock Allan, but simply raises his curiosity to enter the next room. Unlike *Nosferatu*, *Vampyr* is remarkable more for Maté's ingeniously executed high- and low-angle shots and ambitious camera movement, much in the manner of *La passion de Jeanne d'Arc*, than for his trick shots, which are really his and Dreyer's means to pay tribute to Murnau and his cinematographer, Fritz Arno Wagner. It might be said *Vampyr* is a visually progressive vampire film, whereas *Nosferatu* is a visually arresting one.

For example, in his first shot after the shot of the first page of the book, Maté films the nurse looking in on Gisèle from the left side of her bed and then stepping out of the view field on the left: then he pans right, across her in bed and the night table to the door, when the nurse, seen from behind, reenters the vision field, turns her head to look back at Gisèle, opens the door, and leaves the room. The nurse has simply walked around the foot of the bed, but her movement is implicit because out of frame; in contrast, a moving camera shot that shows her moving out one side of the frame and moving back into frame on the other side, is quite complex: it makes camera movement a correlative of the nurse's implicit movement off camera, preserves the visual continuity of a short transitional scene, and involves spectators inferentially in shot composition. Maté complicates the shot further, first by holding it on the nurse, visible in the next room through the open door, and then by panning left to show Gisèle's bed is now empty. The next shot, of Allan reading from *Die Seltsame Geschichte der Vampyre*, intimates where she has gone:

> At night these creatures from the abyss haunt the abodes of the living, where they sow death and decay. A vampire's victim is doomed to perish without hope. A wound on the throat, as from a cat or rat, is the mark of damnation.

Dreyer has now established these book shots as a motif, a choral commentary on the action, and Allan's resource for interpreting events. The motif recurs throughout the film. From his reading Allan now looks up to see Gisèle at the window, alarmed by what she sees and calling out the name of her sister, "Léone!" When he comes to investigate, Maté cuts to a high-angle filtered shot, as if through the frosted glass, to show Léone walking distractedly on the grounds, as if she is sleepwalking. When Allan and Gisèle run outside, they cannot find her. In a reverse point-of-view shot, Maté shows them in a wide shot, looking across the field in the direction of the camera; then, in a mid shot, he films Léone lying on a stone bench, and the Old Woman from the Cemetery, kneeling over her body, presumably having just punctured her neck to ingest her blood, and getting up and, in a pan shot that reveals she realizes Allan and Gisèle have been watching her, walking away. They run to Léone, unconscious on the bench, and are soon joined by an old servant (Albert Bras) and the nurse, who carry her body back to the house. There, from the interior, Maté takes a wide tracking shot of a mysterious young woman outside, visible as she walks past two windows and then enters the house through an open door. From the threshold, he pans left to a set of double doors, and then in a long track-out shot that passes through several connected rooms and doorways he discloses (1) the old servant's wife (N. Babanini), who walks toward the camera, where she meets (2) her husband and the nurse, who carry Léone into the house, camera right, and toward the retreating camera, and (3) Allan and Gisèle at the foot of a staircase, looking as the others arrive and, led by Gisèle, carrying Léone upstairs. Then Maté pans right to follow Allan, who walks back through the doorway, closing the door behind him. From the shot of the woman in the windows to that of Allan closing the door is a very complex single take, comprising a left tracking shot, a left pan shot, a long track-out shot, and a right pan shot. When she regains consciousness, Léone reveals she is not damned and wishes she could die, and immediately afterward starts acting like a vampire, as by eyeing her sister as if she is blood prey.

Maté executes another ambitious fluid shot in a scene in which the village doctor, whom Allan encountered earlier at the derelict house, comes to examine Léone. When the doctor acknowledges him, however, it is simply out of politeness, with no indication he remembers him. First, Maté shoots the doctor in a standard profile mid shot, taking Léone's pulse, following by a close-up of her in obvious discomfort, and then a tracking mid shot of him in profile, walking along the perimeter of room camera right, past the door, to a dresser, on which he places a billfold from his pocket. Here Maté tracks back, camera left, to the door, which opens to show Allan as he enters the room and looks toward the bed, and then he continues to track left to show the nurse sitting at Léonc's bedside. Then he tracks the shot back in the other direction, to Allan at the door, and follows him as he walks over to the doctor at the dresser and asks, "Can't she be saved?" When the doctor responds that she might be saved through a blood transfusion, Maté follows Allan as he walks back toward the bed, at which point the shot ends. This multidirectional tracking shot, forth, back, forth, and back, like the earlier long track-out shot, is a single take, demonstrating Maté's admirable facility for seamless camera manipulation, and also, it should be noted, his and Dreyer's practical commitment to exploit the full potential of whatever tracking infrastructures, such as dollies and other wheeled support vehicles that move on linear and circular tracks, have been built into the set locations to facilitate camera movement.

But these complex tracking shots are functional as well as pragmatic: typically, they are transitional, their movement leading into scenes that are significant to the plot and Allan's quest to differentiate between the natural and the supernatural. For instance, after the doctor tries to persuade Allan to be Léone's blood donor, Maté cross-cuts to a shot of the old male servant as he enters a room, from which he tracks the camera right across the room to Gisèle, seated on the other side. The tracking shot follows not the servant's physical movement across the room but his act of looking across at her. When the shot reaches her, she asks, "Why does the doctor always come at night?" Then Maté cross-cuts to a close-up of Allan, from which he tilts down to show his bare arm in a tourniquet. The preceding tracking shot reveals why the doctor always comes at night and why he was intent on drawing Allan's blood: clearly, the doctor is a vampire whose desire is not to cure Léone but rather to establish a codependent blood relation between her and Allan. For instance, when Allan, recovering from the transfusion, notices his syringe wound is leaking blood, the doctor assures him from the next room, "Nonsense! Your blood is right here!" Maté also uses tracking and pan shots transitionally, but for practical rather than dramatic purposes, such as to follow all levels of characters in their movement toward and away from ordinary things like furniture and doorways. Thus, when Allan poses his question, Maté tracks from a high-angle shot of him reclining in a chair to the doorway where the doctor appears to provide his equivocal response. His fluid camera in *Vampyr* is conspicuous throughout the shot breakdown. Tracking shots always make the transition from one to another shot. But whereas in *La passion de Jeanne d'Arc* the most notable transitions of this kind are from close-up to close-up, in *Vampyr* they are typically close-up to mid shot, and vice versa, but never between close-ups. Dreyer and Maté enhance their supernatural theme by eschewing intimacy. Maté films the Old Woman from the Cemetery feeding on Léone's blood, in the horror genre the most intimate of acts, in a mid shot. The hazy lens filters he uses for all exterior night shots to simulate darkness enhance the distance between spectators and the subjects of the film camera.

> To achieve the unusual photographic quality of *Vampyr*, Dreyer and photographer Rudolph Maté experimented until they found that a piece of tulle placed over the lens of

the camera glowed slightly as the sun or the light from floodlamps shone on it. In this way they achieved a sort of bright foggy light throughout the film exteriors, which created a unique style and tone. Dreyer says, "We created the style day after day. It was not copied from any painter. Reproducing the style time and time again was very hard."[13]

Distancing is also an aspect of the reading of *Die Seltsame Geschichte der Vampyre*, which the old servant takes up, thus removing the knowledge he gains about vampires from Allan. He learns how to kill vampires, with an iron stake through the heart, and about local vampirism.

> Even in these parts, tradition tells how certain areas were haunted by vampires. Just 25 years ago, a murderous epidemic claimed 11 victims in the town of Courtempierre. Doctors assigned the plague a medical name, but a persistent rumour circulated among the people that a vampire was the cause of the scourge. Many firmly believed that vampire to be none other than Marguerite Chopin, who lay buried in the local cemetery.

This information, which corresponds with present phenomena and seems to identify the Old Woman from the Cemetery as Marguerite Chopin, and a vampire, is fraught with dramatic irony. Following his reading, the servant takes up Allan's cause. Investigating a strange noise in the house, he catches the doctor creeping upstairs to Allan's bedroom and, suspicious, follows him. Cross-cutting to show Allan asleep, Maté represents his nightmares in animated shots of a human skeleton, including a close-up of its hand raising the bottle of poison the Old Woman delivered to the village doctor earlier. He cuts from the animation to a close-up of Allan asleep, with a hand entering the vision field to shake him by the shoulder to wake him. Then he tracks back to reveal the hand not of the village doctor or of Death from his dream, but of the knowledgeable servant, who has come to help him. Together they arrive just in time for Allan to prevent Léone from drinking the bottle of poison the doctor has placed on her bedside table. Next he goes after the doctor, but this pursuit takes him into the realm of vampires, spirits, shadows, and special effects.

As Allan searches the house for the doctor, Maté represents his perspective in another 360-degree panoramic tracking shot of a room, this one fast-moving, to evoke his urgency. Then he cuts to a shot of the shadows of the dead on the grounds, that the following shot of Allan looking through an open door reveals to have been from his point of view. Dreyer and Maté's interplay of straight camera shots and special effects is masterful. For example, in a shot of the sickroom, Maté films the old servant sitting in a chair, then tracks to the nurse praying at a *prie-dieu* and, upon hearing Léone call her, to her going to her bedside, then tracks back to the servant. This shot sequence is about succor and empathy, the nature of human beings. But in the next sequence Maté explores supernatural phenomena through special effects. He films Allan running across the grounds. After falling and twisting his leg, he sits on a bench to rest, where in a match dissolve that is the inverse of the earlier match dissolve in which the veteran soldier and his autonomous shadow start to move in unison, a translucent image of Allan's body, representing his spirit or supernatural self, rises from his physical body, making it also translucent, and, leaving it behind on the bench, he continues to search the grounds for the doctor. As a translucent spirit he enters the cellar of the derelict house, where he discovers a suspicious coffin. When he pulls back its cloth cover, he looks down and is shocked to see his own material body inside. This shot was straightforward for Maté: he shoots Allan lying in the yet-to-be-sealed coffin and adds a double-exposure image of him looking at "himself" in the coffin. Logically, it is problematic, however, since there are now three images of him: human being, spirit, corpse. Mimesis in horror films is governed by emotion, not logical supposition.

Lurking in the cellar, Allan makes three startling discoveries: (1) Gisèle is bound and imprisoned in a room; (2) the village doctor, her captor, hides the key to the room inside a grandfather clock; (3) the veteran soldier is the doctor's minion and is currently occupied with securing the wooden lid to the coffin containing Allan's corpse. Each of these shots is from Allan's point of view, which, from the opening shots of the farmer with the scythe, Dreyer and Maté have established as the spectator's. But the point-of-view shot of the soldier covering the coffin is different, not of the translucent spirit Allan but of the dead one: in a mid shot Maté first shows the soldier holding the coffin lid upright in front, with only his fingers visible; then, moving into a close-up, the soldier lowers the lid, still upright, aligning it with the coffin box, until his face appears in a square opening at the top, the glass spy hole designed for observing the corpse in repose; next, he starts to position the lid horizontally, and as he leans over to lower it onto the coffin box, his face is more closely visible in the spy hole. Throughout, the point of view is that of the Allan corpse, which is illogical, of course, yet in the context of the horror genre highly charged emotionally: it provides spectators too with a macabre perspectival correlative of their own death and interment. As the soldier fits the lid in place, Maté cuts to a long-lens interior shot of the Allan corpse, executed from the back of the coffin: by increasing the focal length, he narrows the angle of view along the horizontal subject of the body and enlarges and brings into focus the head and particularly the dead face, now framed in a square of light coming in from the spy hole above. Maté cuts to pan shots of the village doctor observing the work and the soldier walking to the workbench to fetch a hand drill back to the coffin and, in a tilt-down that focuses on his prosthetic leg, pick up his tool kit. Then he cuts back to the interior close-up of Allan in the coffin and cross-cuts to a reverse-angle close-up from the corpse's point of view through the frame of the spy hole, in which the soldier is visible turning the handle of the drill to secure the lid finally. His task completed, he places a candle on the glass and lights it, which Maté films in close-up from below: then, visible from the same perspective, a hand appears in the window frame, to lift the candle to use it as a light source, and then the face, in a diagonal extreme close-up of the Old Woman from the Cemetery, whom spectators can now identify as Marguerite Chopin, vampire progenitor of the Courtempierre contagion, followed by an external close-up of what she sees from her side of the glass, the ghoulish face of Allan Gray appearing to stare back.

Maté exploits his interior and exterior coffins shots for the fullest climactic effects of horror. For instance, after the village doctor commands Gisèle, the soldier, and another minion to carry the coffin to the cemetery, he films the top of the coffin, with Allan's face framed beneath the glass, in an overhead close-up, when the arms of two of the pallbearers enter the shot to lift the box and carry it away. As the coffin crosses the view field, part of an inscription on it becomes legible: *Aus Staub bist du* ("For Dust thou art"). Then Maté takes a moving shot of the ceiling and then treetops, building facades, and the sky, to simulate the corpse's point of view as the coffin is carried through the room, across the threshold, and outside, with intercut close-ups of Allan's face in the window frame, his head now nodding slightly because of the motion of the coffin. His vertical trucking shots of the church steeple to simulate the movement of the subject, the coffin passing beneath it, are especially fine. Executing them would have been easy enough in principle, involving placing the camera upright on a dolly or other vehicle and pushing, pulling, or driving it past the steeple. But the complex oblique as well as vertical perspectives of his resultant shot imply Maté manipulated the camera considerably, such as by executing the shot from a supine position on the dolly, the camera on his chest, in the manner of Karl Freund, who lashed a camera to his chest to get some of the fluid shots in Murnau's *Der letzte Mann* (1924).

In a wide shot Maté shows the pallbearers carrying the coffin into the cemetery, and then he executes a match dissolve to the shot of Allan resting on the bench after he fell in the field, as if the translation of his dead body near this resting place made this image of his living self reappear. Thus, the match dissolve initiates a flashback, based on a distinction between the biological and the supernatural, which implies Allan may be starting to achieve his goal of distinguishing between appearance and reality by experiencing both these mimeses ontologically. Waking up from his revery, Allan alights from the bench and heads to the cemetery, where, looking over a stone wall, he observes, in a wide shot, the old servant, who is using a crowbar to remove a broken stone slab covering a grave, which bears the inscription *Marguerite Chopin*. Allan jumps the wall and runs to help him, by removing slats and eventually the rest of the coffin lid, to reveal the corpse in repose. The servant, who knows the protocol because of his reading of *Die Seltsame Geschichte der Vampyre*, now takes a massive iron spike and, off camera, impales Marguerite Chopin through the heart, a blow that Maté depicts in an abrupt cross-cut to a shot of the sky; he intercuts sky shots throughout this scene and the exterior climactic scenes of the film.

> The special features of Maté's later work, especially in the film "The Passion of Joan of Arc," are destruction of the depth of the shot by "washing" (i.e. putting it right out of focus), mid shots and close-ups taken on the "smooth canvas" of a completely white sky, movement expressed in sharp, frozen turns, and absorption with aerial perspective.[14]

Maté's sky shots, like all his night scenes, are out of focus. Specifically, the moon moves in front of the clouds, giving them focus, and behind them, throwing them out of focus. Maté shows the result of slaying the vampire in an upside-down close-up of Marguerite Chopin's head and torso in the open coffin, looking skyward, which in a match dissolve transform into a white skeleton.

The consequences of the impalement extend into the contaminated community as well. Maté first shows Léone in a mid shot, the nurse sitting at her bedside, asleep, probably after praying for her through the night: she sits up in bed, in the process moving close to the camera, which reveals she has been transformed, is now healthy, and no longer appears demonically possessed, as her utterance, and the nurse's grateful reaction to it, confirm: "I feel strong. My soul is free." Next Maté turns his camera on the village doctor and the veteran soldier in the cellar of the derelict mansion. Visible through a four-paned window, the weather suddenly turns stormy, and, in a match dissolve, the image of a man's giant head appears through the glass, an imposing presence, the facial display identifiable only as Death. The soldier secures the front door, whereas the doctor takes refuge in an adjacent room, locking himself in. Maté focuses his shot on the four-paned window in the top half of the door, behind which the frenetic interplay of intense light and shadow and the appearance of two silhouettes of a raven—"The souls of evildoers . . . are incarnated in birds of prey"[15]—indicate some kind of unspecified phenomena in the room; most likely the doctor is an evildoer who, for now, is managing to weather the storm of Death. The veteran soldier is not so lucky. When the storm passes and the doctor emerges, Maté films him in a circular tracking shot as he runs directly to the door and escapes outside, while the soldier is screaming off camera, and then pans the shot to reveal his dead body, lying upside down on the stairs, first his lower body, his prosthetic leg conspicuous, from which he tilts the camera down his torso to reveal his overturned face with its gruesome death stare. Although the shot is well lighted, the supine body of the veteran soldier now projects no shadow.

Finally, Allan rescues Gisèle. In a close-up of the grandfather clock, Maté films Allan's hand, recognizable from his shirt cuff, in a close-up reaching in for the key to the room where she is imprisoned, from which he pans and tilts to show the hand turning the key in the lock. After an intercut shot of the village doctor engineering his escape by running across the grounds of the mansion to a water mill outbuilding, Maté returns to his close-up of Allan's hands, this time untying the rope that binds Gisèle's hands to an iron grill. Now he cross-cuts to shots of the village doctor in the mill, notably tracking shots of him exploring the facility, scoping it out as a temporary hiding place. While wandering about, he accidentally gets locked into an iron fenced-in area, after the door happens to close behind him. Before he can start to entertain how to get out of there, he notices the servant on a platform higher up in the flour mill and expresses relief he is now to be delivered, not realizing the old man he thinks he knows is actually now a vampire killer. Maté valorizes the servant in his role as the avenger in a spectacular extreme-high-angle shot of him elevated in the crossbeams, in which he looks powerful and dominant over the doctor below. This oblique shot, reminiscent of the shots of the church steeple from Allan's perspective lying in the coffin, serves to reference his role also as a vampire slayer and an avenger for Courtempierre. Rather than responding to his order to free him, the servant activates the mill's elaborate driving mechanism of interlocking gears, water wheels, and grinding wheels. A close-up of the doctor through the bars of his cage reveals his alarm upon realizing he may be trapped. In a low-angle shot Maté discloses a mechanism high above that is starting to release the ground flour into the cage, and cross-cutting to a mid shot, he shows the doctor covered in dust. He draws his camera increasingly close to the doctor's face pressed against the bars, gasping for air, until the cage fills with flour, covering his body almost completely, until only his eyeglasses are visible, then just his hands, held straight up, but now lifeless, holding the bars in a death grip.

Meanwhile, Allan attempts to row Gisèle to safety on the other side of the river, but they become enveloped in mist and disoriented. Their calls for help are answered, however. When they reach the other shore, they discover the ferryman, the Charon figure, has guided them to safety. In the next shot, Maté shows them walking together through the dark and into the light. In its composition the final shot of the film, of the massive gears of the mill mechanism as they grind to a stop, signifies the end, acknowledges *Neue Sachlichkeit* industrial art, and anticipates paintings like Carl Grossberg's *Flywheel with Driving Belt* and *The Paper Machine* (both 1934).

> The last sequence of the film is very formally constructed and gives us, I believe, insight into Dreyer's creative method, one which always tends toward formal control, especially when he is dealing with incident and outward movement rather than people. Here we have the escape of the young people counterpointed with the death of the doctor in the flour mill. The sequence is cross-cut, so that at one moment we see and hear the machinery rhythmically grinding out its white death, and the next we see the young couple gliding slowly on the mist-covered lake, the image being accompanied by a slow, sustained note of music. This combination of shots is repeated in alternation until the couple get out of the boat and go into the sunlit forest.[16]

In their collaborative partnership on both *Vampyr* and *La passion de Jeanne d'Arc*, it was actually Rudolph Maté who exercised control over image form and shot lines, particularly through the exaggeration and distortion of forms and angles, such as in extreme close-up and acute and oblique angle shots, and Carl Theodor Dreyer who managed the larger matters of visual syntax and aesthetics, along with actor performances and *mise en scène* significations.

> On *Vampyr* Maté remarked: "Dreyer and I were sometimes after slightly different things. We didn't always agree—as often happens between artists—and I still don't know who was right. But on *Jeanne D'Arc* on which we worked for seven weeks, we were in complete and absolute accord all the way."
>
> When I recalled the stories of Dreyer forcing Falconetti to spend hours on her knees on the flagstones . . . he was obviously amused, but tactfully made no comment.[17]

The basis of their *gemeinschaftsproduktion* on both films was the framing principle, comprising (1) shot composition, or the aesthetics of the field of view; (2) masking, or the process of blocking the photographic image, including special effects, and *mise en scène*, incorporating rigid structures and enclosures such as doors and windows; and (3) constricting shots and shot angles.

For example, in the opening scene of *La passion of Jeanne d'Arc* Maté films a tight shot of the trial transcript, a small handwritten notebook that, positioned on a diagonal angle by the person who is handling it and leafing through it, fills the frame. In the following shot, a wide tracking shot across the length of the courtroom where Joan of Arc is under trial, and leading up to a track-in close-up shot of Bishop Cauchon, the camera passes a number of jurists in the foreground and soldiers in the background, but in each point along the trajectory, while the constituency of the subjects changes, the number of subjects in the field of view remains quite consistent throughout, between seven and nine, and the jurists keep to the foreground and the soldiers to the background. Thus while the camera is fluid over the protracted shot, the shot composition itself is rather fixed from frame to frame. Dreyer and Maté use an establishing shot, therefore, to introduce spectators to the setting that, excepting Joan's cell and the exterior execution site, dominate the film, and also to usher in a shot repertoire comprising almost exclusively facial close-ups that feature a subject image in the foreground, filling most of the view field, and usually with no actions, subjects, or properties visible in the area behind the image, but rather a nondescript and monochrome background, such as a distant wall, flagstones, or ambient space, a background effect that is most conspicuous in high- and low-angle shots.

Masked and blocked shots are apparent throughout *La passion de Jeanne d'Arc*. For example, in the passing shot that shows the helmets and spear tips of soldiers marching in single file out of the courtroom, the subjects are framed by a doorway, through which they pass one by one: at the end of the shot the door closes behind them, leaving the set of two doors as the frame. In the scene in her cell in which the priest presents her with the forged letter from King Charles VII, the guard outside her door is framed by the spy hole through which he peers. In the first shot, only his right eye and cheek and part of his biretta are visible in the rectangular aperture. In the second shot, the right side of his face is evident: mouth, nose, eye, and part of the biretta. These framing shots are important as signifiers of surveillance and subterfuge, and in identifying the face of the guard. They also set up the arrival of some of the jurists at the cell, as Maté films them entering one by one through the frame of the doorway, the same space through which the guard was spying on her earlier. When the good priest, her faithful counselor, comes to her cell to take her to the torture chamber, Maté first shoots him as he looks through a barred door for a moment, before opening it. Here the framing device signifies his reluctance to perform this task. Joan is similarly framed when she enters the torture chamber with him through a narrow door in the background. She is framed both by the doorway, in which she appears remote in silhouette, and by the dark barrier of jurists standing and sitting in the spectators' gallery in the foreground. All these framing devices signify enclosure, masking, detention, surveillance, and punishment.

La passion de Jeanne d'Arc is a panoply of high- and low-angle shots, and featuring subjects who tend to display themselves in oblique angles gesturally and posturally, as in three-quarter profiles and head tilts. The combination of acute camera angles and acute head and body angles reconfigures the rectangular field of view, subverting the fixed dimensions of the frame. In her many facial close-ups, for instance, Maria Falconetti is shot from every conceivable head angle: together these shots make use of every square centimeter of the frame and the field of view.

In *Vampyr*, Dreyer and Maté compose interior shots against white walls and other white backgrounds, and exterior shots through tulle lens filters and against white skies, most notably in the climax, in which the doctor is asphyxiated in an avalanche of flour. These shots correspond to the nondescript and ambient backgrounds of the close-up shots in *La passion de Jeanne d'Arc*.

> Dreyer and Maté passed a small building that was a factory in which plaster was reclaimed. The whole interior was white and the workmen were covered in white dust, which gave them the idea of using this sense of whiteness as a stylistic element in [*Vampyr*].[18]

Whiteness as a signifier of the nondescript is also evident in the bloodless vampiric faces of Léone, Gisèle, Allan, the village doctor, and Marguerite Chopin, and in the understated performances of Julian West and the other nonprofessional actors Dreyer cast in *Vampyr* and directed to act mainly in a daze. The bland background of the derelict house is prominent also.

Framing and masking devices abound in *Vampyr*, from the beginning when Maté shoots Allan through the window of the hotel door, to the climactic scenes in which he shoots both ways through the window in Allan's coffin lid. His corpse face framed by this aperture is one of the film's most macabre and enduring images. Allan is framed in doorways throughout the film, particularly in the open doorways of the abandoned house. Outside the manor house, framed by the window, he witnesses the murder of Léone and Gisèle's father. The overhead shot of the silhouette of Marguerite Chopin walking through a vanishing-point-perspective cellar door to shake her cane and command the shadow singers and dancers to stop is as visually stunning as the wide shot of Joan in silhouette, as she enters the distant narrow door to her torture chamber.

Whereas in *La passion of Jeanne d'Arc* Maté reconfigures the frame or field of view through extreme close-ups, oblique subject poses, and acute low- and high-angle shots, in *Vampyr* the constricting shots and angles have to do with redefining cinematic space. Maté tends to constrict one kind of space by extending another. For example, the extreme low-angle wide shot of the servant high in the rafters of the flour mill emphasizes the entrapment of the doctor below. Similarly, the extremely long track-out shot in which Maté films the servants carrying Léone's unconscious body through the house after Marguerite Chopin the vampire has attacked Léone on the grounds merely emphasizes her captivity as a chronically ill, bedridden invalid and a vampire. Maté's ambitious tracking shots of the sky, treetops, and architecture, because they are directly linked to Allan's corpse's point of view "looking" through his coffin aperture, are paradoxical.

The framing principle was the greatest achievement of Dreyer and Maté's collaborative partnership on *La passion de Jeanne d'Arc* and *Vampyr*, radically different films that have shot composition, frame reconstruction, fluid camera work, and heterodox camera angles in common.

NOTES

1. William Everson, "Rudy Maté: His Work with Carl Dreyer," *Films and Filming* 2 (November 1955): 7.

2. Herbert G. Luft, "Rudolph Maté Photographed Dreyer's 'Passion of Joan of Arc' and Became a Director on His Own," *Films in Review* 15.8 (October 1964): 481–82.

3. *La passion de Jeanne d'Arc*, subject to government and Catholic Church censorship during production, was completed in 1928, but before its German release, both the original negative and another negative Dreyer reconstructed from outtakes were destroyed by fire. The film had its first screenings in Copenhagen on April 21, 1928, and Paris on October 25, 1928, but thereafter survived only in *bricolage* versions. In 1981, an original Danish copy of the film was found in Norway. The Danish Film Museum and Cinémathèque Française worked to reconstruct the film as closely as possible to its original specifications, notwithstanding the 1927 production censorship. See Tony Pipolo, "The Spectre of 'Joan of Arc': Textual Variations in the Key Prints of Carl Dreyer's Film," *Film History* 2.4 (November–December 1988): 301–24; T. A. Kinsey, "The Mysterious History and Restoration of Dreyer's 'The Passion of Joan of Arc,'" *Moving Image* 1.1 (Spring 2001): 94–107.

4. Susan Sontag, *On Photography* (New York: Farrar, Straus and Giroux, 1973), 104.

5. I have relied on a French-language version of *La passion de Jeanne d'Arc*. All translations and paraphrases of intertitles are my own.

6. Robert Stam, *Subversive Pleasures: Bakhtin, Cultural Criticism, and Film* (Baltimore, MD: Johns Hopkins University Press, 1989), 163.

7. Jean Mitry, *Semiotics and the Analysis of Film*, trans. Christopher King (Bloomington and Indianapolis: Indiana University Press, 2000), 68.

8. Luft, "Rudolph Maté," 484.

9. Sontag, *On Photography*, 70.

10. In *Vampyr* there is a similar scene, in which, in two separate shots, a servant is shown reading a book about vampires and a housefly is visible crawling over his hand.

11. The German, French, and English versions of *Vampyr* were produced in 1931–1932. The original negative of the film in synchronized dialogue and images, however, was lost. Incomplete prints of the German and French versions were the basis of a reconstruction. A new German version appeared in 1998, a collaboration of Deutsche Kinemathek, ZDF/Arte, and Cineteca del Commune di Bolgna, which is the one I have used for chapter 9.

12. In their screenplay of *Vampyr*, Dreyer and Christen Jul write about the farmer with the scythe only: "At this moment he sees a reaper walking along with his scythe over his shoulder. He looks at the man curiously as he walks down toward he ferry. He shouts after him: 'Hullo, you there!' But the reaper, not hearing his cry, continues on his way." Later, when he looks out the window of the inn, Allan Gray, who is named Nikolas in the filmscript, sees only the ferry operator, but not the reaper: "As Nikolas stands waiting, he glances down in the direction of the ferry. The ferryman—who has a white beard—boards the ferryboat, which begins cross-

ing the river." Carl Theodor Dreyer and Christen Jul, "Vampyr: The Screenplay," in *Writing Vampyr*, 4, 5 (New York: Criterion Collection, 2008).

13. Jean Drum and Dale D. Drum, *My Only Great Passion: The Life and Films of Carl Th. Dreyer* (Lanham, MD: Scarecrow, 2000), 154.

14. Vladimir Nilsen, *The Cinema as a Graphic Art: On a Theory of Representation in the Cinema* (New York: Hill & Wang, 1959), 165.

15. J. E. Cirlot, *A Dictionary of Symbols*, trans. Jack Sage, 2nd ed. (London: Routledge & Kegan Paul, 1971), 28.

16. Curtis Harrington, "Ghoulies and Ghosties," *Quarterly of Film Radio and Television* 7.2. (Winter 1952): 201–2.

17. Everson, "Rudy Maté," 7.

18. Drum and Drum, *My Only Great Passion*, 155.

10

Cinematographers as Directors as Cinematographers and the Rebirth of Civilization

The Weimar Republic, 1919–1933, coincided with the final expression of the silent-film era and the transition to film with synchronized sound and dialogue, and with the transition from auteur-generated actuality, documentary, and short films to the collaborative feature-film productions of directors and cinematographers, along with ensembles of actors, and technicians. After the First World War, universally perceived as having marked "the war to end war" and the end of civilization, Germany reconstructed itself in a *zeitgeist* of political rapprochement, social and moral permissiveness, democratically collective self-redetermination. To negotiate their course through the fluid political, social, and moral paradigms of the postwar reconstructed state, Germans came to understand that self-redetermination, as distinguished from self-determination, had to be a collaborative process to be successful. Rather than associating themselves with the old suprasystems of the state, the military, and propaganda, people connected in small groups in the family, school, and workplace, face-to-face groups of friends and followers that, in an evolutionary sense, by facilitating the recognition of facial displays, enhanced the possibility that the community, and by extension a new governing model, would survive. In the arts, as in society, social connections were prominent, but here facial displays had to do as much with mimesis or representation as with freedom of association for purposes of survival. Like the portrait and self-portrait in painting and sculpture and the solo and duet in music and dance, the headshot and close-up in silent film were conspicuous tropes in the collective iconography of Weimar Modernism. In film production this patterning of facial displays on the screen had a counterpart in collaborative cinematography, in which directors and camera operators worked closely together in shot selection, frame construction, lighting, editing, special optical effects, and other aspects of the visual grammar of representation and image sequencing. The face-to-face groups of directors and cinematographers working in concert gave rise to the concepts *filmemacher*, the director and cinematographer in collaboration in the authorship of film, and *kamerateam*, the camera crew comprising the cinematographer and director along with the production ensemble in the coproduction of film. In Weimar film, the elision of *kamera* and *kameraderie* was an experiential reality in a revolutionary kinetic visual culture and film studios that effected the collaborative elisions cinematographer-director, director-cinematographer.

Before examining the abstract concepts of the cinematographer who directs films from the camera and the director who vacates the director's chair to look through the viewfinder, it is necessary to address the careers of the filmmakers under consideration here in reference to three factors: (1) their lives and careers after collaboration; (2) their relation to the rise of fascism, the accession of Hitler, and the transition to the Third Reich; (3) filmmakers' standing in film history.

After collaborating with Ernst Lubitsch on eighteen films, 1916–1923, specifically until the director relocated to Hollywood in late 1922, Theodor Sparkuhl worked at Universum Film AG (Ufa) until 1928, when he accepted an appointment at British International Pictures (BIP), which he held until 1930, and then worked at Braunberger-Richebe in Paris, 1930–1931. In December 1931, having been accepted into the American Quota, the Jewish cinematographer, his Jersualem-born wife, Helen Shahwan, and their five children immigrated to the United States. In April 1933, three months after Hitler was elected chancellor of Germany, Sparkuhl was hired by Paramount Pictures, in Hollywood, where he devoted the rest of his distinguished career, becoming a member of the American Society of Cinematographers (ASC) and photographing fifty-seven films, including *Forgotten Faces* (1936), directed by German *émigré* E. A. Dupont, and William Wellman's *Beau Geste* (1939), starring Gary Cooper. He died of congestive heart failure on June 13, 1946; he was fifty-one years old. Among his many achievements was a new system of aligning the rotation of wheels in moving vehicles in film with the rotation of the recording mechanisms in cameras. The problem was that when wheels turned on screen, particularly spoked wheels, they appeared to move forward initially and then backward. Val Guest wrote:

> But this problem has been solved by Sparkuhl who worked out a colour ratio of wagon wheels to camera wheels. As I am sure this will be of interest to the camera boys over here, this is how he did it:—He painted the first spoke black and the second one green; then one spoke black and the next two green, repeated twice; and finally one spoke black and the next three green, repeated three times. When this was recorded on film the mechanisms of all wheels coincided perfectly. In other words Sparkuhl has at last synchronised the movement of wheels on the screen with the movements of the camera.[1]

Sparkuhl also published in the area of his expertise, on the exploitation of lighting in cinematography, such as his article "Better Ways to Use Your Exposure Meter" (1941), and other writers in the field acknowledged his achievements, like cinematographer William Stull in his articles "How Small Lamps Are Being Used on Major Sets" (1940), "Sparkuhl Builds 35 mm. Developer for Home Laboratory" (1940), and "Proving the New Norwood Exposure Meter on Production" (1941). All these appeared in the prestigious journal *American Cinematographer*.

At Paramount, Sparkuhl was reunited with Lubitsch, who had joined the studio in 1928, and in 1935 he was appointed production manager. When Lubitsch was granted a Special Academy Award in 1937 in recognition of his lifetime achievement, especially in German films, Sparkuhl shared the honor. But the two never worked on another picture together, in part because their careers were winding down. Lubitsch died in 1947, at age fifty-five. Although their *gemeinschaftsproduktion* did not translate overseas to Hollywood, their contribution to film history, especially evident in the distinctive visual syntax of their feature films in narrative, theatrical, and comic genres, is substantial, and their collaborative model, established on eighteen films over seven years, was a *zeitgeist* prototype of progressive filmmaking in Weimar Germany.

After shooting Fritz Lang's *Metropolis* (1927), Karl Freund continued in his position as head of production at Fox-Europa-Film, 1926–1929, and also shot the documentary *Berlin: Die Sinfonie der Gorsstadt* (1927) and four feature films: Lupu Pick's *Eine Nacht in London* (1928), Paul Czinner's *Doña Juana* (1928) and *Fräulein Else* (1929), and, for Gainsborough Studios, in London, Seymour Hicks's *Sleeping Partners* (1930). In 1929 he and his second wife, Gertrude Freund, immigrated to the United States, working briefly at Astoria Studios, New York, before permanently relocating his career to Hollywood, where he was under contract to Universal Studios (1930–1931), Paramount Studios (1931–1935), MGM (1935–1947), and Warner Bros. (1947–1960).

In November 1937, Freund, who was Jewish, had returned to Germany to bring his daughter, Gerda Maria, from his first marriage to Susette Freund, 1915–1918, back to California with him. In late 1941 or early 1942, Susette was sent to Ravensbrück concentration camp, where, determined unfit for labor, she was "selected," solely because she was Jewish, for transportation in March 1942 to Landes-Heil- und Pflegeanstalt, the state sanatorium and mental hospital and a euthanasia center, in Bernburg, where she was executed in a gas chamber.

In 1944 Freund founded the Photo Research Corporation, in Burbank, to manufacture Norwood exposure meters and television cameras. He probably would have encountered Theodor Sparkuhl there, who was an innovator in the use of Norwood exposure meters. William Stull's article on Sparkuhl, "Proving the New Norwood Exposure Meter on Production" (May 1941), complements an article Freund had published the month before in *American Cinematographer*, "A Reflection-Type Meter for Making Incident-Light Readings" (April 1941).

Freund shot fifty-seven films in Hollywood, before turning to television as the director of photography on 150 episodes of *I Love Lucy* (1951–1956). His finest achievement in cinematography was his 1938 Academy Award for best cinematography for Sidney Franklin's *The Good Earth* (1937). He received Academy Award nominations also for Roy Del Ruth's *The Chocolate Soldier* (1941) and Mervyn LeRoy's *Blossoms in the Dust* (1941). His other major films include Robert Z. Leonard's *Pride and Prejudice* (1940), Del Ruth's *Du Barry Was a Lady* (1943), and Richard Thorpe's *The Thin Man Goes Home* (1945). His greatest American film was John Huston's *Key Largo* (1948). He retired in 1960; he died on May 3, 1969, aged seventy-nine. His most enduring contributions to film history, in addition to *Key Largo*, are his German films, most notably Murnau's *Der letzte Mann* (1924) and Lang's *Metropolis* (1927). But his reputation in American cinema also is well deserved. B. R. Crisler, writing in the *New York Times*, calls him "the Giotto of the screen" and observes about his cinematography, specifically his passing shot:

> Mr. Freund, who has been around, has never found a woman who photographs perfectly from all angles. Garbo is the nearest perfect. The still people, naturally, have less complicated problems than the cameraman, who must make allowances for his subject looking up or down, or turning his face to the right or left. Nowadays, faces move in preordained grooves and carefully measured orbits which the camera knows in advance.[2]

Der letzte Mann and *Metropolis* are cinematographically original and avant-garde films not because their shots and angles are not preordained, but because they had never been executed before in film and only Freund and Murnau, Freund and Lang were capable of imagining them.

Fritz Lang's two-part feature film, *Die Nibelungen: Siegfried* (February 1924) and *Die Nibelungen: Kriemhilds Rache* (April 1924), certainly marked the pinnacle of Carl Hoffmann's career as a cinematographer, even though his work on Lang's *Dr. Mabuse der Spieler* (1922), Murnau's *Faust: Eine deutsche Volkssage* (1926), and, as assistant to Karl Freund, E. A. Dupont's *Varieté* (1925), three classic works of German cinema, is surely of enduring merit also.

Cynthia Walk attributes Hoffmann's cinematographic achievement to his work as an *auteur* on one of his earlier films, Karl Heinz Martin's *Von morgens bis mitternachts* (1920):

> As a member of the old guard, Hoffmann's experience encompassed the entire production process. By 1920 he had more than 80 films to his credit with most of the major directors of the period including Rippert, Neuss, Oswald, May, Schünzel, Leni, Murnau, and Lang. Hoffmann's specialty was the film of the fantastic, including special effects developed for the *Homunculus* series, but he also had expertise in other film genres, particularly the detective film. Under the aegis of this veteran cinematographer the adaptation of *Von Morgens bis mitternachts* came to exhibit many sophisticated film techniques.
>
> Hoffmann was the only member of the production team with experience in editing. In this area he intervened to update the filmic dramaturgy of the play by replacing its numbers structure with later developments in narrative cinema.[3]

As a cinematographer, Hoffmann shot 136 films, 1913–1954, from silent actuality shorts to feature color sound films, encompassing the modern history of German film. He worked also as the director of eleven films, 1913–1938. Unlike Theodor Sparkuhl and Karl Freund, Hoffmann did not have to emigrate as the Weimar Republic came to an end, but spent his entire career in Germany. Other than Hans

Schweikart's *Das Fräulein von Barnheim* (1940) and Volker von Collande's *Zwei in einer grossen Stadt* (1942), he appears not to have shot overt wartime propaganda films. Hoffmann married Lilli Lörch in 1908, with whom he had two sons, one of whom, Kurt Hoffmann (1910–2001), was a film director and screenwriter. Carl Hoffmann died on August 5, 1947, aged sixty-six. His legacy in German film history is his facility with special-effects shots, his evocation of emotion through light and shadow and close-ups, and his use of protracted shots.

Fritz Arno Wagner worked with Germany's most innovative, diverse, and eclectic directors and shot several of the most substantial and enduring films of the period: F. W. Murnau's *Nosferatu, eine Symphonie des Grauens* (1922), G. W. Pabst's *Die Liebe der Jeanne Ney* (1927), *Westfront 1918: Vier von der Infanterie* (1930), and *Die 3 Groschen-Oper* (1931), and Fritz Lang's *Spione* (1928) and *M* (1931). He attracted these directors because of his prestigious track record but also because of his versatility, his reputation for shooting with equal facility along the optical and mimetic spectrum from Expressionism to Verism and Naturalism. When in 1936 Wagner wrote from Berlin, "In Germany, during the last few years, the average level of the entertainment film has been considerably improved as a result of State influence,"[4] Hitler and the Nazis had been in power for three years and the Weimar Republic was dead, its social freedoms superseded by fascism. His encoded message hints at the decline of his own career under state repression and points to the emergence of popular entertainment and sociopolitical propaganda as forces designed to reify the creative artistic production of the previous decade.

> His refined sensibility and professional know-how soon came out in film lighting in an era in which impressionism was preferred and his ability to work with light and large shadows was very well spoken of. He was also lucky to work with great directors, like Murnau and Pabst, with whom his aesthetic imagination shone and he applied it in famous scenes for these filmmakers. For example: the well known shot in Murnau's film showing the long shadow of Nosferatu on the staircase wall advancing on his victim. His cinematography for the same director's film *Schloss Vogelód* (1921) was also remarkable with excellent lighting of a castle. The lighting used on the close-ups of the miners was outstanding when he worked with Pabst in *Kameradschaft* (1931) and also in *Die Dreigroschenoper* [1931].[5]

The films he made under the Third Reich and into World War Two—*Flüchtlinge* (1933), *Amphitrion* (1935), *Der Mann der Sherlock Holmes War* (1937), *Robert Koch, der Bekämpfer des Todes* (1939), *Friedrich Schiller* (1940), and *Ohm Krüger* (1941)—were state-influenced entertainments, essentially propaganda films, hardly his art films of the 1920s and early 1930s. After the war, Wagner made documentary films for the American newsreel service *Welt im Bild*, based in Berlin, but these too were propagandistic, regarding democracy, capitalism, and the political realignment of Europe. In 1949, he returned to feature films, shooting *Die Brücke* (1949) and thirty-two other features. But on the set of his final film, *Ohne Mutter geht es nicht* (1958), Wagner suffered a fatal accident when he fell from a camera trolley. He died on August 18, 1958, aged sixty-eight. The tragic circumstances of his death have become the stuff of legend: possibly Germany's greatest cinematographer died while trying to execute a perfect shot.

If *Die Nibelungen: Siegfried* and *Die Nibelungen: Kriemhilds Rache* marked the pinnacle of Carl Hoffmann's achievement as a cinematographer and *Metropolis* the apogee of Karl Freund's achievement, then Günther Rittau, in his capacity as assistant to Hoffmann and Freund on these projects, shares in these artistic triumphs to some degree. But Rittau went on to distinguish himself as principal cinematographer in two groundbreaking German films: Joe May's *Asphalt* (1929) and Josef von Sternberg's *Der blaue Engel* (1930), in which he developed his own visual style through aggressive camera movement and imaginative shots, angles, and lines, such as by working with Erich Kettelhut, a set designer on *Asphalt*, to convert a hydraulic crane into a shooting platform to support a camera and enhance vertical, horizontal, and angular shots. On *Der blaue Engel* Rittau exploited an experimental lens that replicated human eyesight:

> Alexander Walker reports that Gunther Rittau, the cinematographer of *The Blue Angel*, used a special lens that had been given to him by Charles Rosher (who had been the cinematographer for many of Mary Pickford's films). Known as a "Rosher bullseye," the lens has the capability of duplicating human vision by seeming to couple concentration on details directly before it, with only a vague awareness of surrounding information. The result was a clear delineation of Dietrich's main features, combined with a soft-focus look to the rest of her face. The resulting visual image embodied the Dietrich enigma and highlighted the film's polarities.[6]

After the demise of the Weimar Republic, Rittau turned to directing, but his visually spectacular films were state propaganda: *Brand im Ozean* (1939) and *U-Boot Westwkrts!* (1941). The most noteworthy directorial achievement of his later career was the antiwar film *Kinder, Mutter und ein General* (1954–1955). Disillusioned by the *nouvelle vague* of German filmmaking, and experiencing failing eyesight, Günther Rittau retired from filmmaking in the early 1960s. He died on August 7, 1971, age seventy-eight, his legacy film special effects and the mobile camera.

After working as an assistant to Fritz Arno Wagner on F. W. Murnau's *Nosferatu*, Günther Krampf was the principal cinematographer on two major films: Robert Wiene's *Orlacs Hände* (1924) and G. W. Pabst's *Die Büchse der Pandora* (1929). He went on to make eleven feature films and one documentary in Germany, 1929–1932, notably Kurt Bernardt's *Die letzte Kompagnie* (1930), starring Conrad Veidt, and *Kuhl Wampe oder: Wen gehört die Welt?* (1932), with a script cowritten by Bertolt Brecht, Bulgarian director Slatan Dudow's gloomy portrait of a young family, forced to relocate to a homeless camp on the outskirts of Berlin in 1931, struggling with unemployment, social decay, and economic depression as the Weimar Republic starts to collapse. In 1931 Krampf went to England, where he made two films at British International Pictures, which since the mid-1920s had been encouraging international participation and had attracted several German filmmakers, notably

Theodor Sparkuhl and E. A Dupont, the latter of whom made five feature films there, 1926–1931, including *Moulin Rouge* (1928) and *Piccadilly* (1929). At BIP Krampf shot Harry Lachman's *The Outsider* (1931), starring Joan Barry, and Harcourt Templeman and Oscar Friedrich Werndorff's *The Bells* (1931), starring Donald Calthrop. After returning to Germany to shoot a documentary, *Das Kind und die Welt* (1931), and *Kuhl Wampe*, Krampf returned to England, where he spent the rest of his career, making thirty-one feature films, two short films, and one documentary, 1932–1951, at British International Pictures, Gaumont British, Gainsborough Studios, and, mainly, Elstree Studios. He also returned briefly to Germany for the filming of fellow Austro-Hungarian Gustav Ucicky's *Das Madchen Johanna* (1935), a biographical drama about Joan of Arc. Based in London, he shot some eminently British films, including wartime propaganda like *Sabotage at Sea* (1942) and *Warn That Man* (1943), and some classic Ealing comedies such as *Three Cockeyed Sailors* (1940) and *The Black Sheep of Whitehall* (1942), which featured, respectively, the variety stage comedians Tommy Trinder and Will Hay. Krampf shot Leslie Arliss's *The Night Has Eyes* (1942), the film responsible for turning James Mason, who through the 1930s had appeared only in "quota quickies," into a lead actor. Günther Krampf died on August 7, 1950, of pneumonia and other complications following a surgical operation for stomach cancer. He was sixty-one years old. He had just completed shooting Lance Comfort's *Portrait of Clare*, which premiered in November 1950. Another film he had completed appeared posthumously, Lawrence Huntington's *The Franchise Affair* (1951).

After shooting two of G. W. Pabst's greatest and most dissimilar films, the Naturalistic *Die freudlose Gasse* (1925) and the psychoanalytic *Geheimnisse einer Seele* (1926), and also his *Man spielt nicht mit der Liebe* (1926; lost), Guido Seeber shot forty-five feature films, eight short films, and two documentaries, 1926–1937. In 1928–1930 he worked several times with directors Max Obals and Victor Janson, most remarkably in a series of films starring Harry Liedtke. In 1932 Seeber suffered a stroke, from which he recovered enough to continue working at a reduced workload for two years, but when he noticed his health starting to deteriorate, he retired from filmmaking in 1934, or at least he elected to move on as a cinematographer when he accepted a position in October 1934 as the head of animation at Ufa, Neubabelsberg.

Seeber's most enduring contribution to German film history clearly has to do with his exploitation of light variations, assertive camera movement, and framing devices in his shot array. These techniques are most constantly evident in *Die freudlose Gasse* in his strategies of filming the two female leads, Asta Nielsen as Maria Lechner and Greta Garbo as Greta Rumfort.

> Guido Seeber had been working with Asta Nielsen since her early films in Denmark and had been instrumental in her rise as the iconic face of silent-film emotion and eroticism. He shot her as Marie (sic) in *The Joyless Street* in such a way as to create the image of a striking, but aging, femme fatale who was at the same time emotionally complex and sympathetic. And it is in large part due to the camera work that Greta Garbo's character, and her developing star persona, evolve in the film as they do. For example, the use of

> slow motion contributes an intense but ethereal quality to her performance in dramatic moments such as when Grete (sic) Rumfort is pursued by her boss in the office or when Lieutenant Davy chases after her backstage at Frau Greifer's performance hall.[7]

Since his death in Berlin on July 2, 1940, Guido Seeber has received much critical recognition. Some of this has been due to his publications issued when he was most active in his field, such as his book *Der practische Kameraman* (1927) and articles in the journals *Kinotechnik* (1919–1939) and *Filmtechnik* (1925–1935). He is the subject of a documentary film by Helmut Herbst, *Lebende Photographien auf einem laufenden Bande—Guido Seeber 1879–1940* (1979). In 1998 his hometown of Chemnitz dedicated Seeberplatz ("Seeber Center") to honor Guido and his father, Clemens, as pioneers and practitioners of filmmaking, cinematography, and camera technology.

After serving as second-unit camera operator and replacement cinematographer to Karl Freund on *Mikaël* (1924), Rudolph Maté was principal cinematographer on Danish director Carl Theodor Dreyer's *La passion de Jeanne d'Arc* (1928) and *Vampyr* (1932), two of the most ambitious films of the Weimar period. After completing these films, both shot in Paris, he was cocinematographer on other films there: *Liliom*, the last film directed by Fritz Lang before he left for America, and René Clair's *Le Dernier Milliardaire* (both 1934). In 1935 Maté immigrated to the United States to relocate his career in Hollywood, where, as a cinematographer, he made twenty-seven films, 1935–1948, and then, as a producer and coproducer, he made twenty-nine films, two of which he also codirected, 1948–1963. His first significant films as cinematographer were *Dodsworth* (1936) and *Come and Get It* (1936), both directed by William Wyler, who demanded Maté to operate his camera. Maté would go on to become Alfred Hitchcock's cinematographer on his *Foreign Correspondent* (1940), for which he was nominated for an Academy Award, best cinematography. This was the first of five consecutive best cinematography Oscar nominations for Maté. The others were *That Hamilton Woman* (1941); *The Pride of the Yankees* (1942); *Sahara* (1943); and *Cover Girl* (1944). These were major motion pictures, starring, respectively, Vivien Leigh and Laurence Olivier; Gary Cooper; Humphrey Bogart; and Rita Hayworth and Gene Kelly. As a cinematographer, particularly after finding success in Hollywood, Maté considered himself a director of photography and, as such, a film director. Drawing on an interview conducted with Maté at the height of his career, two years before his death, Herbert G. Luft explains his position: "Maté does not regret his shift from cinematography to direction, and regards it as a natural evolution. He says all directors would profit from a knowledge of how the camera works and what it is capable of doing."[8] This was a creative and aesthetic principle he developed in his collaborative partnership over eight years with Dreyer in Germany and France, and it is true of the other major collaborations of directors and cinematographers in the Weimar period. Simply put, the director looks into the camera, and the cinematographer offers direction. Each of them is equally and completely a *filmemacher*. The director of the film envisions it by looking through the lens, and the camera operator, the director of photography, confers with the film director on how their common vision can best be recorded on film, scene by scene, shot by shot. Maté demonstrated his *filmemacher* principle by directing films too, which he did 1947–1963, starting with *It Had to Be You* (1947), codirected with Don Hartman, although most of these—melodramas, thrillers, and westerns—were really B pictures, which was largely the experience of German director E. A. Dupont also in Hollywood. But other German, and Austrian, directors found great success in Hollywood and were consistently on the A-list of film production, notably Ernst Lubitsch, Josef von Sternberg, Fritz Lang, and Billy Wilder, as were some actors, such as Marlene Dietrich and Conrad Veidt, and foreign nationals who had worked in German films, particularly Pola Negri and Greta Garbo. Maté also ventured into directing for television, including seven episodes of *The Loretta Young Show*, 1959–1960.

In the end Rudolph Maté's reputation in German film history depends on two factors: the success he found as a cinematographer in American film, including the five successive Academy Award nominations, and the working relationship based on *gemeinschaftsproduktion* he enjoyed with Dreyer. What was the nature of their collaborative partnership? Dreyer, for example, had a reputation as an autocratic film director, protective of his film property. Consider this account:

> So there were all the producers, actors, cameramen, set designers, and scriptwriters doing exactly what Carl Dreyer wanted for his film. Brainwashing, one of them called it. But he achieved this all so quietly, so politely. Would you mind facing toward the camera just a few degrees more? Let's have the light over here, please, just touching the left arm, if you don't mind. Always he had thought it through, planned it out completely in his head, just the particular camera angle, just the precise placement of a prop, never raising his voice, never seeming to demand even when he was doing just that. It is always *his* set, *his* film, a coworker said, but there was some kind of Dreyer magic that made it all happen so softly that it was all over before anyone realized just exactly what had happened.[9]

The Dreyer magic in bringing all the contributors to a film together derived not from his surface politeness toward them or from a dictatorial determination beneath a show of deference, but from the fact that on *La passion de Jeanne d'Arc* and *Vampyr*, he and Maté worked magic together. These films could not have been made in these forms with any other director or cinematographer. It was the fusion of their filmmaking aesthetics and architectonics, their shared vision of the projects, that created wholly new visual syntaxes and repertoires of camera shots, angles, and movements. The prime example is *La passion de Jeanne d'Arc*, a film comprised of close-ups. Dreyer himself confirms my theory of a common cinematic vision in his comment on this film:

> What streams out to the possibly moved spectator in strange close-ups is not accidentally chosen. All these pictures express the character of the person they show and the spirit of that time. In order to give the truth, I dispensed with "beautification." My actors were not allowed to touch makeup and powder puffs. I also broke with the traditions of constructing a set. Right from the beginning of shooting, I let the scene architects build

> all the sets and make all the other preparations, and from the first to the last scene everything was shot in the right order. Rudolf Maté, who manned the camera, understood the demands of psychological drama in the close-ups and he gave me what I wanted, my feeling and my thought: realized mysticism.[10]

As Dreyer skirted the protocol of set construction, so he effaced the conventional border between the director and cinematographer by letting Maté put together the architectonics of close-up shots, including camera and character movement within individual shots, cross-cutting from one close-up to another, and stretching the frame of some close-ups through tracking, pans, and tilts. Thus, "doing exactly what Carl Dreyer wanted," according to the Drums, is a form of persuasion at best and coercion at worst, whereas, according to Dreyer himself, "he gave me what I wanted, my feeling and my thought," which suggests he and Maté felt and thought the same on this film and the onscreen result was mystic, meaning it was congruent with the spiritual vision of Joan of Arc. Their collaborative partnership was empathetic, based on their ability to understand and share, through creative endeavor, each other's feelings about realizing this film, and ideational, based on their ability to understand and share each other's thoughts and ideas about realizing this film. In this model of *gemeinschaftsproduktion*, which was typical of the Weimar period, the director is a cinematographer and the cinematographer a director. The model also informs the collaborative partnerships of Sparkuhl and Lubitsch; Freund and Lang; Hoffmann and Lang, Hoffmann and Murnau; Wagner and Murnau, Wagner and Pabst, Wagner and Lang; Rittau and May, Rittau and Sternberg; Krampf and Murnau, Krampf and Wiene, Krampf and Pabst; and Seeber and Pabst. Each of these relationships was as idiosyncratic as the personalities of the artists making it up, but also an efficient model of film production and cultural survival in the Weimar Republic. As well as in the abstract theoretical model of collaboration or *gemeinschaftsproduktion*, each of these *filmemacher* relationships can be represented by the films made and also by *the money shot*, by which I mean not the most costly scene to make or the one that made the most money, but (1) the most original and creative shot in a film or films, (2) the shot most likely to hold spectators' attention, (3) the one that best represents the collaborative partnership, and (4) the one that makes the most substantial contribution to the advancement of the film medium in Germany. (See table 10.1.)

In the *gemeinschaftsproduktion* of Ernst Lubitsch and Theodor Sparkuhl, the money shot is a passing shot that exploits the entire axial plane of the field of view and plays with aspect ratio and field size. At a point in the history of silent film when film cameras were stationary, camera movement was limited to pans and tilts, and iris shots, fades, and frames were overused conventional transitional devices, Sparkuhl's camera work in *Die Puppe* (1919) and *Die Bergkatze* (1921) was quite innovative. In *Die Puppe* passing shots involve the movement of actors and properties. All through the film Sparkuhl exploits this movement throughout the field of view: foreground and background, side to side, and along diagonal lines, and he complicates it when the actors are in the field immediately in front of the camera. This camera work is most strikingly evident at the wedding reception Mr. Quaker holds in celebration for

Table 10.1. Money Shot Breakdown

Collaborators	*Film*	*Shot*	*Contribution to Film History*
Sparkuhl-Lubitsch	*Die Bergkatze* (1921)	Aspect-ratio frame shot	Film spectatorship
Freund-Lang	*Der letzte Mann* (1924)	Tilt-tracking revolving-door combination shot	Shot constructiveness
Hoffmann-Lang	*Dr. Mabuse der Spieler* (1922)	Zero-degree action static shot	Shot composition
Wagner-Murnau	*Nosferatu, eine Symphonie des Grauens* (1922)	Reverse-motion special-effect shot	Camera movement through projected image
Wagner-Pabst	***Die 3 Groscher-Oper*** **(1931)**	Angle-reverse angle, shot reverse-shot, frontal-oblique point of view	Shot combination
Wagner-Lang	*M* (1931)	Multiple reflective surface, double-reverse angle shot	Psychological imaging
Rittau-May	*Asphalt* (1929)	Crane shot and dissolve combination	Fluid camera and filmic time
Rittau-Sternberg	*Der blaue Engel* (1930)	Paired track-out shots	Objective camera, subjective response
Krampf-Pabst	*Die Büchse der Pandora* (1929)	*Mise-en-Shot* and crane shot combination	Reverse-angle effect through vectorization
Seeber-Pabst	*Die freudlose Gasse* (1925)	Angle-reverse angle trucking shot sequence	Slow motion
Maté-Dreyer	*La passion de Jeanne d'Arc* (1928)	Close-up shot	High-resolution panchromatic film
Maté-Dreyer	*Vampyr* (1932)	Long lens, short focal length shot	Immediacy through narrowing the angle of view

his daughter, Oss, and her husband, Josef, at which Sparkuhl films the guests on the dance floor in a high-angle shot from a mezzanine and captures their simultaneous movements in a single take. The guests enter the ballroom in pairs in the background and dance the fox-trot in a diagonal line into the foreground and directly in front of the camera, before scattering around the entire floor along the horizontal, diagonal, and vertical axes. Although his camera is fixed, Sparkuhl creates the illusion it is moving around the dance floor. In *Die Bergkatze*, he complicates this illusion by playing with the camera's aspect ratio by using a variety of cookie-cutter masks to alter the dimensions and the configurations of the field of view and the spatial parameters of the frame. Although frame shots were as old as the actuality films of the late 1890s and were always designed to make spectators think about their act of viewing film, Lubitsch and Sparkuhl used frames to prompt viewers to think about spectatorship in radical new ways, because by altering the aspect ratio they destabilized spectatorship, and encouraged spectators to consider the view field as a space for nonhierarchical information, as distinguished from a hierarchy of content. Their money shot is a spectacular diagonal mask shot of thousands of riotous young women who surge across the aspect ratio toward the camera to protest that Lieutenant Alexis is to be sent away. This oblique line symbolizes how Lubitsch and Sparkuhl tend to exploit all spatial axes to simulate camera movement, here in *Die Bergkatze*, and in *Die Puppe* and all their films together.

In the *gemeinschaftsproduktion* of Karl Freund and Fritz Lang avant-garde shots are pervasive, particularly in *Der letzte Mann* (1924) and *Metropolis* (1927), both films shot catalogs. The spectacular opening sequence of *Metropolis*, comprising two master establishing shots, is iconic in German film history. The first is a vanishing-point perspective shot of a tunnel with two phalanxes of men in uniforms of dark overalls and skullcaps, one ending their shift, the other starting theirs, marching in unison. Freund films the workers who are starting their shift as they enter a huge industrial elevator to take them to the subterranean workers city. This appears to be a trucking shot executed on a descending elevator, when in fact the elevator does not move: the simulated movement was effected by elevating the miniature model of the city behind. The shot is intriguing because it is self-reflexive: it demands spectators reflect on how it was constructed. If the opening sequence of *Metropolis* is spectacularly iconic, the opening sequence of *Der letzte Mann* is revolutionary, because it tests the capacity of the fluid camera and ushers in the modern era of cinematography. In an acute low-angle shot executed on ground level, Freund films the descent of an elevator four stories to the hotel lobby. The shot calls attention to how Freund executed it, by slowly tilting down from an extreme low-angle to an eye-level shot. The next shot reveals a bellhop whose job is to keep a revolving door turning. The flickering effect of the glass panels passing in front of the camera is reminiscent of the progression of frames in the camera, or of film passing through a projector in a screening. Freund draws attention to his camera operation. He takes spectators down four floors on an elevator, across a busy hotel lobby, and, in their money shot, a tracking shot, through the revolving doors and into the street.

In his collaborations with both Lang and Murnau, Hoffmann worked on early German adventure spy thrillers, as second-unit camera operator with Freund on *Die Spinnen, 1 Teil: Der Goldene See* (1919) and principal cinematographer on *Dr. Mabuse der Spieler* (1922). Both films are remarkable for their elaborate and prominent special effects, but these ostentatious devices might be viewed today as remnants of the visual spectacle that was much of the silent era, when filmmakers were experimenting with new modes of representation, actuality, and entertainment. *Dr. Mabuse der Spieler* also is a topical film, however, which addresses issues of the social and political unrest in Germany after World War One. For example, when a Mabuse operative, Pesch, posing as an electrician to sabotage the office of police inspector Wenk, is exposed when Wenk returns unexpectedly, Pesch detonates several small bombs to create a smokescreen for his escape through the window. Hoffmann cuts to a wide shot of people in the street, who, having heard the explosions, immediately respond by swarming Pesch and detaining him for the police. The bombing shot is a low-intensity special effect, but the street shot is remarkable too: it alludes to similar acts of subversion in the Weimar Republic, and it urges public vigilance and resistance. In a later scene in contradistinction to this one, Mabuse incites a mob to march out into the streets to demand the release of an unjustly arrested man he has invented named Johannes Gutter, all as an elaborate diversion that frees a sight line for one of his assassins to kill another prisoner, Pesch, who at this point knows too much. These shots also are noteworthy for their topicality. But the Lang-Hoffmann money shot is actually the antithesis of special-effects and propaganda shots like these. Set in Inspector Wenk's office, it features no special effects or surprising cutaway shots. While working at his desk, Wenk hears a cry from the street below and goes over to open the windows to investigate, which an intercut iris shot reveals to be Count Told in an agitated state. Leaving the windows open, Wenk crosses the office and exits through the door opposite, presumably to go downstairs to attend to Told. In his absence, and for a duration of eighteen seconds in which the only action is the movement of the curtains blowing in the windows, yet signifying all the previously completed action in the scene, Hoffmann holds this essentially static shot, which is especially remarkable in a film that relies heavily on cross-cuts to achieve continuity in its fast-moving plot. In other words, Hoffmann could have cut to show Wenk after he leaves the office, running downstairs or into the street and with Told, or returning to the office with him, but instead he abandons spectators to contemplate a protracted static shot of an empty set in which nothing significant appears to happen. This is a money shot in the history of German cinematography because it draws attention to the constancy of camera operation, to the fact that throughout this office scene, including the eighteen-second gap, the camera continues to roll, even when it is recording nothing but drapes fluttering, and because it calls into question the nature of action within the action field, and in of all places an action film, implying it can be minimal as well as explosive, affective as well as special effective: it can be zero-degree action.

Fritz Arno Wagner was such a versatile and inventive cinematographer that he achieved money shots in most of his films. Working with F. W. Murnau on *Nosferatu, eine Symphonie des Grauens* (1922), he achieved iconic shots even within the highly conventional Expressionistic mode of visual representation, notably in the distorted shadow images of Count Orlok. In comparison to Orlok's many projections in silhouette, his demise in a puff of smoke is definitely bathetic. Yet in the preceding scene, in which Ellen allows him to feed on her blood as a means of detaining him until after sunrise, and thus instigating his death, Wagner films two shots of his grotesque shadows in advance of his entering Ellen's bedroom, horribly disfigured on the staircase wall and looming ominously over her door. In the room, Wagner shoots Orlok's shadow as it rapaciously envelops her body, and then directly overhead as, having punctured her neck, he drinks her blood. The three chiaroscuro shots and the shot of him as the prototypical vampire violating her are iconic in the horror-film genre and in German film history. Wagner's overhead mid shot for intimate presence of Orlok feeding on Ellen is much more lurid and disturbing than Rudolph Maté's hazy perspectival wide shot of Marguerite Chopin feeding on Léone in *Vampyr*.

As good as these Expressionistic shots are, Wagner's money shot is of Orlok rising from his coffin in the ship's cargo hold. This reverse-motion special-effect shot, executed by filming with the camera upside down using 35-mm film perforated on both sides, was not new. Georges Méliès was the first to execute it in *Le Déjeuner impossible* (1898), by running the film backward through the camera and then projecting it forward. What makes Wagner's shot original and shocking is not the trick photography but the unforgettable projected image of Orlok rising effortlessly from the coffin. The choreography of the original backward footage of Max Schreck lowered into the coffin with his body perfectly upright and stiff also must have been astonishing.

In the six films Wagner made with G. W. Pabst many of his shots stand out, but two in particular. The first, from *Westfront 1918: Vier von der Infanterie* (1930), is a passing shot remarkable more for its social realism and inscrutable narrative content than for any technical expertise. The setup shot shows a low-ranking soldier, a servant in the officers' mess hall, who, while setting a place at the table, appears to be stealing food from two serving bowls onto a dinner plate he conceals behind his back. In a passing shot, Wagner follows the soldier as he backs out of the mess hall, with the plate still hidden, and in the corridor encounters two officers discussing military strategy. Here he holds the shot on the officers, as if the preceding setup and passing shots of the food thief were simply bridging shots to this one. But suddenly he cuts to an external passing shot of the food thief, a continuation of the earlier shot, still walking backward with his plate of food, until he bumps into the soldier Otto, known as "the student," who, having just run cross-country to deliver an urgent message to headquarters, is exhausted and trying to recover. The server, it turns out, has secured the food to give to the messenger, a human being in need, after headquarters made no allowance for him, despite his brave service. Wagner's passing shot in two intervals is instrumental in concealing and revealing the server's surprising act of charity.

His second remarkable shot in his collaboration with Pabst, from *Die 3 Groschen-Oper* (1931), is the money shot, in which Wagner films the scene, on a high staircase, on which Mackie Messer, who is going into hiding, bids good-bye to Polly Peachum, after he has put her in charge of his operation. Wagner films them in a low-angle shot from behind as they climb the first flight of stairs and in a reverse high-angle frontal shot as they climb the second flight, and then in two high-angle close-ups, a frontal and an oblique angle, as they pause on a landing to talk and whence they part company, Mackie to climb the rest of the way to the street, Polly to climb back down to the warehouse to assume her new responsibilities. Wagner's inventive shot combination—angle-reverse angle, shot-reverse shot, frontal-oblique points of view—is complex and progressive, and a perfect exploitation of the interstitial underworld setting of a leave-taking.

In his collaborative partnership with Fritz Lang, Wagner executed his most momentous shots in *Spione* (1928) and *M* (1931). Although it is derivative of Lang and Carl Hoffmann's *Dr. Mabuse der Spieler* (1922), *Spione* features the most unsettling shot in the silent era of German film. In the climax, Haghi, the villainous counterpart of Dr. Mabuse, hides out in the circus as the clown Nemo, who performs a comic act in which he shoots insects and other pests whenever they distract him from it. But when the police zero in on the circus and surround him onstage and he realizes he has no way of escape, Haghi resolves not to be taken alive: still in performance, he points the gun to his temple, and in the film's final scene, fires it. Edwin S. Porter's shot of the train robber firing his revolver at the camera in the final shot of *The Great Train Robbery* (1903) is iconic, since contemporaneous audiences, whose experience was limited to watching actuality films, as distinguished from narrative films like Porter's, believed he was shooting directly at them. Wagner's shot of Haghi committing suicide onscreen is iconic, since it is self-directed and before the camera rather than directed at the camera, and an original, disturbing, indelible image.

Executed for its shock effect, this shot lacks subtlety. In contrast, the entire shot repertoire of Lang's *M* (1931) is one in which mirror, window reflection, and silhouette shots are prominent yet understated in execution. In the first shot to reveal the face of the murderer, an over-the-shoulder shot, Hans Beckert admires himself narcissistically in a mirror and mugs facial displays as if in concert with a voiceover in which the police graphologist explains his profile of the child killer. But Wagner's money shot is of an unfolding gallery of mirrors in which a fractured image of Beckert's sociopathy emerges. Wagner films Beckert browsing in a J. A. Henckels knife and cutlery shop window. He executes the first shot of the mirror sequence from inside the store through the storefront window, showing Beckert's head framed in a diamond-shaped reflection of some of the knives in the window display, and the second shot, a reverse angle from the outside of the store of this diamond reflection, in which Beckert now discerns the framed reflection of a young girl. Finally Wagner reverses the angle again by returning to the first shot, which is now a reaction shot of Beckert. The knife-edge reflections of Beckert and the girl and volatile camera angles and cuts stress the violence of Beckert and the conflicting perspectives of his pedophilia.

In Joe May's *Asphalt* (1929), Günther Rittau exploited a complete shot repertoire, ranging from an opening-credits montage of intersecting images of the urban environment, to an impressionistic subjective camera, evident throughout in street scenes and fluid shots of traffic and pedestrian movement. For example, after Sergeant Holk first encounters Else Kramer, when she has a minor accident when he is conducting traffic, Rittau films a line of people crossing the street and then people walking along the sidewalk, both in pan shots that, as well as disclosing the bustle of the street, serve as bridging shots to what comes next: bringing the camera to a stop by focusing on a street lamp, he elevates the camera from the base to the electrical lights on top, not by tilting it but by raising it as with a crane, winch, or similar device, keeping it at eye level. Then in a match dissolve the lights, which are off, come on, signaling a time change, from day to night. Would Rittau execute this elaborate shot just to signify the passage of time? Likely, he and May included it as an example of camera movement and the film's innovative cinematography. In this respect the crane shot and dissolve is more a filmic indicator of time than a temporal one. It is a money shot because the crane shot, as distinguished from the elevator shot, was then avant-garde, and the shot subject, a stage property, would seem to be ephemeral and extraneous.

Rittau's artful camera work, less ostentatious than in *Asphalt*, is evident throughout Josef von Sternberg's *Der blaue Engel* (1930), and most graphically in two master track-out shots of Professor Rath at his desk, alone in the classroom: in the first, he has been fired due to the scandal of his relationship with Lola Lola at the Blue Angel; in the second, in the climax of the film, he has died, after having experienced a mental breakdown onstage earlier that evening and having returned to the school, as it were to reclaim his former life before surrendering it to death. The two structurally parallel track-out shots are significantly different in execution. In the first, Rath stands at his desk, and Rittau films him in three-quarter profile in a wide shot and tracks back to the third row of desks, when Rath sits down, and then back to the sixth and final row, when the shot fades to black. In the second, Rittau tracks back from the first row slowly to the last row, and then fades to black. The associational difference between the shots, that the subject does not move at the halfway point of the second track-out, is highly emotive, signifying death. Rittau's objective camera depersonalizes his subject in distinctive ways in the two shots, and the parameters of spectatorship, how spectators perceive the subject, also are different: the first is a standard reaction shot, showing how Rath responds to the news of his dismissal, the second a vanishing-point perspective shot designed to provoke an emotional response from the audience.

In Robert Wiene's *Orlacs Hände* (1924), Günther Krampf exploits a stationary camera and executes standard special effects. Otherwise, his film space comprises mainly passing shots and perspectival shot sequences. In G. W. Pabst's *Die Büchse der Pandora* (1929), however, Krampf exercises an interactive and inventive camera. His money shot shows Anna arriving at Casti Piani's gambling ship, Lulu's refuge after her murder conviction and her flight from custody, as a crew member leads Countess Anna Geschwitz down two flights of stairs to the gambling room. Because the wooden treads of the stairs have no risers, Krampf is able to execute the shot by filming through the spaces between the treads. With the camera positioned at floor level on the landing, he uses a wide shot to film the crewman and Anna, followed by two other crewmen carrying her luggage, walking down the first flight of stairs and toward the camera, and then as the crewman and the others turn on the landing and walk in the other direction to the next flight of stairs, the change in the staircase vectorization and the direction of movement of the characters creating the illusion of a reverse-angle shot. But when Anna takes her first step onto the second flight of stairs, Krampf lowers the camera, as distinguished from tilting it down, below floor level to shoot the rest of her descent through the spaces between the wooden treads. The shot is aesthetically distinctive because of Krampf's creative exploitation of the constricted space of a set property, and his amalgamation of a *mise-en-shot* with a crane shot.

Guido Seeber executed highly creative shots in the films he made with both Lang and Pabst. Although it is one of Lang's early films, *Das wandernde Bild* (1920) features some remarkable live-action external shots. For example, the third shot of the film is of a train interior, in which Irmgard Vanderheit stands at an observation window at the end of the car. Seeber shoots her first in a wide shot through two panes of glass, that is, from an adjoining car's observation window and through her window. Then he cuts to a close-up of Irmgard in three-quarter profile directly through her window. This glass-filtered perspective is beautiful and visually intriguing, and it is pertinent to the film's theme of surveillance, but it is most noteworthy because, as in all the outward-looking shots on the train, this on-location shot has a live moving backdrop, as distinguished from a traveling matte. The perspectival and focal balance Seeber maintains in these outward-looking train shots between characters and moving backgrounds is masterful.

His greatest cinematography is apparent in *Die freudlose Gasse* (1925), one of the most visually complex films of the Weimar period. Throughout, his fluid camera is active, perhaps most remarkable in pan, tracking, and close-up shots executed with variable lens speeds. In the first of these shots, an establishing shot in which Frau and Herr Lechner and Counselor Rumfort and his daughter Greta walk home to Melchiorgasse, which they enter by passing under an archway, Seeber films them in a close-up and in slow motion. In the final slow-motion shot, Frau Greifer checks the appearance of Josef Geiringer, the lecherous butcher, before he meets with Greta Rumfort, and she places a flower on his lapel. After she slips the stalk about halfway through the buttonhole and lets go of it, it drops the rest of the way from its own weight, only in slower motion. Seeber executed both these slow-motion shots by cranking the camera at a quicker pace than normal, so that in projection the film would appear to run slower than normal. In between these two shots, Seeber executed his money shot, a sequence of three shots, and one of the most inventive in German film history. The master shot shows Frau Greifer in her car as she returns to Melchiorgasse, passing a group of working-class people who are queued up outside Geiringer's butcher shop for rationed meat. The first shot shows the car moving toward the camera and turning into Melchiorgasse and past the queue. The second shot, in reverse angle, from Greifer's perspective, guided by the car's turning arc, is a close-up trucking shot that swings past the individual faces, including those of Maria, Greta, and Else, illuminated by the car's headlights, and, at the completion of the arc, in slow motion. This trucking shot is innovative because Seeber is deliberately overcranking the camera to produce an arresting visual effect. He described his technique simply as getting "the crankcase 'into position.'" But Seeber's slow-motion photography was truly revolutionary in the evolution of modern cinematography.

In *La passion de Jeanne d'Arc* (1928), Carl Theodor Dreyer and Rudolph Maté's pervasive use of close-ups, in combination with other shots and angles and an ambulant camera, define the film's entire aesthetic and visual syntax: (1) facial close-ups and head-and-shoulders and extreme close-ups of actors without makeup and shot with light-sensitive, high-resolution panchromatic film to record the subtle gradations in skin tone and gestural movement; (2) variations in high- and low-contrast lighting for the purposes of shaping the *mise-en-scène* of large-scale concrete medieval architecture, and exposing skin imperfections; and (3) extreme low-angle "frog perspective" shots, including shots in which the camera was lowered into a hole to augment the angle and depict Joan's judges and interrogators as inimically as possible. By filming actors without makeup, Dreyer and Maté recognized the *Neue Sachlichkeit* movement and conventions of portraiture with subjects on a spectrum from plain to grotesque. Composed primarily of close-ups, *La passion de Jeanne d'Arc* revolutionized shot composition and film analysis in international film. Maté's money shot here is his and Dreyer's entire shot breakdown.

In Dreyer's *Vampyr* (1932), Maté demonstrates his facility with special effects and other high-intensity, suspense-generating circus shots within the horror genre. For example, when Allan Gray enters the derelict house of the vampire village doctor, Maté shoots his look around the first room in a 360-degree panoramic point-of-view tracking shot that ends by showing him walking out of the camera's view field. He uses the shot again later to show his search of another room in the house, only this time he tracks it more quickly to evoke the urgency of his surveillance at this point. He would have executed these shots either literally, by running a camera dolly along a circular track in the room or on a dolly with turning wheels. His money shot in this film, however, is the entire sequence of point-of-view shots of the "dead" Allan Gray externally through the glass window, the spy hole, at the head of his coffin and internally and from his perspective within the coffin looking out through the glass. The sequence includes shots, from Allan's point of view, of the soldier, the village doctor's assistant, as he lowers the coffin lid, aligns it, and screws it in place. Of greater technical complexity are the external shots of Allan's face visible in the frame of the window: for these Maté used a long lens that shortened the focal length of the camera, thus narrowing the angle of view and, with directed lighting framing it in a square of light, made it appear vivid, close to the glass, and particularly terrifying.

All these money shots are of enduring merit, both as instances of *kameraführung* ("camerawork") and because of the outstanding films in which they appear, of which they are representative components and the films are conserved artifacts within the history of cinema. These shots are technically and aesthetically superlative visual kinetic art. Nearly a century after the shots were executed, spectators can view them again; react to them emotionally, intuitively, sensually, and intellectually; analyze them; understand how they were constructed and how they function cinematically; and even experience them much as contemporaneous audiences first experienced them. If the current "visual culture historicizes the idea of visuality,"[11] then the enduring merit of *kameraführung* has to do with the fact that the images the movie cameras first recorded are iterative, preserving their original visuality in the artifact of film. Thus, in the close-ups in *La passion de Jeanne d'Arc*, spectators today see the "real" Maria Falconetti, "the image" of Joan of Arc, and "an image" that Rudolph Maté recorded iteratively on high-resolution 35-mm panchromatic film, a historicized visuality. Likewise, in the shot of the vampire rising from his coffin in *Nosferatu, eine Symphonie des Grauens*, spectators today see the "real" Max Schreck, "the image" of Count Orlok, and "an image" that Fritz Arno Wagner recorded iteratively on 35-mm film perforated on both sides, by positioning the camera upside down, a reverse-motion shot that extends back to Méliès's *Le Déjeuner impossible* (1898). In these respects, the history of film is a perceptual continuum of images, angles, shots, and movements, whose visuality transcends temporal abstractions like *history* and *time*. Can visuality cut across political abstractions too, like *Weimar Republic* and *Third Reich*? Images, angles, shots, and movements persist in their visuality, according to the working model of *the persistence of vision*, whereas these political systems endure in *historicity*. Consider this passage, in which Albert Speer recalls Adolf Hitler's first days in office in 1933:

> Every evening a crude movie projector was set up to show the newsreel and one or two movies. In the early days the servants were extremely inept at handling the apparatus. Frequently, the picture was upside down or the film strip broke. . . .
>
> Hitler preferred light entertainment, love, and society films. All the films with Emil Jannings and Heinz Rührmann, with Henny Porten, Lil Dagover, Olga Tschechowa, Zarah Leander, or Jenny Jugo had to be procured as quickly as possible.[12]

Did Hitler watch Henny Porten in E. A. Dupont's *Die Geierwally* (1921) and *Das alte Gesetz* (1923), and Pabst's *Skandal um Eva* (1930), Lil Dagover in Lang's *Der müde Tod* (1921) and Murnau's *Herr Tartüff* (1925)? Did he watch Emil Jannings in Lubitsch's *Madam Dubarry* (1919) and *Anna Boleyn* (1920), Murnau's *Der letzte Mann* (1924), *Herr Tartüff*, and *Faust: Eine deutsche Volkssage* (1926), and E. A. Dupont's *Varieté* (1925)? If "revues with lots of leg display were sure to please him,"[13] was he pleased more by Olga Tschechowa's earthy turn as leggy dancer Parysia in Dupont's *Moulin Rouge* (1928) than by her demure performance as Baroness Safferstätt in Murnau's *Schloss Vogelöd* (1921)? Did he find Marlene Dietrich's performance as Lola Lola in Josef von Sternberg's *Der blaue Engel* (1930) pleasing? Did he like the scene in which Emil Jannings as Professor Rath blows on a photo of Lola Lola to lift her appliqué skirt to reveal her "leg display"? Did he note cinematographer Günther Rittau took this shot and perhaps later pave the way for him to continue his career by making World War Two propaganda films? When his inept servants installed film upside down in the movie projector, was he reminded of how Fritz Arno Wagner executed the reverse-motion shot of Max Schreck in *Nosferatu*? Was he amused, perhaps, when he reflected on the irony that in *Le Déjeuner impossible* Georges Méliès got the shot by running the film backward through the camera? Clearly, my ironic rhetoric here notwithstanding, the answers to these queries have little to do with the history of Weimar cinema.

More pertinent to film history was the fascist suppression of the German film industry and of the distribution of international films in Germany, such as when Hitler and members of his National Socialist German Workers' Party (NSDAP) disrupted the German premiere of Lewis Milestone's film *All Quiet on the Western Front*, in Berlin, on December 4, 1930, and facilitated the fascist promotion of propaganda and disinformation films such as director Leni Riefenstahl's *Triumph des Willens [Triumph of the Will]* (1935), a promotional documentary about Hitler and the Third Reich, and documentary filmmaker Walter Ruttman's *Deutsche Waffenschmieden [German Armories]* (1940) and *Deutsche Panzer [German Tanks]* (1940). S. S. Prawer notes, variously, "that films with a strong Jewish presence were not immediately banished from German screens,"[14] yet "that the involvement of men and women with Jewish ancestry ended, for the German film industry, in 1933."[15] Prawer further cites the examples of Fritz Lang, who decided to emigrate from Germany, even though the authorities had granted him an official dispensation even though he had a Jewish mother, and the director Reinhold Schünzel, who was issued a "special license" to continue making films, provided they were *Heimatfilme* ("home films"), which were sentimental popular films with idealized local settings. Yet "the last film he directed, *Land der Liebe* (*Land of Love*, 1937), was truncated by the Nazi censorship and briefly shown before disappearing from German screens."[16] Schünzel, who was also an actor and screenwriter, had played Tiger Brown in *Die 3 Groschen-Oper* (1931) and had directed and written *Viktor und Viktoria* (1933), which was the inspiration for English director Victor Saville's *First a Girl* (1935), and also for American director Blake Edwards's *Victor and Victoria* (1982). After his experience with Nazi censorship and the suppression of *Land der Liebe*, Schünzel left Germany in 1938 for America. In Hollywood, his first acting role was in Fritz Lang's propaganda film *Hangmen Also Die!* (1943), and he exacted at least a show of personal revenge in taking the role of General Ludendorff in John Farrow's comic parody *The Hitler Gang* (1944).

Other film artists exercised different forms of dissent to Hitler's rise to power in 1933. For example, Gustav von Wangenheim, who had starred as Hutter in *Nosferatu*, was the founder and director of Truppe 31, 1928–1933, a theater company formed in a Communist cell in the artists' colony in Berlin. After the Nazis disbanded the company in 1933, Wangenheim emigrated to Moscow, returning to Berlin in 1945. Many filmmakers and actors left Germany in 1933, such as Lang, whereas others left much earlier. Notably, F. W. Murnau relocated to Hollywood in 1926, after completing *Faust: Eine deutsche Volkssage* (1926), and where he made *Sunrise: A Song of Two Humans* (1927), arguably one of his greatest films, which received Academy Awards for best picture, best actor (Janet Gaynor), and best cinematography (Charles Rosher and Karl Struss). Murnau had designed the film and screenwriter Carl Meyer had written the script back in Berlin, where Rosher traveled to discuss the shot breakdown and lighting. But they took their property to America. Murnau and Meyer knew the film could never have been made without interference in Germany. At Fox Film Corporation, however, Murnau worked with complete artistic freedom; his producer, William Fox, let him work independently and just submit the final cut. From Hollywood, Murnau continued to influence German filmmaking, in diaspora in the late 1920s. For instance, his use of an animated intertitle in *Sunrise* influenced E. A. Dupont in his design of a kinetic intertitle in his *Moulin Rouge* (1928), made at British International Pictures.[17]

The mass migration of filmmakers and other artists away from the Weimar Republic in the late 1920s and early 1930s and away from the Third Reich took two directions: diasporic and retrospective, notably in the films of German director Hans-Jürgen Syberberg (1935–), such as *Hitler, ein Film aus Deutschland* (1978), about whose body of work Fredric Jameson has noted:

> After the war it became clear that: 1) the history of high culture was not a very reliable guide to German social history generally; 2) the canon of this stereotype excluded much that may be more relevant for us today (e.g., expressionism, Weimar, Brecht); and 3) the Germany of the economic miracle, NATO, and social democracy is a very different place from rural or urban central Europe in the period before Hitler. So people stopped blaming Wagner for Nazism and began a more difficult process of collective self-analysis which culminated in the antiauthoritarian movements of the 1960s and early 1970s. It also generated a renewal of German cultural production, particularly in the area of film.[18]

The alternative to "collective self-analysis" for Germany is reification, the effacement of the means of cultural production, which Jameson exemplifies as "expressionism, Weimar, and Brecht." For Jameson's categories, I would substitute my own of *Neue Sachlichkeit* ("New Objectivity"), *gemeinschaftsproduktion* ("teamwork of coproduction"), and *zusammenarbeit* ("community production"). All the films of the Weimar period exemplify German cultural production, as distinguished from historical representation, and including historicized visuality.

They also signify the rebirth of civilization in Germany, after World War One, in the Weimar Republic, and after the Third Reich, the Second World War, and the Holocaust, in "collective self-analysis," as distinguished from cultural reification, in which images, camera shots and angles, visuality, the cinematography of film, and the cultural production of the past, are crucial. Noting that *Neue Sachlichkeit* was not limited to the Weimar Republic but was part of a wider European phenomenon, Olaf Peters observes, "On the one hand, it cannot simply be equated with a democratic stance; on the other, it enjoyed a complex afterlife in Germany after 1933 as a mentality and attitude in a variety of cultural fields."[19] The enduring visuality of the films of the Weimar period, comprising reiterative images, camera shots and angles, and cinematography, is mnemonic of this way of thinking about cultural production as teamwork and community work. During the Third Reich, National Socialist art theorists and curators tried to appropriate *Neue Sachlichkeit* under the rubric of traditional German Romanticism, as a means of cultural reification, but the historicized visuality of New Objectivity survived after World War Two in the art movements of Europe and in the Socialist Realist art of the German Democratic Republic.[20] The destruction of the Berlin Wall in 1989 and the reunification of West Germany and the GDR in 1990 were crucial symbolic events in restoring "New" Objectivity in Weimar.

How does the restored, as opposed to reified, visuality of Weimar film contribute to civilization?

> When Cézanne painted three apples set out on a white tablecloth, he was using objects with no *a priori* significance. But, through his composition, the interplay of shape and colour, he provided them with a *value* and a *meaning*. Which derive entirely from the pictorial expression given specific form in the painting.
>
> In the same way, the specificity of the cinema consists in giving a metaphorical, symbolic or other significance to objects, actions or facts which have no other meaning than that they are objects or actions, and which find themselves involved in a flow of meaning which suddenly turns them into signifying elements.[21]

Although one might counterargue three painted apples, regardless of their degree of mimesis, are identifiable as such only because they have a referent, three organic apples, Mitry persuades that Cézanne's painted apples are self-referential because of their original composition and form. Whereas in painting self-referentiality arises from the application of paint to the surface of a canvas, in cinema self-referentiality arises from the imprinting of images onto the surface of film stock. Therefore, film images of objects and actions have no referent, not the actors, costumes, properties, sets, lighting, and so on, and thus become signifying elements only through the movement of the mechanisms of the film camera, film-editing equipment, and film projector.

Mitry's conclusive model of filmic representation as a signifying system eliminates *the real* and *the image* referents from his preliminary model, leaving only self-referential *images*, or the visuality of film composition. Thus, in the master close-ups in *La passion de Jeanne d'Arc*, spectators in the context of the rebirth of civilization after the Weimar Republic and after the Third Reich see neither the real Maria Falconetti nor the image of Joan of Arc but only an image that Rudolph Maté recorded reiteratively on high-resolution 35-mm panchromatic film. In the master shot of the vampire rising from his coffin in *Nosferatu* spectators in the context of this rebirth of civilization see neither the real Max Schreck nor the image of Count Orlok but only "an image" Fritz Arno Wagner recorded reiteratively on double-perforated 35-mm film in an upside-down camera. The original visuality of images in film artifacts resides in cinematography.

The context or frame of reference of civilization is similarly reiterative or self-referential and self-signifying. How did German society and culture under extreme duress, censorship, disinformation, and repression during the Weimar Republic and the Second World War contribute to preserving, recovering, or regenerating civilization? German society and culture survived the traumas of economic volatility, runaway inflation, dictatorship, world war, and genocide through *gemeinschaftsproduktion* ("teamwork of coproduction") and *zusammenarbeit* ("community production"), of which the collaborative partnerships of *filmemacherin* are emblematic, such as Theodor Sparkuhl and Ernst Lubitsch; Karl Freund and F. W. Murnau; Carl Hoffmann and Fritz Lang; Fritz Arno Wagner and G. W. Pabst; Günther Rittau and Josef von Sternberg; Günther Krampf and Robert Wiene; Guido Seeber and Pabst; Rudolph Maté and Carl Theodor Dreyer. Mainly German society and culture survived because their frame of reference was a civilization with no referent in historical events, including trauma, but only the resolve to reiterate its image.

NOTES

1. Val Guest, "Correspondence," *The Cine-Technician* (November–December1943): 132.
2. B. R. Crisler, "The Friendly Mr. Freund: A Chapter from the Past Which Remains Very Much in the Present Tense," *New York Times* (November 21, 1937): 178.
3. Cynthia Walk, "Cross-Media Exchange in Weimar Culture: *Von Morgens bis Mitternachts*," *Monatshefte* 99.2 (2007): 185.
4. Fritz Arno Wagner, "I Believe in the Sound Film," trans. A. L. H. Moore and S. P. Larcombe, *Film Art* 8.111(1936): 12.
5. H. Mario Raimondo-Souto, *Motion Picture Photography: A History, 1891–1960* (Jefferson, NC: McFarland, 2007), 235.
6. Sybil DelGaudio, *Dressing the Part: Sternberg, Dietrich, and Costume* (Madison, NJ: Fairleigh Dickinson University Press, 1993), 33.
7. Noah Isenberg, *Weimar Cinema: An Essential Guide to Classic Films of the Era* (New York: Columbia University Press, 2009), 140.
8. Herbert G. Luft, "Rudolph Maté Photographed Dreyer's 'Passion of Joan of Arc' and Became a Director on His Own," *Films in Review* 15.8 (October 1964): 490.
9. Jean Drum and Dale D. Drum, *My Only Great Passion: The Life and Films of Carl Th. Dreyer* (Lanham, MD: Scarecrow, 2000), 2.
10. Carl Theodor Dreyer, *Dreyer in Double Reflection: Carl Dreyer's Writings about the Film (om Filmen)*, trans. Donald S. Skoller (New York: Perseus, 1973), 50.
11. Laura U. Marks, "An Interview with Laura U. Marks," interview by Margaret Dikovitskaya, *Visual Culture: The Study of the Visual After the Cultural Turn*, by Dikovitskaya, 216 (Cambridge, MA, and London: MIT, 2005).

12. Albert Speer, *Inside the Third Reich: Memoirs*, trans. Richard Winston and Clara Winston (New York: Macmillan, 1970), 36.

13. Ibid., 36.

14. S. S. Prawer, *Between Two Worlds: The Jewish Presence in German and Austrian Film, 1910–1933* (New York and Oxford: Berghahn, 2005), 189.

15. Ibid., 190.

16. Ibid., 190.

17. Paul Matthew St. Pierre, *E. A. Dupont and His Contribution to British Film:* Varieté, Moulin Rouge, Piccadilly, Atlantic, Two Worlds, Cape Forlorn (Madison, NJ: Fairleigh Dickinson University Press, 2010), 76.

18. Fredric Jameson, *Signatures of the Visible* (New York and London: Routledge, 1992), 86–87.

19. Olaf Peters, "New Objectivity and 'Totalitarianism': The Reception of Weimar's Modernity in the Third Reich and the German Democratic Republic," in *New Objectivity: Modern German Art in the Weimar Republic 1919–1933*, ed. Stephanie Barron and Sabine Eckmann, 77 (New York: Prestel, Los Angeles: Los Angeles County Museum of Art, 2015).

20. Ibid., 81.

21. Mitry, *Semiotics and the Analysis of Film*, 246.

Filmography

CARL THEODOR DREYER

Mikaël, Carl Theodor Dreyer (dir.), Karl Freund and Rudolph Maté (cins.), Universum-Film AG (Ufa), September 1924. Feature.

La passion de Jeanne d'Arc, Carl Theodor Dreyer (dir.), Rudolph Maté (cin.), Société générale des films, 1928. Feature.

Vampyr, Carl Theodor Dreyer (dir.), Rudolph Maté and Louis Née (cins.), Tobis Filmkunst, May 1932. Feature.

FRITZ LANG

Die Spinnen, 1 Teil: Der Goldene See, Fritz Lang (dir.), Karl Freund, Carl Hoffmann, and Emil Schünemann (cins.), Decla-Bioscop AG, October 1919. Feature.

Harakiri, Fritz Lang (dir.), Max Fassbender and Carl Hoffmann (cins.), Decla-Bioscop AG, December 1919. Feature.

Die Spinnen, 2 Teil: Das Brillantenschiff, Fritz Lang (dir.), Karl Freund (cin.), Decla-Film-Gesellschaft Holz, February 1920. Feature.

Das wandernde Bild, Fritz Lang (dir.), Guido Seeber (cin.), May-Film, December 1920. Short.

Der müde Tod, Fritz Lang (dir.), Bruno Mondi, Erich Nitzschmann, Herrmann Saalfrank, Bruno Timm, and Fritz Arno Wagner (cins.), Decla-Bioscop AG, October 1921. Feature.

Dr. Mabuse der Spieler, Fritz Lang (dir.), Carl Hoffmann (cin.), Uco-Film GmbH, April 1922. Feature.

Die Nibelungen: Siegfried, Fritz Lang (dir.), Carl Hoffmann, Günther Rittau, and Walter Ruttmann (cins.), Decla-Bioscop AG, February 1924. Feature.

Die Nibelungen: Kriemhilds Rache, Fritz Lang (dir.), Carl Hoffmann and Günther Rittau (cins.), Decla-Bioscop AG, April 1924. Feature.

Metropolis, Fritz Lang (dir.), Karl Freund, Günther Rittau, and Walter Ruttmann (cins.), Universum-Film AG (Ufa), January 1927. Feature.

Spione, Fritz Lang (dir.), Fritz Arno Wagner (cin.), Universum-Film AG (Ufa), March 1928. Feature.

M, Fritz Lang (dir.), Fritz Arno Wagner (cin.), Nero-Film AG, May 1931. Feature.

Das Testament des Dr. Mabuse, Fritz Lang (dir.), Fritz Arno Wagner and Károly Vass (cins.), Nero-Film AG, April 1933. Feature.

ERNST LUBITSCH

Ich möchte kein Mann Sein, Ernst Lubitsch (dir.), Theodor Sparkuhl (cin.), Projektions-AG Union (PAGU), October 1918. Feature.

Die Austernprinzessin, Ernst Lubitsch (dir.), Theodor Sparkuhl (cin.), Projektions-AG Union (PAGU), June 1919. Feature.

Madame Dubarry, Ernst Lubitsch (dir.), Theodor Sparkuhl (cin.), Projektions-AG Union (PAGU), September 1919. Feature.

Die Puppe, Ernst Lubitsch (dir.), Theodor Sparkuhl (cin.), Projektions-AG Union (PAGU), December 1919. Feature.

Sumurun, Ernst Lubitsch (dir.), Theodor Sparkuhl (cin.), Projektions-AG Union (PAGU), September 1920. Feature.

Anna Boleyn, Ernst Lubitsch (dir.), Theodor Sparkuhl (cin.), Universum-Film AG (Ufa), December 1920. Feature.

Die Bergkatze, Ernst Lubitsch (dir.), Theodor Sparkuhl (cin.), Projektions-AG Union (PAGU), April 1921. Feature.

JOE MAY

Asphalt, Joe May (dir.), Günther Rittau (cin.), Universum-Film AG (Ufa), March 1929. Feature.

F. W. MURNAU

Der Gang in der Nacht, F. W. Murnau (dir.), Max Lutze (cin.), Goron Film, January 1921. Feature.

Schloss Vogelöd, F. W. Murnau (dir.), Lásló Schäffer and Fritz Arno Wagner (cins.), Uco-Film GmbH, April 1921. Feature.

Nosferatu, eine Symphonie des Grauens, F. W. Murnau (dir.), Fritz Arno Wagner and Günther Krampf (cins.), Jofa-Atalier Berlin-Johannisthal, February 1922. Feature.

Die Finanzen des Grossherzogs, F. W. Murnau (dir.), Karl Freund and Franz Planer (cins.), Universum-Film AG (Ufa), January 1924. Feature.

Der letzte Mann, F. W. Murnau (dir.), Karl Freund (cin.), Universum-Film AG (Ufa), December 1924. Feature.

Herr Tartüff, F. W. Murnau (dir.), Karl Freund (cin.), Universum-Film AG (Ufa), November 1925. Feature.

Faust: Eine deutsche Volkssage, F. W. Murnau (dir.), Carl Hoffmann (cin.), Universum-Film AG (Ufa), October 1926. Feature.

G. W. PABST

Die freudlose Gasse, G. W. Pabst (dir.), Guido Seeber, Curt Oertel, and Robert Lach (cins.), Sofar-Film-Produktion GmbH, May 1925. Feature.

Geheimnisse einer Seele, G. W. Pabst (dir.), Robert Lach, Curt Oertel, and Guido Seeber (cins.), Neumann-Filmproduktion, March 1926. Feature.

Die Liebe der Jeanne Ney, G. W. Pabst (dir.), Robert Lach and Fritz Arno Wagner (cins.), Universum-Film AG (Ufa), December 1927. Feature.

Die Büchse der Pandora, G. W. Pabst (dir.), Günther Krampf (cin.), Nero-Film Studio, January 1929. Feature.

Tagebuch einer Verlorenen, G. W. Pabst (dir.), Sepp Allgeier and Fritz Arno Wagner (cins.), Pabst-Film, September 1929. Feature.

Die 3 Groschen-Oper, G. W. Pabst (dir.), Fritz Arno Wagner (cin.), Tobis Filmkunst, February 1931. Feature.

ARTHUR ROBISON

Schatten: Eine nächtliche Halluzination, Arthur Robison (dir.), Fritz Arno Wagner (cin.), Pan Film, October 1923. Feature.

JOSEF VON STERNBERG

Der blaue Engel, Josef von Sternberg (dir.), Günther Rittau and Hans Schneeburger (cins.), Universum-Film AG (Ufa), April 1930. Feature.

PAUL WEGENER

Der Golem: Wie er in die Welt kam, Paul Wegener and Carl Boese (dirs.), Karl Freund and Guido Seeber (cins.), Projektions-AG Union (PAGU), October 1920. Feature.

ROBERT WIENE

Orlacs Hände, Robert Wiene (dir.), Hans Androschin and Günther Krampf (cins.), Berolina Film GmbH, September 1924. Feature.

Works Cited

Anscombe, G. E. M. *Intention*. 2nd ed. Cambridge, MA: Harvard University Press, 1963.

Arijon, Daniel. *Grammar of the Film Language*. Beverly Hills, CA: Silman-James, 1976.

Arnheim, Rudolf. *Film als Kunst: Mit einem Vorwort zur Neuausgabe*. Munich: Hanser Verlag, 1974.

Bader, Graham. "Life in the Democracy and the Aftermath of War," in *New Objectivity: Modern German Art in the Weimar Republic 1919–1933*, edited by Stephanie Barron and Sabine Eckmann, 130. New York: Prestel, Los Angeles: Los Angeles County Museum of Art, 2015.

Baldi, Pierre. "Surprise: A Shortcut for Attention?" In *Neurobiology of Attention*, edited by Laurent Itti, Geraint Rees, and Joh K. Tsotsos, 24–28. Amsterdam: Elsevier, 2005.

Barthes, Roland. *Image—Music—Text*, translated by Stephen Heath. New York: Hill & Wang, 1977.

Bergstrom, Janet. "Sexuality at a Loss: The Films of F. W. Murnau." *Poetics Today* 6.1/2 (1985): 185–203.

Binding, Karl, and Alfred Hoche. *Allowing the Destruction of Life Unworthy of Life: Its Measure and Form*, translated by Cristina Modak. 1920. N.p.: Suzeteo Enterprises, 2012.

Blessing, Jennifer. *Rrose Is a Rrose Is a Rrose: Gender Performance in Photography*. New York: Guggenheim Museum, 1997.

Bretschneider, Jürgen, ed. *Ewald André Dupont: Autor und Regisseur*. Munich: Edition Text and Kritik, 1992.

Brown, Blain. *Cinematography Theory and Practice: Imagemaking for Cinematographers, Directors, and Videographers*. Amsterdam: Elsevier, 2002.

Cirlot, J. E. *A Dictionary of Symbols*, translated by Jack Sage. 2nd ed. London: Routledge & Kegan Paul, 1971.

Corrigan, Timothy. "Teaching Film Auteurs." In *Teaching Film*, edited by Lucy Fischer and Patrice Petro, 20–21. New York: Modern Language Association of America, 2012.

Crisler, B. R. "The Friendly Mr. Freund: A Chapter from the Past Which Remains Very Much in the Present Tense." *New York Times* (November 21, 1937): 178.

Dämonische Leinwand. DVD. Directed by Peter Buchka. Munich: Kick Film, 1998.

DelGaudio, Sybil. *Dressing the Part: Sternberg, Dietrich, and Costume*. Madison, NJ: Fairleigh Dickinson University Press, 1993.

Dikovitskaya, Margaret. *Visual Culture: The Study of the Visual after the Cultural Turn*. 2005; Cambridge, MA: MIT, 2006.

Dreyer, Carl Theodor. *Dreyer in Double Reflection: Carl Dreyer's Writings about the Film (om Filmen)*, translated by Donald S. Skoller. New York: Perseus, 1973.

Dreyer, Carl Theodor, and Christen Jul. "Vampyr: The Screenplay." In *Writing Vampyr*, 4, 5. New York: Criterion Collection, 2008.

Drum, Jean, and Dean D. Drum. *My Only Great Passion: The Life and Films of Carl Th. Dreyer*. Lanham, MD: Scarecrow, 2000.

Eckmann, Sabine. "A Lack of Empathy: On the Realisms of New Objectivity," in *New Objectivity: Modern German Art in the Weimar Republic 1919–1933*, edited by Stephanie Barron and Eckmann, 27–39. New York: Prestel, Los Angeles: Los Angeles County Museum of Art, 2015.

Eisner, Lotte H. *The Haunted Screen: Expressionism in the German Cinema and the Influence of Max Reinhardt*, translated by Roger Greaves. Rev. ed. 1952. Berkeley and Los Angeles: University of California Press, 1969.

———. *Murnau*. Rev. ed. 1964. Berkeley: University of California Press, 1973.

Elsaesser, Thomas. *Weimar Cinema and After: Germany's Historical Imaginary*. London and New York: Routledge, 2000.

Everson, William. "Rudy Maté: His Work with Carl Dreyer." *Films and Filming* 2 (November 1955): 7.

Fairservice, Don. *Film Editing: History, Theory and Practice; Looking at the Invisible*. Manchester: Manchester University Press, 2001.

Finkelstein, Haim. "Dalí and *Un Chien andalou*: The Nature of a Collaboration." In *Dada and Surrealist Film*, edited by Rudolf E. Kuenzli, 128–41. Cambridge, MA, and London: MIT, 1996.

Franklin, James C. "Metamorphosis of a Metaphor: The Shadow in Early German Cinema." *German Quarterly* 53 (March 1980): 176–88.

Freund, Rudolf. "M: Mörder unter uns." In *Deutsche Spielfilme von den Anfängen bis 1933: Ein Film Führer*, edited by Günther Dahlke and Günter Karl, 254–57. Berlin: Henschelverlag Kunst und Gesellschaft, 1988.

Furness, R. S. *Expressionism*. The Critical Idiom 29. London: Methuen, 1973.

Gehler, Fred. "Die Bergkatze." In *Deutsche Spielfilme von den Anfängen bis 1933: Ein Filmführer*, edited by Günther Dackel and Karl Günther, 52. Berlin: Henschelverlag Kunst und Gesellschaft, 1988.

Gifford, Don. *The Farther Shore: A Natural History of Perception, 1798–1984*. New York: Random House, 1990.

Grob, Norbert. "'Bringing the Ghostly to Life': Fritz Lang and His Early Dr. Mabuse Films," translated by Julian Raymer. In *Expressionist Film: New Perspectives*, edited by Dietrich Scheunemann, 87–105. Rochester, NY: Camden House, 2003.

Guest, Val. "Correspondence." *The Cine-Technician* (November–December1943): 132.

Hake, Sabine. "Self-Referentiality in Early German Cinema." *Cinema Journal* 31 (Spring 1992): 37–55.

Hans, Anjeana. "'These Hands Are Not My Hands': War Trauma and Masculinity in Crisis in Robert Wiene's *Orlacs Hände* (1924)." In *The Many Faces of Weimar Cinema: Rediscovering Germany's Filmic Legacy*, edited by Christian Rogowski, 102–15. Rochester, NY: Camden House, 2010.

Harrington, Curtis. "Ghoulies and Ghosties." *Quarterly of Film Radio and Television* 7.2. (Winter 1952): 191–202.

Isenberg, Noah. *Weimar Cinema: An Essential Guide to Classic Films of the Era*. New York: Columbia University Press, 2009.

Jameson, Fredric. *Signatures of the Visible*. New York and London: Routledge, 1992.

Jochum, Norbert, ed. *Das wandernde Bild: Der Filmpionier Guido Seeber*. Berlin: Elefanten, 1979.

Kaes, Anton. "The Cold Gaze: Notes on Mobilization and Modernity." *New German Critique* 59 (Spring–Summer 1993): 105–17.

Kinsey, T. A. "The Mysterious History and Restoration of Dreyer's 'The Passion of Joan of Arc.'" *Moving Image* 1.1 (Spring 2001): 94–107.

Kobel, Peter, and the Library of Congress. *Silent Movies: The Birth of Film and the Triumph of Movie Culture*. New York: Little, Brown, 2007.

Koebner, Thomas. "Murnau—a Conservative Filmmaker? On Film History as Intellectual History." In *Expressionist Film: New Perspectives*, edited by Dietrich Scheunemann, 111–23 (Rochester, NY: Camden House, 2003).

Koepnick, Lutz. *The Dark Mirror: German Cinema between Hitler and Hollywood*. Berkeley: University of California Press, 2002.

Konigsberg, Ira. *The Complete Film Dictionary*. New York: New American Library, 1987.

Krampf, Günther. "The Curse of Dialogue." *World Film and Television Progress* (April 1936–March 1937): 4.

Kreimeier, Klaus. *The Ufa Story: A History of Germany's Greatest Film Company, 1918–1945*, translated by Robert and Rita Kimber. Berkeley: University of California Press, 1999.

Laoghaire, Liam Ó. "Jannings: The Portrait of an Actor." *Irish Monthly* 78.926 (August 1950): 388–91.

Legendary Sin Cities: Paris, Berlin, Shanghai. DVD. Directed by Marrin Canell and Ted Remerowski. Toronto: Demi-Monde Productions, 2004.

Luft, Herbert G. "Rudolph Maté Photographed Dreyer's 'Passion of Joan of Arc' and Became a Director on His Own." *Films in Review* 15.8 (October 1964): 481–90.

Makela, Maria. "New Women, New Men, New Objectivity." In *New Objectivity: Modern German Art in the Weimar Republic 1919–1933*, edited by Stephanie Barron and Sabine Eckmann, 54. New York: Prestel, Los Angeles: Los Angeles County Museum of Art, 2015.

Marks, Laura U. "An Interview with Laura U. Marks," interview by Margaret Dikovitskaya. *Visual Culture: The Study of the Visual After the Cultural Turn*, by Dikovitskaya, 216. Cambridge, MA, and London: MIT, 2005.

McCallum, R. Andrew. "Instance-Based State Identification for Reinforcement Learning." In *Advances in Neural Information Processing Systems 7*, edited by Gerald Tesauro, David Touretzky, and Todd Leen, 377–400. Cambridge, MA, and London: MIT, 1995.

McCormick, Richard W. "Desire versus Despotism: The Politics of *Sumurun* (1920), Ernst Lubitsch's 'Oriental' Fantasy." In *The Many Faces of Weimar Cinema: Rediscovering Germany's Filmic Legacy*, edited by Christian Rogowski, 67–83. Rochester, NY: Camden House, 2010.

McGilligan, Patrick. *Alfred Hitchcock: A Life in Darkness and Light*. New York: HarperCollins, 2003.

Mertins, Detlef. "Anything But Literal: Sigfried Giedion and the Reception of Cubism in Germany." In *Architecture and Cubism*, edited by Eve Blau and Nancy J. Troy, 219–51. Montreal: Center Canadien d'Architecture, Cambridge, MA, and London: MIT Press, 1997.

Metzger, Rainer. *Berlin: The Twenties*, translated by Clare Costa. 2006. New York: Abrams, 2007.

Mitry, Jean. *Semiotics and the Analysis of Film*, translated by Christopher King. Bloomington and Indianapolis: Indiana University Press, 2000.

Mückenberger, Christiane. "Der letzte Mann." In *Deutsche Spielfilme von den Anfängen bis 1933: Ein Film Führer*, edited by Günther Dahlke and Günter Karl, 110–12. Berlin: Henschelverlag Kunst und Gesellschaft, 1988.

Naylor, Gillian. *The Bauhaus*. London: Studio Vista; New York: Dutton, 1968.

Nilsen, Vladimir. *The Cinema as a Graphic Art: On a Theory of Representation in the Cinema*. New York: Hill & Wang, 1959.

Noack, Frank. *Emil Jannings: Der erste deutsche Weltstar*. Munich: Collection Rolf Heyne, 2012.

Peters, Olaf. "New Objectivity and 'Totalitarianism': The Reception of Weimar's Modernity in the Third Reich and the German Democratic Republic." In *New Objectivity: Modern German Art in the Weimar Republic 1919–1933*, edited by Stephanie Barron and Sabine Eckmann, 78. New York: Prestel, Los Angeles: Los Angeles County Museum of Art, 2015.

Pipolo, Tony. "The Spectre of 'Joan of Arc': Textual Variations in the Key Prints of Carl Dreyer's Film." *Film History* 2.4 (November–December 1988): 301–24.

Prawer, S. S. *Between Two Worlds: The Jewish Presence in German and Austrian Film, 1910–1933*. New York and Oxford: Berghahn, 2005.

Raimondo-Souto, H. Mario. *Motion Picture Photography: A History, 1891–1960*. Jefferson, NC: McFarland, 2007.

Reisz, Karel, and Gavin Millar. *The Technique of Film Editing*. 1953. London and New York: Focal, 1968.

Rogowski, Christian. "Introduction: Images and Imaginaries." In *The Many Faces of Weimar Cinema: Rediscovering Germany's Filmic Legacy*. Ed Rogowski, 1–12. Rochester, NY: Camden House, 2010.

Roth, Lynette. "New Identities: Type and Portraiture." In *New Objectivity: Modern German Art in the Weimar Republic 1919–1933*, edited by Stephanie Barron and Sabine Eckmann, 259–69. New York: Prestel, Los Angeles: Los Angeles County Museum of Art, 2015.

Rutherford, Anne. "Teaching Film and Mise-en-Scène." In *Teaching Film*, edited by Lucy Fischer and Patrice Petro, 299–310. New York: Modern Language Association of America, 2012.

Schanze, Helmut. "On Murnau's *Faust*: A Generic Gesamtkuntswerk?" In *Expressionist Film: New Perspectives*, edited by Dietrich Scheunemann, 223–33. Rochester, NY: Camden House, 2003.

Sebeok, Thomas A. *Global Semiotics*. Bloomington and Indianapolis: Indiana University Press, 2001.

Seeber, Guido. "Trick und Ton." *Das wandernde Bild: Der Filmpionier Guido Seeber*, edited by Norbert Jochum, 125. Berlin: Elefanten, 1979.

Shklovsky, Viktor. *Literature and Cinematography*, translated by Irina Masinovsky. 1923. Champaign, IL: Dalkey Archive, 2008.

Silberman, Marc. "What Is German in the German Cinema?" *Film History* 8.3 (1996): 297–315.

Skal, David J. *Hollywood Gothic: The Tangled Web of Dracula from Novel to Stage to Screen*. New York: Norton, 1990.

Solomon, Alicia. *Re-Dressing the Canon: Essays on Theater and Gender*. London and New York: Routledge, 1997.

Sontag, Susan. *On Photography*. New York: Farrar, Straus and Giroux, 1973.

Speer, Albert. *Inside the Third Reich: Memoirs*, translated by Richard Winston and Clara Winston. New York: Macmillan, 1970.

Stam, Robert. *Subversive Pleasures: Bakhtin, Cultural Criticism, and Film*. Baltimore, MD: Johns Hopkins University Press, 1989.

Stetler, Pepper. "Man and Machine." In *New Objectivity: Modern German Art in the Weimar Republic 1919–1933*, edited by Stephanie Barron and Sabine Eckmann, 203–28. New York: Prestel, Los Angeles: Los Angeles County Museum of Art, 2015.

Stiasny, Philipp. "Humanity Unleashed: Anti-Bolshevism as Popular Culture in Early Weimar Cinema." In *The Many Faces of Weimar Cinema: Rediscovering Germany's Filmic Legacy*, edited by Christian Rogowski, 48–66. Rochester, NY: Camden House, 2010.

St. Pierre, Paul Matthew. *E. A. Dupont and His Contribution to British Film*. Madison, NJ: Fairleigh Dickinson University Press, 2010.

———. *Mediate! Digital Perspectives on Canadian Media History*. Dubuque, IA: Kendall Hunt, 2013.

———. *Music Hall Mimesis in British Film, 1895–1960: On the Halls on the Screen*. Madison, NJ: Fairleigh Dickinson University Press, 2009.

Wagner, Fritz Arno. "I Believe in the Sound Film," translated by A. L. H. Moore and S. P. Larcombe. *Film Art* 8.111 (1936): 8–12.

Walk, Cynthia. "Cross-Media Exchange in Weimar Culture: *Von Morgens bis Mitternachts*," *Monatshefte* 99.2 (2007): 177–93.

Weber, Nicholas Fox. *The Bauhaus Group: Six Masters of Modernism*. New York: Knopf, 2009.

Weillett, John. *The Weimar Years: A Culture Cut Short*. London: Thames & Hudson, 1984.

Index

About the Author

Educated at the University of British Columbia (B.A., Hon.), Queen's University (M.A.), and the University of Sydney (Ph.D.), professor of English, Simon Fraser University, Vancouver, **Paul Matthew St. Pierre** specializes in New Zealand, Australian, and Pacific literatures, biosemiotics, and performance studies. He is editor of *Dictionary of Literary Biography, Volume 352: Twentieth-Century British Humorists* (2010) and author of *Janet Frame: Semiotics and Biosemiotics in Her Early Fiction* (2001), *E. A. Dupont and His Contribution to British Film* (2010), *Music Hall Mimesis in British Film: On the Halls on the Screen* (2009), *A Portrait of the Artist as Australian: L'Oeuvre bizarre de Barry Humphries* (2004). He is a painter and installation artist.